THE EMOTIONAL LIFE OF THE GREAT DEPRESSION

THE EMOTIONAL LIFE OF THE GREAT DEPRESSION

JOHN MARSH

OXFORD
UNIVERSITY PRESS

OXFORD
UNIVERSITY PRESS

Great Clarendon Street, Oxford, OX2 6DP,
United Kingdom

Oxford University Press is a department of the University of Oxford.
It furthers the University's objective of excellence in research, scholarship,
and education by publishing worldwide. Oxford is a registered trade mark of
Oxford University Press in the UK and in certain other countries

First Edition published in 2019

Impression: 1

Published in the United States of America by Oxford University Press
198 Madison Avenue, New York, NY 10016, United States of America

British Library Cataloguing in Publication Data
Data available

Library of Congress Control Number: 2019950500

ISBN 978–0–19–884773–1

DOI: 10.1093/oso/9780198847731.001.0001

Printed and bound by
CPI Group (UK) Ltd, Croydon, CR0 4YY

Acknowledgments

Thanks to Debra Hawhee, Nora Marsh, Jason Maxwell, Jacquelyn Norton, and the two anonymous readers for Oxford University Press.

Margaret Walker, "Lineage" from *This Is My Century: New and Collected Poems* (University of Georgia Press, 1989). Chapter 2 and parts of chapter 6 draw heavily upon work previously published in *Arizona Quarterly* and *American Literature in Transition* (Cambridge University Press, 2019), respectively, both reproduced with permission.

Contents

List of Figures

I

Introduction

On October 24, 1933, the former Associated Press reporter Lorena Hickok, en route from Washington, D.C. to Minneapolis, Minnesota, stopped to send a letter to her new boss, Harry Hopkins. What she had to say, she wrote, "could not very well be said over the telephone," so she had chosen "to add another letter to the stack."[1]

Over the summer, her boss, Hopkins, had been appointed director of the Federal Emergency Relief Administration (FERA in the alphabet soup of New Deal acronyms). With unemployment near 25 percent and crop prices at historic lows, some 18 million Americans—or roughly one in six families—lived in dire poverty.[2] Hopkins, as head of FERA, would oversee the distribution of hundreds of millions of dollars in federal relief funds to individual states, most of which had long since exhausted their own resources; the states would then distribute those funds to individuals and families in need.

In August, not long after taking charge of FERA, Hopkins had hired Hickok to travel the country and investigate what she came to call, somewhat cynically, "the relief show."[3] By this Hickok meant how well—or, as often as not, how poorly—local agencies, using those federal funds, met the needs of those who sought relief. More generally, Hopkins wanted Hickok to investigate the state of the union during its moment of crisis. "What I want you to do," he told her,

> is to go out around the country and look this thing over. I don't want statistics from you. I don't want the social worker angle. I just want your own reaction, as an ordinary citizen.
>
> Go talk with preachers and teachers, businessmen, workers, farmers. Go talk with the unemployed, those who are on relief and those who aren't. And when you talk with them don't ever forget that but for the grace of God you, I, any of our friends might be in their shoes. Tell me what you see and hear. All of it. Don't ever pull your punches.[4]

The Emotional Life of the Great Depression. John Marsh, Oxford University Press (2019).
 DOI: 10.1093/oso/9780198847731.001.0001

By the time she left for Minneapolis in October, Hickok had investigated an infamous slum in Washington, D.C., "the Alleys"; in late summer, she had made a trip through Pennsylvania, West Virginia, Kentucky, New York, and Maine. And in Minneapolis, she would begin a six-week journey through the plains states: Minnesota, North Dakota, South Dakota, Nebraska, Iowa, and then back to Minnesota.

In the letter she sent en route to Minneapolis, Hickok wrote Hopkins that before she left Washington, Louis Howe, who had craftily managed Franklin Roosevelt's political career for the last twenty years, had asked her "to do some special work for him while I was in the middlewest." Howe was "interested in finding out what sort of treatment people are getting from government representatives who deal with them directly when they ask for help." "He feels it is a matter of great importance," Hickok added, "and I certainly agree with him." Meanwhile, Henry Morgenthau, head of the Farm Credit Administration, another New Deal program, this one devoted to extending low-interest loans to farmers at risk of losing their mortgaged farmland to foreclosure, had "also asked me to pass on anything I might hear about the workings of his department out there."[5] Hickok, loyal to Hopkins, and conscious of who paid her salary, wanted to clear such requests with him.

Everyone in Washington, it seemed, wanted to see and hear what Hickok heard and saw while "in the middlewest." One can rather easily guess why: because the Midwest was exploding.

In January 1933, Ed O'Neal, head of the usually politically placid American Farm Bureau Administration, had told Congress, "Unless something is done for the American farmer we will have revolution in the countryside in less than twelve months."[6] O'Neal may have exaggerated, but not by a lot. In August 1932, seeking prices for their crops that would keep them and their families alive, farmers in Sioux City, Iowa declared a farm strike, blocking the roads into town and turning back trucks carrying produce to market.[7] At roughly the same time, Sioux City dairy farmers called their own strike, which quickly spread to nearby communities and states. When striking dairy farmers caught trucks trying to deliver milk to cities, however, they did not merely turn the trucks around. At a time when some people literally starved to death and millions more went hungry, strikers poured the milk out by the side of the road. It formed brilliant white pools in the ditches.[8]

In addition, that winter, as Ed O'Neal warned Congress of revolution in the countryside, farmers across the Midwest, but especially in Iowa, had occasionally assembled to prevent banks from selling off the hundreds of thousands of mortgaged farms that had gone into foreclosure. At bank auctions, groups of farmers would gather by the hundreds, one would bid pennies for the property and everything on it, while the others would intimidate outsiders from bidding anything more. And just like that, an evicted farmer owned his farm again.[9] In a similar vein, farmers would gather in courtrooms to intimidate judges who processed foreclosure claims. Occasionally, they did more than merely intimidate. In April 1933, after the new Roosevelt administration had taken office, farmers in Le Mars, Iowa kidnapped a judge from his bench after he refused to suspend foreclosure proceedings against mortgaged farms. The farmers drove the judge to the outskirts of town and went through the motions of lynching him from a telegraph pole.[10]

Then, in the fall of 1933, just before Hickok left for the Midwest, and with the clock counting down, farmers did everything they could to make good on the revolutionary prediction O'Neal had made. In September, Illinois dairy farmers voted to withhold milk from Chicago until they got the prices they wanted. "Farm War On" the *Chicago Tribune* declared.[11] That same month, the National Farm Holiday Association, the closest thing farmers had to a union, declared a national strike.[12] A few days earlier, the governor of North Dakota—the governor, mind you—joined farmers in that state in declaring a wheat embargo until prices rose. Unlike governors in other states, the governor of North Dakota threatened to call out the National Guard not to keep the roads open, thereby allowing farmers to deliver their crops to markets, but to patrol the roads, making sure that trucks and trains crossing the bridge over the Red River into Minnesota did not contain wheat. In strike parlance, the National Guard would be the picket.[13] In October, dairy farmers in Wisconsin renewed their milk strike. In late October and early November, they started bombing creameries.[14]

Into this developing revolution drove Lorena Hickok in a used Chevrolet Cabriolet nicknamed "Bluette."[15] She would leave the Midwest impressed less by the militancy of farmers than by their incredible suffering. Three incidents from her first week in North Dakota suggest both how the Great Depression had begun to affect Americans *and* how the Great Depression had begun to affect those, like Hickok, whose job it was to document how it affected others.

After speaking with Minnesota governor Floyd Olson, Hickok left for Bismarck, North Dakota. From there she drove to Dickinson, North Dakota to a rural church that doubled as the county relief agency. "Grouped about the entrance to the church," she wrote Hopkins back in Washington, "were a dozen or more men in shabby denim, shivering in the biting wind that swept across the plain." "Farmers, these," she commented, " 'hailed out' last summer, their crops destroyed by two hail storms that came within three weeks of each other in June and July, now applying for relief." Hickok sat in with the relief investigator who took down their stories. "Again and again on the application appeared the statement, 'Hailed out. No crop at all.' " "Of the men I saw this afternoon," she wrote, "none had any income." "For themselves and their family they need everything," Hickok observed. "Especially clothing." Although only October, it was already bitterly cold in North Dakota. When Hickok returned to her car from the church, she "found it full of farmers, with all the windows closed. They apologized and said they had crawled in there to keep warm."[16]

After Dickinson, Hickok drove to Minot, North Dakota, in the northern part of the state. At the relief office in Minot, she met "a quiet, mild-mannered, Scandinavian wheat farmer seeking a loan." "He'd been 'hailed out again,' " he said. His assets, Hickok listed, included thirty head of cattle, sixteen horses, some hogs, some farm machinery, a tractor—"which he hadn't used for several years because he couldn't afford to"—and 320 acres of land. His liabilities, meanwhile, had accumulated: "Bank of North Dakota, mortgage on a quarter section of his land, $800; farm implement company, $400; blacksmith, $300; hardware company, for spare parts, tools, etc. $1000; back taxes, $600; U.S. feed and seed loans, $500. A total of $3,600." "During the conversation," she wrote,

> the secretary of the Farmers' Loan Association, taking his application, asked:
> "How are you fixed for the winter in food and clothes for your family?"
> The man didn't answer. Instead, his eyes filled up with tears—which he wiped away with the back of his hand.
> The question was not repeated. And for the second time since I've been on this job I found myself blinking to keep tears out of my own eyes.[17]

It must have taken a lot for Hickok, who spent years honing a persona of the hard-boiled reporter, to admit to having to blink back tears. (She never tells Hopkins of the first time she had to.) At least, as Hickok observes, the investigator had the decency not to repeat the question.

From Minot, Hickok drove to Bottineau, North Dakota, flush against the Canadian border. "I visited this afternoon," she wrote her close friend, the first lady, Eleanor Roosevelt, whom she had met while working as an Associated Press reporter, "one of the 'better' homes of people on the relief

Figure 1.1. Lorena Hickok (on the left) with Eleanor Roosevelt in 1935.
Source: Bettmann/Contributor/Getty Images

rolls" (see Figure 1.1). Hickok observed that no real repairs had been made to the house in years. The kitchen floor had been patched up with tin can lids and old automotive license plates; newspapers had been stuffed into cracks in the walls where plaster had fallen away; and daylight shone beneath a crack in the door. "And in that house," Hickok wrote, having earlier observed that winter had already arrived, and that the previous winter the temperature had dropped to 40 degrees below zero and stayed there for ten days, "two small boys . . . were running about without a stitch on save some ragged overalls. No shoes or stockings. Their feet were purple with cold." Hickok noted—with horror—that the mother was going to have another baby in January. "In that house!" she exclaimed. "This, dear lady," Hickok informed the first lady, "is the stuff that farm strikes and agrarian revolutions are made of."[18]

From Sioux City, Iowa, in late November, Hickok confessed to Hopkins, "sometimes I feel damned ashamed for drawing down the salary I get for—just going around and observing!"[19] She need not have felt ashamed. Hopkins evidently felt her salary was money well spent. Over time, he did not rely on Hickok and her observations alone. Eventually, he hired sixteen field investigators—including a young Martha Gellhorn—to circulate about the country and take the American temperature.[20] He did so because, as Louis Howe and Henry Morgenthau also knew, how Americans felt about the Great Depression mattered intensely. How well did state and local relief agencies meet the needs of suffering Americans? Would Americans continue to suffer quietly? Or would they, like farmers in the Midwest, revolt? How did they feel about the president and the New Deal? Most importantly, when and from where would they summon the "animal spirits," as the economist John Maynard Keynes would put it a few years later, that would lead the country out of its torpor and into recovery?

No one could answer those questions definitively, but more so than perhaps at any other point in American history, the future of the country seemed to depend upon the emotional life of ordinary Americans.

Contemporary psychologists somewhat faddishly speak of emotional intelligence: the "ability to monitor one's own and other people's emotions, to discriminate between different emotions and label them appropriately, and to use emotional information to guide thinking and behavior."[21] By that definition, Hickok had emotional intelligence to spare. Everywhere she went, in every report she wrote, she sought to discern how Americans felt, to label those feelings, and to speculate about what sort of actions those feelings would produce. "I have an idea that the chief trouble with the people in South Dakota," she wrote Hopkins in November 1933, "the thing that is behind whatever unrest there is in the state, is sheer terror. Those people are afraid of the future. Some of them are almost hysterical."[22] She could also use emotions to guide thinking and behavior. After spending a week in North Dakota watching farmers freeze, Hickok lost her temper. "I wish I could find words adequately to express to you the immediate need for clothing in this area," she wrote to Hopkins. "All I can say is that these people have GOT to have clothing—RIGHT AWAY."[23] The outburst worked. On the strength of its emotional urgency, and its appeal to human decency, the letter passed from Harry Hopkins to Louis Howe all the way to Franklin Roosevelt. On the copy of the report in the Roosevelt archives, a note appears indicating that the president himself called the head of state relief in North Dakota to see that farmers did indeed get clothing and other supplies at once—RIGHT AWAY.

Reading the reports that Hickok sent to Hopkins, however, and that Roosevelt administrators like Louis Howe and Henry Morgenthau vied to get their hands on, the term emotional intelligence acquires another meaning. Not intelligence in terms of individual ability or knowledge but intelligence in terms of information. George Gallup would start his public opinion polling firm in 1935, but prior to that, basic information about how Americans felt either did not exist, came filtered through mediums like newspaper editorials or partisan journalism, or, like election results, arrived too infrequently to reveal very much at all. Hickok and other investigators filled that void in information. They were spies, if you like, though spies out to help those whom they spied on.[24] Indeed, the reports that Hickok, Gellhorn, and others wrote for Hopkins offer some of the most insightful, moving writing about American life during the Great Depression in the then scant public record.

For all of their work, however, the emotional life of ordinary Americans during the Great Depression—and extraordinary ones, for that matter—remains something of a mystery. One knows that Americans suffered during the Great Depression, but what does that mean? Suffer how? Suffer what? Did they suffer equally? And what did they make of their suffering? Did they do anything besides suffer? Inspired by field investigators like Hickok, this book sets out to answer those questions.

The Conventional Wisdom

If answers to these questions do not come immediately to mind, thereby making a book like this one necessary, that may be because of the role the Great Depression has come to play in American history. If people have thought about the Great Depression lately, they have likely thought about it in the context of the Great Recession, when the latest economic catastrophe earned comparisons to the earlier one. In the wake of the Great Recession of 2008, that is, the Great Depression has often functioned less as history than as history lesson, and such an approach usually flies too far above the everyday life of the period to provide an intimate view of how ordinary people experienced it. In *After the Music Stopped: The Financial Crisis, the Response, and the Work Ahead*, for example, Alan S. Binder repeatedly refers to the Great Recession as the "Great Depression 2.0."[25] Indeed, in the midst and aftermath of that recession, economic historians returned to the Great Depression with newfound urgency. Liaquat Ahamed's *Lords of Finance* and, especially, Barry Eichengreen's *Hall of Mirrors* explored how an earlier generation of politicians and central bankers had, as Ahamed's subtitle put it, "broke the world" and then struggled to put it back together again. Still more urgently, these books asked if the latest generation of politicians and central bankers had learned anything from how their forebears had responded to the previous economic catastrophe. More to the point, they asked if they had learned the right lessons.

Scholarship rarely gets more relevant. Too often, however, in focusing on policy, on the decisions of elites and central bankers, these books tended to quantify rather than describe the experience of those who lived through the Great Depression. In the opening pages of *Lords of Finance*, for example, Ahamed, adopting a global perspective on the Great Depression, writes that by 1931,

> production in almost every country had collapsed—in the two worst hit, the United States and Germany, it had fallen 40 percent ... Armies of the unemployed now haunted the towns and cities of the industrial nations. In the United States, the world's largest economy, some 8 million men and women, close to 15 percent of the labor force, were out of work ... Gangs of unemployed youth and men with nothing to do loitered aimlessly at street corners, in parks, in bars and cafes. As more and more people were thrown out of work and unable to afford a decent place to live, grim jerry-built shantytowns constructed of packing cases, scrap iron, grease drums, tarpaulins, and even of motor car bodies had sprung up in cities such as New York and Chicago—there was even an encampment in Central Park ... In the United States, millions of vagrants, escaping the blight of inner-city poverty, had taken to the road in search of some kind—any kind—of work. Unemployment led to violence and revolt. In the United States, food riots broke out in Arkansas, Oklahoma, and across the central and southwestern states.[26]

Similarly, in *Hall of Mirrors*, Eichengreen recounts how "just as the US treasury allowed Lehman Brothers to fail in September 2008 in part to make a political statement and correct the moral hazard created by its earlier bailout of Bear Stearns," in 1933 the Reconstruction Finance Corporation allowed Guardian Trust, a Michigan Bank, "to go under." "This was a disaster of miscalculation and obduracy all around," Eichengreen concludes, reciting the grim economic statistics then facing the nation. "By February of 1933 industrial production in the United States had fallen to just 53 percent of its 1929 level. Prices had collapsed. Unemployment was approaching 25 percent. The banking system was allowed to disintegrate over the misplaced priority attached to moral hazard."[27]

Eichengreen is right, and Ahamed paints an accurately grim if nevertheless blurry picture. The problem, however, lies in the fact that while economic indicators like how much industrial production had fallen off, whether prices had collapsed, what number unemployment approached, and how many millions of vagrants had taken to the roads mean a great deal to economists and policymakers, and indirectly to everyone who seeks to avoid recessions and depressions, they only vaguely represent the experience of people who lived out those economic indicators, who lost jobs, who could not feed their families for what their crops sold for, who watched their savings disappear in bank failures, or who—one by one and not by the millions—took to the roads. It sounds sloganeering to say it, but the economy does not matter, people do—or the economy matters because people do. Economists know that as well as others, but their reliance on numbers rather than stories can obscure that basic truth. "You can pity six men," Harry Hopkins wrote in his 1937 memoir, *Spending to Save*, "but you can't keep stirred up over six million."[28] As the Great Recession has come to frame histories of the Great Depression, however, readers have been asked to pity 6 million men rather than six. Ironically, in such accounts, that mythic figure of the Great Depression, the forgotten man, risks being forgotten yet again.

Earlier histories of the Great Depression, those that predate the Great Recession, do not suffer from this problem to nearly the same extent. In seeking to tell the story of "the ordeal of the American people," as one of the most famous histories of the Great Depression puts it, many of them draw on the reports Hickok wrote for Hopkins and, whether consciously or not, strive to represent the emotional ordeal of the American people in the Great Depression as well.[29] Yet while these works acknowledge the emotional lives of Americans, they suffer from their own limitations and contribute to keeping the emotional life of Americans in the shadows. As a rule, these works tend to focus on a handful of emotions, on what I have come to think of as the canon of Great Depression feelings. Like canonical books of the Bible, this canon includes only those sacred Great Depression emotions accepted as genuine. These canonical emotions comprise—and rarely stray far from—despair, fear, anger, and, following the election of Roosevelt in 1932, hope. Of these, though, fear and despair have become hyper-canonical, the ur-emotional texts of the Great Depression. Moreover, these emotions have come to define the literary canon qua canon of the period as well. Although, as I argue later in this book, it hits other emotional notes, the novel that has outlived and defined the decade of the 1930s better than any other, John Steinbeck's *The Grapes of Wrath*, survives in the cultural imagination—despite a title that promises anger—as a book principally about despair. In sum, the conventional wisdom would have you believe that during the 1930s Americans felt despair and fear to the exclusion of all other emotions. That same conventional wisdom would also have you believe that sometimes they went to the movies, but only to escape their despair and fear.

Of course, the conventional wisdom is not wrong. If fear and, especially, despair dominate popular histories of the Great Depression, that is because those emotions largely did define the decade. In writing to Eleanor Roosevelt of the dust storm that overtook her outside Huron, South Dakota, Lorena Hickok speaks of her own brush with "desolation, discomfort, and misery," as if those emotions, those synonyms for despair, wandered the landscape like figures out of the Bible.[30] And so they did.

That said, although fear, despair, and other canonical emotions capture an essential, perhaps the defining part of life in the Great Depression, they leave out a lot, too. By the time Hickok made it to Sioux City, Iowa in late November, for example, she had found intimations of optimism. The farm strike had started in Sioux City and, Hickok reminded Hopkins, "it was a hotbed of 'the reds'"—that is, communists.[31] But the arrival of the Civil Works Administration (CWA), a predecessor to the Works Progress Administration, both of which tried to put the unemployed and the needy to work, had pacified many of those inclined to rebel. Instead of surplus goods from the grocery store, which they had received on relief, CWA workers would earn wages, which they could spend how they pleased. "The CWA gangs, some 20 men," Hickok wrote Hopkins, "were putting in shoulders along an old and rather narrow paved road. It was a nasty morning. Cold. And sleet. But they looked cheerful. Thirty-hour week, 40 cents an hour—CASH, instead of grocery orders."[32] In other Iowa towns—Des Moines, Ottumwa—the CWA seemed to have the same good effect. In early December, Hickok returned to Sioux City to report on the area two weeks after the CWA had arrived. "You get a feeling of optimism all through the area," she wrote. "All the little towns have got out Christmas tree decorations. They've strung evergreens above Main Street." "I hope I'm not unduly optimistic," she added, "but it does look darned good."[33]

Earlier in the month, Hickok had found an even more surprising emotion than optimism. In South Dakota, she met a woman "who has ten children and is about to have another." She had so many children, Hickok observed, "that she didn't call them by their names, but referred to them as 'this little girl' and 'that little boy.'" Hickok added, "And despite the fact that her husband was out of work and that they had no money and were terribly ragged, she seemed contented and happy enough. 'This (White River) used to be quite a town,' she said cheerfully, 'but it's kinda gone down hill lately.' "[34]

I do not think the Great Depression made many people content or happy, or if that is too high of a bar to clear, that many people had their contentedness or happiness left untouched by the Great Depression. But its presence on the plains of South Dakota serves as a warning not to rule anything out.

To put it plainly, the emotional life of the Great Depression ranged beyond the canonical emotions, beyond despair and fear, and to understand it, one must understand them, too. In sum, when the Great Depression appears only in the guise of macroeconomic lesson, or when it appears only in the costumes of its most familiar emotions, much of the decade remains lost to us.

So What?

Although the details of how Americans responded to the Great Depression may seem of interest to only a small group of historians and literary critics or those, like me, who cannot stop thinking about the decade, in fact they concern anyone who cares about contemporary life in the United States. Indeed, the Great Depression matters, and continues to matter, for a host of reasons.

It matters economically. Economists understand how capitalism works precisely because it failed so spectacularly during the Great Depression. It matters ethically. The Depression poses, in dramatic and sweeping terms, the question of what responsibility one has to relieve the suffering of another, and what role the state can play in discharging that responsibility. The stakes, quite simply, could not be higher. Those stakes perhaps explain why historians focus so intently on the widespread despair of the decade. Without despair, without suffering, the question of who owes what to whom would lose much of its urgency. In any case, rarely did Americans get so clear a chance as they did during the Great Depression to test the proposition that, as Michael Ignatieff famously put it, needs make rights.[35] In revisiting the Depression, when so many needed so much, readers today retake that test.

And it matters politically. With apologies to Arthur Miller, the Great Depression is the American crucible: a test the country survived, but also a crisis in which events and responses to those events interacted to produce something new, to produce, really, the country Americans live in today. The Great Depression, Ahamed writes, "was the seminal economic event of the twentieth century."[36] In many ways, it was the seminal political event, too. Nearly every one of the political fights that make newspapers today—over taxation, the budget, the role of government, on and on—began or drew blood during the Great Depression. As a result, the 1930s represents a decade we can never understand fully enough, if, that is, we wish to understand ourselves and the origin of our own political divides. To study it is to study us.

Admittedly, these reasons for why the Great Depression matters can seem suspiciously high-minded; at times, they read like reasons why the Great Depression *should* matter rather than reasons why it really matters. For that, one must confess that the Great Depression might matter most of all because it offers a terrifying yet enthralling glimpse into the fragility of economic life. The journalist and literary critic Edmund Wilson called the Great Depression *the American Earthquake*.[37] It is an apt metaphor. Like an earthquake, everyone felt the Great Depression. Like an earthquake, it caught everyone off guard. And like an earthquake, it devastated lives and landscapes. (Like an earthquake, it also had aftershocks.) And if you are at all like me, you cannot help but wonder how people, in the midst of that chaos, responded emotionally to the destruction that followed. How did it feel to lose a job, lose a home, to not have enough to eat? How did it feel to *not* suffer those fates yet know that they could visit you at any moment? And how did it feel to live among so many undone by economic disaster?

The Great Depression matters because it provides a horrible but natural experiment for answering such questions, in part because those who lived through it left behind so many documents—from diaries to gangster films to the great American novel—attesting to how they felt about what happened to them. In his 1931 poem "Papermill," to take but one example, Joseph Kalar writes of a factory once alive with sound and motion but that now, after the Depression, lies in a "clammy silence." Kalar composes the poem almost exclusively in the present tense, as though time, like the factory, has also stopped. The whole scene is, as the refrain of the poem puts it, "Not to be believed." In the closing lines of the poem, Kalar turns to the workers of the mill, who offer their own variation on the refrain:

Where once feet stamped over the oily floor,
Dinnerpails clattered, voices rose and fell
In laughter, curses, and songs. Now the guts
Of this mill have ceased their rumbling, now
The fires are banked and red changes to black,
Steam is cold water, silence is rust, and quiet
Spells hunger. Look at these men, now,
Standing before the iron gates, mumbling,
"Who could believe it? Who could believe it?"[38]

In reading "Papermill," one feels pity for the tragedy that befalls the workers and, if Aristotle is right about tragedy, fear that there but for the grace of God go I. (I may not work at a paper mill, but my job could suddenly disappear one day, too.) But, in keeping with the Aristotelian theme, what one may feel above all is catharsis, which does not mean the purification or purgation of emotion but the "clearing up" or "clarification" of something, in this case, the perception and apprehension of an emotion.[39] Yes, one thinks, it would be unbelievable for a once thriving mill to close and take with it a whole way of life. Or, if, like many of the men and women I grew up around in northeastern Ohio in the 1970s and 1980s, you yourself stood outside the gates of a closed factory, you would think, if you had not before, that yes, when the mill closed, at first it was simply unbelievable.

The Great Depression matters, then, and perhaps matters most of all, because it represents economic catastrophe, and one understandably wonders what it feels like to live through economic catastrophe. In reading of the Great Depression and, especially, in reading the literature of the Great Depression, you are like an athlete training for a race that others have run before you but that, with any luck, you will never have to run yourself, or never run again.

All of which raises the question of whether economic catastrophe on the scale of the Great Depression could happen a second time. Are we right to wonder what it would feel like to live through a Great Depression? Or, if it is never wrong to wonder, is our fear justified?

Yes and no. The discrete events that caused the Great Depression in the United States—a stock market crash, a banking crisis, and, to a lesser extent, accompanying recessions in European nations that dried up markets for American goods—could happen again and, to some extent, have happened again. Between October 2007 and February 2009, the S&P 500 lost over half its value. That could not match the Great Crash of 1929, in which the

S&P 500 lost almost all its value.[40] Yet without the safeguards put in place to prevent a second Great Depression, the most recent stock market crash, like the earlier one, might simply have kept crashing. Much the same might be said for a banking crisis. During the Great Recession, hundreds of banks closed. During the Great Depression, thousands did. As I discuss in Chapter 3, a provision of the 1933 Banking Act, the Federal Deposit Insurance Corporation, which insures individual bank deposits, likely kept the number of bank failures in the hundreds instead of the thousands. It no doubt saved Americans from a familiar Great Depression scene: depositors lining up to withdraw their savings from banks while they still could. Moreover, what economists call automatic stabilizers, things like unemployment insurance—another piece of 1930s legislation—and food stamps, which increase as the economy recesses, cushion the blow of economic shocks. Without them, again, the Great Recession might have turned into a Great Depression. Even with them, we felt—to invoke an earthquake metaphor—the ground shake.

On the other hand, as Ahamed and Eichengreen both argue, for the most part central bankers and politicians have learned their lessons from the Great Depression, especially when it comes to monetary policy and the need for the federal government to spend in order to get private businesses spending again.[41] Furthermore, economies no longer strain under the golden fetters of the gold standard, which constrained policymakers in the 1930s as they sought to combat the Depression.[42]

A theme emerges here. As the Great Recession demonstrates, the crises that caused the Great Depression did not disappear with it. They appear to go hand in hand with capitalism. The stock market will crash again; banks will make bad bets; and economies will fall into recession. But policymakers have gotten better at dealing with such crises. To continue the earthquake metaphor, the nation has constructed economic buildings that bend.

Or so one hopes. No matter how important the lesson, countries rarely learn anything by heart. Twenty-five senators and 171 congressional representatives voted against the Emergency Economic Stabilization Act of 2008. Some of them wanted a better bill; some of them wanted no bill at all. Those who wanted no bill at all did not see why taxpayer money should go toward bailing out sinking Wall Street banks, even if the sinking banks threatened to take the rest of the economy down with them.[43] Righteousness, as I argue in Chapter 2, is a powerful emotion. Just as the Reconstruction Finance Corporation let the Guardian Trust bank fail in 1933 to avoid creating moral hazards, some legislators would gladly cut the nation's nose off to spite its face.

Be that as it may, we do not need a Great Depression—or a Great Recession—to experience economic catastrophe. In any given month, recession or no, well over 1 million people lose their jobs.[44] With the number of foreclosures lower than ever, some 60,000 homeowners still file for foreclosure every month.[45] True, a Great Depression or Great Recession magnifies suffering. It makes it that much more difficult, for example, to find a job. (At the start of the Great Recession, on average two people applied for every job opening; by the end, six people did. If the unemployment rate correlates with the job-seekers rate, during the Great Depression the ratio of those seeking jobs to job openings must have risen well into the teens.)[46] If economic catastrophe visits enough people, it gets called a recession or depression. But just because economic catastrophe does not rise to a critical mass does not make it any less catastrophic for those whom it does visit. And even if it does not visit you, the prospect that it might creeps up on you in quiet moments. That makes the earthquake metaphor still more fitting. During the Great Depression and, to a lesser extent, during the Great Recession, the earthquake struck. It does not need to strike, though, for one to register its presence. Every time businesses fail, or the stock market dips, the ground rumbles, and you remember that fault lines run beneath you, too.

Methodology

In *The Beauty of a Social Problem*, Walter Benn Michaels has recently—and provocatively—argued that our feelings about a social problem like unemployment are "beside the point because how we feel about the unemployed has no connection at all to anything we might do about unemployment." Michaels goes so far as to argue that a focus on the plight of the victims of unemployment may distract us from the inexorable function of unemployment. Regardless of how we feel about the unemployed, that is, "there would still be (our economy would still need) unemployment."[47] "Capitalism likes it," he writes, "whether we do or not." The social problem, he continues, "cannot be addressed by having better" attitudes toward it.[48] In other words, Michaels argues, forget how you or others feel about capitalism or its victims. It makes no difference. Focus instead on the injustices of capitalism.

Although he does not say so explicitly, I cannot imagine Michaels would have kind words to say about a project like this one. To the extent that a book focuses on how people felt about capitalism, or how they felt during a moment in the history of capitalism in which social problems proliferated, the book would merely distract from what matters, which is capitalism qua capitalism.

By now, it should probably not surprise anyone that Michaels and I will disagree about the importance of feelings to social problems. For Michaels, feelings accomplish nothing; they are where social change goes to die. For me, they accomplish much more; they are, perhaps, where social change is born.

As opposed to Michaels, I would argue that how we feel about the unemployed profoundly affects what we do about unemployment. In 1935, for example, a majority of legislators and the president of the United States, presumably with the support of the American people who elected them, acknowledged that since the economy needs unemployment, the unemployed cannot therefore be held responsible for their unemployment. In other words, the unemployed should be pitied and not blamed. As a result, the country made unemployment insurance part of the Social Security Act. From then on, when you lost your job, you would not be cut loose but, rather, would receive cash for a limited number of weeks, ideally until you could find another job. To put it another way, the social problem was indeed addressed by having a better attitude toward it. True, our better attitude did not rid the world of the social problem, but it did improve the lives of those subject to it and, if you believe that automatic stabilizers like unemployment insurance keep recessions from becoming depressions, it improved the lives of everyone else, too.

Perhaps more seriously, it seems hard to see how individuals would conclude that capitalism is a problem in the first place without referring to their feelings about it, without, that is, consulting their sense of anger or injustice that it arbitrarily subjects some people but not others to social problems like unemployment and poverty, or their sense of fear that it might subject them to the same. In short, capitalism may be a problem. But if it is it will be because our feelings tell us so.

Convinced, therefore, that it matters unto itself and for Americans today, in what follows I explore how Americans in and out of political power responded emotionally to the Great Depression. I draw on an eclectic archive of sources: the ravings of a would-be presidential assassin, *Superman* comics,

Christian sermons, Orson Welles's *War of the Worlds*, sociology textbooks, stock market investment handbooks, diary accounts of bank runs, a Cleveland serial murderer, the 1931 New York City polio outbreak, pulp magazines, psychological case studies of the unemployed, the discovery of the Big Bang, the construction of the Empire State Building, Jesse Owens's record-setting long jump at the 1936 Berlin Olympics, King Edward VIII's abdication from the throne to marry a twice-divorced American woman, an account of a five-month stay alone at the South Pole, success manuals, and, in concert with all these, the imaginative literature of the period, everything from obscure Christian apocalyptic novels and H.P. Lovecraft short stories to classics like John Steinbeck's *The Grapes of Wrath* and Richard Wright's *Native Son*.[49]

I use these sources to tell the story of the Great Depression through its quintessential emotions. In the background, emotions like despair and anger never fall out of the picture for long. Individual chapters, however, foreground emotions like righteousness, panic, fear, awe, love, and hope. The list includes emotions one likely thinks of when one thinks of the Great Depression (fear, anger, and, to a lesser extent, hope) but also the emotions one may not (righteousness, panic, awe, and love). And unlike Hopkins and Hickok, I am not only interested in the emotional life of ordinary Americans, but also extraordinary ones, including those in power, those whose own emotional response to the Great Depression—and the policies those emotions generated—would influence how others experienced the decade. Throughout the book I attend to how emotions translate into actions, into what people or nations do under their influence. In the conclusion to the book, I consider further the relationship between feelings and social problems, examining how all six of the emotions I discuss in the book led to the passage of the Social Security Act of 1935 and shaped its final form. That said, as I also argue in Chapter 8, emotions do not always translate into actions, nor do they have to, I believe, to justify their study.

The overall arc of the book is, roughly, from the negative to the positive emotions.[50] That is, the book advances from righteousness, panic, and fear through awe, love, and hope. Within each chapter, I give roughly equal weight to politics (including economics), popular culture, and literature, going wherever I find the most interesting and revealing examples of the emotion taken up in that chapter. Although it may sound pretentious, I have imagined each chapter as a piece of music, with variations on a single emotional theme provided by different texts and events, each of which nevertheless adds up in the end to a broader statement about the period and the emotion. Each chapter, in addition to its more esoteric sources, discusses one or two classics of Great Depression literature: F. Scott Fitzgerald's "Babylon Revisited" (righteousness); Richard Wright's *Native Son* (panic); H.P. Lovecraft's "The Thing on the Doorstep" (fear); John Steinbeck's *The Grapes of Wrath* and James Agee and Walker Evans's *Let Us Now Praise Famous Men* (awe); John O'Hara's *BUtterfield 8* and Mary McCarthy's "The Man in the Brooks Brothers Shirt" (love); and Isaac Asimov's "Liar!" (hope). The approach, I hope, shines a new light on the Great Depression but also on these classic works of literature.[51]

In drawing on such a variety of sources, I offer a different way to think about influence or historical connection than is usual. From one perspective, that is, little—besides the emotion itself—can seem to link these divergent examples to each other. In Chapter 2 on righteousness, for example, I make no claim that Joseph Zangara (the would-be presidential assassin), Franklin Delano Roosevelt, Jerry Siegel and Joe Shuster (the co-creators of *Superman*), classical economists, Christian millenarians, or F. Scott Fitzgerald were in conversation with each other, shared intellectual origins, or were, except in the most superficial ways, even aware of each other's existence. Yet by choosing such a motley cast of actors, I hope to show how a given emotion pervaded the decade, infusing the familiar and the strange. Each chapter focuses on a major event of the 1930s—in the case of righteousness, the initial response to the Great Depression on the part of the Hoover administration—and then looks outward to analogous figures, texts, and events. In short, by demonstrating the breadth of an emotion, I hope to demonstrate its depth, its centrality. To the extent that the disparate figures I gather under one roof shared an emotion, they also shared a connection. They responded to their very different worlds in remarkably similar ways.

The book covers the period 1929 to 1941. The starting date likely requires little enough justification. Although the stock market crash did not singlehandedly cause the Great Depression—the economy had technically entered a recession in August of 1929, two months before the crash—most of those who lived through the Great Depression dated its start to the crash.[52] When the Great Depression ends, however, is far less clear. A case can be made for September 1, 1939, when Germany invaded Poland and, two days later, Great Britain and France declared war on Germany. That date offers a close less because, at that point, the United States saw the war as its fight than because the war solidified its recovery from the recession of 1937–8 and, more generally, from the Great Depression itself.[53] (In 1940, the unemployment rate, adjusted for federal relief work, would fall below 10 percent; in 1941, it would fall to 6 percent, its lowest point since 1929.)[54] To draw the line in September 1939 or, arbitrarily, at December 31, 1939, however, cuts off works of literature—Richard Wright's *Native Son* (1940) most prominently but others as well—whose themes definitively ground them in the Great Depression proper. Like other historians, then, I let the Japanese attack on Pearl Harbor on December 7, 1941 mark the end of the Depression. The next day, the United States declared war on Japan and, three days after that, Germany declared war on the United States. Wars should not always define the starts and stops of history, but in this case the Second World War probably does.

Fixing dates for when the Great Depression starts and stops does have a disadvantage, though, which is that it can leave the impression that the period contained within those dates represents a unified, static whole. To some extent, of course, the period represents just that. In later decades, people would refer to *the* Depression or *the* 1930s as though they were in fact a unified, static whole. Yet as my reference to the recession of 1937–8 might suggest, that unified, static whole experienced almost constant internal change. To put it plainly, the worst, early years of the decade differed from the middle years of the decade, and the middle years of the decade differed from the later years. More to the point, these differences would affect how people experienced the decade emotionally. Some emotions, like righteousness, arose most intensely early in the decade; others, like fear, panic, and awe, span the decade, though different events within the decade would provoke those emotions, and they would play out under very different circumstances; still other emotions, like love and hope, more closely follow the ups and downs of the decade. In any case, it pays to remember that when one speaks of the 1930s, or the Great Depression, one speaks of a single era, but also of an era that evolved over time.

For readers who may know only the barest outlines, *The Emotional Life of the Great Depression* can serve as an introduction to the 1930s. Although not necessarily in chronological order, over the course of the book I treat the major events of the period: the stock market crash; the initial response to the depression by Herbert Hoover and his administration; the widespread poverty; the election and re-election of Franklin Roosevelt; the bank holiday; the birth of the New Deal; the Dust Bowl; the 1936 Berlin Olympics; the ups and downs of the recovery; and the descent into the Second World War.

By focusing on the emotional origins and implications of these events, however, the book seeks to freshen up these somewhat shopworn conventions of Great Depression history. In addition, I treat movements and events—the polio scare of 1931, the evangelical belief in the second coming of Christ, the founding of Alcoholics Anonymous—that have not attracted as much attention but that, to my mind, reveal as much about the decade as the banner events.

For academics, the book contributes to some of the exciting research into emotion and affect that has occurred in various scholarly fields over the last two decades. It makes this contribution less by delving into the biology, psychology, and theory of emotions—though it does a little of that—and more by demonstrating what a focus on the emotions can bring to the writing of cultural history. The book does not seek, as an earlier generation of work on the emotions did—I am thinking in particular of Ronald de Sousa, Martha Nussbaum, and Antonio Damasio—to rehabilitate emotions generally over against something like reason.[55] Rather, believing that argument safely made, this book sets out to explore the political and cultural origins and effects of emotions.[56] The upshot is a new take on the Great Depression, one that emphasizes its major events (bank panics, unemployment, the Dust Bowl) but also, and perhaps even more so, its sensibilities, its structures of feeling.

I should add, too, that while I am interested in what makes the Great Depression unique, I am also interested in what makes it commonplace. By that I mean each decade or period of history doubtless has its own amalgam of emotions, with each particular emotion having greater or lesser potency in the blend. Indeed, that is what allows us to speak of an era at all. And I believe the emotions I filter out and examine in this book—despair and anger but in more depth righteousness, panic, fear, awe, love, and hope—together compose the peculiar emotional blend of the Great Depression. (That each of the emotions I select would come together in the passage of the 1935 Social Security Act, to my mind the signature legislative achievement of the decade, confirms, for me, their particular importance to the decade.) That said, I do not think these emotions were in and of themselves peculiar to the 1930s. Obviously, individuals felt emotions like righteousness and love before and after the Great Depression. The same goes for the other emotions. That commonality of emotions is what makes the Great Depression recognizable. We can understand what people felt then because we feel similar emotions today. What makes the Great Depression unique, however, in addition to the specific potency and blend of its emotions, are the social and historical stimuli that elicited those commonplace emotions. We may feel what those during the Great Depression felt, but the events that provoked those feelings will differ. In the chapters to come, I try to do justice to both the unique and the common, to what made those who lived through the Depression like us, but also to what made them unlike us, if only because they lived then and we live now.

Still, in writing this book, I have been surprised by how much I have learned not just about the decade but also about the emotions in and of themselves. Above I suggested that, when it comes to politics, to study the Great Depression is to study us. That thought has turned out to have another meaning, one having to do with what makes the Great Depression recognizable. The book explores how panic works, what it means to fear something, to feel in awe of something, to hope for something, and—silly as it may sound—what it means to love someone. In taking up the emotional life of the Great Depression, one can learn a lot about the Great Depression. But one can learn a lot about the emotional life in general, too, which has not changed as much as we might think between then and now.

Caveats

Although I tell many different stories in the chapters to come, I return more often than not to one very familiar story of the 1930s, that of economics. That drift toward economics is true for the content of the book; that is, many of the stories I tell have to do with economics. It is also true for the interpretive frame of the book; that is, even those stories that do not have an obvious relationship to economics nevertheless turn into, in my telling, a story about economics. Not always, but often enough that readers might notice a trend.

I return so often to economics partly because of training, partly because of temperament, but mostly because I believe the age—the Great Depression—demands it. It goes without saying that a lot happened during the 1930s that had less rather than more to do with economics, developments that shaped the lives, profoundly or negligibly, of those who lived through the decade. A very partial list would include the rise of fascism in Europe; lynchings; the Black Legion; the birth of the freeway; the surge in high school attendance and graduation; mail-order homes; the electric washing machine and refrigerator; Tampax; Alfred Kinsey's course on marriage at Indiana University; the Book of the Month Club; miniature golf; dance marathons; commercial air travel; talkies; the introduction of frozen vegetables to grocery stores; and for that matter, grocery stores; Pearl S. Buck's *The Good Earth*; *The Jack Benny Program*; the sudden popularity of downhill skiing after the 1932 winter Olympics in Lake Placid, New York; the Lindbergh kidnapping; Mickey Mouse; the end of Prohibition; Roosevelt's fireside chats; contract bridge; bank robbers; Hervey Allen's *Anthony Adverse*; the Chrysler Airflow and the streamline aesthetic more generally; night baseball; bingo; Monopoly; Margaret Mitchell's *Gone with the Wind*; radio ventriloquists; the disappearance of Amelia Earhart somewhere over the Pacific Ocean; Joe Louis versus Max Schmeling; the New York World's Fair; deep-sea exploration; Seabiscuit; on and on. I treat some of these and, with no small agony, neglect others. The point, however, is that one could turn any one of these events into a story about economics, but probably not without losing something meaningful about how people at the time experienced them. Conscious of this inclination to see things economically, I have tried to keep it in check and, more importantly, not to let it distort what I do discuss or how I discuss it. When a wider frame seems called for, I summon it. Yet more so than most decades, the 1930s seems defined by economics. I am convinced, then, that a book about the decade, especially one written for general readers and scholars alike, should be so defined as well. That is why I take up texts and events that have more to do with the economy, and why I tend, even when discussing texts and events that seem to have less to do with the economy, to nevertheless view them with economics in mind.

Across the chapters, I trust poets like Joseph Kalar and storytellers like John Steinbeck to have discerned the emotional life of the decade better than most, and here too I should offer a caveat. This faith in the perceptiveness of writers may strike some as critically naïve. They will wonder, rightly, about how works of literature relate to the world they purport to describe. In a poem like "Papermill," for example, when Joseph Kalar describes the disbelief among workers newly confronted with their shuttered factory, how much confidence can we have that that disbelief truly existed among workers and, by contrast, how much suspicion should we have that it existed merely as an invention or projection of Kalar himself? That is, does Kalar perceive disbelief, or project it onto others? Does the disbelief originate with him or with workers? Can literature reliably reveal the emotions of ordinary Americans? Or does it really only reveal the emotions—or the emotional projections—of its author?

I fall on the side of those who believe writers do at least as much perceiving as they do projecting. Even if they did only project, their work would still count as evidence of how the decade affected people emotionally. But the literature they wrote, which expressed those emotions, would only represent themselves and their emotional response to the decade. Instead of looking outward, literature would turn inward, back on the author. Yet I believe a work of literature represents more—and more people—than just its author. So yes, I think disbelief did exist among workers, and Joseph Kalar perceived and described it. I do not take this position on faith alone, though, or because I would prefer it to be true, though I admit I do prefer such a vision of literature. In each chapter, I look to the non-literary events and incidents of the decade, from politics, economics, and popular culture, to act as a check on the literature. If the events and incidents correspond to what the literature says, then I believe we can take the literature to describe the emotional life not just of one person, its creator, but of many people.[57] Of course, if the events and incidents differ from what the literature says, and it happens, I say so.

Finally, an episode from early in the 1930s raises the question of whether one can speak of a single emotional life of the Great Depression and, if not, how one approaches the fact that some emotional lives obviously mattered more than others during this period. I refer to Mexican repatriation, when, during the early years of the Great Depression, some 450,000 Mexicans and Mexican Americans returned (or were returned) to Mexico from the United States. Some left voluntarily. Others were encouraged to go. Still others were rounded up and deported.

During the Hoover administration in particular, local officials did not want to provide aliens with scarce relief funds, while local and federal officials alike—the latter led by the secretary of labor, William N. Doak—believed that aliens took jobs from American citizens and made the already bad unemployment problem worse. Therefore, local and federal officials often came together to deport Mexicans who had entered the country illegally.[58] Officials lacked the manpower to accomplish this task on their own, however, so they hoped that by staging well-publicized raids and deportations, they could intimidate as many aliens as possible into leaving the country. One Los Angeles city official, Charles P. Visel, who collaborated with Federal Bureau of Immigration agents to conduct such raids, including an infamous one staged in City Plaza in February 1932, even coined a term for these efforts: "scareheading."[59]

With the exception of lynching, which occurred periodically throughout the decade, Mexican repatriation offers as stark a contest as I know of the question of whose emotions mattered in the 1930s. Mexican and Mexican-American workers and families feared hunger, eviction, and unemployment as much as white workers and families. Yet it was the concern that white workers might go jobless and their families might not get enough to eat, or might get evicted, if relief funds went to aliens, that drove policy. Quite simply, both white and brown people were scared during the early years of the Great Depression. Only one group, however, was scared of being deported from the country, or scared of their lives being made intolerable if they avoided deportation and chose to remain in the country. Only one group, therefore, had their fears exploited in order to lessen the fears of another.

In less barefaced ways, this story repeats itself across the decade. The emotions of white men mattered more than the emotions of white women, which mattered more than the emotions of black men, which mattered more than the emotions of black women, on and on. That goes for policy and, to a lesser extent, for literary and popular culture, too. Rare is the mainstream representation of African Americans in love, or Latinos feeling hope. I do not believe, as a result, that we should value the emotional life of white men, for example, any less. Just because their fear received priority did not mean they experienced it any less profoundly, and because it did receive priority, if we want to understand what happened in the decade, we have to understand those fears. In what follows, however, I have tried not to assume that the emotions of some matter more than the emotions of others, and I have tried, equally, to remain alert to the emotional lives of those whose emotions, at the time, were thought to matter less.

Hickok Revisited

On December 12, 1933, seven weeks after she left Washington, D.C. for the Midwest, Lorena Hickok wrote Harry Hopkins one last letter from the region. She was leaving Minnesota that day and promised to be in Washington by the end of the week.[60] Once in Washington, she did not take much of a break for the holidays. Indeed, she had no permanent residence in the city. While there, she stayed at the White House as a guest of Eleanor Roosevelt.

Just as well, then, that Hickok spent virtually all of 1934 on the road, crisscrossing the country in the used Chevy Cabriolet, until it suffered an accident in Arizona in May and Hickok replaced it with a gray Plymouth she nicknamed "Stepsister."[61]

Her mood tended to reflect the mood of wherever she stopped. On April 11, 1934, Hickok wrote Hopkins from Houston, Texas. "At no time previously, since taking this job," she observed, "have I been quite so discouraged as I am tonight." "Texas," she concluded, "is a Godawful mess." The city had run out of relief funds, the state had fallen to political infighting, and "in the meantime," she prayed, "God help the unemployed."[62] "I've been out on this trip now for a little more than two weeks," she added. "In all that time I've hardly met a single person who seemed confident and cheerful." In Houston, however, she did meet an enthusiast for Mussolini and, discouraged by everything she had seen elsewhere, confessed her own occasional enthusiasm for dictatorship—albeit a Roosevelt dictatorship. "And honestly, after nearly a year of traveling around this country, I'm almost forced to agree with him," she wrote Hopkins of the Mussolini supporter. "If I were twenty years younger and weighed 75 pounds less, I think I'd start out to be the Joan of Arc of fascism in the United States."[63]

By June, though, her mood had lifted. From Florence, Alabama, she wrote with unabashed awe about "the New Deal's most magnificent project," the Tennessee Valley Authority (TVA), the federal government's grand experiment in economic modernization often—and rightly—attacked as socialistic. "A Promised Land," Hickok wrote Hopkins in Tennessee, in prose rising to the occasion, "bathed in golden sunlight, is rising out of the grey shadows of want and squalor and wretchedness down here in the Tennessee Valley these days." True, she admitted, "all over the state, in rural areas, the story is the same—an illiterate, wretched people, undernourished, with standards of living so low that, once on relief, they are quite willing to stay there the rest of their lives. It's a mess." "But then—there's the TVA," she exclaimed. "Gosh, what possibilities!"[64] Of the 10,000 men the TVA had put to work, "thousands of them," Hickok enthused, "are residents of the Valley, working five and a half hours a day, five days a week, for a really LIVING wage. Houses are going up for them to live in—better homes than they have ever had in their lives before. And in their leisure time they are studying—farming, trades, the art of living, preparing themselves for the fuller lives they are to lead in that Promised Land." "You are probably saying," Hickok anticipated, " 'Oh, come down to earth!' But that's the way the Tennessee Valley affects one these days."[65] She admitted that not everyone got "so excited about it as I do," but "the people—the people as a whole—are beginning to 'feel' already the presence of the TVA."[66]

As her letters suggest, wherever she went, and she went virtually everywhere, Hickok honored the emotional life—and range—of Americans during the Great Depression. As in Tennessee, she sometimes found excitement. More often than not, as in Houston, she found pessimism and gloom. Above all, though, she sought to fathom the country—and its people—in what Roosevelt in his First Inaugural Address called this "dark hour of our national life."[67] She sought to understand the many and various ways ordinary people responded to extraordinary times.

Her example suggests what an emotional approach to the Great Depression can mean for how one understands this period in American history, especially if one remains open to feelings other than just despair and fear. As psychologists understand them, emotions principally help human beings to appraise their environment and adapt their purposes to it. "From an emotional reaction," Richard Lazarus wrote in his influential 1991 book *Emotion and Adaptation*, "we can learn much about what a person has at stake in the encounter with the environment or in life in general, how that person interprets self and world, and how harms, threats, and challenges are coped with. No other concept in psychology is as richly revealing of the way an individual relates to life and to the specifics of the physical and social environment."[68] In other words, emotions disclose the self and the world, the person and the person in history.

A former journalist, Hickok seemed to grasp, intuitively, the adaptive purposes of emotion. She understood that how people felt revealed what had happened to them. And she understood that how people felt also revealed what people might do about what had happened to them. She saw that emotions unlocked history.

We pick up where she left off.

2

Purging the Rottenness from the System

The Blessed and the Damned in the Great Depression

When we think of the Great Depression, we tend to think of the lost and bewildered: the stoic but dazed "Migrant Mother" in Dorothea Lange's famous photograph; the Muncie businessman who took books out of the library, sat up nights reading them so that he might understand "the big things [that] were happening," but who soon gave up after realizing "they're too big for us anyway"; or Sewell Avery, the Chicago businessman who, at the beginning of the Great Depression, led the turnaround of the Montgomery Ward department store, nevertheless confessing that "To describe the causes of this situation is rather beyond my capacity. I am unfortunate in having no friends that seem able to explain it clearly to me."[1] Perhaps the title of Sherwood Anderson's 1935 travelogue summarizes this sense of bewilderedness best: *Puzzled America.*

Doremus Jessup, the aged, flinty New England newspaper editor and main character of Sinclair Lewis's *It Can't Happen Here* (1935), would certainly consider himself a citizen of that country. Early in Lewis's novel, Doremus considers how life has changed since the onset of the Great Depression. He laments the impossibility of planning for the future, regretting his share in "the insecurity, the confusion, the sense of futility in trying to do anything more permanent than shaving or eating breakfast, that was general to the country."[2] In addition to robbing him of the capacity to act, the Great Depression has robbed him of the capacity to know. He complains, "And for a newspaper editor—for one who must know, at least as well as the

The Emotional Life of the Great Depression. John Marsh, Oxford University Press (2019).
 DOI: 10.1093/oso/9780198847731.001.0001

Encyclopaedia, everything about local and foreign history, geography, economics, politics, literature, methods of playing football—it was maddening that it seemed impossible now to know anything surely." A couple of paragraphs below this one, he extends the circle of his ignorance:

> The coming and the going of the N.R.A., the F.E.R.A., the P.W.A., and all the rest, had convinced Doremus that there were four sets of people who did not clearly understand anything whatever about how the government must be conducted: all the authorities in Washington; all of the citizenry who talked or wrote profusely about politics; the bewildered untouchables who said nothing; and Doremus Jessup.[3]

According to Doremus, the Great Depression has uncovered the abyss of ignorance that lies below the thin surface of knowledge in the United States. The Depression, Doremus concludes, has revealed that no one knows anything, including those whose job it is to know something. At best, Doremus believes, those living through the Great Depression could say "I know that I know nothing," as Socrates put it. Except for them, ignorance, instead of the starting place for inquiry, as it was for Socrates, becomes the finish line of existence.

Lewis, through Doremus, articulates the anxieties of many thoughtful Americans during the Great Depression. Yet not everyone, and certainly not "all of the citizenry who talked or wrote profusely about politics," shared Doremus's sense "that it seemed impossible now to know anything." For some, just the opposite occurred. The Depression reinforced their understanding of how the world worked and confirmed their most sacred beliefs. This emotional response to the Great Depression looks very different from the bewildered emotional response of liberals like Doremus Jessup, migrant mothers, Indiana businessmen, and Chicago millionaires. It looks like nothing so much as righteousness—an imperfect term that nonetheless captures the sense of confidence and comfort that comes from being on the right side of a question, on the side of truth.

If the psychologist Jonathan Haidt's thesis in *The Righteous Mind* is correct, righteousness is one of the most common—and most troublesome—emotions in contemporary life. Curiously, however, even after the emotional and affective turn in literary studies and critical theory in the last two decades, few critics or theorists have explored righteousness. Perhaps that is because of its association with religion, which in the main critics and theorists neglect, but for whatever reason this particular ugly feeling has received little attention.[4]

When it comes to the Great Depression, however, that will not do, for at times during those years, righteousness functioned as something like the national emotion.

In Miami, Florida, on February 15, 1933, a thirty-three-year-old naturalized immigrant, Joe Zangara, read in the morning paper that the newly elected president, Franklin Roosevelt, would give a speech that evening at Bayfront Park. Zangara arrived early so he could sit close to Roosevelt, and as the president finished his speech, Zangara stood on his chair and fired five shots at the president. He missed Roosevelt but injured five others, including the mayor of Chicago, Anton Cermak. Immediately arrested, Zangara, an anarchist of sorts, but also clearly deranged, later told reporters, "I don't know whether or not I shot Mr. Roosevelt, but I want to make it clear I do not hate Mr. Roosevelt personally. I hate all presidents, no matter from what country they come, and I hate all officials and everybody who is rich."[5] At his sentencing hearing, his defense attorney asked him if he wasn't sorry he tried to kill Mr. Roosevelt. "No, no, no—I am only sorry because I did not kill," Zangara responded. "I am sorry about nothing. Put me in the electric chair."

Zangara did not get his wish; instead, he was sentenced to eighty years in prison.[6] A few weeks later, however, after Cermak died of his wounds, Zangara was retried for murder. He remained defiant—and in absolutely no doubt about the righteousness of his cause, either his hatred for the rich and powerful or his urge to act on it. "I feel I have a right to kill him," Zangara said, meaning Roosevelt. "I feel that many years. It was right. I know they give me electric chair, but I don't care—I'm right."[7] Less than two weeks later, when the state of Florida did execute him, his last act as a free man was to stride across the room and hand his manifesto, in which, the papers reported, "he had set forth his philosophy on capitalism," to the prison superintendent.[8]

Although of an altogether less violent and crazed sort, righteousness occasionally consumed the man whom Zangara sought to kill, too. Two weeks prior to the election of 1936, employers in Detroit tried to scare workers against voting for Franklin Roosevelt by raising alarms about the recently passed Social Security Act of 1935. The employers slipped a note into pay envelopes warning that "Effective January, 1937, we are compelled by a Roosevelt 'New Deal' law to make a 1 percent deduction from your wages and turn it over to the government. Finally, this may go as high as 4 percent." Workers, the note claimed, had no guarantee they would ever see the money again.[9]

In a speech at Madison Square Garden on the eve of the 1936 election, Roosevelt pounced. In an oddly vague use of the word, Roosevelt boasted that his administration had restored "peace" to the American people, by which he seems to have meant economic security, functioning local government, a promise to stay out of war, and a grab bag of other benefits like "protection of their currency, the ending of long hours of toil, the abolition of child labor, the elimination of wild-cat speculation, [and] the safety of their children from kidnappers." Peace, however, Roosevelt declared, did not come easy. "We had to struggle," he said, "with the enemies of peace—business and financial monopoly, speculation, reckless banking, class antagonism, sectionalism, war profiteering." He added, explicitly associating the perpetrators of "the current pay-envelope campaign" with these enemies of peace:

> Never before in all our history have these forces been so united against one candidate as they stand today. They are unanimous in their hate for me—and I welcome their hatred.
>
> I should like to have it said of my first Administration that in it the forces of selfishness and lust for power met their match. I should like to have it said of my second Administration that in it these forces met their master.[10]

Although I admire Roosevelt as much as anyone, here as elsewhere he could sometimes fall under the spell of righteousness, which tends to simplify the world and populate it with comic book villains and heroes rather than real people. As Kim Phillips-Fein makes clear in her history of business-led opposition to the New Deal, those who opposed Roosevelt, including the Detroit industrialists who conducted the pay envelope scheme, were not "the enemies of peace"; they were simply enemies of the New Deal.[11] More generously, they considered themselves friends of the Constitution, which, they thought, Roosevelt and his administration violated at every turn. Their pay envelope tactics may have crossed a line, but they acted out of principle—that government is best which governs least—and not, as Roosevelt had it, a cartoonish "selfishness and lust for power."

Or consider *Action Comics No. 3*, from August 1938, which carried the third installment of Jerome Siegel and Joe Shuster's *Superman*. In "The Blakely Mine Disaster," reporter Clark Kent, Superman's alter ego, learns that a miner has been trapped in a cave-in. Superman saves him, but he learns that the cave-in occurred because "the owner disregarded the mine's dangerous conditions."[12] Clark Kent interviews the mine owner, Thornton Blakely, who expresses neither sympathy nor regret for endangering his workers. "There are no safety hazards in my mine," he tells Kent. "But if there were—what of it? I'm a businessman, not a humanitarian."[13] Superman, fired by his own righteousness, sets out to teach Blakely a lesson.

That night, dressed as a miner, Superman crashes a party at the Blakely estate. Blakely, thinking the miner has come to see how the other half lives, decides to entertain his bored guests by showing them how miners live. "We'll make merry in the bowels of the earth," he declares, moving the party to the mine.[14] Once there, Superman engineers a cave-in. When Blakely tries to sound the alarm, he discovers that it, like the other safety devices in the mine, has rusted. The partygoers, including Blakely, must dig themselves out. They quickly tire. "Think of the miners," one says, "They have to do this 14 long hours each day."[15] Soon enough, the partygoers give up and settle in to die. "Oh," Blakely despairs, "if only I had this all to do over again!—I never knew—really knew—what the men down here have to face!" "That's all I've been waiting to hear!" Superman says, and allows the partygoers to be saved.[16] Several days later, Blakely tells Clark Kent, "You can announce that henceforth my mine will be the safest in the country, and my workers the best treated."[17]

Superman and the president notwithstanding, perhaps the most notorious group to feel deeply their own righteousness during the Great Depression was communists. The communist of the 1930s, however, is a familiar, possibly overfamiliar figure of Great Depression righteousness. Fortunately, as Joe Zangara, Superman, and the president show, communists did not have a monopoly on righteousness during the Great Depression. Other groups—in this chapter, I explore classical economists, religious fundamentalists, and repentant Lost Generation exiles—also felt the righteousness of their beliefs, and none hesitated to judge those who had fallen from the truth. That last part is crucial. The righteous know themselves by their opposite, those who behave in sinful or iniquitous ways. Righteousness, then, is at times indivisible from shame. For the righteous, those who have fallen from the truth, will, like contemptuous mine owners, eventually see the light, regret their misbehavior, and feel deeply shameful about it—and if they don't, they should. Righteousness therefore also implies the need for atonement, and what connects classical economists, religious fundamentalists, and Lost Generation exiles, including F. Scott Fitzgerald, who imaginatively described the emotional lives of those exiles under the pressure of the Great Depression, is their view of the Great Depression as punishment for past excesses, punishments that must be endured, even embraced, for a good life to resume. A sense of righteousness, that is, would invite many people to read what happened to the economy in the 1930s as a morality tale, with clear lessons about right and wrong, good and bad. And because it tends to rationalize the suffering of others, this righteous view of the economy would have—and to no small extent continues to have—disastrous consequences for ordinary Americans. Indeed, as I show in the first section, out of a sense of righteousness, policymakers during the early years of the Great Depression convinced themselves that by doing nothing about the failing economy, they did everything they could and should do about it lest they reward sinners and punish saints. Their decision changed history.

The Liquidationists

For many people, one of the enduring mysteries of the Great Depression is why the federal government did not do more to try to rescue the economy when it began to crash. In his popular work of populist history, *A People's History of the United States*, Howard Zinn offers one answer when he writes that "Clearly, those responsible for organizing the economy did not know what had happened, were baffled by it, refused to recognize it, and found reasons other than the failure of the system."[18] In this version of history, Herbert Hoover fares especially poorly. When he is not ordering out the cavalry to evict an encampment of impoverished World War One veterans (known as the Bonus Army) from Washington, D.C., he is leading—if that is the right word—"the inaction of the government in helping."[19] A 1933 cartoon by the great Daniel Fitzpatrick captures the populist belief in Hoover and his administration's indifference to economic suffering and obtuseness to economic reality.[20] In the cartoon, two tramps sit outside a Hooverville reading a newspaper with the headline "Hoover Speech." "It seems there wasn't any depression at all," one says to the other. As the example of Zinn suggests, Hoover's reputation has not improved much since.

Although not necessarily inaccurate, this story of the ignorant, baffled, and indifferent federal response to the Great Depression leaves out much. At least initially, Hoover broke with his advisors who urged inaction, though his efforts ultimately accomplished little. Moreover, such an account obscures how even those who *did* counsel doing nothing—most famously, Andrew Mellon—thought they were very much doing something by doing nothing. In short, few were ignorant, baffled, or indifferent. In retrospect, that may have been the problem.

Foremost among those who preached doing something about the Great Depression by doing nothing were classical economists. Although not trained as an economist, Andrew Mellon, the banker, industrialist, and secretary of the treasury during the first years of the Great Depression, very much spoke their language. It was Mellon who contributed one of the most famous quotations to emerge from the period. In his memoir of those years, Hoover reported that in response to the catastrophic slump, Mellon had only one formula: "Liquidate labor, liquidate stocks, liquidate the farmers, liquidate real estate."[21] On its face, Mellon's prescription looks bad enough. He treats human beings—laborers, farmers—as objects to be liquidated, belonging to the same category as stocks and real estate. Nor is *liquidate* a verb most people will have heard all that often, or, if they have, they will have heard it used in the sense of "to dispose of or get rid of, as by killing." Obviously Mellon did not want to kill farmers and laborers. So what did he mean?

Mellon had made his millions as a banker. For him, to liquidate meant to convert assets into cash and, relatedly, to settle the accounts of a bankrupted business by apportioning those liquidated assets to its creditors. In other words, Mellon was calling for Hoover to let bankrupt businesses go bankrupt, and for them to get what they can for their assets, until the market bottoms out. For that to happen, Mellon believed, the slump must proceed unmolested by government intervention. Hoover reports that Mellon "felt that the government must keep its hands off and let the slump liquidate itself." Hence Hoover's reference to Mellon as belonging to the "leave-it-alone-liquidationists." Mellon, Hoover writes,

> insisted that, when the people get an inflation brainstorm, the only way to get it out of their blood is to let it collapse. He held that even a panic was not altogether a bad thing. He said: "It will purge the rottenness out of the system. High costs of living and high living will come down. People will work harder, live a more moral life. Values will be adjusted, and enterprising people will pick up the wrecks from less competent people." He often used the expression, "There is a mighty lot of real estate lying around the United States which does not know who owns it," referring to excessive mortgages.[22]

By "inflation brainstorm," Mellon means something like what Alan Greenspan later famously dubbed "irrational exuberance": when optimism about the future of the economy leads people to bid up assets beyond a reasonable value. The market inevitably corrects such exuberance, and when it does, prices fall, sometimes disastrously. As Mellon states, however, a market correction "was not altogether a bad thing." "Values," Mellon declares, "will be adjusted." As prices fall back to their pre-inflated level, enterprising people can gather up the pieces and make something new. For Mellon, one man's panic and crash is another man's opportunity.

But when Mellon insists "values will be adjusted," he means moral values in addition to economic ones. And his language suggests that he conflates the two; in fact, that they are negatively correlated. In the boom, prices go up and morals deteriorate. In the crash, prices come down and morals return. Hence Mellon's association of "high costs of living" and "high living." Both rose together, and both must simultaneously return to earth. And when they do, Mellon believes, people "will work harder, live a more moral life." In general, Mellon suggests, prosperity has coddled and corrupted people; the slump will reform them.[23] It will restore order, morality, and prosperity. Thus a panic, the precursor to a slump, "was not altogether a bad thing," as Mellon has it.

Despite taking such a hard line, Mellon, as Hoover recognized, "was not hard-hearted. In fact he was generous and sympathetic with all suffering." His formula for responding to the crashing economy—leave-it-alone—arose not from indifference to suffering but from sympathy for it. "He felt," Hoover reports, "that there would be less suffering if his course were pursued," and in this feeling he reflected perfectly the economic orthodoxy of the day.[24] Regardless of their effect on morals, slumps had critical, ultimately beneficial work to do. They must be left alone to do it.

Or so some of the leading economists of the day argued with more or less one voice; and while they might not have conflated economic and moral values as explicitly as Mellon did, they nevertheless spoke of the Great Depression as a timely corrective for past misdeeds.[25] In 1934, for example, the economic faculty of Harvard University published *The Economics of the Recovery Program*, a collection of essays that promised to "analyze, in the light of economic experience and principle, the present economic policy of this country with reference to the goal of recovery."[26] The lead essay of the collection, written by Joseph Schumpeter—one of the most important economists of the twentieth century—questioned the wisdom of any efforts on the part of the federal government to intervene in the economy. Indeed, when people are most tempted to fiddle with the economy—during slumps—that is precisely when, Schumpeter argued, they should most keep their hands off of it.

For Schumpeter, slumps occur because of overinvestment in certain sectors of the economy or because of an overly bubbly enthusiasm for future prosperity. During a boom, Schumpeter observes, "an increasing volume of business is being done on the assumption that things will continue to boom. A superstructure of such transactions rises above what is substantially sound and comes down with a crash."[27] Because crashes are inevitable and corrective, Schumpeter tends not to speak of depressions or slumps but of "readjustments" and "adjustments," and they are not to be avoided but endured, even welcomed. (Fittingly, Schumpeter is best remembered today for his phrase "creative destruction.") Speaking of "the recurrent troubles of capitalist societies," Schumpeter asserts, "They are but temporary. They are the means to reconstruct each time the economic system on a more efficient plan."[28] "[D]epressions are not simply evils," Schumpeter continues, "but—perhaps undesirable—forms of something which has to be done, namely, adjustments to previous economic change."[29] As a result, recovery must "come of itself" and not from what Schumpeter calls "artificial stimulus," that is, government intervention. He explains, "For any revival which is merely due to artificial stimulation leaves part of the work of depressions undone and adds, to an undigested remnant of maladjustment, new maladjustment of its own which has to be liquidated in turn, thus threatening business with another crisis ahead."[30] Schumpeter mixes all sorts of metaphors here—artificial stimulation, undigested remnant, maladjustment, liquidation—but his meaning is plain. In Mellon's terms, slumps are not the rottenness; they purge the rottenness from the system.

Schumpeter and Mellon spoke with such certainty because their account made good economic sense but, even more so, because they believed they had history on their side. For evidence, both referred to the Panic of 1873, which was, until the Great Depression of the 1930s, known as the Great Depression. Like its later version, it left widespread bankruptcy, unemployment, and deflation in its wake. The economy shrank for over five consecutive years, but then, just as suddenly, it bounced back, and prosperity returned. Soon enough, Mellon reminded Hoover, "the whole system was working at full speed."[31] Schumpeter drew a similar moral. In the section of his essay titled "The Upshot," he declared: "There is no reason to despair—this is the first lesson to be derived from our story. Fundamentally the same thing has happened in the past, and it has—in the only two cases which are comparable with the present one—lasted just as long." "In *all* cases," he added, "recovery came of itself." Indeed, "recovery is sound only if it does come of itself."[32]

Unfortunately, while "Always historicize" is usually good advice, in the case of the Great Depression, it was not. The Great Depression was not a "readjustment." By 1934, when Schumpeter and his colleagues published *The Economics of the Recovery Program*, the Depression had wiped out nearly *all* of the gains the economy had made since the end of the last recession in 1923. It could not, therefore, simply be an ordinary correction. Still, as one contemporary economist observes, "The advocates of the 'liquidationist' point of view during the Great Depression were mistaken, but not crazy."[33] Prior to the Great Depression, a liquidationist view did seem to explain the ups and downs of the business cycle. In the case of the Great Depression, however, this time really was different.

For Schumpeter, there may not have been any reason to despair, but there was reason to atone. Although they felt no personal shame for their conduct during the Great Depression, economists like Schumpeter and liquidationists like Mellon nevertheless believed that the Great Depression arose because of the excesses of the 1920s. (Somewhat more generously, Schumpeter refers to these excesses not as "high living" but as "error and misbehavior.") For both Mellon and Schumpeter, hard times had, by necessity, to follow good times, which were made good in part by people not behaving—or investing—well enough. Fittingly, a later economist, Walter S. Salant, would refer to the liquidationist school of economics as the "crime and punishment" theory of business cycles.[34] Slumps, including the Great Depression, were punishments for past economic and moral looseness.

To put it plainly, then, according to the liquidationists, the economy had to atone for its misdeeds. So too did the American people, even though they may not have erred or misbehaved or even shared in the wealth of the boom. They still had a price to pay.

Economists like Schumpeter and would-be economists like Mellon reveal a number of things about how righteousness works. First, righteousness emerges not from the self alone but the self in tune with some higher power, someone or something that guarantees the truth and lies beyond appeal; usually, as with the religious, that higher power is God, but it does not have to be. For Schumpeter and Mellon, their authority was classical economics, the irresistible force of business cycles, supply and demand. Second, righteousness usually requires concrete evidence that irrefutably reveals the authority of a higher power in action. For Schumpeter and Mellon, evidence for the authority and truth of classical economics came from history itself. Untouched, the Depression of 1873 eventually broke, and prosperity followed. Third, righteousness often requires sacrifice on the part of the righteous. That is, the righteous witness others succumbing to temptation, from which they hold themselves back. For Schumpeter and Mellon, that temptation was, on the way up, high living and mortgaged real estate, and, on the way down, compassion—the impulse to intervene in the economy and relieve suffering before the work of slumps or adjustments (or what have you) could finish. Schumpeter and Mellon resisted those temptations and derived sober authority from it. All of these elements combine to warrant the final and most important characteristic of righteousness, which is a willingness—at times an eagerness—to judge others who disobey the dictates of a higher power or, what amounts to the same thing, succumb to temptation. If someone is right, and thus righteous, someone else must be wrong. In other words, the righteous know themselves through the wicked; in this case, those who sought to get rich quick during the boom and those, the misguided bleeding hearts of the New Deal, whose sympathy and economic policies would only prolong suffering by delaying true prosperity. One struggles to imagine an emotion more perfectly suited to rationalize the suffering of the Great Depression. To a certain extent, Hoover resisted its pull. He would do something instead of nothing. But primed to do nothing, he exaggerated the momentousness of what he did do.

The Eschatologists

Some economists may have responded righteously to the Great Depression, but they had nothing on evangelical Christians, whose faith, far from wavering during the onslaught of the Depression, only grew stronger. During the 1930s, Christian fundamentalists believed that mankind was living through its last days. They did not mean this metaphorically. As they saw it, God had lost patience with a sinful mankind, and the signs of the times, including the Great Depression itself, all pointed to an imminent Apocalypse.

Many fundamentalist Christians viewed with horror America's slide into modernity and immorality in the 1920s. For them, too many people, especially young people, lived "fast" lives—smoking, drinking, dancing, and going to movies. Worse, in high schools and universities, the young studied Darwin, and their faith suffered accordingly. Worse still, instead of condemning such trends, fundamentalists charged, the modern Church sought to get in step with them. Apostasy, in other words, ruled the day, just as the Bible said it would, and widespread apostasy, as the Bible also said, inevitably preceded the Apocalypse.

Moreover, the political developments of the 1930s—Benito Mussolini's rise to power, Adolf Hitler's driving Jews back to Palestine, the consolidation of godless communism in the Soviet Union and its spread across the globe, the increasing prospect of world war, the droughts and plagues of grasshoppers in the American dust bowl, and the alleged drift of the United States toward dictatorship—also seemed to fulfill what the New Testament prophets had predicted millennia ago. To fundamentalists, even the blue eagle of the National Recovery Administration, which was supposed to signal that businesses had complied with federal economic recovery policies, instead invoked the mark of the beast that the author of the Book of Revelations warned of, and thus confirmed mankind's drift into the end days.[35] No less a figure than H.L. Mencken, no friend to organized religion or fundamentalism, eventually came to think that the fundamentalists might have been onto something. The New Testament, Mencken wrote in 1932, "offers precise and elaborate specifications of the events preceding the inevitable end of the world," and he observed "that a fair reading of them must lead any rational man to conclude that those events are now upon us. If the Bible really is the Word of God... then it is plain as day that the human race is on its last legs."[36]

And then there was the Great Depression itself. "You must know this," the apostle Paul wrote, "that in the last days distressing times shall come," and distressing times—in the form of an unprecedented and inexplicable economic collapse—had indeed come.[37] In the grip of the Depression, evangelicals did not hesitate to draw apocalyptic conclusions. The United States, the editor of the *Sunday School Times* told his readers in 1933, was being judged for its sins, and the trial of the Great Depression proved it.[38] Similarly, E.W. Crowell, a Baptist pastor from Jackson, Michigan, began his 1938 sermon, titled "Why God Is Judging America," with the following passage from the prophet Hosea: "The Lord hath a controversy with the inhabitants of the land, because there is no truth, nor mercy, nor knowledge of God in the land. By swearing, and lying, and killing, and stealing, and committing adultery, they break out, and blood toucheth blood. Therefore shall the land mourn."[39] In short, America had sinned and, as the Great Depression showed, the day of reckoning had come.

For premillennial fundamentalists, then, the Apocalypse was nigh. The end days, however, had a silver lining; two in fact. The first was the rapture. During the rapture, which would precede the Apocalypse proper, all true Christians would ascend to heaven, leaving behind an impious remnant to suffer through seven years of tribulation (pestilence, war, famine, and death) and rule by the Antichrist. The second was the second coming of Christ, who, after the rapture and the tribulation, would return to Earth and usher in a millennium of peace and prosperity, at least for those who had not succumbed to the lures of the Antichrist during the years of tribulation.

Nothing captures this premillennial worldview quite so well as the Carter Family's "No Depression (in Heaven)," one of the most moving or, depending on your perspective, disturbing songs of the decade. The Carter Family—A. P. Carter, his wife Sara Carter, and his sister-in-law Maybelle Carter—recorded the song in New York City in June 1936. (Sara Carter sings.) The first verse associates the arrival of the Great Depression with the end times as predicted in the Bible. The second verse imagines the glories that await Christians in heaven, and the third verse describes the apocalypse itself, which will send millions of the damned to hell.[40] Neither the plucky guitar melody, nor the unperturbed monotone in which Sara Carter dispatches the unregenerate to their fate—it sounds like she is reading the shipping forecast—seem at all appropriate to the horror of the last verse. But the millions of the damned deserved their fate. As did the saved. Indeed, to focus on the violence and suffering of the final verse misses the point of the song. For the Carter Family, and for those who listened to the song, the Depression meant hunger and death. But for the Carter Family, and many of their listeners, the Great Depression also promised salvation. Hence the title of the song ("No Depression (in Heaven)") and the chorus, when the rest of the Carters join Sara to describe how they will leave this world for their final one in heaven.[41] In short, the destruction of one world would lead to the birth of a new and better one. God promised.

This premillennial way of viewing the world hanged on a sort of delayed gratification. For the small band of believers whom Christ would take up to heaven during the rapture, things—manners, mores, and in general life on earth—had to get worse before they would get better. In fact, things getting worse were signs that they would henceforth get very much better. In addition, by denying themselves pleasures here on earth, believers laid them up—tenfold—in heaven. The same delayed gratification applied for the apostates who would witness the rapture, dramatically confront the errors of their ways, and then give themselves to Christ. True, they would have to live through the seven indescribably awful years of the tribulation, during which time the Antichrist and his legions would persecute those who committed themselves to Christ, but soon enough Christ would return to defeat the

Antichrist and establish His kingdom of peace and prosperity on earth. Whether saints or converts, pre- or post-Apocalypse, one must suffer now to thrive later.

Fundamentalists half-heartedly fought the satanic forces that drove the earth toward its last days; they also thrilled at the prospect of the rapture and the second coming. In 1932, the founder of the Dallas Theological Seminary wrote of Franklin Roosevelt's victory in the presidential election, which supposedly brought mankind that much closer to the Apocalypse, "As these dark days grow darker, we are feeling the certainty of His soon return."[42] The pastor of the Hollywood Presbyterian Church offered a similar interpretation of the election returns. "The results of the past election in our country," he told readers of the *King's Business*, one of the more influential fundamentalist magazines in the country, "must confirm the conviction that we are living in the end days of human government in the earth... Surely the Lord must be at hand!"[43]

Almost by definition, religious fundamentalists exuded righteousness, and as with classical economists, that righteousness entailed doling out judgment on (at best) the mistaken and (at worst) the wicked. That formula drives the premillennial fiction written and published during the Great Depression. These novels confirm the righteousness of the saved even as they underscore the disgracefulness of the profane. By dramatizing the rewards the righteous will receive *and* the shame and regret that unbelievers will feel after Christ returns, these novels also help readers imagine such powerful emotions in the here and now, while they still have a chance to do something about them.

Take Forrest Loman Oiler's 1937 novel *Be Thou Prepared for Jesus Is Coming*. (My first edition of the book is inscribed "To Merle/from/Thelma/Merry Christmas/1938.") The novel concerns the Kolzon family: John, Miriam, and their three children, Frank, Jane, and Ann. John, Miriam, and their youngest daughter, Ann, all fervently believe in Christ; their older children, Frank and Jane, do not. After graduating from high school, Frank and Jane leave their parents' homestead for the city, where they work at banks and live fast lives, "going to dances, playing cards, smoking and tearing around and becoming more worldly, daily," their mother laments. In time, Frank embezzles money from his bank and is imprisoned, while Jane, we are told, "stayed in the city and went from bad to worse."[44]

Years pass, and a literally wandering Jew, Joel Levi, joins the family. One day, with a neighbor named Acy, Joel and Miriam drive to town "to take some produce to the village and some provisions to the Agnes Mission, to help feed the hungry and needy."[45] During the services, Miriam persuades Acy, usually indifferent to Christ, "to confess and accept the Lord Jesus as your Savior."[46] She has no such luck with Joel, much to his immediate dismay, because at the moment Acy converts, there is, as the novel describes it: "(AN INSTANEOUS OCCURRENCE!)" In other words, "a transition of the saints"—that is, the rapture.

With the main characters from the first third of the book—Ann, John, and Miriam—ushered off the earth, the book switches perspectives to Frank, Jane, and Joel, especially their newfound regret at having ignored Miriam's counsels. On his drive home from the village, for example, Joel "could not keep from thinking of Miriam's last words: '*Don't miss this chance*' and of what an idiot he had been in his indifference and stubbornness."[47] "Joel Levi and millions of others in the world," the narrator explains, "had missed their chance of becoming a part of the Bride. They had failed to accept the Lord Jesus Christ as the Son of God and to live in readiness, as a bride would, in expectation of her lover's coming."[48] Jane, in a chapter titled "The Prodigal Daughter," is also "completely awakened to what had transpired. She became fully resigned to the situation, remembering the warning she had heard from her mother, time and time again, and like millions of others had heedlessly disregarded."[49]

The remainder of the novel plays out the end days according to the Biblical prophecies: the rise of the Antichrist; his torture of the Jews and those, like the newly converted Jane, who refuse to take the mark of the beast; the battle at Armageddon between the armies of the Antichrist and Christ himself; Christ's victory and the establishment of His kingdom on earth; and finally His judgment of the dead.

Unsurprisingly, perhaps, but nevertheless compellingly, the novel is suffused with shame and regret, but mostly—and finally—righteousness. Midway through the novel, Jane is captured by the Antichrist and confined to a small prison on top of a skyscraper "for the rest of her natural life."[50] There she is visited by a demon that tempts her to commit suicide. She resists and is visited by an angel, who leads her on a guided tour through the Jerusalem of the New Testament (where she witnesses the crucifixion of Christ), then hell, and finally heaven. In hell, the angel shows her the daily arrival of the 30,000 unsaved and recently dead who "had refused their chance for eternal happiness" and now despair at their eternal fate. Among them is Herman Zolk, a wealthy oilman whom Miriam had earlier tried to save at one of his grand parties but who rebuffs her and dies before he can "think of such serious matters."[51] Seeing Herman in hell, Jane observes that in his life Herman had "gave thousands of dollars to the poor and to the missionaries." Surely, then, "there is some hope for him," she thinks. None, the angel replies. "Herman missed the one and only really important requisite. He rejected the Lord Jesus Christ as his Savior."[52] Like others in hell, Herman must live with the consequences of his rejection.

Those who are condemned to hell must live with the consequences, but Jane learns that some of those in heaven do too, for not all experience heaven equally. While showing Jane around heaven, the angel points out a group of "ministers, settlement workers, Sunday school teachers, and missionaries" who "seemed to be wishing that they had labored more earnestly and with perpetual zeal in their tedious tasks of feeding God's Word to souls in need of divine food."[53] If the soldiers in God's army regret their wasted lives on earth, think how the insurance men, bankers, unemployed, and retired, who similarly neglected their opportunities to save others, must feel. In heaven, some of these last are even denied crowns and reduced to "merely looking-on," while those who saved other souls are granted crowns and a closer seat to and a better view of Christ. "If you had your life to live over," the angel asks one of these mere onlookers in the cheap seats, "would you do it differently?" "Yes, indeed," he responds. "I had no idea of these wonderful things in store for the saints."[54] He, of course, is not among them.

As if to drive home the point still further, *Be Thou Prepared for Jesus Is Coming* does not end, like the other major work of premillennial fiction published during the Great Depression, Dayton A. Manker's *They That Remain* (1941), with a vision of Christ's peaceful and prosperous kingdom come but with a vision of Christ the righteous judge mercilessly dispatching souls to hell. At the end of the novel, Herman Zolk returns, standing before Christ's throne awaiting His judgment, pleading for forgiveness. Zolk claims he "was a wealthy oil man, generous—." "Yes, Herman Zolk," Christ replies, "I know all about it. You, like millions of others here, had good intentions. You didn't appreciate God's goodness to you." Christ explains that Zolk was too busy with a big gathering to hear the messenger—Miriam Kolzon—whom God had sent to offer him salvation. When Zolk asks why God could not have sent a messenger before, when he was less engaged, Christ loses patience. "You are one of those who *expected God to suit your convenience*," he tells Zolk. "What a mistake! Then, too, you were money-mad and would never have listened to my messengers." Christ asks, "How could you refuse your God?" Zolk says he is sorry. Christ says, "Not as much as I." At which point, Zolk is sent to hell for all eternity.[55]

Frank Kolzon, bank embezzler, fares even worse. He stands before Christ's throne awaiting His judgment:

> "Mighty God," he admits, "I robbed my bank but—"
>
> "Yes, Frank Kolzon, I know all of the circumstances. Like millions of others in this throng, there is absolutely no use for you being lost but you wouldn't listen to your saintly parents or even to your sister Jane. With every privilege, there was added responsibility, and because of that intimate knowledge and lack of interest you will receive more severe punishment than if you had never heard the message of salvation."
>
> "Oh God, have mercy, I'm sorry—"
>
> "Your excuses are lame. You are a thief and a robber and tried to enter some other way. Depart!"[56]

In his judgment of Frank, Christ sounds like the Christ of the parable of the faithful servant. To whom much is given—in this case, opportunities to hear the gospel—of him much will be required. And much greater will be the judgment against him if he does not seize his opportunity. As for Frank, *Be Thou Prepared* insists, so for all those who, despite the manifest signs of Christ's return during the Great Depression, persisted in lives of sin and sacrilege.

Fundamentalists seem to have always dreamed—and continue to dream, to judge from the success of the *Left Behind* series of novels—of the rapture and the second coming. Still, the chaos and fear of the Great Depression intensified the emotions surrounding this dream. Prophecies about the second coming of Christ not only made sense out of the chaos of the Great Depression; they also promised an escape from it.[57] (Recall "No Depression in Heaven.") The imminent arrival of Christ also ensured that those who behaved shamefully would receive their punishment, and forever after regret it, while those who gave themselves to Christ would receive their eternal reward. To many who lived through it, that is, the Depression could seem strikingly unjust, with its capricious ruining of good men and women and occasional rewarding of bad. In fact, or so fundamentalists could hope, it began the process of separating the sheep from the goats, the blessed from the damned.

Although in some, perhaps most respects they could not have less in common, when it comes to righteousness fundamentalists and classical economists spoke a similar language. Both resisted temptation, both delayed gratification, and both judged those who did not behave as virtuously as they did. Although the economists might not have used just that word, both evangelicals and economists believed that Americans had sinned and would have to pay for those sins. For the economists, the sin consisted in high costs of living and high living, as Mellon put it. For the fundamentalists, the sin was high—read ungodly—living, plain and simple. Most importantly, both groups believed the Depression was punishment for those sins. Finally, economists and fundamentalists may have had different gods and different notions of virtue. The economists worshipped prosperity and the market, while the fundamentalists stuck to God and godliness proper. But both groups believed that, ultimately, virtue would be rewarded and sins punished. As a result, both groups viewed the Depression as something necessary, even, in the end, something beneficial. So long as Americans took what they had coming, the Depression would lead to something better, whether renewed prosperity or the second coming. You might call this the righteous view of the Great Depression; you might also call it the punitive—or redemptive—view of the Great Depression. By that view, the road to redemption, economic and spiritual, ran through suffering.

The Babylonians

The punitive view of the Great Depression must have had a powerful emotional pull on the American people, because it shows up in the unlikeliest of places, including in what would become one of the canonical short stories of the 1930s, F. Scott Fitzgerald's "Babylon, Revisited."[58] In Fitzgerald's story, which originally appeared in the *Saturday Evening Post* in February, 1931, Charlie Wales returns to Paris to reclaim his nine-year-old daughter, the significantly named Honoria, from his sister-in-law, Marion. Honoria is placed with Marion after Helen, Honoria's mother and Charlie's wife, dies as a result of drunkenly wandering around in a Paris snowstorm after being locked out of their apartment by an angry and equally drunken Charlie. After her death, Charlie enters a sanitarium and sobers up, but Marion still holds him responsible for her sister's death and is therefore reluctant to return Honoria to him.

If the guiding metaphor of Mellon and Schumpeter was liquidation, turning assets into more liquid cash, the guiding metaphor of Fitzgerald's "Babylon Revisited" is dissipation, turning all-too-liquid cash—and existence—into nothing. Wandering around Montmartre, the setting for his previously dissolute Paris life, Charlie reflects, "All the catering to vice and waste was on an utterly childish scale, and he suddenly realized the meaning of the word 'dissipate'—to dissipate into thin air; to make nothing out of something."[59] Indeed, the story repeatedly hints of Charlie's dissolute, shameful past, beyond his indirect responsibility for Helen's death. In the opening scene, he returns to the Ritz bar, where he meets Alix, a bartender whom he knows from the old days. Charlie stops at one drink ("I'm going slow these days"), and Alix congratulates him. "You were going pretty strong a couple of years ago," Alix says, and then asks him about conditions in America.[60] "I haven't been to America in months," Charlie says. "I'm in business in Prague, representing a couple of concerns there. They don't know about me down there," he adds. The implication is that if the concerns in Prague knew about Charlie's behavior in Paris, they would not trust him with their business.

But Charlie reveals the most about himself—his past and his present—when he contrasts himself with others. Still in the bar, Charlie watches "a group of strident queens installing themselves in a corner," and his response is telling: "'Nothing affects them,' he thought. 'Stocks rise and fall, people loaf or work, but they go on forever.'"[61] Unlike the strident queens, that is, Charlie has been deeply affected by the crash. Unlike the strident queens, too, who are "installing" themselves in a corner of the bar, Charlie has renounced living his life in bars. (He takes just one drink every afternoon, he insists, "so the idea won't get too big in [his] imagination.")[62] The scene closes with Alix asking Charlie if he is in Paris for long. When Charlie responds that he is "here for four or five days to see my little girl," Alix exclaims, "Oh-h! You have a little girl." The exchange illustrates how much Charlie has changed, and how anxiously he needs to assert that change. In all of the years of Alix serving him drinks, his daughter apparently never came up. Now, though, his daughter further distinguishes him from the strident queens. He is heterosexual, and in a reversal of his dissipated years, when he made nothing out of something, he has instead made something, a daughter, out of nothing. As Andrew Mellon predicted, the Depression did purge the rottenness out of the system—or out of Charlie, anyway, since the strident queens appear not to have gotten the message. After the crash, Charlie does indeed "work harder" and "live a more moral life."

At bottom, "Babylon Revisited" is about the past, whether it can be outlived or made amends for. The answer is no. Charlie takes Honoria to Le Grand Vatel, "the only restaurant he could think of not reminiscent of champagne dinners and long luncheons that began at two and ended in a blurred and vague twilight."[63] Even there, though, he runs into "sudden ghosts out of the past: Duncan Shaeffer, a friend from college. Lorraine Quarrles, a lovely pale blonde of thirty; one of a crowd who had helped them make months into days in the lavish times of three years ago."[64] Charlie puts these ghosts off, which prompts Lorraine to write him later at his hotel, hoping to rekindle their relationship and reminding him of events he would prefer to forget. "We *did* have good times that crazy spring," she writes, "like the night you and I stole the butcher's tricycle, and the time we tried to call on the president and you had the old derby rim and the wire cane." "His first feeling," Charlie thinks upon receiving the letter, "was one of awe that he had actually, in his mature years, stolen a tricycle and pedaled Lorraine all over the Étoile between the small hours and dawn. In retrospect it was a nightmare...How many weeks or months of dissipation to arrive at that condition of utter irresponsibility?"[65] In other words, Charlie is ashamed of his past, and ashamed of his association with the people of his past. Children ride tricycles and play dress-up, not adults.

But Lorraine (and Duncan) will return to do more damage than just remind Charlie of his shamefully childish Paris years. In order to regain custody of Honoria, Charlie must convince his righteous sister, Marion, that he has changed and can now care for his daughter. In doing so, Fitzgerald not so subtly nudges readers, Charlie will reclaim his Honor(ia). Marion, however, remains bitter about Charlie's role in her sister's death and skeptical that he has genuinely forsaken his drunken past. In a discussion with Marion and her husband Lincoln regarding his paternal fitness, Charlie reflects: "He knew that now he would have to take a beating. It would last an hour or two hours, and it would be difficult, but if he modulated his inevitable resentment to the chastened attitude of the reformed sinner, he might win his point in the end." And he does win the point in the end, persuading Marion to release Honoria to him.

When he returns to the apartment the next day to arrange the details, however, his ghosts return. Seated with Marion in the living room, having just agreed on the day he will come back to take Honoria, Duncan Shaeffer and Lorraine Quarrles arrive, obviously drunk, bearing a dinner invitation for Charlie. Their arrival frightens the children and shocks Marion, who associates Charlie with their loutishness and instantly reverses her decision to trust Charlie with his daughter.

After the incident, Charlie retreats to the Ritz bar, where he runs into Paul, the owner. Their exchange provides the final, revealing gloss on the story:

> "It's a great change," [Paul] said sadly. "We do about half the business we did. So many fellows I hear about back in the States lost everything, maybe not in the first crash, but then in the second. Your friend George Hardt lost every cent I hear. Are you back in the States?"
>
> "No, I'm in business in Prague."
>
> "I heard that you lost a lot in the crash."
>
> "I did," and he [Charlie] added grimly, "but I lost everything I wanted in the boom."
>
> "Selling short?"
>
> "Something like that." [66]

Short selling is an investing strategy that profits from a drop in the price of a stock. For example, say a stock is trading at $10 per share. A short seller will borrow 100 shares of that stock from a broker, agree to pay the shares back to the broker in, say, a month, then immediately sell the shares for $1,000. In a month, if the price of the stock has dropped to $8, the short seller buys 100 shares for $800, returns the shares to the broker, and has pocketed $200. If, however, the price of the stock rises to $11, the speaker must buy 100 shares for $1,100, and he is out $100. In a booming market, when most or all stocks rise, it is a losing strategy.

Charlie does lose everything selling short, but not quite in the sense that Paul means. He has a different kind of asset in mind than stocks. Charlie lost a lot of money in the crash, but he lost everything he wanted—his wife and, especially, his daughter—in the boom. In the delirium of the boom, that is, Charlie thought the value of his wife and daughter would drop or, at least, not rise. They did not matter to him then, and he could not ever imagine them mattering to him. When he chose, when he was done with his life of dissipation and irresponsibility, he could buy them back and still come out ahead—that is, he could short sell them. But their price did not drop. It rose. So much so that now he cannot reacquire them for love or money. His wife is dead, and he has given up custody of his daughter with no prospect of reclaiming her.

Not for nothing, then, does Charlie fantasize about a return to "character." Early in the story, at dinner with Honoria, he feels a "great wave of protectiveness" go over him. "He thought he knew what to do for her. He believed in character; he wanted to jump back a whole generation and trust in character again as the eternally valuable element. Everything else wore out."[67] According to Charlie's logic, the problem with his generation is its lack of character, its penchant for stealing tricycles or getting in drunken fights that result in accidental deaths. That may be true, but it subtly implies that the ills of an entire generation—including the Great Depression—result from a lack of character. Conversely, it suggests that those same ills might be solved through a reassertion of character. Just as the United States was debating ending the real gold standard, Charlie believes it would—or should—adopt another: "the eternally valuable element" of character. Such moralizing recalls Andrew Mellon's inference that the Depression was brought on in part by "high living," or E.W. Crowell's assertion that God is judging America for its sins.

Whether and to what extent Fitzgerald shares Charlie's belief in character as an explanation of the ills of the present does not matter all that much—though it would be in keeping with Fitzgerald's self-assessment of himself as a "moralist." At the least, Fitzgerald must have known it would appeal to the readers of the *Saturday Evening Post*. In the same issue that "Babylon Revisited" appeared, the editors published an unsigned editorial ("The Dole Evil") arguing against the federal government providing relief for the needy because doing so would undermine "responsibility," both of the poor who receive relief funds and of the wealthy who would feel relieved of their responsibility to take care of the poor.[68]

In "Babylon Revisited," responsibility is synonymous with character, and an appeal to virtues like responsibility or character during the Great Depression signaled, as the editors of the *Saturday Evening Post* understood, a certain attitude toward it.[69] According to this view, irresponsibility and lack of character caused the Great Depression, and a return to responsibility and character would solve it. To be sure, unlike fundamentalists or the liquidationists, Fitzgerald never explicitly states that the crash and depression were judgments for living "utterly irresponsibly," as Charlie puts it—but Fitzgerald nevertheless implies as much on every page. He has turned Lost Generation dissipation into an economic morality tale.

Consider his title. In Revelation, that favorite book of the Bible for fundamentalists, Babylon is "the great city which rules over the kings of the earth," until, that is, God judges and punishes it for its sins.[70] "[H]er sins are heaped high as heaven," the author explains, "and God has remembered her iniquities."[71] Revelation also outlines the retributive justice that fundamentalists and economists alike used to describe the Great Depression: "As she glorified herself and lived luxuriously, so give her a like measure of torment and grief."[72] The same could be said of Charlie. During the boom, he glorified himself and lived luxuriously. After the crash, he must receive equal parts torment and grief. But having so suffered and repented, he can now cast judgment on the wicked whom he has left behind: queens who establish themselves in the corners of bars and exiles who refuse to grow up, all of whom, somehow, have brought the Great Depression upon themselves and others.

The Keynesians

To be sure, not everyone in the 1930s viewed the Great Depression as righteous punishment for American sins, whether moral, economic, or both. Christian sermons, the oral histories of ordinary people during the Great Depression, the fireside chats of Franklin Roosevelt, or the proletarian fiction of the day reveal much more sympathy for the victims of the Great Depression than righteous judgment—though the proletarian fiction (and the fireside chats, for that matter) are not without their own kind of righteousness. Even so, the righteous view of the Great Depression had many and various believers. John Maynard Keynes had these believers in mind when, in one of his first written responses to the Great Depression, "An Economic Analysis of Unemployment," published in 1931, the same year as "Babylon Revisited," he warned against the tendency to see the Depression as the logical and necessary reaction to the boom. "It seems an extraordinary imbecility," he wrote,

> that this wonderful outburst of productive energy should be the prelude to impoverishment and depression. Some austere and puritanical souls regard it both as an inevitable and a desirable nemesis on so much overexpansion, as they call it; a nemesis on man's speculative spirit. It would, they feel, be a victory for the mammon of unrighteousness if so much prosperity was not subsequently balanced by universal bankruptcy. We need, they say, what they politely call a "prolonged liquidation" to put us right. The liquidation, they tell us, is not yet complete. But in time it will be. And when sufficient time has elapsed for the completion of the liquidation, all will be well with us again.[73]

For the most part, Keynes won this argument. With the exception of the scarce remaining Marxist economists, today few mainstream economists view "impoverishment and depressions" as inevitable, and fewer still as desirable. Still, as the recent Great Recession shows, with its outbursts against subsidizing "the losers' mortgages" and its solemn talk of the need for austerity after so much profligacy, the punitive view of depressions and recessions continues to attract converts, perhaps because it appeals to our righteous, if mistaken, belief in a just world, the view that people—and nations—reap what they sow. If something bad happens, like a depression, it must have happened because of something bad we—or, more often, someone else—did.[74] In ordinary times, a righteous belief in a just world can be a dangerous illusion. In times of mass suffering, however, it can turn into an economic and moral disaster. At best, it can lead to inaction. At worst, it can lead people to justify others' suffering.

My point is not that recklessness and misbehavior do not happen or do not have broad economic implications. (The deliberate mislabeling of subprime mortgage-backed collateralized debt obligations that led to the near collapse of the financial sector in 2008 comes to mind.) Nor is it that such behavior should go unpunished. Nor, finally, do I think human beings will rid themselves of the ugly emotion of righteousness any time soon. Even warnings against righteousness like Keynes's (or this one) smuggle in their own sort of righteousness. Rather, my point is righteousness, by justifying misfortune, risks turning the economy into a morality tale when it is no such thing.

If not a morality tale, then what kind of story does the economy tell? Here too Keynes helps. His great insight is that the economy is more like an occasionally balky machine than a vengeful God. It can be tinkered with, and perhaps even tuned to accord with whatever sense of fairness and justice we can agree to. The economy does not, however, have a moral life of its own. It does not punish sin, decadence, or debased character.[75] Then and now, economies crash because opportunities for investment recede, aggregate demand falls, and unemployment rises, which makes everything worse. As everyone, even Doremus Jessup, should now know, economies do not crash because they have punishments to dole out or moral weights to balance.

3

"I Saw One Woman Faint"

Toward a Sociology of Panic

In the late 1930s, a young man named Robbins had everything. His father was an executive at a large, thriving company. His family had money and belonged to the right church. Just twenty years old, Robbins drove his own car and owned his own stocks. He was a junior at Princeton. He read the popular magazines (*Esquire*, *Reader's Digest*, *Colliers*) and the daily newspapers, but few books beyond the ones assigned to him. Still, he did not think this indifference to book learning would do him much harm. He imagined a future in advertising. He liked to play tennis.[1]

On the night of October 30, 1938, Robbins and a college friend were driving home from visiting a girlfriend in another state. As they approached the New Jersey border, they turned the car radio to the local CBS station. An orchestra played a tango for a minute or two, until it was interrupted by a news flash. An astronomer had observed "several explosions of incandescent gas, occurring at regular intervals on the planet Mars." The gas appeared to be hydrogen and was "moving towards the earth with enormous velocity."[2]

It was probably nothing to worry about. Indeed, Robbins and other listeners had grown used to these sorts of interruptions. In September, Adolf Hitler had announced his intention of reclaiming—by force if necessary—what he called the Sudetenland, the section of Czechoslovakia inhabited by German speakers. The British prime minister Neville Chamberlain and other European leaders rushed to Munich to meet with Hitler, and over the next few days the radio routinely broke into broadcasts to report on efforts to stave off war. Then as now, the station would soon return to its regular program.

On this night, too, the music returned, but shortly thereafter the announcer interrupted yet again to report that the "Government Meteorological

The Emotional Life of the Great Depression. John Marsh, Oxford University Press (2019).
 DOI: 10.1093/oso/9780198847731.001.0001

Bureau has requested the large observatories of the country to keep an astronomical watch on any further disturbances occurring on the planet Mars."[3] The announcer also promised a forthcoming interview with a Princeton astronomer, Professor Pierson, whose name Robbins thought he had heard around campus.[4]

Soon, things began to spin out of control. During the interview, Professor Pierson was told that a meteor had landed within twenty miles of Princeton, and the radio correspondent informed listeners that "a huge flaming object, believed to be a meteorite, [had fallen] on a farm in the neighborhood of Grovers Mill, New Jersey," just "twenty-two miles from Trenton." The correspondent rushed to the scene, where he described, amid noises of a crowd and police sirens, the truly incredible things he saw.[5]

Now Robbins and his friend began to worry, especially when the meteorite turned out not to be a meteor but a huge metal cylinder that emitted a curious hum. They really began to worry when its top unscrewed and something with tentacles, big as a bear and glistening like wet leather, wriggled out of the capsule. The creature was followed by "a humped shape" with "a small beam of light against a mirror." As the correspondent on the scene breathlessly described the scene, suddenly fire flashed from the mirror, incinerating everything and everyone in its path. "Good Lord," the radio correspondent shrieked, "they're turning into flame!"[6]

The broadcast from the scene cut off, but the announcer back in New York mournfully reported "at least forty people, including six State Troopers, lie dead in a field east of the village of Grovers Mill, their bodies burned and distorted beyond all recognition."[7] The commander of the State Militia at Trenton, New Jersey came on the air to announce that the governor was placing "the counties of Mercer and Middlesex as far west as Princeton, and east to Jamesburg, under martial law." The roads would be closed, and the State Militia would evacuate the area.[8]

At this point, Robbins and his friend were distraught. His family lived in the area that fell under martial law. He stopped at a drugstore to use the phone. On his way in, he told the four people in the store about the news. In the phone booth, he could not place his call; the lines were jammed. Back in the drug store, the patrons had turned on the radio, and now they too were anxiously listening. Not thinking entirely clearly, Robbins and his friend decided to drive back and rescue the girlfriend. The two raced back across the state line listening to the radio, and when the secretary of the interior made an announcement to the whole nation, urging calm, Robbins concluded that we—the United States, humanity—were finished. An "invading army from the planet Mars," as Robbins later put it, would soon conquer the country, in all likelihood the world. Robbins "could not bear to hear the worst," so he turned off the radio and prayed. "I was waiting for doom to strike," he remembered. "I could practically smell the gas."[9]

Eventually, Robbins turned the radio back on, and by switching to other stations, which were not covering the catastrophe, he and his friend figured out that they were not listening to news of an apocalyptic Martian invasion but to a radio play, Orson Welles's adaptation of H.G. Wells's *War of the Worlds*.[10]

If he felt embarrassed about having fallen for the hoax, Robbins could take comfort that he was not alone. The next day, newspapers across the country reported on the nationwide panic caused by the play. The *New York Times* told of a woman who "walked into the West Forty-seventh Street police station dragging two children. She said she was ready to leave the city." In Washington Heights, a man ran into the Wadsworth Avenue Police Station "white with terror, shouting that enemy planes were crossing the Hudson River and asking what he should do."[11] The Associated Press reported that in Pittsburgh, a "man returned home in the midst of the broadcast and found his wife, a bottle of poison in her hand, screaming: 'I'd rather die this way than like that.'"[12] In Indianapolis, "a woman ran into a church screaming: 'New York destroyed; it's the end of the world. You might as well go home to die. I just heard it on the radio.'"[13] As Welles himself later boasted, exaggerating, as only he could, for effect, "Houses were emptying, churches were filling up; from Nashville to Minneapolis, there was wailing in the street and the rending of garments."[14]

Journalists and media critics now think decidedly less of the story of the radio play that supposedly caused a "Wave of Hysteria over Nation," as one newspaper declared at the time.[15] Recently, W. Joseph Campbell, professor of communications at American University, referred to the panic broadcast as "a media-driven myth" and included it among his list of ten of the greatest misreported stories in American journalism. According to Campbell and other scholars, newspaper editors exaggerated the panic because it made good copy, and because they could not resist an opportunity to swat the new medium of radio, which was cutting into circulation, on the nose.[16]

If these critics doubt the story itself, they think even less of the academic study, *The Invasion from Mars: A Study in the Psychology of Panic*, written by Hadley Cantril and published by Princeton University Press in 1940, that in many respects inaugurated—regrettably so for many scholars—the field of mass communication studies. According to Joy Elizabeth Hayes and Kathleen Battles, Cantril started from the premise that some listeners lacked "the critical ability to distinguish fact from fiction" and, thus, his study contributed to "the idea that, by the 1930s, radio broadcasting was a centralized, self-contained, one-way form of communication that enthralled listeners."[17] Cantril's study therefore epitomized the so-called hypodermic needle model of communication, which, as Michael J. Socolow observes, "posited that the media injected ideas, more or less directly, into the consciousness of the audience."[18] In the field of contemporary communication studies, where no one simply passively consumes popular culture but must always "talk back" to it, an argument like Cantril's can seem as elitist and out of fashion as a top hat.

In fact, though, Cantril's study is more sophisticated than its later caricatures would suggest. True, in seeking funding from the Rockefeller Foundation for his study, and in seeking to establish his own reputation, Cantril may have exaggerated the panic caused by the broadcast. (Privately, he referred to his project as the "Mass Hysteria Study.")[19] He certainly played up the parallels between the response to the *War of the Worlds* broadcast and German propaganda for all they were worth.[20] And, to be sure, Cantril started from the premise that some listeners lacked "the critical ability . . . to distinguish between reality and fiction."[21] But evidently some listeners *did* lack the critical ability to distinguish fact from fiction. Perhaps not the millions that Cantril, working from phone surveys conducted after the broadcast, estimated, and perhaps not even the hundreds of thousands that newspapers led readers to believe, but certainly tens of thousands of people. Moreover, Cantril fought against the widespread perception that those who panicked were merely stupid. Writing in the *New York Herald Tribune*, the columnist Dorothy Thompson asserted that Welles and the *War of the Worlds* broadcast "have shown up the incredible stupidity, lack of nerve and ignorance of thousands." "Such glib generalizations," Cantril averred, "are not only wrong but dangerous, both theoretically and socially."[22]

Cantril brought a similar skepticism to the question of panic. As his colleague on the project, Paul Lazarsfield, observed, the fact that people panicked is not compelling. Indeed, given the realism of the play, panic was inevitable.[23] What was compelling is why some people panicked and others did not. Cantril thus shifted the question of panic to the question of standards of judgment and critical ability. How did people distinguish between fact and fiction? Who was more likely to take fiction as fact? Could people learn to be more critical? Based on his survey data and interviews, Cantril concluded that those with more years of formal education did a better job of recognizing the play as a play, but as with the case of Robbins, the Princeton undergraduate, education did not always suffice. Cantril further speculated, based on interviews with those who took the broadcast at face value, that the widespread economic and political insecurity of the Depression had something to do with why people panicked. Jitters, as he quoted the columnist Heywood Broun, had come home to roost. During the Depression, people had come to expect the worst, so why not Martians?[24]

One can learn a lot about the Great Depression from *War of the Worlds* and *Invasion from Mars*: the rise of radio and mass communication; how economic insecurity and, especially, the prospect of war in Europe, may have changed how people inhabited the world; and, not least, what many Americans feared. Some feared Martians, while others feared a cowed and credulous people who could be made to panic over the invasion of make-believe Martians. In addition, one can learn about the emotion of panic itself. In any reckoning of the emotional life of the Great Depression, as *War of the Worlds* and *Invasion from Mars* both indicate, panic figures prominently. During the decade, Americans tried to evacuate cities after hearing a fictional radio play, sold stocks for whatever they could get, made runs on insolvent and solvent banks alike, took justice into their own hands, and, in countless ways, responded to events with something less than reason and equanimity. If it was the red decade, it was also the panic decade. In 1932, Americans could have gone to theaters and seen the uneven film *American Madness*, directed by Frank Capra, which features a bank run. In 1935, the poet Archibald MacLeish staged his first play, called, simply enough, *Panic!* Everyone knew what he meant.

In what follows, I try to get to the bottom of whether people did in fact panic during the Great Depression, what made them panic, and what a diverse group of people—sociologists, economists, diarists, presidents, and protest novelists—thought that propensity to panic on the part of Americans meant. In short, I argue that, even more than most emotions during the period, panic preoccupied Great Depression writers. Yet like Cantril, many writers and legislators during the Great Depression concluded that in order to understand why so many people panicked during the 1930s, they had to go beyond a reductive explanation of panic that chalked it up to the stupidity, irrationality, or baseless fears of those who did panic. Like Cantril, they had to develop a sociology of panic, an understanding of the processes governing this widespread social phenomenon. In doing so, many rejected the heuristic of panic altogether; others revised it so much as to make it unrecognizable. Their conclusions offer some of the most fascinating glosses on some of the major events of the period, including, as the first section of this chapter documents, the inaugural event of the Great Depression, the stock market crash of 1929. Their conclusions would also fundamentally change the texture of American life. The Banking Act of 1933, for example, which created the Federal Deposit Insurance Corporation, and which kept commercial banks from investing their own funds in the stock market, emerged principally out of concerns over what happens when Americans supposedly panicked about their bank deposits. And while it led to no new legislation, Richard Wright's theory of racial panic offered readers a whole new way to think about American race relations.

But first, there was the crash.

The Crash

On September 3, 1929, the long bull market of the 1920s reached its zenith. After nine years of mostly uninterrupted growth, the Dow Jones Industrial Average peaked at 381.[25] It declined in fits and starts for the next six weeks, until October 24, 1929, Black Thursday, when at the opening bell the race to sell began. Within hours, the market lost 11 percent of its value. At noon, leaders of the largest banks and investment houses met, which gave hope to traders that something would be done to stop the free fall. In the event, the banking houses pooled hundreds of millions of dollars and started buying stocks.[26] The gambit worked. Confidence was restored. During the afternoon, prices climbed, and the Dow made back almost half of its morning losses.

On Friday and Saturday, the market held. But come the start of the week, the liquidation resumed. On Monday, October 28, the Dow Jones fell 38 points. The next day, it fell an additional 31 points. All told, the Dow Jones fell from 326 at the opening of trading on the morning of Wednesday, October 23 to 230 at the close of trading on Tuesday, October 29, a loss of around 30 percent of its value in a week, which added up to tens of billions of dollars (hundreds of billions of dollars adjusted for inflation).

Then and now, most observers described this race to sell as a panic. "Wall Street in Panic as Stocks Crash," the *Brooklyn Daily Eagle*, an afternoon paper, reported on Thursday, October 24. On the 25th, across the Atlantic, the London *Daily Mail* announced "Deluge of Panic Selling Overwhelms Market." The same day, back in the United States, a Boston investment trust took out an advertisement in the *Wall Street Journal* that read: "S-T-E-A-D-Y everybody! Calm thinking is in order. Listen to America's greatest bankers."[27] The implication was that stocks fell Thursday morning not because they were grossly overvalued and investors suddenly realized this, but because investors panicked and ignored America's greatest bankers, who apparently knew best what stocks were worth.

The stock market crash of 1929 is commonly credited with starting the Great Depression, and though the crash did not singlehandedly cause the Depression, it did help turn an ordinary recession into an unprecedented economic disaster. At the time, many wished to ascribe the crash to the irrational behavior of panicked investors. As we shall see, however, that story, even for those who wanted to tell it, was not quite so simple.

No one represents the evolving view of the stock market crash, and the role that panic did or did not play in it, better than Irving Fisher. At the time, Fisher was an esteemed professor of economics at Yale University, and today he is acknowledged as one of the most important economists of the twentieth century, not least for his role in bringing mathematics to the dismal science. For decades, though, Fisher was simply known as the batty professor who made one of the worst predictions in economic history. In fact, he made several infamous predictions.[28] In New York on October 16, 1929, Fisher addressed the monthly meeting of the Purchasing Agents Association and declared "stocks had reached a permanently high plateau."[29] Even worse, on October 23, 1929, Fisher addressed the District of Columbia Bankers Association. In that speech he walked listeners through the economic reasons why the rise in the market since the war had been "justified," but the timing of his speech was disastrous. The next day, what would turn out to be Black Thursday, the *New York Times* carried an account of Fisher's speech under the headline "Says Stock Slump Is Only Temporary." In the article, Fisher is quoted as saying how he did not see how a collapse of "60 to 80 points on the Dow Jones barometer could be expected."[30] That morning alone, newspaper in hand, investors watched the Dow drop almost 40 points. By the end of trading the next Tuesday, it had fallen 100 points. By November 13, it had fallen an additional 31 points. When it bottomed out in June 1932, it had not fallen 40 points. It had fallen to around 40 points. In retrospect, Fisher was right that the Dow Jones would not fall 60 to 80 points. When it was all said and done, it had fallen five times that far.

As his truly woeful predictions suggest, the stock market crash caught Fisher off guard. Throughout the fall of 1929 he had insisted that corporate earnings and the prospect of still greater corporate earnings had justified stock prices. True, price-to-earnings ratios looked historically high, possibly even unprecedented, but Fisher thought that plowed-back earnings, mergers, scientific research and invention, industrial management, labor cooperation, the dividends of prohibition, and seven years of stable money more than accounted for that. In other words, this time really was different. Before the crash proper, Fisher blamed the smaller declines throughout the months of September and October on what he called the "lunatic fringe": the "thousands of small and inexperienced investors [who] try to scramble aboard the stock market bandwagon from time to time, hanging on by their eyelids, that is, inadequate margins and lacking needed specific knowledge of the stocks they thus overbuy." Fisher concluded, however, that the market would be stronger for shaking out these "reckless speculators."[31]

As the market continued to fall, though, well beyond what a shaking out of reckless speculators would account for, Fisher turned to other explanations for the inexplicable crash. In early November, he settled on one in particular: panic. He told the *New York Herald Tribune*: "It was the psychology of panic. It was mob psychology, and it was not, primarily, that the price level of the market was unsoundly high... the fall in the market was very largely due to the psychology by which it went down because it went down."[32] Although this last sentence seems gnomic, Fisher is basically saying that the market acquired its own momentum. It went down—for whatever reason—which persuaded investors that it would continue to go down. Trying to beat the fall, investors sold out, which, of course, drove prices down, which convinced still more investors that prices would fall, and they responded by selling out, which drove prices down, on and on. Throughout all of this, though, the market—and its underlying economic soundness—had not changed. Investors had. In short, they panicked.

According to this school of thought, the market crashed not because there was a bubble, but because people *thought* there was a bubble and, once the so-called bubble began to pop, this confirmed others in their suspicion that there was a bubble, so they began to sell as well. Moreover, even if you did not think there was a bubble, others clearly did, so you would be wise to sell too. In other words, everyone, at the same time tried to leave by the same door, which, as fire marshals can tell you, is a recipe for panic. By this account, the stock market crash illustrates the power of collective behavior, of the psychology of panic. If enough people think something is true, it may as well be true, even if it is not.

For behavior to count as panic, most dictionaries insist, it must have something irrational and extravagant about it. Either the fear that inspires the panic must be unfounded, and a moment's pause would reveal this, or the fear that inspires the panic must lead to counterproductive behavior. For Fisher, the crash was a textbook example of panic in both senses. The fear was unfounded: according to Fisher, the price level of the market was not unsoundly high. There was no bubble. And the fear was counterproductive: the fear that the price level of the market *was* unsoundly high led to frantic selling, which, like a contagion, spread to other investors, thus undermining what in reality (or so Fisher thought) was a legitimate level of prices. For Fisher, then, panicked investors needlessly crashed the stock market.

This explanation, it should be noted, attracted immediate ridicule. In response to Fisher's assertion that the crash owed to "mob psychology," the editor of the *Commercial and Financial Chronicle* wrote, "The learned professor is wrong as he usually is when he talks about the stock market."[33] Yet focus for a moment on Fisher's original explanation of the crash, that it was the "psychology of panic." It may seem plainly wrong, as the editors of the *Commercial and Financial Chronicle* concluded, but from Fisher's perspective it made perfect sense. Assume for the moment, as many economists now believe, and at the time Fisher fervently believed, that the stock market in 1929 was not as grossly overvalued as the conventional wisdom holds. In a book he wrote in the months following the crash, *The Stock Market Crash—and After*, Fisher insisted "that between two-thirds and three-fourths of the rise in the stock market between 1926 and September, 1929, was justified."[34] (Other, later economists would put the fraction even higher.)[35] On January 2, 1926, the Dow Jones stood at 159. On September 3, at its peak, it had risen to 381. By Fisher's calculation, the Dow should have been somewhere between 307 and 326. On January 2, 1930, around the time Fisher sent his book to press, it was 244.[36] As Fisher saw it, then, the psychology of panic drove stock prices significantly lower than where they belonged.

A chart Fisher placed at the beginning of *Stock Market Crash—and After* makes the same point (see Figure 3.1). The chart purports to depict how far stock prices depart from where the fundamentals of the economy predict

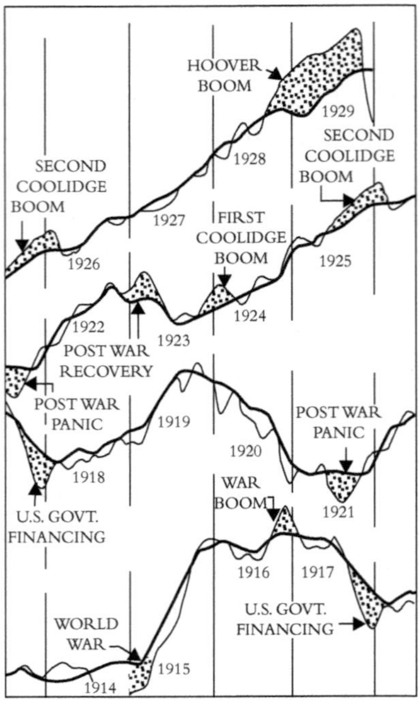

Figure 3.1. Chart from Irving Fisher's *Stock Market Crash—and After.*
Source: Irving Fisher, *The Stock Market Crash—and After* (New York: Macmillan, 1930)

they should be. (Fisher based his chart on the research of the statistician and investor Karl Karsten, who started one of the first—if not the first—hedge funds.) In the upper right-hand corner, stock market prices for 1928 and 1929 initially soar beyond their line of fundamentals. After the crash, however, they dive below where Karsten (and Fisher) believed they belonged. The area in white thus documents the harm that panic has done to the stock market: if not for it, the actual value of stocks would be closer to the bold line. That is why Fisher could conclude his 1930 book with the soon-to-be infamous prediction that "For the immediate future, at least, the outlook is bright."[37] Relative to their actual value, Fisher believed, stocks were now cheap. Sooner or later investors would come to their senses, put panic aside, and figure this out. When the future arrived, of course, it looked anything but bright. Stocks, it turned out, had a long way left to fall.

When it comes to the actual values of stocks at the time, it does not matter all that much whether Fisher was right or wrong. I happen to think he was more right than wrong; stocks—and the underlying economy—need not have fallen as far as they did.[38] The Great Depression is full of tragedy, but the greatest is that it need not have been as "great" of a depression as it was. A combination of bad luck and bad policy turned a normal recession into a decade-long disaster. In any event, what does matter—at least for the purposes of this chapter—is the extent to which for Fisher emotion functioned as a heuristic, or as a way to make sense of the otherwise inexplicable. Whatever did not make sense or departed from what it should be could be chalked up to emotion, especially panic. According to Fisher, investors were "over-enthusiastic" on the way up, which led them to drive up prices higher than where they belonged.[39] More seriously, investors panicked on the way down, driving stocks below where they belonged. In both cases, what Fisher called the "'psychological short swing'" was to blame.[40] If something, say, stock prices, did not make sense, if reality did not follow rational predictions, then something irrational and distorting must explain why. For Fisher, after the crash, that something was panic.

To his credit, Fisher ultimately acknowledged his misplaced faith in panic as the sole explanation for the stock market crash. To be sure, he never abandoned panic entirely, but like others I explore in this chapter, he started to look behind it, into the reasons for it. In *Stock Market Crash—and After*, Fisher listed eighteen possible "causes for the crash," accepting some, rejecting others. In the end, Fisher settled on the "chief cause" of the crash in "the unsound credit situation," by which he meant the truly spectacular amount of investment that took place in borrowed money, so-called margin trading, which left investors vulnerable to large drops in prices.[41] Instead of buying stocks outright, margin traders buy stocks and use them as collateral to borrow still more stocks. Trading on margin can magnify gains, but it can also magnify losses. If, for example, I use $10 of my own money as collateral to buy $100 worth of stock, I do very well if the price of the stock rises by 10 percent to $110. I could return the $90 worth of borrowed stock to my broker and still have $20, my original $10 plus the $10 by which the stock increased.[42] I have doubled my investment. If I only invested my $10, however, without using it as collateral, I would have only made $1 by the 10 percent increase in prices.

The problem, of course, is that in margin trading, drops in prices can quickly bankrupt investors. In the example above, if, instead of rising to $110, the value of the stock fell to $90, my original investment would disappear. From my broker's perspective, the collateral I deposited with him—my initial $10—is gone. The stock is only worth $90 now, or how much he leant me. To keep trading, I would need to raise more collateral. (The term of art is "receiving a margin call.") To meet it, perhaps I dip into my savings. Or maybe I sell other stocks. If I cannot raise the collateral, however, the broker will sell off the stocks that remain in order to recover his loan. In that case, like it or not, I will be selling stocks. *That* term of art is called "distress selling," and, like panic, it can achieve its own momentum. If many people trade on margin, and prices fall, they may all have to sell at once, which can drive prices lower, which will lead to more margin calls and more distress selling, which will drive prices lower, which will lead to still more margin calls and still more distress selling, on and on until everyone is bankrupt. "Between the loans on a stock market and the stock market price levels," Fisher observed in 1933, "there could not be a better example of a vicious spiral."[43]

A "vicious spiral" is what, after calling the learned professor wrong as he usually is, the *Commercial and Financial Chronicle* had in mind when it insisted in early November that the crash "was not due to mob psychology" or "the psychology of panic," as Fisher claimed. Rather, its editor insisted, "the mob held on to the last minute with the greatest tenacity and finally got sold out instead of selling out."[44] Fisher admits "that there may be some substance to this view," but he refuses to admit "there was no *panic* at all."[45] Not everyone who traded on margin during the Great Crash faced bankruptcy. But they might if they did not sell. They owed much more than they owned. Hence panic—or what looked like panic. In other words, Fisher seems to feel, overleveraged investors feared that they *might* be sold out and, so, panicked and sold out. In a speech before the American Statistical Association, Fisher argued, "it was just because there were great chances to make money such as have seldom if ever, in the aggregate, occurred before in the history of the world that so many people were eager to profit by them and went into debt for this purpose."[46] And it is debt that creates the conditions for panic. "Anxiety is always present, or should be," Fisher wrote in 1933, "in the person who has a margin account."[47] It did not help, Fisher felt, that interest rates were "artificially low," and investors could borrow cheaply.[48] In any case, Fisher concluded, it was no longer a "lunatic fringe" that had speculated with borrowed money and brought the market down with them. It was most everyone.

Still, Fisher believed, now that the speculators had sold out or been sold out—take your pick—those who had, for the moment, stepped in to buy stocks after the initial crash would insure greater stability in the market. "They will be much more cautious than holders who bid up the stock price level," Fisher hoped, "and will buy less on borrowed money." He admitted that this "contraction in demand . . . may prevent prices for a long time from regaining their old height on the new plateau," but he had no doubt that in the long run prices would return to that plateau.[49]

Of course, as the *Commercial and Financial Chronicle* might have put it, the learned professor was wrong again. The market continued to plunge. In addition to having to acknowledge his misreading of the stock market, in a few years Fisher would also have to acknowledge his misreading of the entire economy, too. In another speech to the American Statistical Association, in March 1933, Fisher ate crow. Speaking of the fact that "all would-be economic forecasters have for the last four years failed dismally to tell the business man what to expect," Fisher argued that it "is well that we face these failures and that, when we fail, we confess it with due humility." "I confess it," he added, in a line that must have been difficult but nevertheless liberating to write.[50] His error, though, led to one of the real breakthroughs in thinking about the business cycle. In a 1933 book, *Booms and Depressions*, and a widely cited article in the journal *Econometrica*, Fisher developed a debt-deflation theory of the Great Depression, which, as he summarized it, focused on "the important role of over-indebtedness and its tendency to break down the price level through distress selling, contraction of deposit currency, and slackening of velocity."[51] Basically, Fisher argued, what happens in a deflating stock market—forced selling and a driving down of prices—can happen to an entire economy, and keep happening, longer than anyone, including insightful Yale economists, would ever have thought possible. John Maynard Keynes would shortly come to the very same conclusion.

Only when Fisher revised the heuristic of panic, though, did he begin to understand why the stock market crashed and why the economy behaved the way it did. Or, since he continued, rightly, to view emotion and panic as part of the business cycle, only when he stopped viewing them principally as causes did he begin to understand why the economy boomed and, even more so, why it fell into depression. Emotions like panic could cause markets to crash; but certain real economic forces (debt, distress selling) created the conditions that led people to panic. The same could be said about emotion and the economy writ large. If capitalists grow pessimistic and do not believe the economy will grow, they will not invest money in their own businesses, thus assuring that the economy does not in fact grow. (Keynes referred to the motivating emotions that underlie an economy as "animal spirits.") In other words, pessimism, like panic, only looked causal.[52] Even pessimism and animal spirits traced back to other, very much material forces, and, in theory anyway, were subject to those same material forces.[53]

It took Fisher longer than most to come to this realization about the minimal role panic played in the stock market crash; or, if you prefer, the realization that panic was not a cause but an effect of the crash. Still, it was an essential realization. It forecast the one that the federal government would soon make about another plague of panics during the Great Depression, bank runs.

"You People Must Have Faith"

On June 5, 1931, Benjamin Roth, then a lawyer in the industrial city of Youngstown, Ohio, started keeping a diary. In his foreword, he wrote, "For the first time in my personal business life I am witnessing a major financial crisis. I am anxious to learn the lessons of this depression." Unlike those past middle age, for whom the crisis would only mean "tragedy and disaster," Roth thought he was young enough to learn valuable lessons from the experience. "With this thought in mind," he wrote, "I am going to write down brief accounts of developments as they occur from time to time."[54]

Among other developments, Roth could watch the banking crisis as it battered Americans during the early years of the Great Depression. On July 30, 1931, Roth noted almost in passing the "numerous bank failures" and their effect on spending.[55] On August 5, the failures, which until then had mostly affected banks in St. Louis, Chicago, and outlying areas, finally hit Youngstown. The first banks to wobble were the savings and loan companies, which had made bad loans on real estate, as Roth explains. "The town is stunned," Roth wrote, "by the news that the Home Savings & Loan Co. has suspended payments and would demand 60-day notice of withdrawals." Other banks followed suit. These banks, Roth noted, had "earned their money by lending on real estate." But, as he also observed, correctly, mortgages "are not a good investment for a bank which has agreed to pay out its deposits on demand." With "the coming of the depression people stopped paying their mortgages—mortgages became frozen and the banks had no way to get cash." Thus, "for the past three days, these institutions have been besieged by hysterical depositors demanding their money."[56]

Figure 3.2. Photograph of depositors in front of the closed American Union Bank in New York City, April 1932.
Source: National Archives (12573155)

But the crisis—and the hysterical depositors—would not stop with savings and loan banks. On August 17, Roth noted that the local newspaper carried "the news that four of the largest commercial banks in Toledo, Ohio, closed their doors (total deposits over $100 million)."[57] On August 18, he observed, apropos of Youngstown and its bank closings: "This town is fast becoming panic-stricken."[58]

Roth could not know it, but he and the city of Youngstown were caught in by far the most catastrophic and prolonged banking crisis in U.S. history (see Figure 3.2). From 1930 to 1933, over 9,000 undercapitalized and over-leveraged banks failed, with deposits in those banks amounting to nearly 7 billion dollars.[59] (That is well over 100 billion in inflation-adjusted dollars.) Over a couple of days and sometimes even hours, millions of Americans could only watch as their savings simply disappeared. The crisis culminated in early 1933 with first the state of Michigan, then adjoining states, and finally the whole of the United States ordering banks to close so that federal authorities could sort out the solvent from the insolvent ones. More than any other event in the Great Depression, even the stock market crash, the banking crisis, as Roth observes, grew out of and gave rise to panic, and few other events in the Great Depression can reveal as much about the emotion as the banking crisis and the psychological and legislative attempts to dispel it. It too reveals what Irving Fisher eventually learned: what at first looks like panic may not be entirely so.

Throughout the month of August, Roth followed reports of bank closures in the state. His entries on August 22 and 25 illustrate what made the banking panic so devastating. On August 22, he wrote:

> There is a quiet but steady stream of depositors at every bank in Youngstown this morning quietly withdrawing their funds. The closing of banks in Toledo and Warren received much publicity and distrust of all banks is growing like a cancer. It is a movement which feeds on itself and is hard to stop. At the Dollar and Union Banks there are about 4 or 5 depositors at each withdrawal window. There is no excitement but a quiet look of intensity on the faces of both depositors and bank officials. Even the strongest banks can't keep this up long. They do not have enough cash to pay everybody . . . It is hard to rent a safety box today because there has been such a demand by hoarders. Actually the liquid cash of the bank is being transferred from the bank vaults to the private safety vaults where it is taken out of circulation and becomes sterilized.[60]

On August 25, he was much more succinct: "Everyone is afraid of the banks."[61]

Roth, admittedly no poet, nevertheless captures, with his metaphors of cancer and sterilization, the twin problems posed by the banking crisis. Just as cancerous cells can metastasize and spread to other parts of the body, destroying previously healthy cells, so too can bank panics spread and destroy not just unhealthy banks but healthy ones too.

As Roth outlines, the roots of the banking crisis lay in banks taking on too much risk and paying for it when the economy crashed. Banks pay you interest for depositing your money with them. They do not do this out of the goodness of their hearts, but because they take your money and lend it out at higher interest rates than the one that they pay you, thereby making a profit for themselves and their shareholders. At any given time, a bank retains only a small percentage of its deposits as capital, say 10 percent. These reserves allow it to meet the day-to-day demands of its depositors. The bank lends out the other 90 percent of its assets at interest. However, if a bank makes bad loans, or if a Great Depression turns once good loans into bad loans, and those to whom it has loaned money no longer pay their loans, the bank may find itself in trouble. With no or little money coming in, it will quickly run through its capital reserves, and once those are depleted, it can no longer pay interest to you nor, if it has completely run through its reserves, can it even produce your savings if you show up asking for them. At that point, the bank must close, and the prospect of it closing fuels bank panics. Depositors race to the bank to get their money before the money runs out, which, of course, only hastens the bank's failure.

That is what happened to the Savings and Loan Companies in Youngstown and elsewhere in 1931. They took in money from depositors, loaned most of it out for real estate, but when people lost their jobs or businesses during the Depression, they could no longer make their mortgage payments, leaving banks with little or no income. The banks could foreclose on the properties and sell them in order to raise cash, but in a Depression no one would buy them, except at a tremendous loss to the banks. These properties were, in Roth's terms, "frozen." The Savings and Loan Companies in Youngstown did not close, but they did stop paying interest on deposits and required customers to wait sixty days before withdrawing money. (The banks needed that time to raise it.) More often, however, as Roth describes, banks would simply close. When that happened, depositors could not access their money, and they could not know how much of their money would remain when the bank opened again, if it ever did.

The truly malignant feature of bank panics, though, is that as soon as one bank closes, or even threatens to close, it imperils the rest. A bank that has made good loans, retains more of its capital, or has more capital to begin with, can nevertheless fall prey to a panic. Weak or strong, as Roth observes, no bank can withstand everyone asking for their money at once. Yet that is just what happens during a bank run. A depositor in Youngstown notices that the Savings and Loan Companies have closed, or he reads of bank closings in nearby cities, and he begins to worry about his bank and his own money. Just to be safe, he withdraws his money and stashes it in a safety deposit box. The problem, of course, is that if enough people think that way, they all descend on the bank at once, demanding their money. Meanwhile, other people see depositors lined up outside a bank, desperate to withdraw money, and think they had better withdraw their money, too. So off they go to their bank, bringing more people with them, until every bank in town, in the state, and in the country faces a panic, and many banks close altogether. Thus bank runs, in Roth's apt metaphor, are a cancer.

For this reason, the British journalist Walter Bagehot outlined in his 1873 book 65 *Lombard Street* what has come to be known as Bagehot's Dictum, which holds that to dispel a banking panic one must dispel the fear of loss that drives it. Therefore, central banks ought to lend liberally to banks in trouble.[62] When the public perceives that it can access its money whenever it likes, calm will return. In theory, the Federal Reserve of the United States was created in 1913 to make good on Bagehot's Dictum. It would act as lender of last resort to banks facing runs. But not all banks during the early years of the Great Depression belonged to the Federal Reserve system, which meant they could not borrow money from it, and even when banks did belong to it, they oftentimes did not have sufficient assets to allow the Fed to loan funds to them. In addition, banks were sometimes reluctant to apply to the Federal Reserve. If its application was made public, people might think the bank was in trouble, which would cause depositors to make a run on it, thereby undoing whatever temporary aid the loan from the Federal Reserve offered.

Yet bank runs can have less obviously dramatic though equally pernicious effects. As Roth notes in his last sentence quoted above, when depositors withdraw their savings from banks and stash it in safe deposit vaults, that is that much less money the bank can lend to people or businesses for the sake of investment. The money becomes sterilized, unable to infect—and beget—other money. To make things worse, in order to withstand runs, banks may begin to hoard reserves themselves. In their annual report for the year 1933, the Federal Reserve Board included a fascinating chart documenting how much of the money it had printed remained outside Treasury and Federal Reserve banks at any given time; in other words, how much money, and of which denominations, was in circulation and not, say, in safe deposit vaults or under mattresses (see Figure 3.3). Throughout 1931 and again in 1933, notice the ascent in the number of \$50 bills and higher that Americans had withdrawn from banks. No other denomination, with the exception of \$20 bills, was withdrawn nearly so quickly. As the Federal Reserve Board report pointed out, "The increase in large denominations clearly indicates that most of the currency withdrawn represented funds taken out for hoarding."[63]

To be sure, the problem during depressions is not primarily a lack of money but rather a lack of profitable investments; even so, the hoarding of money, by diminishing credit, does not help matters. (Among other ills, it drives up interest rates and creates deflation.) Therefore, in a series of speeches given in early 1932, as the banking crisis worsened, Herbert Hoover took to the radio to spell out the dangers of hoarding. "I am convinced," he said,

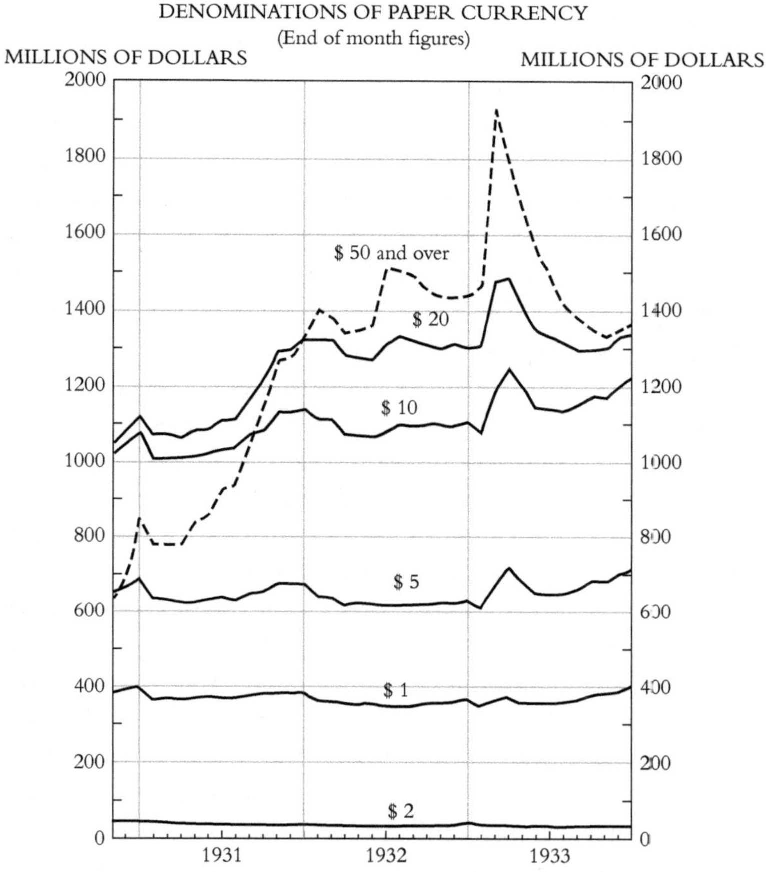

Figure 3.3. Federal Reserve Board chart depicting denominations of paper currency in circulation outside banks.

Source: Twentieth Annual Report of the Federal Reserve Board Covering Operations for the Year 1933 (Washington, D.C.: G.P.O., 1934)

> that citizens hoarding currency or money do not realize its serious effect on our country... Every dollar hoarded means a destruction of from $5 to $10 of credit. Credit is the bloodstream of our economic life. Restriction or destruction of credit cripples the revival and expansion of agriculture, industry, commerce, and employment.[64]

With some cause, many people scoffed at Hoover's diagnosis of the causes of the Depression. Many people had no money whatsoever, to hoard or not, and the rhetorically tone-deaf Hoover could not imagine what his speech would sound like to them. Even so, Hoover is not wrong about the hazards of hoarding. It does harm the economy. His solution, however, illustrates why bank panics could prove so hard to contain. Hoover urged Americans "to put their dollars to work—either by conservative investment, or by deposit in sound institutions," which sounds good, but with banks failing right and left, who could be sure which institutions, if any, were sound, and which unsound? Depositors did not have access to a bank's balance sheets. As Roth notes, in the absence of information about the soundness of any given bank, it made more sense to withdraw your money from it and stash it in a safe deposit vault, whose soundness or unsoundness you could easily judge. Better safe, so to speak, than sorry.

In the event, none of Hoover's efforts, neither speeches nor the Reconstruction Finance Corporation, a federally funded program begun in early 1932 that would lend money to banks when the Federal Reserve could not, could halt the banking crisis. Indeed, over the next two years, Roth records the slow, accumulating wreck of bank closures and hysteria that played out in Youngstown and across the country. On October 15, 1931, his worst fears came to pass. In addition to three other banks, his bank, the Dollar Bank, "the Gibraltar of Youngstown," closed.[65] The two remaining banks, he observed, "are besieged by depositors seeking to withdraw their deposits. I do not see how it can last. The town is panic-stricken and the streets are crowded with people excitedly discussing the situation."[66]

In the months that followed, nothing much changed. On November 12, Roth observed, "The banks are still closed."[67] And a week later: "The banks remain closed."[68] In December, Roth heard that "The Commercial Bank and the (now closed) First National Bank will combine and reopen on January 4th as a new bank."[69] When the new bank did open, it started "with a bad run."[70] Finally, on May 18, 1932, seven months—yes seven months—after it closed, Roth's bank, the Dollar Savings and Trust Co., the Gibraltar of Youngstown, reopened. Even so, depositors could only withdraw 10 percent of their savings. After an initial run, Roth noted, the bank settled "down to normal business."[71]

Just when it appeared that the worst of the crisis had passed, though, at least in Youngstown, anyway, it returned. On January 23, 1933, Roth observed, "bank closings are again coming to the front."[72] A month later, he wrote:

> Without any warning this morning 69 banks in Ohio including three in Youngstown restricted withdrawals to approximately 5% of deposits. All day in the Union National Bank bedlam reigned with hundreds in line clamoring

> for money. There was no violence but I saw one woman faint. The same thing was happening in every other city of Ohio.[73]

It is not quite right to say, as Roth does, that the bank closings in Ohio came "without any warning." Two weeks earlier, with scores of banks, including its largest, in trouble, the state of Michigan declared a bank holiday, closing every bank in the state for eight days. Other states, including Ohio, soon followed suit. By the time Franklin Roosevelt took office on March 4, 1933, thousands more banks had forbidden or restricted withdrawals and most states had closed their entire banking systems.

In his first official act as president, Roosevelt declared a national bank holiday. Every bank in the country would close for four days. (A few days later, Roosevelt extended the banking holiday for an additional three days.) During that time, Roosevelt announced, officials in the Treasury Department would examine banks and determine which ones were fundamentally sound and which ones were not. (States would examine banks that did not belong to the Federal Reserve System.) Over the coming days, solvent banks would open, and the federal or state government would reorganize or close insolvent ones.

Roosevelt devoted the first of his fireside chats entirely to the banking crisis, and his rhetoric reveals a great deal about how emotion drove the crisis, and how despite the bedlam and fainting women that characterized it, panic may not have been the best description of that emotion. Over the radio, in a relaxed but still urgent tone that may have gone far toward reassuring Americans, Roosevelt promised to explain the crisis "for the benefit of the average citizen." (As Will Rogers shortly thereafter quipped, "He made everyone understand it, even the bankers.")[74] Roosevelt then gave an abbreviated though perfectly lucid lecture about banking in America.

> Because of undermined confidence on the part of the public, there was a general rush by a large portion of our population to turn bank deposits into currency or gold—a rush so great that the soundest banks couldn't get enough currency to meet the demand. The reason for this was that on the spur of the moment it was, of course, impossible to sell perfectly sound assets of a bank and convert them into cash except at panic prices far below their real value.[75]

To solve this dilemma, Roosevelt described recently passed legislation—the Emergency Banking Act of 1933—that "allows the twelve federal reserve banks to issue additional currency on good assets and thus banks that reopen will be able to meet every legitimate call." "I can assure you, my friends,"

Roosevelt closed, "that it is safer to keep your money in a reopened bank than it is to keep it under the mattress."[76]

Comforting words, but would they convince Americans? As Roosevelt's acting comptroller of the currency later remembered, "No one knew how the public would react when banks reopened. If they demanded their money they either had to have it or the reopening would be a failure."[77] Adding to the uncertainty of how the public would react was that if someone stopped to think about it for even a moment, they would realize that the federal and state governments could not possibly judge the soundness (or unsoundness) of literally tens of thousands of banks in under a week. Or they could, but the examination would be cursory and rely almost exclusively on information the banks themselves provided. Moreover, what if the assets a bank held were not perfectly sound? What if the prices a bank could fetch for them were not "panic prices far below their real value" but simply their new value? Roosevelt, that is, assumed that the economy would improve, but nothing guaranteed that it would. In essence, that is, Roosevelt bluffed, except that he backed up his bluff with billions of dollars. When the banks did open, people would, in fact, be able to withdraw their money. But that is less because their bank was judged sound than because Roosevelt instructed the Federal Reserve and the Reconstruction Finance Corporation to approve every request from banks for more funds. Basically, the federal government would turn on the currency spigot and banks could absorb as much as they needed to make good on their depositors' claims.

In the event, the federal government did not need to drench banks with currency. When the banks reopened, depositors lined up, not to withdraw money but to return it. Evidently, they believed their bank had been judged sound. Look again at the Federal Reserve chart for 1933. After the bank holiday in March of 1933, large bills returned to the banks. The bluff worked. Or, rather, the steps the federal government took to stop the panic worked. In his fireside chat, Roosevelt predicted that "when the people find that they can get their money—that they can get it when they want it for all legitimate purposes—the phantom of fear will soon be laid," and so it was.[78] Bagehot was right.

As the noted historian Charles A. Beard and his co-author, George H.E. Smith, observed at the time, "the sudden nationwide holiday performed the same function for the bank panic as may a slap in the face for a person gripped by unreasoning hysteria."[79] It is a nice analogy, but it does not do justice to those who hurried to withdraw their money during the months and years leading up to the 1933 bank holiday. As we have seen, those who lined up outside of banks to withdraw their money may have panicked, in a manner of speaking, and no doubt things got unruly and maybe a woman or two fainted, but their choices were neither unreasoning nor hysterical. Rather they were caught in a classic Prisoner's Dilemma, wherein two individuals acting purely rationally may nevertheless betray their best interests.

Perhaps to avoid judging people—like me—who would withdraw their money from banks, in his fireside chat Roosevelt rarely used the word *panic*, and then only in the context of banks, not depositors. Instead, he chose words like *rush* and, most often, the more dignified *fear*. In doing so, Roosevelt echoed his Inaugural Address from the previous week, in which he asserted, possibly with the banking crisis in mind, that the only thing Americans had "to fear was fear itself—nameless, unreasoning, unjustified terror." Although as I write in Chapter 4, that is not quite true—Americans had plenty to fear beyond just fear itself during the Great Depression—Roosevelt did put his finger on the principal cause of the banking crisis, which was not panic per se but fear and, in the case of the banking crisis anyway, neither nameless, unreasoning, nor unjustified fear. Panic implies hysteria and irrationality. Fear acknowledges a genuine threat, which people might act rationally by acknowledging.

True, Roosevelt believed that in the case of the banking crisis, that threat was exaggerated. In the closing lines of his fireside chat, Roosevelt lectured his listeners: "You people must have faith; you must not be stampeded by rumors or guesses. Let us unite in banishing fear."[80] In the days that followed, Americans may have resisted being stampeded by rumors or guesses, and they may have united in banishing fear, but all that was made easier because the source of their rumors, guesses, and fear—that their bank would fail and take their money with it—had been banished for them, and in a way that none could have done for themselves. In the days after the banking holiday, the federal government informally guaranteed bank deposits. A few months later, with the passage of the Glass-Steagall Act, the federal government made those guarantees formal, insuring bank deposits up to $2,500. Basically, if your bank failed, the federal government would return your deposit. (In an effort to keep banks from taking on too much risk, the Act also barred commercial banks that received federal deposit insurance from speculating in the stock market.) That promise spelled the end of the banking crisis. In making it, the federal government acknowledged the good reasons Americans had to panic, which amounted to admitting that they hadn't really panicked at all.

As with Irving Fisher, though, legislators, including Roosevelt, could only make progress when they stopped ascribing individual behavior to panic and similarly irrational emotions. To call it hoarding, for example, as Hoover did, implies greed but also emotional excess, a perverse, even hysterical attachment to money.[81] Unsurprisingly, depositors did not recognize themselves in Hoover's characterization of them as hoarders. Hoarders are mad; those making runs on banks were wise. Only when Roosevelt acknowledged the legitimacy of their fears and addressed its causes did they abandon their supposed panic and, for that matter, their hoarding.

Thus far, we have examined two instances—the stock market crash and bank runs—when observers concluded that panic may not have described well the phenomenon at hand. In the next and final section of this chapter, I show how one of the most famous works of Great Depression fiction also revised the conventional wisdom about panic.

Laboring under Too Much Emotion

In "How Bigger Was Born," his account of the genesis and composition of *Native Son* (1940), Richard Wright spoke of his desire to elicit certain emotional responses from Bigger, and in the first part of the novel no emotional response, with the possible exception of hatred, is elicited from Bigger more often than fear.[82] Indeed, *Native Son* provides perhaps the definitive example of fear—and then panic—in all of American literature: when Bigger carries Mary Dalton to her bedroom, lingers to molest her, and is discovered by her blind mother, a scene I examine in some detail below. Yet the novel contains numerous smaller examples, too. In addition to giving the novel the title of its first section, the word *fear* appears roughly 120 times in the text, while *afraid* and *scared* log in at forty-eight and forty times, respectively. In the next chapter, I parse more closely the difference between fear and panic, but for now my interest lies in when fear passes over into panic, when, that is, fear leads Bigger to behave wildly and irrationally.

Although Wright occasionally uses the word *panic* to describe that behavior, he more often than not opts for *hysteria* or its variant *hysterical*, a term with an admittedly fraught gendered history, and which Wright likely picked up from his reading of Freud. Nevertheless, the term, like panic, bears for Wright the same burden of irrational and extravagant fear that overtakes the thinking and conscious self. For example, early in the novel, as Bigger and his friends contemplate robbing Blum's store, one of the friends, Gus, hesitates to undertake the robbery. Like Bigger, he is afraid, and his fear simultaneously angers and outrages Bigger. The narrator speaks of the "hysterical tensity of [Bigger's] nerves," and in the course of confronting Gus, hysteria overcomes Bigger. Quite simply, he loses it: "He faced Gus, his eyes red with anger and fear, his fists clenched and held stiffly to his sides."[83] Later still, when Gus does in fact arrive at the pool hall for the robbery, Bigger attacks him. Wright describes Bigger laughing, "softly at first, then harder, louder, hysterically; feeling something like hot water bubbling inside of him and trying to come out." Eventually, Bigger punches Gus: "he had struck him really before he was conscious of doing so"; afterwards, he humiliates him by holding a knife to his throat, then forcing Gus to lick it.[84]

At moments like these, when Bigger is overcome by emotion, especially an emotion like hysteria, Wright experiments with how to depict what Bigger feels and how intensely he feels it. On the one hand, Wright has to convey that Bigger *is* overcome by emotion and, as a result, does not think entirely clearly. On the other hand, if Wright is too articulate about what Bigger is feeling during these moments of intense, overwhelming emotion, he undermines the effect of Bigger becoming overcome by intense emotion. By definition, Bigger ought not to be able to describe what happens to him when he loses control of his emotions. Trying to square this circle, Wright often leaves a reader wondering where Bigger's consciousness leaves off and where the narrator's description of his consciousness begins. Occasionally, as in the scene when Wright describes Bigger's hatred and fear of Gus, Wright articulates Bigger's feelings more clearly than Bigger, or anyone, ever could in the moment. ("He hated Gus because he felt that Gus was afraid.") When his emotions reach a pitch, however, Wright sensibly departs from trying to describe what Bigger thinks or feels at all. Sometimes, Wright resorts to simile: "feeling something like hot water bubbling inside of him and trying to come out." Other times, especially in the early pages of the novel, as when Bigger attacks Gus in the pool hall, Wright presents the scene objectively. We stay with Bigger until the moment that Bigger loses consciousness, after which we watch him from the outside as he panics and behaves hysterically, violently. When we do get a glimpse inside his head, as when Bigger thinks he has struck Gus "before he was conscious of doing so," it is only to render how little consciousness Bigger has of his behavior.

Later, after the emotional storm, the subjective view returns. The point is that when Bigger panics, or behaves hysterically, he loses his mind. Fittingly, it disappears from the narration as well.

It can come as a surprise, then, when during the most hysterical passage in the novel and, as I say, the most definitive example of panic in all of American literature, that Wright departs from this narrative technique and, for the whole of the long scene, leaves us trapped in Bigger's head. As Mary loses consciousness on the way from the car to her room, Bigger and his consciousness—"a mingled feeling of helplessness, admiration, and hate"—takes over.[85] To a certain extent, like elsewhere in the novel, fear drives Bigger to behave as he does. When he wrestles a drunken Mary out of the car in the driveway, he "wondered what a white man would think seeing him here with her like this. Suppose Old Man Dalton saw him now? Apprehensively, he looked up at the big house. It was dark and silent."[86] But Bigger is also plainly "excited" by Mary.[87] At one point, fully passed out, Mary's lips, "faintly moist in the hazy blue light, were parted and he saw the furtive glints of her white teeth," which is a wonderful detail, revealing, as it does, how much Mary has exposed herself to Bigger, how much this titillates him, and how much of a threat her whiteness—here in the form of the glittering of her teeth—poses to Bigger.[88] The scene that follows, when Bigger molests Mary, can be hard to read; perhaps because of this, or because critics believe the meaning is self-evident, few have looked at it or the scene that follows in much detail. Yet it can tell us a lot about panic and how to narrate it. Here is the passage:

> He kissed her again and felt the sharp bones of her hips move in a hard and veritable grind. Her mouth was open and her breath came slow and deep.
>
> He lifted her and laid her on the bed. Something urged him to leave at once, but he leaned over her, excited, looking at her face in the dim light, not wanting to take his hands from her breasts. She tossed and mumbled sleepily. He tightened his fingers on her breasts, kissing her again, feeling her move toward him. He was aware only of her body now; his lips trembled. Then he stiffened. The door behind him had creaked.
>
> He turned and a hysterical terror seized him, as though he were falling from a great height in a dream. A white blur was standing by the door, silent, ghostlike. It filled his eyes and gripped his body. It was Mrs. Dalton. He wanted to knock her out of his way and bolt from the room.[89]

Wright can occasionally strive for one effect too many in his prose, but here he has pared everything down to the bone. Notice how he uses syntax to achieve the effect of dread and then horror. Most of the sentences in the first paragraph follow a simple subject-verb-object structure, with Bigger as the subject manipulating the world—in this case Mary—around him. Mary intrudes as a subject long enough to toss and mumble sleepily, but Bigger reasserts himself. ("He tightened his fingers on her breasts.") As the scene progresses, Wright focuses Bigger and his "awareness" exclusively on Mary's body. So too ours. For a moment ("his lips trembled") we may or may not step outside of Bigger's awareness, but that merely sets up the bombshell that follows. Instead of doing this or that to Mary, here he "stiffens," an intransitive verb, the "Then" at the beginning of the sentence signaling that something has interrupted his domain over Mary's body. He is no longer initiating the action but responding to it. Finally, magnificently, Wright shifts the subject of his sentences. Now it is the door that does something: "creak." The creaking door suggests another agent in the room, Mrs. Dalton. The shift toward other subjects and agents continues in the paragraph that follows. It is Bigger who turns, but it is a "hysterical terror" that seizes him. Then "a white blur" stands by the door. Suddenly, the room has filled up. While the scene concludes from Bigger's perspective—we learn that he "wanted to knock her out of his way and bolt from the room"—he has traded his status as subject and doer for object and done to. He has also begun to panic. The two are related.

At this point, Wright describes Bigger's wild response in excruciating detail. As often happens when one panics, Bigger begins to repeat himself. After Mrs. Dalton appears, we are told, "He waited tensely, afraid to move for fear of bumping into something in the dark and betraying his presence." A few lines later, he thinks: "He wanted to move from the bed, but was afraid he would stumble over something and Mrs. Dalton would hear him, would know that someone besides Mary was in the room." He does worse than repeat himself. As Bigger panics at the sight of Mrs. Dalton—"Frenzy," we are told, "dominated him"—he "frantically" grabs a pillow and unwittingly smothers Mary. After Mrs. Dalton leaves, and Bigger remains undiscovered, Bigger observes, "He felt he had been in the grip of a weird spell and was now free," which describes well the suspension of consciousness—or the hyperconsciousness that goes beyond consciousness—that characterizes panic. Unfortunately, Bigger will once again fall into the grip of that spell. When he discovers that Mary is dead, panic—and repetition—returns: "His hand moved toward her, but stopped in mid-air. He blinked his eyes and stared at Mary's face; it was darker than when he had first bent over her. Her mouth was open and her eyes bulged glassily. Her bosom, her bosom, her—her bosom was not moving!"[90]

Unlike earlier scenes, especially in the pool hall, where Wright steps outside of Bigger as he behaves hysterically, from this point on Wright locks readers into Bigger's consciousness as he responds to his newly dire situation. For the next half dozen pages, as Bigger realizes what he has done and blunders about trying to clean up the mess, readers come along for the panic-stricken ride. In many ways, these pages disturb even more than the initial molestation and murder. We stay with Bigger as he hatches and follows one bad—irrational, counterproductive, doomed—idea after another. Panicking, Bigger first stuffs Mary's body into her half-packed trunk, which is strange indeed. If he simply wants to hide her body to buy time, he does not need to put her in the trunk. He then drags her to a basement boiler room, where he—again, needlessly—attempts to burn her body in the coal furnace. (Wildly, he concludes, "That was the safest thing of all to do.") Then, because he was, as the narrator puts it, "tired and scared, and because her feet were nearer, he pushed her in, feet first," which meant that he would have to decapitate her to make her fit in the furnace. At one point, the family cat, wandering in from an Edgar Allan Poe short story, confronts Bigger as he conducts his gruesome work in the basement. At arguably his most hysterical, Bigger wonders whether he should catch the cat, kill it, and put it in the furnace too, and he makes a move to do so until he remembers, "Cats can't talk."[91] Before leaving the house, he foolishly takes Mary's purse. (Later, the missing purse will lead the police to conclude, briefly, that Mary has absconded, but at the time Bigger is not thinking that far ahead.) The next morning, he disposes of the purse and his bloody knife in a garbage pail. (The police will later find both, and they will surface at his trial.) All the while, he cooks up a half-baked plan to implicate Jan, Mary's communist boyfriend, repeating to himself, like a comforting mantra, "Reds'd do anything. Didn't the papers say so?"[92] It never occurs to him that Jan may have an alibi, as he does.

In sum, Bigger behaves, let us say, less than rationally in these moments, but I do not think Wright wants us to find fault with him. Few people can calmly and thoroughly cover up an accidental murder. Rather, Wright offers a masterful portrait of a mind in the grip of panic, with its tendency to repeat phrases, its irrationality, and its propensity for shortcuts that in the end only complicate things. In addition, Wright adds a new dimension to panic; namely, that one of its sources, and certainly one of the things that makes it worse, is race. Indeed, the desire to violate racial taboos at least in part puts Bigger in Mary's room in the first place, where, of course, he panics when he is discovered by Mrs. Dalton and inadvertently kills Mary. (For her part, Mary also wants to violate racial taboos by treating Bigger like a harmless victim, but as she may or may not ever learn, he is not.) But after the murder, Wright shows how Bigger suffers a kind of racial panic that drives his hysteria and inexplicable actions, as in this unnerving passage, complete with simile, after he has killed Mary but before he has decided what to do about it: "He stood with her body in his arms in the silent room and cold facts battered him like waves sweeping in from the sea: she was dead; she was white; she was a woman; he had killed her; he was black; he might be caught; he did not want to be caught; if he were they would kill him."[93] Here, Wright almost certainly makes Bigger's consciousness altogether too orderly. The sequential arrival of facts—like waves in Wright's metaphor—seem more like axioms in a mathematical proof. In any case, these cold facts and the panic they inspire explain much of Bigger's otherwise inexplicable—and needlessly violent—actions that follow.

For all the power of these scenes, I want to argue that Wright saves his most compelling illustration of racial panic and, especially, hysteria for the conclusion of the novel. As I have explored elsewhere in this chapter, many in the 1930s, from actual sociologists to drafters of banking legislation, struggled to arrive at a sociology of panic, to describe and understand the forces that produced this powerful emotion, one that seemed to arise at every meaningful turn in the decade. They did not work in a vacuum, however, and many of them confronted an existing if, they nevertheless felt, occasionally flawed existing academic literature on panic, which oftentimes went under the heading of the study of collective behavior or the behavior of crowds. Wright, in particular, had a ringside seat for scholarly theorizing about collective behavior. Biographers have known about his connections to the University of Chicago School of Sociology for decades, and while most scholars have focused on what Wright took from the Chicago School and its theory of race relations, the sociologist most closely associated with the Chicago School of Sociology, Robert Ezra Park, also studied what he called collective behavior. Another pioneer in the field, Herbert Blumer, also of the University of Chicago, began his work just as Wright began *Native Son*.

The study of collective behavior dates at least as far back as Gustave Le Bon's *The Crowd: A Study of the Popular Mind* (1895). Famously, Le Bon explained the wild behavior of large groups of people by arguing that joining a crowd radically changed the otherwise sensible individuals who formed it. The "fact that [individuals] have been transformed into a crowd," Le Bon argued, "puts them in possession of a sort of collective mind which makes them feel, think, and act in a manner quite different from that in which each individual of them would feel, think, and act were he in a state of isolation."[94] In a crowd, Le Bon argued, conscious personality disappears and an atavistic unconscious personality appears. "Our savage, destructive instincts," he wrote, "are the inheritance left dormant in all of us from the primitive ages. In the life of the isolated individual it would be dangerous for him to gratify these instincts, while his absorption in an irresponsible crowd, in which in consequence he is assured of impunity, gives him entire liberty to follow them."[95] Not surprisingly, Freud admired Le Bon's work. In the former's terms, when we join the crowd, we shed our civilizing Ego and free our primitive Id.[96]

The University of Chicago sociologist Robert Ezra Park incorporated Le Bon's thinking about crowds into his 1904 dissertation, *The Crowd and the Public*, and afterwards regularly offered a course at the University of Chicago of the same name.[97] With a slightly better opinion of them than Le Bon, Park (along with his co-author Ernest W. Burgess) argued that crowds embody social unrest but also the possibility for social reformation. He emphasized, as well, the "circular reaction" of collective behavior, or how "social unrest...is transmitted [and reinforced] from one individual to another."[98] In other words, Park noticed how one may be drawn into crowds; or, put differently, how the behavior of crowds infects others. Nevertheless, like Le Bon, Park distinguished, as in the title of his dissertation and his class, between the irrational, impulsive crowd and the rational, deliberative public. In particular, Park emphasized the role that newspapers play in forming that deliberative public. But newspapers often failed in keeping the public critical, and "when the public ceases to be critical," Park wrote, "it dissolves or is transformed into a crowd."[99] Despite some minor differences, Park's views about crowds often dissolve into Le Bon's. In short, neither thinks much of them, and both think that civilization will—or should, anyway—evolve beyond them.[100]

Yet few represented the conventional wisdom about collective behavior, then or, perhaps, now, better than Park's colleague at the University of Chicago, Herbert Blumer. For decades, his frequently reprinted 1939 essay, "Collective Behavior," offered the last word on the subject. Under the heading of "Collective Behavior," Blumer, looking back on the panic-stricken decade, included many of the phenomena we have already witnessed in this chapter: "a highly excited mob, a business panic, a state of war hysteria, a condition of social unrest."[101] In seeking to explain these phenomena, Blumer, like Park, emphasized the contagious nature of collective behavior, going so far as to borrow Park's term "circular reaction," which, Blumer argued, was "a type of interstimulation wherein the response of one individual reproduces the stimulation that has come from another individual and in being reflected back to this individual reinforces the stimulation."[102] In a helpful aside, Blumer argued, "one sees the process [the reflection and intensification of feeling] amidst cattle in a state of alarm. The expression of fear through bellowing, breathing, and movements of the body, induces the same feeling in the case of other cattle who, as they in turn express their alarm, intensify this emotional state in one another."[103] Later in the essay, Blumer will refer to the more intense version of circular reaction as "social contagion."[104] "Under such conditions," he writes, opting for a different metaphor, "the given kind of behavior will spread like wildfire."[105]

Like Park, Blumer emphasized the difference between the collective behavior of crowds and the individualized behavior of a public. "Individuals in the public," Blumer observed, optimistically, "are likely to have their self-consciousness intensified and their critical powers heightened instead of losing self-awareness and critical ability as occurs in the crowd."[106] By contrast, in moments of "pure circular reaction"—that is, when someone has been swallowed up by the crowd—an individual may "embark on lines of conduct which [he or she] previously would not likely have thought of, much less dared to undertake."[107] "Impulses which ordinarily would be subject to a severe check by the individual's judgment and control of himself," Blumer wrote, "now have a free passage to expression." It should not be surprising, he concluded, "that much of the actual behavior should be violent, cruel, and destructive."[108] Like Le Bon and Park, Blumer thought crowds robbed human beings of their humanity, turned them into beasts, though on second thought, the comparison may not do justice to beasts.

In Blumer's description of the atavistic crowd, readers will instantly recognize the climax of Nathaniel West's *The Day of the Locust* (1939), in which a crowd at a movie opening, touched off by a rumor that "a pervert attacked a child," riots and devolves into a smothering—and literal—circle of reaction, hysteria, and violence.[109] West's novel should remind us that though we remember the Great Depression for its populism, some had doubts about the wisdom and worth of the people. (It would take too long to list the Frank Capra films from this period that portray mobs in all their furious irrationality. I mention *American Madness* above, but mention should also be made of *Mr. Deeds Goes to Town*, *Mr. Smith Goes to Washington*, and *Meet John Doe*, and these are just the more famous examples.) In 1936, Carl Sandburg published his populist book-length poem *The People, Yes*. Reading West after reading Blumer, one imagines that West could just as easily have titled his novel *The People, No*.

In *Native Son*, Wright provides an equally disturbing portrait of the hysterical, contagious crowd and those who pander to it. From his jail cell, after his capture, Bigger is shown—by district attorney Buckley—"the streets below crowded with masses of people in all directions." "See that, boy?" Buckley says. "Those people would like to lynch you." A little later, Bigger hears "the faint excited sound of mob voices coming through the concrete walls of the building," and from this moment on the mob functions as a loud if simple-minded Greek chorus to the drama of settling Bigger's fate that occupies the third and final section of Wright's novel.[110] Later, on his way to court, Bigger will be struck on the head by one member of the mob. And after being made to re-enact his crime at the Dalton's house, so that the newspapers can get their pictures and further inflame public opinion, the mob will burn a cross atop an adjacent building, thereby aborting whatever spiritual rebirth Bigger may have initially contemplated. In his opening statements at Bigger's trial, Buckley plays directly to the mob, which, evidently, has nothing better to do than gather outside the courthouse all day long.

> "It is not often," Buckley continued, "that a representative of the people finds the masses of the citizens who elected him to office standing literally at his back, waiting for him to enforce the law..." The room was quiet as a tomb. Buckley strode to the window and with one motion of his hand hoisted it up. The rumbling mutter of the vast mob swept in. The court room stirred.
>
> "Kill 'im now!"
>
> "Lynch 'im!"

Rebuked by the judge for the theatrics of his opening statement, district attorney Buckley apologizes: "I'm very sorry, Your Honor," he says. "I was laboring under too much emotion."[111]

In essence, laboring under too much emotion is precisely what Max, in his closing argument to save Bigger's life, identifies as the problem afflicting not just Buckley but the mob, the court, indeed the nation itself. In most ways, the mob in *Native Son* resembles the mobs of Le Bon, Park, and Blumer. They say and do things en masse that they would never say or do individually. Unlike Park and Blumer, however, Wright does not distinguish between an irrational, impulsive crowd and a rational, deliberative public, and he especially does not follow Park or Blumer in believing that the newspaper engenders the latter. In "How Bigger Was Born," Wright describes how when he "was halfway through the first draft of *Native Son* a case paralleling Bigger's flared forth in the newspapers of Chicago."[112] Wright refers here to the case of Robert Nixon, who was accused and convicted of the murder—beating to death by brick, just as Bigger kills Bessie with a brick—of a white woman in her apartment. Newspaper coverage of the Nixon case, and newspaper coverage of the Bigger Thomas case in *Native Son*, does not cultivate rational, deliberate thought among a public so much as it does actively undermine it.[113]

In other respects, however, Wright more or less traces Le Bon, Park, and Blumer in his sketch of the hysterical crowd. Like district attorney Buckley, the crowd in *Native Son* "labors under too much emotion" and not enough reason. Under the weight of that emotion, it behaves violently—or would if given the chance—and in ways that the individuals who compose it would not, in all likelihood, be capable of on their own. Indeed, Max recognizes from the start that the problem he faces in his defense of Bigger is the hysterical crowd itself, which will settle for nothing less than Bigger's execution, and whose blood thirst infects others as well. Indeed, this view of the crowd lies behind Max's choice to avoid a jury trial. Max concludes that an impartial jury could not exist. Its twelve members would merely represent a smaller version of the mob that gathers outside the courtroom. His strategy, then, is plain, and takes a page out of Le Bon et. al.: isolate from the crowd those who will determine Bigger's fate. A jury is a good start, but too numerous to remain immune to the hysteria of the crowd. Better still a single man, the judge, who may be quarantined from the crowd and appealed to rationally.

Indeed, quarantining the judge from "too much emotion" drives Max's whole defense. Invoking the historical injustice of slavery and its aftermath without immediately naming it, Max nevertheless insists, "I do *not* claim that this boy is a victim of injustice, nor do I ask that this Court be sympathetic with him." Avoiding the legacy of historical injustice or the possibility of sympathy may seem like an odd strategy, but for Max both raise the possibility of what Max calls "the mire of blind emotion."[114] For Max has a reading of the hysterical crowd—and of race relations in the United States—that blames both on an excess of emotions. Midway through his defense, Max addresses the judge: "Let me, Your Honor," he says,

> dwell a moment longer upon the danger of looking upon this boy in the light of injustice. If I should say that he is a victim of injustice, then I would be asking by implication for sympathy; and if one insists upon looking at this boy as a victim of injustice, he will be swamped by a feeling of guilt so strong as to be indistinguishable from hate.[115]

For Max, whites in the United States do not wish to confront the historical injustice of slavery. "Of all things," Max says, "men do not like to feel that they are guilty of wrong, and if you make them feel guilt, they will try desperately to justify it on any grounds; but, failing that, and seeing no immediate solution that will set things right without too much cost to their lives and property, they will kill that which evoked in them the condemning sense of guilt."[116] In other words, white guilt—and, relatedly, sympathy—leads to fear and hatred of blacks. Just as a man haunted by the ghost of someone he has wronged will seek to thrust the ghost out of sight, so too will whites seek to thrust out of sight the race whom they have wronged. It is a form of racial panic. But the ghost—in Max's analogy, blacks—does not rest quietly. Thrust out of sight, segregated, they too strike out with fear and hatred. But the fear, hatred, and violence of the ghost only leads to more guilt, fear, and hatred on the part of whites, which, of course, leads to more fear, hatred, and violence on the part of blacks. Hence the climax of Max's speech: "Your Honor, I'm trying to wipe out this circle of blood, trying to cut down into this matter, beneath hate and fear and guilt and revenge and show what impulses are twisted."[117] Hence, too, Max's appeal to let Bigger live. More killing will reinforce—rather than begin to wipe out—the circle of blood.

In his defense, Max joins two circles: the circular reaction of Le Bon, Park, and Blumer, and the circle of blood of his own invention. The first explains how an entire community—the white citizens of Chicago—comes to lose its rationality, panics, and begins to behave hysterically. The second, the circle of blood, explains why the first, the circular reaction, happens in the first place. In mob justice—and the racial panic and hysteria it makes possible—lie absolution; or, if not absolution, at least avoidance. One can surrender to the crowd, to the sweet oblivion of emotion. "It is not my duty here, today," Max tells the judge, "to say how this great problem can be solved. My job is to show how nonsensical it is to seek revenge on this boy under the pretense that we are making a great fight for justice. If we do that, we shall merely be hypnotizing ourselves, and to our own ultimate disadvantage."[118] Notice that word "hypnotizing." Le Bon, Park, and Blumer each used hypnosis to describe the loss of consciousness and suggestibility that supposedly characterized crowds. So too Max, except for Max, at the moment of the trial, everyone belongs to the crowd. Everyone would prefer revenge, the mire of blind emotion, and hypnotic release to a conscious, rational confrontation with the reality of race in America. Everyone, he hopes, except the judge.

For all that he borrows from them, by now it should be clear where Wright departs from Le Bon, Park, and Blumer. Unlike Le Bon, Park, and Blumer, Wright—in the person of Max, at least—does not settle for an atavistic explanation of the hysterical crowd; that is, that the crowd releases individuals from, in Freudian terms, civilization and its discontents. Rather, Max favors an historical rather than an evolutionary or strictly psychoanalytic account of the hysterical crowd. In *Native Son*, one joins the crowd because it frees one from responsibility. In racial panic lies freedom; or, at least, evasion.

Not all critics admire Max's approach to defending Bigger's life. Still others insist on establishing a distance between Max and Wright, with the latter inviting judgment of the former, and, indeed, Wright composed *Native Son* just as he lost patience with the Communist Party, so one can imagine him losing patience with the levelheaded but nevertheless still communist Max. As it happens, I admire Max's defense, and to my mind the Wright of "How Bigger Was Born" sounds an awful lot like the Max of the closing argument of *Native Son*, which, for that matter, sounds an awful lot like a close reading of the novel *Native Son*. But that is neither here nor there. My point is only to observe that like Hadley Cantril, Irving Fisher, Franklin Roosevelt, or, say, the drafters of the FDIC provision of the Glass-Steagall Act, Wright sought to go behind or beyond existing approaches to collective behavior and panic. In Wright's case, he sought the racial origins of that panic.

Like others during the 1930s, Wright concluded that simply saying that those who panicked behaved irrationally would not do. That was not the end of the story but the beginning.

4

Fear Itself

Polio, Unemployment, and Other Things on the Doorstep

On September 5, 1934, a Cleveland man searching for driftwood along the Lake Erie shore stumbled across what he thought was a tree trunk. Up close, though, it turned out to be the rotting legs of a woman, severed at the waist and knees. A few days later, the upper torso—cut off at the waist and missing its head—was found on the beach. Not long after an upper arm washed up. A coroner, looking at the body parts under a microscope, saw distinct knife marks, which indicated that someone had deliberately dismembered the body. The woman was never identified, though, and the crime went unsolved.[1]

A year later, in the Kingsbury Run section of the city, then (and now) an industrial neighborhood not all that far from downtown, a boy looking for a lost softball at the bottom of a hill found a naked, headless corpse. Thirty feet away, at nearly the same time, two other boys glimpsed another headless corpse. When the police arrived, they discovered that in addition to being decapitated, the bodies of the two male victims had been castrated. The genitals were found nearby, as was the head of the first corpse but, weirdly, not the second head. As with the corpse found on the beach, the heads from both corpses had been neatly removed from the bodies. This time, however, one of the bodies was identified. It belonged to twenty-nine-year-old Edward W. Andressy, a minor criminal who made his home in what was then called the Roaring Third, a neighborhood of bars and tenements adjacent to Kingsbury Run.

Then, one night in January, in an area of the city just northwest of Kingsbury Run, dogs in the neighborhood would not stop barking, and in the morning residents discovered why. Someone had left two half-bushel

The Emotional Life of the Great Depression. John Marsh, Oxford University Press (2019).
 DOI: 10.1093/oso/9780198847731.001.0001

baskets filled with human body parts—the lower half of a female torso, two thighs, and a right arm and hand—neatly wrapped in newspapers, including one bearing that day's date, January 26, 1936. A little less than two weeks later, the rest of the body—everything except the head—turned up not far away. This time, the corpse turned out to belong to Florence Polillo, an occasional waitress, barmaid, and prostitute who, like Andressy, was not unknown to the police. Whoever dismembered her body had also carefully removed her entire reproductive system.

Separated by years, none of these gruesome murders had yet been linked. All that would change on the morning of June 5, 1936, when two boys walking through Kingsbury Run discovered a man's head rolled up in his own pants. The next day, two local workers found the rest of his body. This corpse would never be identified. By then, no one could fail to connect the string of murders and decapitations, and the local newspapers began to refer—not inappropriately—to a "human butcher." The next month, a headless corpse—this one badly decayed—turned up on the west side of the city.

It got worse. On September 10, 1936, a vagrant passing through Kingsbury Run found a torso—headless, armless, and legless—floating in a stagnant creek. In the same water, police later found the lower half of the legs but no head. Like some of the earlier male victims, this one had been castrated. The autopsy also suggested that the victim had been alive when he was dismembered—whether conscious or not no one could or wanted to say.

With five corpses discovered in one year—and six total beginning with the body of the woman found by the lake in 1934—the Cleveland newspapers did not temper their coverage. An editorial in the *Cleveland News* on September 12, 1936—two days after the latest victim appeared—set the tone:

> Why these dead? Why this darkest of all Cleveland murder mysteries? He kills for the thrill of killing. He kills to satisfy a bestial, sadistic lust for blood. He kills to prove himself strong. He kills to feed his sex-perverted brain the sight of a beheaded human. He must kill. For decapitation is his drug, to be taken in closer-spaced doses. Yes, he will kill again. He is, of course, insane.[2]

Another paper declared:

> Of all horrible nightmares come to life, the most shuddering is the fiend who decapitates his victims in the dark, dank recesses of Kingsbury Run. That this creature, sly, crafty, inhumanly skilled in butchery, is a menace to every man, woman and child who walks the streets of Cleveland does not have to be emphasized.[3]

In fact, it did have to be emphasized, for the human butcher had not—thus far anyway—proved a menace to every man, woman, and child in Cleveland. Both of the bodies that could be identified, and the neighborhoods where they were found, suggested that the human butcher was a menace to a rather narrow class of minor criminals and socially dispossessed. And the corpses that could not be identified also confirmed as much. They remained unidentified. Evidently, no one missed them. Indeed, such a gulf separated most residents of Cleveland from the Kingsbury Run section of the city that one newspaper, the *Cleveland Press*, induced a reporter to visit the neighborhood and describe it for those—the majority of Clevelanders—for whom it existed, at most, as a neighborhood seen from a train window.

On Friday, September 11, 1936, William Miller published his front-page article, which had the arresting lead, "Last midnight I went down in Kingsbury Run." He continued: "Kingsbury Run, that lonely, mysterious gully where prowls a mad butcher. Four of his headless victims have been found there. He has killed two others." In the article that follows, Miller describes his own passing fears and the more permanent ones of residents of Kingsbury Run. As for the former, Miller describes—some might say exaggerates—how fear feels and eventually overtakes the body. Near the outset of the piece, he writes "that if you enjoy feeling your flesh creep—feeling the small hairs rise on your neck and your heart pounding with shameless fear—if that's what you like, just take a midnight tour through Kingsbury Run!" Later, he writes of making his way down an overgrown path, "Every step your feet took forward your heart was going the other way." A flare of flame out of a nearby foundry made "our shadows turn somersaults."

More convincingly, Miller describes the fear of residents themselves. For his midnight tour, Miller enlists the help of two local boys to show him around. They talk, Miller writes, "of 'him'—that unknown person or thing whose specialty is removing the heads of homeless tramps." "Every kid around here is in bed or at home early these nights," the boys add. In addition to scaring the permanent residents of Kingsbury Run, the "thing" had also scared off its temporary ones. Those made homeless by the Depression had set up shantytowns in Kingsbury Run, until the human butcher had, Miller reports, driven many of them away. "Fear," he concludes, "is over the Run like a living thing."

Fear provides the final note of the article, too. His tour complete, and once again overlooking Kingsbury Run from an elevated road, Miller sees another car parked below "where ours had been." "You knew it was just a curiosity seeker," he writes, "but you couldn't help thinking, 'It might be... someone else.'"[4]

This chapter is about fear and, leaving aside the human butcher for a moment, Miller's report of his midnight descent into Kingsbury Run suggests the many forms that fear can take. According to psychologists, fear exists along a spectrum of proximity.[5] On the end of the spectrum, fear arises from an unexpected and immediate threat: finding a corpse instead of a softball, the flaring of a flame, or someone shouting, "Boo!" When this happens, one is startled, and the response bypasses conscious thought. Once the shock passes, however, the fear and its physiological responses pass too. This end of the fear spectrum is reserved for fright, or a sudden, intense feeling of fear. Somewhere along the middle of the spectrum lies the form of fear that arises not from something that has happened but something that might happen: the possibility that a human butcher might jump out from behind a bush, or the thought that a car might belong to a human butcher. The physiological responses include the ones Miller describes: creeping flesh, rising hair, pounding heart. That feeling is what most of us talk about when we talk about fear. Call it terror, or extreme fear. On the far end of the spectrum lies a more prospective fear, not of what has happened or what might happen but what may happen; for example, the fear on the part of residents when a serial killer stalks their neighborhood. Call this end of the spectrum dread, or an intense apprehension about potential threats.

In this chapter, I examine what scared Americans during the Great Depression, and with one or two exceptions, I focus on dread, the more prospective and less immediate end of the spectrum of fear: not flares of flame or human butchers jumping out from behind bushes, but the knowledge that somewhere in this city a human butcher plies his craft. As I suggest in my introduction, and discuss at greater length in my conclusion, fear—of unemployment, of impoverished old age, and of what people subject to or afraid of those horrors might do—would drive many of the legislative initiatives of the 1930s, including the Economic Security Bill of 1935, otherwise known as Social Security. In this chapter, I focus more on how fear works, on its inner logic.

I derive its inner logic by examining two fears in particular: polio and unemployment. Polio, I argue, frightens because it exposes the fragility of the human body. By the 1930s, scientists had developed vaccines for pertussis (whooping cough) and diphtheria. (Although doctors did not regularly administer such vaccines until the 1940s.) Vaccines for other communicable diseases, though, like measles, mumps, tuberculosis, tetanus, rubella, and polio, were years or decades away. As a result, these diseases sickened, killed, and scared many more people than they do today. The same goes for osteomyelitis, septicemia, pneumonia, and other bacterial infections, which, in the days before penicillin—it did not appear on the domestic market until well into the war years—regularly and casually killed people. Of the communicable diseases, however, polio seems to have scared people the most during the Great Depression, as a particularly alarming epidemic in New York City in 1931 illustrates. (Many New Yorkers in the 1930s would have remembered the ghastly polio outbreak of 1916.) In addition to scaring people, polio can help us understand how fear works. When we fear something, like polio, we often fear it because it reveals our body to be weaker and more defenseless than we supposed.

Not even polio, however, could compete with the most common fear of the Great Depression, unemployment, and for good reason. Not only was it widespread—the unemployment rate rose into the teens and twenties in the first half of the decade—but for years virtually no safety net (no unemployment insurance, no food stamps) existed to catch people when they fell. In this chapter, I examine unemployment and the fear of unemployment among the middle class, not because unemployment and the fear of unemployment among the working class does not matter, but only because the former has, over the years, received comparatively less attention and, therefore, may revitalize our understanding of this somewhat shopworn fear of the Great Depression. Like polio, unemployment can, ultimately, threaten the body. (People really did starve during the Great Depression.) In the accounts I examine, however, unemployment threatens something less substantial but no less meaningful than our body: our place in the world, our sense of identity.

After examining each of these fears, polio and unemployment, I argue that what they have in common, and what a reading of the pulp literature of the day confirms, is a concern for the purity and autonomy of being, the nature or essence of a person, and the dread that such being might be violated and despoiled by impersonal but nevertheless malevolent forces. I do not claim that this fear was unique to the 1930s, but it does seem to have become more general and more intense during the decade.

A fear that the integrity of being would be violated is obviously and somewhat crudely the case with the human butcher who stalked Cleveland during the middle years of the 1930s. Indeed, one of the things that disturbs us so much about the Cleveland serial killer is how casually and cruelly he treated something—the body—that we invest with such dignity and sacredness. In this respect, "the human butcher" is an apt nickname. He treated human beings like animals, like meat. The other things that people feared during the Great Depression—disease, unemployment—did not treat human beings with the obvious contempt that the human butcher did, but they were in their way akin to human butchers in their indifference to human life and, thus, at times, could be just as frightening.

In his inaugural address of 1933, President Franklin Roosevelt asserted his "firm belief that the only thing we have to fear is fear itself."[6] In a bit of unguarded optimism, Roosevelt meant that though the nation faced any number of what he called "the dark realities of the moment," nothing had fundamentally changed about the country or its economy, nothing, anyway, that government could not fix. As years passed, though, and times remained tough, if Americans thought of Roosevelt's words, they may have come to doubt their wisdom. During the Great Depression, as this chapter shows, Americans had plenty to fear beyond fear itself.

After the sixth body appeared in Kingsbury Run in September 1936, the human butcher went on to murder at least six more people over the next two years. Then he stopped. Although the police had dozens of suspects, some more likely than others, they never brought charges against anyone. In all likelihood, the killer remained free.

"Don't Ever Kiss Your Children or Allow Them to Be Kissed"

Like baseball, polio arrives with the warm weather. On March 30, 1931, the *New York Times* reported its first annual case of infantile paralysis, as poliomyelitis was then more commonly known. Curiously, the case the *Times* reported on did not occur in New York City but in Rhode Island. The obituary ("Girl, 14, Dies of Poliomyelitis") is terse. It says only that "Barbara Jones, 14-year-old daughter of Mayor Frederick A. Jones of Cranston, died at Jane Brown Memorial Hospital today of infantile paralysis. She was a freshman in Cranston High School, where she ranked high in scholarship. She had been ill about a week."[7] The *Times* picked up the story from the Associated Press. It likely did so not because of how the girl died—deaths from polio were rare but not uncommon—but because of who her father was; that is, the story is not about infantile paralysis but about the mayor of a sizable city in the northeast and his grief for the loss of his young daughter.

If that seems strange in light of what would happen over the coming summer, when New York would experience its worst polio outbreak since the devastating one of 1916, recall that by 1931 polio had all but dropped out of public consciousness. Indeed, when polio made news in recent years, it did so because of how little news it had made. On January 1, 1931, the health commissioner of New York City, Dr. Shirley W. Wynne, said that "the city was fortunate in having only seventy-nine" cases of infantile paralysis in the previous year, and though "the incidence of this disease was expected to be high in 1930, only eight more cases were reported here than in 1929, when the number was seventy-one, of which twenty-five were fatal."[8]

That optimism began to change as the summer of 1931 progressed. In June, the *Times* reported on another victim of infantile paralysis, Louise Hohne:

> After oxygen had been administered to 4-year old Louise Hohne of 215 Fourth Avenue, Brooklyn, for more than twenty-four hours in the Kings County Hospital, physicians there last night expressed the hope that she might recover from infantile paralysis.
>
> The child was taken ill last Saturday and was removed to the hospital Wednesday afternoon. She was then in a coma.
>
> At the hospital she was treated with a respirator. After four hours of treatment color returned slowly. During Wednesday night she mumbled a few words. A physician and nurse were in constant attendance. One of her parents was at her bedside constantly.
>
> About noon yesterday Louise showed signs of consciousness. She asked for something to eat and liquid nourishment was given to her.
>
> Dr. Ruben Budnowitz and Dr. Thomas Fry are in attendance, with a day and night nurse. Because her parents are not in financial position to pay for her treatment, the city will defray the expense.
>
> Both doctors last night expressed satisfaction at her progress and said there was hope of recovery.[9]

As the story suggests, Louise Hohne suffered through the classic symptoms of the most serious type of infantile paralysis. Roughly one to three weeks prior to falling ill, Hohne would have contracted the virus from another person, whether through direct contact or, less likely, by consuming tainted food or water. On Wednesday, when she took ill, Hohne would probably have suffered from fever, fatigue, headache, vomiting, stiffness in the neck, and pain in the limbs. Her parents may have thought she had a bout of the flu.

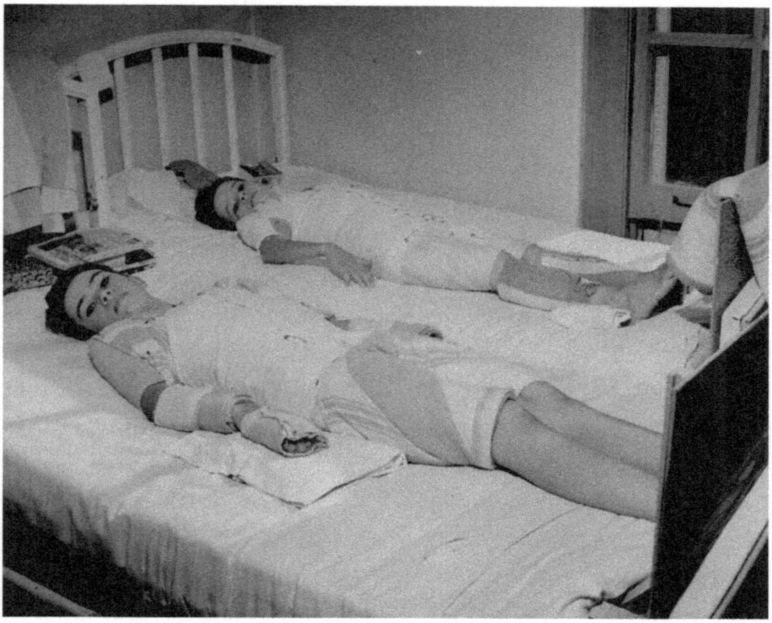

Figure 4.1. Two young polio patients press their legs against wooden footboards. The treatment—and others—was pioneered by an Australian nurse, Sister Elizabeth Kenny, who developed a following during the 1930s.
Source: Ed Clark/LIFE Images Collection/Getty Images

Over the coming days, though, her symptoms would not have improved and, before anyone knew what was going on, her stiffness and pain would have hardened into paralysis. The polio virus, that is, quickly attacks and destroys nerve cells and muscle tissue, usually in the hips, ankles, and feet. Some children fully recover, but others are left with withered limbs and a lifelong disability (see Figure 4.1). In the worst cases, such as Hohne's, the paralysis spreads to the muscles of the diaphragm, which makes breathing impossible. When people die from polio, they usually asphyxiate. Hence the infamous iron lung, which, using changes in air pressure, artificially inflates and deflates the lungs, thereby breathing for those who could not. (The *Times* refers to it as a respirator.)

Sadly, the optimism on the part of Hohne's doctors proved unfounded. Two days later, the *Times* reported her death.[10] As Hohne's case reveals, not even the leading edge of polio treatment—artificial respirators—could save the lives of those who contracted the virus. As her case reveals, too, a child could be healthy one week and dead the next.

In July, the *Times* reported a happier story concerning infantile paralysis: how a mechanical lung rushed from New York City to Connecticut saved the life of an eight-year-old boy, Arthur Ahearn.[11] Two days later the *Times* reported that Ahern—the spelling had changed—still lived, but the newspaper never reported whether he ultimately lived or died.[12]

Soon, however, the narrative of infantile paralysis that summer changed from one of individual cases to one of the beginnings of an epidemic. On July 18, the *Times* reported that the Health Department of the City had asked the "medical societies of the Greater New York . . . to obtain the prompt reporting of new cases of infantile paralysis which may develop this Summer." The same article reported that the number of cases of infantile paralysis in 1931 (171) had already exceeded the number of cases for 1929 (71) and 1930 (78), with, worryingly, much of the summer and early fall remaining, when the virus thrived.[13] On July 25, the *Times* reported "New York City has the largest number of cases of infantile paralysis, or poliomyelitis, in several years."[14]

As the epidemic worsened, Dr. Wynne, the health commissioner of the city, advised residents on "general preventative measures": "strict attention to cleanliness, guarding against flies, keeping children from crowds, and normal care in food and water."[15] If these recommendations seemed vague, that is because, as the *Times* also reported in August, scientists were largely in the dark about the disease. "After three years of experimentation," the *Times* wrote, "research experts of the National Institute of Health admitted today that they had failed to find the cause, methods of communication or cure for infantile paralysis." "DISEASE BAFFLES SCIENTISTS," as the headline put it.[16] Similarly, in October, a Dr. Robert Kingman published an article in the Brooklyn *Daily Eagle* under the headline, "Infantile Paralysis a Medical Mystery."[17]

This lack of knowledge about the disease left communities vulnerable to polio epidemics, and as became increasingly clear to everyone in 1931, New York City, particularly the borough of Brooklyn, had an epidemic on its hands. In late July, public health officials requested that parents from the city not visit children they had sent upstate to summer camps lest they bring the disease with them. The same article noted that thus far in July, 373 cases of infantile paralysis had been reported. On July 27 alone, 89 cases of polio were reported in the city, including 69 in Brooklyn. As the article observed, "this figure [89] is 11 more than were reported in the city throughout 1930."[18] Thus far, the epidemic had not matched the horrifying one of 1916, which sickened some 9,000 people, of which over 2,400 died.[19] Still, in July

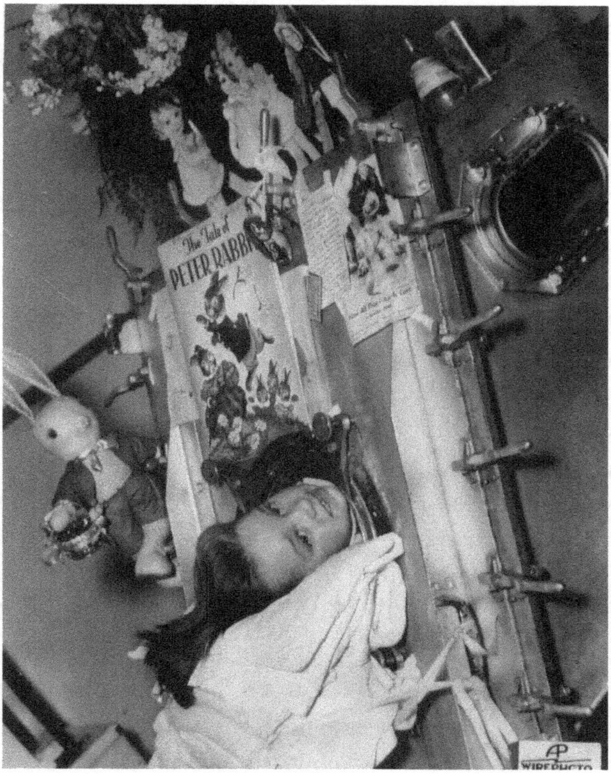

Figure 4.2. A child in an iron lung at Johns Hopkins Hospital.
Source: Steve Degenaro

alone 688 cases occurred, with 508 in Brooklyn. And as Dr. Wynne pointed out, true to the name infantile paralysis, "most of those afflicted with the disease were under 5 years of age."[20] As in later outbreaks, hospital rooms would be lined with as many iron lungs as hospitals could obtain, the heads of children poking out from the top like magician's assistants waiting to be sawn in half (see Figure 4.2).

In a story that only could have occurred in the Great Depression, in early August the *Times* reported on a Staten Island family "whose ten-month old son Theodore died in his mother's arms Thursday as moving men were evicting the family from their home." Generously, or so the *Times* thought anyway, the landlord told the family they "could remain in the house until Monday." At that point, grieving for the death of their child, and facing eviction, another one of their children, "Minnie, 3 years old, was taken ill, and at Seaview Hospital was found to be suffering from malnutrition with symptoms of infantile paralysis."[21]

On August 5, 111 new cases were reported, bringing the total in the city since July 1 to 1,013 (and 1,047 since the new year). At this point in the epidemic, real fear set in, especially on the part of authorities. Summer camps everywhere barred visitors from the city, and a camp in Vermont went so far as to bar children from the city. In Brooklyn, the center of the outbreak, Dr. John Oberwager, of the New York City Department of Health, addressed several thousand concerned parents and warned them against kissing their children. When a mother in the audience "asked whether it was safe for her husband to kiss their baby when he returned home from work," Dr. Oberwager replied: "Don't ever kiss your children or allow them to be kissed, now or at any other time. It is a legal, moral, parental duty. A kiss is the easiest way of spreading disease."[22] This advice may have seemed extreme, but given how the disease spread, or was thought to spread, it made sense. A booklet issued by the Department of Health "warned that patients carry germs of the disease in their mouths and noses for several days after the fever; [and] that the germs may be present in the noses and mouths of members of the family of those who are ill and may be carried in mouths of healthy persons."[23]

In the event, August 5 turned out to be the high water mark—in terms of daily reported cases—of the epidemic. By then, the city had 1,570 cases, all but 34 since July 1. Still, the epidemic had by no means receded. On August 17, 87 new cases were reported.[24] The next day, there were 79.[25] On September 1, Dr. Wynne delayed the opening of the school year by a week.[26] By September 3, 2,892 cases had been reported in the city.[27] On September 22, however, the *Times* gratefully reported "Paralysis Recedes with Cool Weather." By that point, 3,508 cases had occurred.[28] But the *Times* may have been premature in calling the recession of the disease. Over 500 cases would yet be reported. All told, by the end of 1931, the city counted 4,087 cases of infantile paralysis. Happily, and as opposed to the 1916 outbreak, only 490 of those who contracted the disease died, thanks in no small part to the widespread use of iron lungs.[29]

When the narrative of a disease comes to revolve around the number of cases, the individuals who fall ill to the disease can too easily get lost in those numbers, obscuring the human drama associated with each so-called case. One would do well to remember, then, that each instance of polio involved more or less the same fear and, often enough, grief that the parents of Louise Hahn experienced early in the summer. To put it bluntly, children died, by the hundreds, and many more sickened and were disabled, and each death or illness battered the parents of those children, not to mention the children themselves. In addition, one has to calculate the dread of parents whose children did not contract polio during the epidemic but might. In short, parents in New York City in the summer of 1931, especially certain neighborhoods of the city, must have lived in a state of near constant dread. Every time a child coughed or looked tired, a chill must have gone down their spine.

All of this raises the question, though, of whether polio should have scared parents in 1931—and, for that matter, later summers—as much as it did. In the early days of the New York City outbreak, Dr. Charles F. Bouldan, the director of health education for the Health Department, tried to calm fearful parents. He pointed out that "so far there had been only 500 cases," which, in a city of 1.5 million children under 15 years of age, meant that only one in 3,000 had contracted the disease. (Dr. Bouldan had no way of knowing it, but by year's end, the ratio would be one in 367, which is a slightly less reassuring number.) He also observed that compared to measles, which in the United States killed 1,000 children annually, polio seemed relatively benign.[30] Similarly, Dr. Wynne "counseled parents not to be frightened, pointing out that with ordinary precautions the disease was not very contagious." Like Dr. Bouldan, Wynne also observed that "other contagious diseases were often far more prevalent."[31]

Later critics echo these warnings that the public may have overreacted to the polio threat. In addition, they accuse charities like the March of Dimes, started by Franklin Roosevelt in 1938 as the National Foundation for Infantile Paralysis, with deliberately stoking public fear about the disease in order to raise money to fight it. Oftentimes, these critics make arguments similar to Drs. Bouldan and Wynne, which is that little distinguished polio from other infectious diseases, especially in prevalence and morbidity, yet polio commanded a disproportionate share of attention and public and private aid. Worse still, critics charge, polio may have received the attention and funds it did because it tended to affect the middle class, who had the resources, social and economic, to make it into more of an existential threat to public health than it was. As Gareth Williams writes in *Paralysed with Fear: The Story of Polio*, "the fear of polio [was] deliberately played up, by an organization [the March of Dimes] prepared to steamroller its way through American society to achieve its goal of conquering polio."[32]

Although those who charge the National Foundation for Infantile Paralysis with deliberately exaggerating fears of polio have a point, those who make that charge also risk dismissing the genuine horror people had of polio and the reasons they had for it. As its name suggests, infantile paralysis primarily targeted children. An analysis in September of 1931 would show that 54 percent of all cases affected children under age five, and 83 percent affected children under age ten.[33] Adding to fears, no one knew exactly what caused infantile paralysis or quite how it spread. The August booklet issued by the city hinted at what turned out to be true. Nearly everyone is infected by the polio virus, but usually only a few of those infected will develop any symptoms at all. (That, by the way, is why the disease primarily affected children. Most adults had previously—and unknowingly—contracted the virus and built up an immunity to it.) Moreover, most of those who did get sick as a result of the virus did not experience paralysis, meaning, in most cases, they thought they had the flu. Yet everyone—those made sick by the virus and those who did not know they had it—could equally infect others. As in the HIV crisis of the 1980s and 1990s, perfectly healthy people, ignorant of the fact that they carried a virus, could pass it on to others. If so, to recall Dr. Oberwager's address to Brooklyn parents, it made a certain amount of sense not to let your children be kissed by anyone. That is, no one could know who carried the virus, which made it difficult to guard against. Finally, while most people who suffered from polio recovered without any lingering effects, many did not. Famously, Franklin Roosevelt, who contracted the disease in 1921 at age thirty-nine, never wholly regained the use of his legs. The same was true for many others. Each neighborhood would have one or more children who walked with crutches or a limp, a constant reminder of what the virus could do and what could befall your child. More than a few children spent the rest of their lives in an iron lung. And many, of course, like Louise Hahn, died. In short, and with no offense to measles, polio seemed reverse engineered to terrify parents. You can accuse the foundations of fear mongering, but I suspect most parents did not need the hard sell.

Whether you think polio was exaggerated or not, parents during the Great Depression feared it. And though neither the city nor the nation would experience another epidemic quite as bad as the one in 1931, at least during the Great Depression, fear of the disease lingered. More than just showing what those in the Great Depression feared, however, polio shows how fear works. As I discuss above, fear usually takes one of two forms: terror, or the fear of a sudden, specific stimuli; and dread, the fear of a looming, prospective threat. In a way, the latter is more psychologically destructive than the former. With the exception of those who suffer post-traumatic stress disorder, terror passes. By contrast, dread, particularly during anxious times, is a way of life. Unlike, say, the sudden appearance of a bear, in which case one is eaten or escapes, with anxiety and dread you cannot escape—or suffer—unless and until the threat manifests, which it never may, or disappears. Until it does, it—and the fear it engenders—simply lingers.

The polio epidemic of 1931 indicates two additional ways that fear works. First, although we fear a variety of things, at bottom, as with polio, many of our fears have to do with the body, with what illnesses, injuries, and, finally, death might do to our physical selves. Polio, which twists and deforms human bodies, plays on this fear perfectly. Second, we fear what may harm us, and what may harm us—like the polio virus—by definition lies beyond our control. After all, if we could control something or someone, it could not threaten us, and we would not fear it. As with polio, what we fear may strike at any moment, and we can do little to nothing about it. It transcends us. What we fear—and fear itself for that matter—therefore diminishes us. Polio targeted children, which made it even more dreadful because some children, especially the very young, could not understand what befell them. But fear makes children of us all. Fear reveals and exploits our vulnerability. It exposes our helplessness.

In the next section of this chapter, I explore another prominent fear of the Great Depression, perhaps the prominent fear of the Great Depression: unemployment. Unemployment, and the prospect of unemployment, also illustrates the helplessness and, to a certain extent, anxiety about our exposed bodies that lie behind fear. In this respect, unemployment, that quintessential Great Depression fear, may have more in common with polio than it might seem. Even more so, though, unemployment exposes the fragility of our identities, the precarious and contingent place we occupy in any given community.

Fear of Falling

In 1989, Barbara Ehrenreich famously diagnosed a "fear of falling" that had supposedly defined the inner life of the middle class for a generation or more. By middle class, Ehrenreich meant those people whose "economic and social status is based on education rather than the ownership of capital or property."[34] (Elsewhere, Ehrenreich refers to this group as the professional-managerial class.)[35] The middle class included everyone from schoolteachers to professors to corporate executives. This stratum of the middle class, Ehrenreich argues, is haunted by its own precariousness. "Its real 'capital,'" she writes, "is knowledge and skill . . . And unlike real capital, these cannot be hoarded against hard times, preserved beyond the lifetime of an individual, or, of course, bequeathed."[36] Because members of the professional-managerial class cannot guarantee that they will continue to succeed, or that their children will succeed as they did, there is, as Ehrenreich observes, "the fear, always, of falling."

In the bulk of her book, Ehrenreich explores the repercussions of this fear of falling. It is not, she admits, "a pretty story." Tracking the inner life of the professional-managerial class from the 1960s through the 1980s, Ehrenreich argues that its consciousness of itself as a precarious but nevertheless elite class "has led to—and sometimes helped to justify—the adoption of the kind of political outlook appropriate to an elite, which is a conservative outlook, and ultimately indifferent to the nonelite majority."[37] In short, as Ehrenreich tells it, the professional-managerial class in the second half of the twentieth century could have allied with the poor and working class against the rich, thereby making its condition slightly less precarious, but instead it emulated—culturally, ideologically, and ultimately politically—the rich, and it pays for it, cruelly, with more precariousness.

As a result of Ehrenreich's argument, the "fear of falling"—the fear "of misfortunes that might lead to a downward slide"—has gotten a bad reputation, at least as that fear manifests itself among the middle class. Thanks to Ehrenreich, it implies smugness, complacency, and selfishness on the part of those who feel it. In this section, I set out to rehabilitate the fear of falling and those subject to it, especially as that fear showed up in the 1930s. To be sure, no one likes the middle class. (I exaggerate.) But I would like to approach them, especially as one glimpses them in the 1930s, with slightly less judgment and slightly more sympathy. I take this approach not because a fear of falling among the middle class in the 1930s necessarily led to less smugness, complacency, and selfishness than it would later. It did and it did not. Rather, I take it because during the Depression, people from across classes, including and especially the professional-managerial class, had a legitimate fear of falling, and instead of lamenting its politically conservative outcomes, I would like to take it seriously as a fear.

One does not have to look hard for stories of how unemployment afflicted the working class during the Great Depression. They are ubiquitous and horrifying. Stories of how unemployment affected the middle class, however, have attracted less attention. In what follows, I explore how a number of writers—popular novelists, academic sociologists, and federal relief investigators—represented unemployment and the fear of falling among the middle class.[38] All agree that unemployment unravels the comforting identity individuals have wound, layer by layer, around themselves. Yet each, depending on when in the decade they wrote, offered different conclusions about how catastrophic and final this unraveling would be.

Hardy Perennials?

All but forgotten today, or consigned to the status of the lover of a slightly better-known writer (the children's book author Mabel Louise Robinson), Helen Hull wrote seventeen novels during the middle decades of the twentieth century, including *Heat Lightning*, from 1932, which was a Book-of-the-Month Club selection. While the Great Depression for the most part remains in the background of that book, her next novel, *Hardy Perennial* (1933), moves it to the foreground. The novel concerns Cornelia Prescott, the vaguely dissatisfied wife of Horace Prescott, an executive at a Ford Foundation-like granting agency. Horace returns to Manhattan from a trip abroad with a new secretary, Miss Brusello. Cornelia fears that Miss Brusello has designs on Horace, and that Horace is insecure and vain enough to succumb to them. Their prospective affair, however, which casts a constant shadow over the book, turns out to be a McGuffin for the real crisis in the novel, when through an unlikely series of events Horace is pushed out of his executive position at the foundation and finds himself, during the worst years of the Great Depression, with no other prospects.

The novel generates considerable suspense about when, exactly, the sword of unemployment will fall on Horace. A third of the way through the book, before he can appoint Horace acting president, the president of the foundation dies, and Horace, having accumulated enemies on the board of trustees, suddenly feels exposed. "Just at this moment," he exclaims to Cornelia, "with everything in the air! It's preposterous! Cornelia, it won't make any difference, will it? Don't look at me as if you wanted to cry. Say it won't."[39] But of course it will.

Although Horace does not lose his job immediately, his prospects—for the presidency of the foundation, for continued employment—immediately dim. Worse, Cornelia can glimpse the difference unemployment might make to Horace in Ellery, a friend of the family and a former broker who has lost his job and grown desperate. Unemployed, alienated from his wife, adrift in "a horrible world of nightmares," Ellery seeks out Cornelia for courage and faith. "Give me a good reason for wanting to live," he demands. "It's not reason," she responds, somewhat feebly, "It's just wanting to live," and their conversation reveals one reason why so many people—even those who would not necessarily starve—feared unemployment as much as they did.[40] As Ellery describes it, unemployment robs you of your identity and a will to live. "But I don't [want to live]," he tells Cornelia:

> I'm sick of it. I tell you, Cornelia, I've had a look into what's under the surface. Most folks stay on top and never know. As long as you're busy, making money, spending it, feeling a fine fellow because you're smarter than some other fellow— But that's all over. The world's gone to pot. I'm part of the ruins. Clear 'em away![41]

In the same conversation, Ellery will say: "All I do know is that I've walked the town, in and out offices, I've written letters, I've seen men. I have nothing to sell. And it's no comfort that there are lots like me. I'm superfluous and useless."[42] At times, Ellery can seem sniveling, but these lines haunt. Hull, through Ellery, suggests that as much as unemployment threatens material comfort—and that threat is real enough—at bottom it threatens your sense of belonging, your place in the community. Unemployed, you have nothing to offer the community, and the community has no need of you. It is a form of exile. As if to confirm the point, Ellery will later die in a car accident, driving to Maine where he plans to buy a general store and "be of some use."[43] Although speaking of the specific conditions of his accident, Horace's description of his death—"the Depression really got him finally, didn't it?"—is nonetheless apt.[44]

Eventually, Hull drops the sword of unemployment on Horace, and for a while it looks as though the Depression will finally get him, too. Not only does Horace not receive a promotion to acting president, but his bureau—the foreign office—is closed, and he loses his job outright. If the prospect of losing his position makes Horace distraught, actually losing it throws him into despair. "You'll find something else as good—or better," Cornelia insists. "Of course I'll find something," Horace confirms. But then he "turned, his face altering as if a wind of fear blew over it," and, perhaps with men like Ellery in mind, who do not in fact find something, he collapses.[45]

Cornelia, heretofore adrift in her life and marriage, finds renewed purpose in tending to "Horace's needs" and his confidence, which indeed breaks after he loses his job. Oddly, this reversal of fortune merely confirms the thesis of the book, which is that individuals flourish when they have a use, when they are employed at some meaningful task, and wither when they are not. Unemployed, Horace begins to wither. "'What am I going to do?' Horace asks, dully. 'How can I go asking for work?'"[46] Later, he fears he is "too old, too old to start again." Later still, after the family has retreated to its cabin in the woods, and Horace has sent out letters inquiring about jobs, Cornelia worries:

> Nothing will come of those letters, she thought. He's hiding, because the self he took abroad is stripped and shivering. He was what he had, so triumphantly. She breathed in fear with the damp smell of the sea's margin. We all do that, dress up in what we possess, in what we have accomplished, to show the world. But Horace—it was not armor that he wore, within which he existed, complete; stripped of which he could step out, naked, alert. More like the bark of a tree, the shell of a tortoise, built cell by cell. Stripped of it, had he life enough—.[47]

Cornelia, fearing that Horace does not have life enough, that he will come to the suicidal despair that Ellery the unemployed broker did, does not finish the thought. Nevertheless, her metaphors—unemployment and loss of status as weakness, vulnerability, bodily decay—weirdly links it with polio. Unemployment, like disease, exposes one to the malevolence of the world, and unemployment, like disease, threatens first identity but eventually life itself. The novel links polio and unemployment still further. One of its subplots concerns Horace and Cornelia's sons, David, who contracts polio in a 1927 outbreak, survives after a brush with death, but lives with the effects ever after. Just as Cornelia nurses David through that crisis, she will nurse Horace through his. Like father like son.

Just as it appears that Hull will follow the narrative of unemployment into genuine despair, however, the gods intervene. Cornelia, keeping a promise she made to the president of Horace's foundation before he died, drives out to his estate to pick up some rare flower seedlings. While there, his widow asks if Cornelia thinks Horace would like to write a biography of the former president. The widow would pay. And just like that, Horace has solved the problem of unemployment—or, rather, Cornelia has solved it for him. Things may look bleak, the novel assures readers, but no one stays down for long. Winter, the Great Depression, descends upon us all, but, like a "hardy perennial," some of us—Horace but Cornelia most of all—return to life in the spring. One of the last lines of the novel is Cornelia commenting on the seedlings: "They stand a lot." Readers are to gather that humans do, too.

By letting the gods intervene, however, by saving Horace from unemployment and the relief rolls, the ending of *Hardy Perennial* is in many ways more frightening than if it had just followed Horace and Cornelia into unemployment and despair. That fate, the novel suggests, is so terrible that it must not be shown. Or, by contrast, it is a fate so familiar or cynical that it would not provide a sufficiently thrilling denouement, so, instead, it gets reduced, in Ellery, to a subplot, to a foil. Despite and perhaps because of the ending, though, what emerges from Hull is how deeply a sense of self is tied to use, and how catastrophically unemployment undermines the identity of those upon whom it falls. The novel shows that individuals, at least the professionals who people Hull's novel, do not fear unemployment because they will starve, but because they will not be the same people afterwards. Their whole being is tied to their employment.

In his study of unemployment, the Yale sociologist E. Wight Bakke started from a similar premise, though he ultimately concluded that people could adapt to unemployment, could assume new identities. In 1940, Bakke published two significant if now largely forgotten books—*Citizens without Work* and *The Unemployed Worker*—that drew on his eight years of research among the unemployed in New Haven, Connecticut. In his research, Bakke attempted nothing less than to document how unemployment affected individual workers and their families during the 1930s.[48] Although marred by patches of academic prose—it existed back then, too—the books offer glimpses into the lives of countless people as they navigated the economic pressures of the Great Depression. Few books reveal the era better than these.

In *The Unemployed Worker*, the second of the two volumes, Bakke writes of the Cohens, a professional family that, as he put it in a subtitle to the section, "Loses Its Social Status." In 1924, as Bakke tells it, Mrs. Cohen married Mr. Cohen, a professional musician with his own orchestra, at least in part because he offered her better prospects than the man she claimed she really loved, a lowly cabinetmaker. This choice would come back to haunt them both. In the meantime, though, Mr. Cohen earned a professional salary, which paid for a suitably middle-class life for Mrs. Cohen and their two sons: a car; an attractively furnished house in a nice neighborhood; and a maid who came daily to tend the house and children. For her part, Mrs. Cohen played cards and belonged to clubs.

Then the Depression hit, undercutting Mr. Cohen's orchestra. Theaters stopped using musicians, and the rich stopped throwing dances. The orchestra was forced to disband. For three months, the family lived on savings, but after they exhausted those funds, their lives began to unravel. They sold their car; they let the maid go; they took out loans; they cashed in an insurance policy; eventually, they appealed to Mr. Cohen's family for help. And whereas before Mr. and Mrs. Cohen mostly got along, now they argued, viciously. Forced to keep house and care for the children, Mrs. Cohen resented her husband for, as Bakke paraphrases her, "losing his job and destroying the fairly comfortable routine to which she had become accustomed."[49] For his part, Mr. Cohen resented his wife for her selfishness. Before long, they stopped speaking to each other. Soon, they slept in separate rooms.

Not long after, though, they reconciled, until, that is, Mr. Cohen abandoned hope of finding work as a musician and considered taking a job at a department store unloading trucks. Mrs. Cohen rebelled. If she had wanted to marry a common laborer, she said, she would have married the cabinet-maker. Above all, she feared what a husband who worked unloading trucks would mean for her social status. As Bakke summarizes her argument with Mr. Cohen, "Didn't he know why she had married him? What would her friends say? What would her family think?" She packed her bags and took the children to her parents in Massachusetts. "When he got a job that would support them decently," she said, "he could send for them—not before."[50]

Despite these warnings, Mr. Cohen took the job. He did not experience the loss in status nearly as acutely as his wife did. He felt like "he was making his own way and could support his family."[51] And here it—the marriage—would have ended, except that, as Bakke tells it, "at some point in [her] experience away from home [Mrs. Cohen] gave up the hope that she was to continue to be the wife of a professional man and determined to return to the task of building her home on the basis of actual possibilities."[52] In the end, the Cohens adjusted their sights downward. Despite opportunities to return to the orchestra, Mr. Cohen remained in his more stable job at the department store, and the family reconciled itself to that life. They "reorganized their home so that its activities and status are typically working-class rather than professional."[53] In short, as Ehrenreich might put it, they fell. But, as Bakke would respond, they survived the fall.

Bakke was an economist, but he never abandoned his training in sociology. In his two masterful books from 1940, he was interested, more than anything else, in how workers adjusted to unemployment. (The word *adjust* or *adjustment* appears countless times in the two books.) In other words, he tracks what resources—economic, political, psychological, and familial—workers brought to unemployment, and how they changed or adjusted when it appeared. The story of the Cohens shows this interest perfectly. The "family is an adjustable institution," Bakke writes of the Cohens.[54] "Unemployment did not destroy this family because the human beings who constituted it were able to modify their objectives in line with possibilities."[55] Bakke acknowledges that other families did not fare as well as the Cohens. Indeed, that the Cohens may not even be "typical" when it comes to "the effects of unemployment on family life."[56] (The more typical version of the story, he acknowledges, ends when Mrs. Cohen leaves home—and does not come back.) But the Cohens, in allowing their illusions to be destroyed and adjusting, downward, their family status, suit his argumentative purposes.

Hull and Bakke tell similar stories about unemployment and its effect on individual or family identity. They conclude their stories, though, in different ways, and one suspects the difference owes, at least in part, to when each told their stories. Hull, writing in the early 1930s, as the initial waves of unemployment continued to stagger and drown people, tries to save its main characters from the worst because the worst, as the character of Ellery demonstrates, is simply catastrophic. By contrast, Bakke, who published his books on unemployment in 1940, has the advantage of hindsight. He knows as well as anyone how unemployment can devastate lives, but he also knows that some people—not everyone, but some people—survive it. They adjust, to use his favorite word. They forge new identities. In short, for Bakke unemployment is not, as it is for Ellery, or as it looks to be for Horace, the end of the world.

My final foray into unemployment among the middle class comes from earlier in the decade and, not surprisingly, it shares the darker view of it on display in Hull. Unlike Hull, though, it offers no easy way out. Perhaps because its author, forced to describe reality, could not plot her way out of the ongoing catastrophe.

As I detail in the introduction, in 1933, at perhaps the very nadir of the Great Depression, the newly elected Franklin Roosevelt created the Federal Emergency Relief Administration, the office that would distribute relief funds to the unemployed. Within weeks of its creation, the head of the relief agency, Harry Hopkins, hired the former Associated Press reporter Lorena Hickok to travel the country and report back to him about what she saw. While visiting Atlanta in January 1934, Hickok for the first time confronted the problem of white-collar workers on relief, many of whom, Hickok notes, had finally "reached the end of their resources."[57] "The plight of some of them," she wrote Hopkins, "is pitiable," and then offered the following story as illustration:

> For instance, a man in his late fifties, a salesman all his life. He paid cash for his home, now mortgaged, sent his two sons through college, and believed, when he lost his job something over a year ago, that he had enough to live on the rest of his life. His investments went bad, however. One of his sons is studying to be a priest in Washington and [he] cannot help him financially. The other boy, a graduate of Georgia Tech, is out of work and has been for a long time. Out of the money he borrowed on his home, the old man had supported himself, his wife, his son, and the latter's wife and two children until the day before yesterday. At first he asked only for a little coal, saying he thought he could still get credit at the grocery store—always hoping that his son, at least, would get a job. Night before last, however, he called up the investigator and told her the grocery store had cut him off. The investigator told me that on her first visit, when she was getting the family background, this man's wife suddenly burst into tears and left the room.[58]

The investigator Hickok mentions refers to the person—usually a young woman who had graduated from college—hired by the relief agency to confirm that a family had exhausted its savings and therefore qualified for relief. The investigator told Hickok, by way of illustrating how shameful previously professional families found their new lot, that "A couple of times lately I've found myself in a most embarrassing predicament. I discovered that I was being sent to investigate people I had known all my life—one man whose son I had once been engaged to!"[59]

In April 1934, in Birmingham, Hickok made a more systematic study of the problem of white-collar relief. To learn more, she spoke with "a certified public accountant, an insurance man, a pharmacist, a couple of engineers, an architect, a musician, a pawnshop clerk, and a masseur," all of whom had gone on relief. "Generally," she told Hopkins, "they were dumb with misery."[60] Hickok noted the difficulty in "getting white-collar people to apply for relief at all. God how they hate it!" Indeed, their shame—or pride—kept them from seeking much-needed help. "I simply had to murder my pride," Hickok quotes one of the engineers. An insurance man tells her, "We'd lived on bread and water three weeks before I could make myself do it." In particular, the white-collar unemployed resented the practice of investigators asking for the names of neighbors as references. "Good God," Hickok quotes one of them, "can't they realize that the very last people in the world we want to know we are on relief is any of the neighbors?" Sympathetically, Hickok admitted to Hopkins: "it is about as stupid [a practice] as any I ever heard of."[61]

The other problem Hickok observes is what she calls "adequacy"; namely, those with white-collar backgrounds received the same relief funds as those from other classes, which did not enable them to sustain—or easily sustain—their white-collar lives. Although that did not keep many from trying to keep up appearances, especially when it came to housing. "To white collar people," Hickok observed, "it's damned important to live in a decent house or apartment, in a decent neighborhood."[62] "They've somehow managed—" she added, speaking generally of white-collar families on relief, "God knows how—to keep up that much of their standards of living before they came onto relief. And they'll do it after they're on relief, even if they starve."[63] She did not exaggerate about starving. She spoke with one young man who paid $3 in rent out of the $4.80 his family, including a wife and a seven months' old baby, received in relief money per month, which left next to nothing for food. "Most of the time we honestly don't have enough to eat," he told Hickok. "My wife is losing all her teeth. I got a relief order for her to go to a doctor. He said it was due to bad and insufficient diet. Well, she's nursing the baby, for one thing. Because we can't afford to buy enough milk for the baby."[64] With a mixture of pity and admiration, Hickok commented on the situation: "Well, I suppose another family—not a white-collar family—might have broken down, let themselves be evicted, moved into cheaper quarters. But these people won't. Apparently they won't even let themselves be starved to it."[65]

For Hickok, the dominant emotional note among those white-collar families who fall was pride. But in that pride lay a real sense of fear: of what the neighbors might think, of how far one might fall, and of what indignities one will have to suffer. Unlike Bakke, the story that emerges from Hickok's investigations into white-collar workers who lose their jobs is not one of adjustment but of a stubborn refusal to adjust. In short, families clung to their identities as professionals and professional families. Indeed, in seeking to maintain their distinction from blue-collar families, white-collar families lived in worse circumstances—except for housing—than many blue-collar ones. In other words, they paid for their pride, their unwillingness to adjust, in hunger.

Although they draw different conclusions about it, Hull, Bakke, and Hickok tell remarkably similar stories about unemployment during the

Great Depression. That story goes something like this: during the Depression, unemployment befell even those—professionals—whose education and training was supposed to defend them from such catastrophes. And when that happened, their education and training could suddenly seem paper thin, no longer a defense against economic chaos but a point of entry. Moreover, if polio threatened the body, unemployment threatened status and identity. Eventually, it went after the body, too, but its most immediate threat was to a way of life. No wonder people feared it as much as they did.

Both polio and unemployment revealed how few and comparatively flimsy were the barriers humans could build between themselves and the world. In the final section of this chapter, I want to suggest that all of these fears—of polio, of unemployment, for the body, for identity, for human vulnerability—come together in the weird fiction of the 1930s, which, as a matter of course, pictured a world of human bodies and identities under threat by forces beyond their control.

Glub Glub

In 1944, the literary critic Edmund Wilson reviewed a number of new anthologies of horror stories, including *Creeps by Night* (edited by the noir writer Dashiell Hammett) and *Great Tales of Terror and the Supernatural*, still considered one of the best such anthologies ever compiled.[66] In the review, Wilson wondered how ghost stories survived—and lately seemed to thrive—in the age of electric light. Ghosts, the thinking went, required darkness. "If you can reach out and press a button and flood every corner of the room," Wilson wrote, "leaving the specter quite naked in his vector, or if you can transfix him out of doors with a flashlight, his opportunities for haunting are quite limited."[67] Wilson offered two explanations for this mystery. The first, that readers sought evidence of another world because their own world presented them with nothing but social confusion and blocked political progress, is interesting but not overly convincing, unless Wilson simply means that ghost stories allow readers to escape their own disappointing realities, but one suspects he means more. His second explanation, however, has more to recommend it. Writing amid the Second World War, Wilson speculated that we read ghost stories out of an

> instinct to inoculate ourselves against panic at the real horrors loose on the earth—Gestapo and G.P.U., tank attacks and airplane bombings, houses rigged with booby traps—by injections of imaginary horrors, which soothe us with

> the momentary illusion that the forces of madness and murder may be tamed and compelled to provide us with a mere dramatic entertainment.

Wilson called it "homeopathic horror."[68] We scare ourselves with invented monsters to keep from being scared by real ones.

If Wilson had expanded his scope beyond the Second World War, his theory of homeopathic horror might have made even more sense. Indeed, the age of horror stories truly arrives with the Great Depression, when horrors economic and political roamed the earth in alarming numbers. That is a demand-side explanation—as real horrors multiplied, individuals sought fictional, homeopathic ones—but there is a supply-side explanation as well. Horror, like pornography, quickly takes advantage of new media, and during the 1930s new media, specifically film and radio, thrived. Unsurprisingly, then, horror also thrived. During the 1930s, most of the horror classics appeared on film for the first time or were revived: *Dracula* (1931), *Dr. Jekyll and Mr. Hyde* (1931), *Frankenstein* (1932), *Island of Lost Souls* (1932), *The Mummy* (1933), *Mad Love* (1935), *The Wolf Man* (1941), and, by all accounts, the most disturbing of the lot, Tod Browning's *Freaks* (1932). On the radio, then just coming into its own as a medium, both *The Shadow* and *Lights Out, Everybody* enjoyed long and popular runs.

In addition to its success in film and on radio, horror and its sister genre, weird fiction, continued to flourish in print. As its practitioners and readers described it, weird fiction mixed a number of pulp modes—horror, supernatural, science fiction—into one distinctive blend. It found a home in the pulp magazines of the 1920s and 1930s, especially *Weird Tales*, which, under its editor, Farnsworth Wright, published the writers now inextricably associated with the genre, including Robert Howard, Henry S. Whitehead, August Derleth, Clark Ashton Smith, Robert Bloch, and, above all, H.P. Lovecraft, whose 1927 essay "Supernatural Horror in Literature" all but defined the genre.[69]

Over the years, weird fiction has won many converts, though few would describe many of the stories as genuinely scary. As Wilson wrote in his 1944 review of a number of the new horror anthologies, he "found it very hard to believe that any of these particular tales could scare anybody over ten."[70] He further accused their authors of failing "to lay hold on the terrors that lie deep in the human soul and that cause man to fear himself."[71] Much the same could be said of weird fiction. In a follow up to the piece, Wilson had even less kind things to say about Lovecraft in particular. "The principal feature of Lovecraft's work," Wilson wrote, "is an elaborate concocted myth which provides the supernatural element for his most admired stories. This myth assumes a race of outlandish gods and grotesque prehistoric peoples who are always playing tricks with time and space and breaking through into the contemporary world, usually someplace in Massachusetts."[72] Wilson later took Lovecraft to task for "his incessant effort to work up the expectations of the reader by sprinkling his stories with adjectives" such as horrible, terrible, frightful, and others. "Surely one of the primary rules for writing an effective tale of horror is never to use any of these words—especially if you are going, at the end, to produce an invisible whistling octopus."[73] Lovecraft's reputation has since risen—these days infinitely more people read him than Wilson—but, as Wilson shows, he is not to all tastes. From a contemporary perspective, Lovecraft and, for that matter, other weird fiction of the 1930s, can seem more farcical than fearsome.

Still, these stories do occasionally frighten, and for reasons that may refine a homeopathic theory of horror during the Great Depression. As Wilson describes it, for horror to be homeopathic, any old horror will do. Regardless of what you fear in the real world, the Mummy or the Wolf-Man or anything sufficiently scary will inoculate you against your fears. Yet it seems more likely that a relationship exists between what individuals in the Great Depression feared and what literature arose to inoculate them against that fear. In other words, to inoculate yourself against polio, scientists eventually learned that you should ingest some of the polio virus and not, say, the measles virus. To nullify what ails you, that is, you have to treat yourself with what ails you. "Like cures like," as the original homeopaths of the nineteenth century believed. The same relationship, it would seem, would apply to fear.

What do the examples of polio and unemployment suggest that people feared during the Great Depression? Principally, the degeneration of the human body and the violation of personal identity. People have always feared these things, of course, but they seem to have especially feared them during that decade. (Consider how many of the horror movies I list above feature stories of ordinary people somehow or other twisted into awful monsters.) And while these particular fears can take many forms—Dracula has those teeth for a reason—several variations of them arise in some of the better weird fiction of the 1930s. In the remainder of this chapter, I look at one classic story from that literature, H.P. Lovecraft's "The Thing on the Doorstep." This story brings together the two fears thus far discussed in this chapter, polio and unemployment; or, better said, the story drills down to the source of those two fears, which is at bottom a concern for the contingency of being, the terrifying vulnerability of both body and identity.

"The Thing on the Doorstep," published in *Weird Tales* in 1933, is one of Lovecraft's best stories. It succeeds largely because the occasionally cumbersome mythology and creatures that Wilson regretted about Lovecraft remain in the background—no whistling octopuses—but also because the story is genuinely disturbing. In it, an architect named Daniel Upton narrates the tale of his friend Edward Derby. From youth, Edward is a precocious, sickly, and, we are told at several points in the story, weak-willed young man who dabbles in poetry and—this being an H.P. Lovecraft story—black magic, an interest Daniel shares. Daniel and Edward spend many evenings together, Edward announcing himself—this will matter—with "a characteristic way of ringing the doorbell or sounding the knocker that grew to be a veritable code signal."[74]

In his late thirties, Edward marries a young woman, Asenath Waite, who also dabbles in black magic. Indeed, as Daniel describes her, Asenath is "a genuine hypnotist," capable of inducing "a distinct feeling of exchanged personality—as if the subject were placed momentarily in the magician's body and able to stare half across the room at her real body." As a result of this dark parlor trick, Asenath "often made wild claims about the nature of consciousness and about its independence of the physical frame." For Asenath, however, consciousness cannot, alas, exist independent of gender. The "crowning rage" of Asenath, we are told, "was that she was not a man," since, she believes, only "a male brain had certain unique and far-reaching cosmic powers."[75]

Physically, Asenath is "dark, smallish, and very-good looking," but also "one of the Innsmouth Waites," about which, Daniel says, "dark legends have clustered for generations." In addition, Asenath is the daughter of the deceased Ephraim Waite, also of Innsmouth, who, like his daughter, practiced black magic. (Here Lovecraft refers to an earlier story of his, "The Shadow over Innsmouth.")[76] The black magic, Daniel thinks, may explain the changes he sees overtaking his friend. Whereas before Edward could not drive a car, now he drives Asenath's, "handling it like a master, and meeting traffic entanglements with a skill and determination utterly alien to his accustomed nature." Worse, in addition to driving Asenath's car, he starts to resemble her physically—or, worse still, her father Ephraim. In the third year of his marriage, things, Edward tells Daniel, have gone "too far," and he begins to "talk darkly" to his friend "about the need of 'saving his identity.' "[77]

By this point, readers have likely figured out what is happening to poor Edward Derby, even if it takes his friend a while longer. In any case, the horrible plot is revealed when Daniel is summoned to rural Maine to rescue Edward, who stumbles "out of the woods with delirious ravings and screaming...for protection."[78] On the car ride back from Maine, Edward tells his story. Asenath "was getting hold of him, and he knew that someday she would never let go." "She constantly took his body," he explains, "and went into nameless places for nameless rites, leaving him in her body and locking him upstairs—but sometimes she couldn't hold on, and he would find himself suddenly in his own body again in some far-off, horrible, and perhaps unknown place."[79] Later Edward speculates that Ephraim Waite, not his daughter Asenath, is ultimately responsible for his plight. Ephraim, Edward claims, found "the formula." "On, on, on, on—body to body to body—he means never to die," Edward tells his friend. "The life glow—he knows how to break the link."[80] In short, Ephraim Waite, wanting to live forever, exchanged bodies with his daughter, Asenath, whom he locked in an attic and killed. Unsatisfied with the female brain, however, Ephraim-now-Asenath courted and married Edward and has begun to take over his body.

Just as Edward reveals this horrible plot to his friend, though, "the thing happened." "Derby's voice...was shut off with an almost mechanical click."[81] Although Daniel only suspects it at this point, Asenath—or rather Ephraim—has repossessed Edward's body, like a car someone has missed payments on. "The face beside me," Daniel observes, "was twisted almost unrecognizably for a moment, while through the whole body there passed a shivering motion—as if all the bones, organs, muscles, nerves, and glands were readjusting themselves to a radically different posture, set of stresses, and general personality."[82] "This man," Daniel concludes after the repossessed Edward takes the wheel of the car, "for all my lifelong knowledge of Edward Pickman Derby, was a stranger—an intrusion of some sort from the black abyss."[83] (By the way, note Edward's middle name: Pickman. Lovecraft was not always subtle.)

The road trip from hell—appropriate given what Edward-cum-Ephraim had got up to in Maine—concludes, and in the months ahead the story reaches its awful conclusion. A few months after the return trip from Maine, Edward calls on Daniel to reclaim some books he had lent him, but he does "not even bother to give the old three-and-two signal when ringing the doorbell." He does not bother, of course, because he does not know the signal. He is Ephraim in Edward's body. A few months after that, though, Edward, announcing himself with his familiar signal, calls on Daniel and informs him that, employing some black magic of his own, he has banished Asenath-cum-Ephraim for good, and before she-slash-he could complete the transformation. Edward has evidently spoken too soon, though, for in time he begins to feel Asenath-cum-Ephraim "tugging" at his brain. He is committed to an insane asylum, where, when Daniel visits him, he repeats phrases such as "I had to do it" and "it'll get me... it'll get me... down there... down there in the dark."

At this point, things turn truly weird. Edward regains his sanity, but as becomes clear when Daniel visits him in the asylum, he is not Edward. The next night, Daniel receives a telephone call, but all he hears is silence and "a sort of half-bubbling noise—'*glub... glub... glub*'—which had an odd suggestion of inarticulate, unintelligible word and syllable divisions."[84] The caller hangs up. Later that night, Daniel hears someone ringing his doorbell and knocking at his door—"doorbell and knocker both, plied alternately and uncertainly in a kind of weak desperation, *and each trying to keep to Edward's old signal of three-and-two strokes*."[85] At first, Daniel thinks that Edward has reoccupied his body, until he remembers that Edward is still locked up in the asylum. When he opens his door, he discovers a dwarfed, grotesque, malodorous corpse—the thing on the doorstep of the title—wearing one of Edward's overcoats. "As I stepped unsteadily forward," Daniel relates, "the figure made a semi-liquid sound like that I had heard over the telephone—'*glub... glub...*'—and thrust at me a large, closely written paper impaled on the end of a long pencil."[86]

The note is from Edward-slash-the corpse of Asenath. It instructs Dan to "go to the sanitarium and kill it. Exterminate it. It isn't Edward Derby any more. She got me—it's Asenath—and she has been dead three months and a half." Derby's letter explains that he killed Asenath and buried her in the cellar. But not even death could stop her pursuit of his body. Fearing what is coming, he snaps and commits himself to the insane asylum, but Asenath finds him there. "Then it came—" he writes, "I found myself choked in the dark—in Asenath's rotting carcass down there in the cellar under the boxes where I put it. And I knew she must be in my body at the sanitarium." So he claws his way out of his grave and, unable to talk on the phone, writes his friend a letter and delivers it. "Kill that fiend if you value the peace and comfort of the world," he tells his friend. "See that it is cremated. If you don't, it will live on and on, body to body forever, and I can't tell you what it will do."[87]

Having read the note, the narrator decisively passes out, and when he wakes up, the thing at his doorstep has "died" and lies inert. Soon thereafter, Daniel visits the asylum and shoots Edward-cum-Ephraim, as Edward-cum-the rotting corpse of Asenath instructs him to do, an event that provides the wonderful opening line of the story: "It is true that I have sent six bullets through the head of my best friend, and yet I hope to shew [sic] by this statement that I am not his murderer."[88] As for the thing on the doorstep, "What they finally found inside Edward's oddly assorted clothes was mostly liquescent horror. There were bones, too—and a crushed-in skull. Some dental work positively identified the skull as Asenath's." In other words, everything Edward says in his note is true.

To my mind, "The Thing at the Doorstep" has two genuinely frightening moments: the first is when the reanimated yet rotting corpse, which Lovecraft does well to describe as a "liquescent horror," attempts to communicate ("*glub . . . glub*") with the narrator; and the second is during the car ride home from Maine when Edward's voice is "shut off with an almost mechanical click," and his body repossessed by Ephraim. Asenath's revivified—and reoccupied corpse—frightens because it grotesquely reminds us of the eventual fate of our own body. It too shall become a "liquescent horror." As for the scene in the car when Edward switches off and Ephraim switches on, it also frightens because, like death, it suggests the fragility of our bodies and identities. Both scenes amount to the same thing. They demonstrate how outside forces may impose upon us. Within the terms of the story, they show that we are not as autonomous as we like to believe and that the everyday nature of our lives invites us to think. True, most of us will not marry someone intent on swapping personalities with us, and fewer still will wake up in the body of an interred, decomposing corpse. But Lovecraft worked in symbols, and both images—the corpse and the personality that switches on and off like a record player—suggest our essential vulnerability and exposure to the more malign powers of the universe.

In his biography of Lovecraft, S.T. Joshi argues that "The Thing at the Doorstep" "is one of his [Lovecraft's] poorest later efforts."[89] Joshi complains that "the basic scenario of the story" is "obvious" and is executed with an "utter lack of subtlety"; that it is marred by "poor writing"; and finally that the story does not take up Lovecraft's great theme, cosmicism. The first two charges may or may not have merit, though in truth "The Thing at the

Doorstep" seems no more obvious and poorly written than any other Lovecraft work. The last charge, however, of failing to take up cosmicism, seems to rest on a narrow understanding of cosmicism. By cosmicism, Lovecraft apparently meant the worldview that followed from taking the long view of the universe and the place of humanity in it. In short, next to the former, the latter mattered not a whit. (You occasionally see cosmicism referred to by more revealing terms such as cosmic indifferentism or cosmic horror.) The French novelist Michel Houellebecq, whose first book was a critical appreciation of Lovecraft, ably summed up cosmicism when he writes that Lovecraft believed "the human race will disappear. Other races will appear and disappear in turn. The sky will become icy and void, pierced by the feeble light of half-dead stars. Which will also disappear. Everything will disappear."[90] Instead of simply sketching the "the blackness of space illimitable" to horrify readers, as he did in his very early short story "The Music of Erich Zann" (1922), Lovecraft invented his roster of whistling octopuses, as Wilson dismissed them, to make the same point.[91] Space and time are infinite. Other races had preceded human beings, and other races would replace them. But in any case the universe did not evolve for our sake, and if one truly grasped this "terrifying" fact, as Lovecraft wrote in the opening paragraph of his most famous story, "The Call of Cthulhu" (1928), it would drive one mad.[92]

But you do not need whistling octopuses to generate cosmic horror. Anything that puts human beings in their proper—that is, meaningless—place will do, including, as in "The Thing at the Doorstep," death and, relatedly, the precarious contingency of our very being. In other words, Ephraim Waite is simply another species of whistling octopus, which explains why the narrator of the story routinely speaks of his own cosmic horror when he confronts Ephraim in the body of Edward. In the car ride home from Maine, after Ephraim has repossessed Edward's body, Daniel thinks:

> Just where the supreme horror lay, I could not for my life tell; yet there swept over me such a swamping wave of sickness and repulsion—such a freezing, petrifying sense of utter alienage and abnormality—that my grasp of the wheel grew feeble and uncertain. The figure beside me seemed less like a lifelong friend than like some monstrous intrusion from outer space—some damnable, utterly accursed focus of unknown and malign cosmic forces.[93]

Later, he speaks of the new Edward as "a stranger—an intrusion of some sort from the black abyss" and, thus, when in his presence, his "feeling of elusive cosmic horror increased."[94] Near the climax of the story, Daniel confesses that the new Edward "filled me with the same dim feeling of blasphemous alienage and ineffable cosmic hideousness."[95] He fears, too, that the same forces that threatened Edward now threaten him. "There are horrors," the narrator writes, "beyond life's edge that we do not suspect, and once in a while man's evil prying calls them just within our range. Ephraim—Asenath—that devil called them in, and they engulfed Edward as they are engulfing me."[96] Daniel reassures himself that, unlike Edward, "his will is not weak," and therefore he is safe, but against cosmic forces like the ones Ephraim summons and represents, individual will does not much matter. Eventually, we are all engulfed, by one thing at the doorstep or another.[97] Perhaps it is a malevolent sorcerer from someplace in Massachusetts, or perhaps unemployment, polio, or the death of a child, but something inevitably comes. If one believes Edmund Wilson, the liquescent horrors merely soothe our fears about the other ones.

Cosmic Triggers

Although I cannot put him in Cleveland at the time of the human butcher murders, the writer and occasional mystic Robert Anton Wilson strangely brings the themes of this chapter together in one person. Wilson was born in Brooklyn in 1932. In 1934, at the age of two, he contracted polio, and he walked with a limp the rest of his life. (He would eventually die, as many of those who initially survived polio did, from a later manifestation of the disease, called post-polio syndrome.) In the second volume (1995) of his *Cosmic Trigger* series, a work of spiritualism, futurism, and memoir quite unlike any other book written in the twentieth century, Wilson recalls of his boyhood days in Depression Brooklyn that many "regularly died of tuberculosis . . . and children had dozens of diseases now abolished. I myself survived measles, German measles, mumps, flu (still a major killer in those days), rheumatic fever, whooping cough, diphtheria and polio."[98] "People," he adds, "were always dying of influenza and pneumonia and other diseases related to lack of heat in winter. Every head cold created minor panic because it might develop into one of those killer diseases."[99] People were also always expecting the worst, he observes, "because all they had known in all their lives were deadly diseases and grinding poverty. Optimism was a sign of insanity."[100]

Wilson and his family had moved to Garrison Beach from another, better neighborhood in Brooklyn (Flatbush) after his father lost his job during the Great Depression. At the time of his birth, Wilson recalls,

> The Depression had already brought unemployment to many, but not to my family. My father had a good job somewhere—I haven't a gopher's notion of what he was working at, but I dimly remember a very early time when I felt that we were safe from the God-awful things the Depression was doing to some of our relatives.
>
> Then suddenly the Depression turned around and dumped its Golden Turd of the Week on us, too. The company my father had been working for went out of business and he and hundreds of others found themselves without jobs. We moved to Garrison Beach where rents were very low because only the poor Irish Catholics lived there.[101]

Within several years during the Great Depression, then, Wilson suffered two of its more frightening tragedies, polio and unemployment.

Unsurprisingly, or so I would like to claim, Wilson peppers his prose with references to H.P. Lovecraft, including the opening sentence of the first volume (1977) of *Cosmic Trigger*: "As the late, great H.P. Lovecraft might begin this narrative: It is now nearly 13 years since the ill-fated day when I first began investigating the terrible legends surrounding the enigmatic Bavarian Illuminati."[102] (For the record, that is a very good Lovecraft impersonation.) Like a character out of a Lovecraft story, too, for a span of years in the 1970s Wilson, while experimenting with LSD, suspected—at least, he could not rule it out—that he could telepathically communicate with extraterrestrial intelligences from the distant star Sirius. To be sure, the intelligences he encountered seemed far more benign—even welcoming—than the malevolent alien-gods with whom a Lovecraft character usually communicates, but that, I think, is a difference in degree and not kind. Indeed, I want to suggest that Wilson may not have gone as far off the rails as this brief description of his experiments with LSD and intergalactic communication might suggest.

To be sure, the LSD no doubt accounts for much of the reason why Wilson believed he spoke with aliens, and as he diminished his use of the drug the aliens seem to have had far less to communicate to him. But I do not think one can ascribe Wilson's openness to extraterrestrial intelligences exclusively to drugs. Rather, the early events that befell Wilson during the Great Depression—unemployment, polio—could make extraterrestrial forces seem less rather than more extraordinary. As Lovecraft knew, nothing terrified readers more than the suspicion that the universe exercised infinitely more influence over them than they did over it. I have suggested that polio and unemployment gave rise to similar epiphanies and so similar fears.

In the case of someone like Robert Wilson, who absorbed his share of the sort of suffering the Great Depression had to offer, it may have seemed natural to assume outsized, supernatural forces bearing down on human lives. After all, and especially after the trauma of the Great Depression, to believe in extraterrestrial forces may have seemed no more absurd than to believe in all the other organisms—human, viral, and economic—that also impinged on lives during this most fearful of all decades.

5

Awe

Toward a Depression Sublime

In 1930, astronomers discovered the planet Pluto. With apologies to Pluto, a mere planet would prove the least of the wonders astronomers would discover during the years leading up to and following the stock market crash in October 1929.

Possibly the most wondrous came in 1925, when Edwin Hubble, working at the Mount Wilson Observatory in California, showed that many of the stars visible from earth with a telescope were not in fact stars within our galaxy, the Milky Way, but, rather, were self-contained nebula—so-called "island universes"—lying outside our galaxy. In other words, they were other Milky Ways. The discovery changed everything. Instead of living in a universe with one galaxy and hundreds of billions of stars, we lived in a universe with countless galaxies, each of which had its own hundreds of billions of stars.

That meant that the universe, instead of being hundreds of thousands of light years in diameter, as astronomers had previously thought, was millions or tens of millions or even hundreds of millions of light years in diameter. Indeed, no one could say for sure, because as the power of telescopes increased, so did the size of the universe. In a 1932 article in *Scientific American*, the astronomer Henry Norris Russell guessed that based on what astronomers could then see, the universe must be at least 250 million light years across. Yet the universe almost certainly kept going past what telescopes could reveal. "The material universe," Russell wrote, "extends beyond the utmost limits of observation. We have sounded its depths with the longest line that human skill has yet devised—perhaps with the longest that human means can supply—and our final report is 'No Bottom.' "[1]

The Emotional Life of the Great Depression. John Marsh, Oxford University Press (2019).
 DOI: 10.1093/oso/9780198847731.001.0001

As news of what Hubble had found trickled into the mainstream press, journalists and scientists struggled to convey his astounding findings. On December 15, 1930 the *New York Times* reported that Hubble and his partner, Milton L. Humason, had estimated "the limits of Creation to be equal to 10 followed by 33 ciphers light-years from the Earth." The headline read, "Limits of Creation, in Light Years, Estimated at 10,000,000,000,000,000, 000,000,000,000,000,000."[2] But not even all those ciphers could make plain the overwhelming size of the universe. They just looked like a bunch of zeroes on a column of newsprint. In another 1932 article from *Scientific American*, Sir James Jeans, former secretary of the Royal Astronomical Society and, at the time, a research associate at the Carnegie Institution of Washington, offered the following illustration to describe the size and population of the universe as Hubble and other astronomers then understood it. Imagine a sphere about a mile in diameter. Then take 300 tons of apples, or about 1,800,000 individual apples, and dump them into the sphere so that each apple is about ten yards apart from each other. "This sphere," Jeans wrote, "is the range of vision of the 100-inch telescope; each apple is a nebula containing matter enough for the creation of several thousand million stars like our sun; and each atom in each apple is the size of a solar system with a diameter equal to, or slightly larger, than that of the earth's orbit."[3] As a journalist for the *New York Times* would write in 1939, these discoveries established a new, outsized, and slightly terrifying cosmic order: "the great spiral nebulae with their billions upon billions of giant and supergiant stars and suns, alongside each of which our solar system is but a speck of dust in infinite space."[4]

More sobering news waited. In 1929, a few years after he had confirmed that the universe was substantially larger and inestimably more populated by stars than all but a handful of people had suspected, Hubble showed that those stars did not stay in place but, rather, raced away from the earth (and each other) at tremendous speeds (see Figure 5.1). Our own galaxy, Hubble estimated, moved through space at a velocity of approximately 100 miles per second. That insight buttressed a hypothesis offered in 1927—and more widely publicized in 1931—by the Belgian priest and astronomer George Lemaître, who, working from insights gleaned from Albert Einstein's recently confirmed theory of general relativity, posited that the universe must constantly expand outward. That is, "space itself," as Henry Norris Russell wrote in 1932, "is expanding and carrying the nebula with it."[5]

Figure 5.1. Albert Einstein (left) and Edwin Hubble (back row, between Einstein and Walter Sydney Adams, the man in the hat) at the Mount Wilson Observatory circa 1931.

Source: PictureLux/Hollywood Archive/Alamy Stock Photo

To illustrate that counterintuitive idea, the astronomer Sir Arthur Eddington famously likened the universe to a rubber balloon. "Imagine the galaxies to be embedded in the rubber," he told a Cambridge, Massachusetts audience in 1932. "Now let the balloon be steadily inflated; that's the expanding universe." "As the balloon dilates," he added, "the rubber stretches, and the galaxies embedded in it recede from one another."[6] In other words, although in

1929 Hubble had hesitated to assert it, by 1931 it seemed certain that the universe, already bigger than anyone thought, was getting bigger, much bigger, by the second.

Astronomers had yet more in store. The expanding universe suggested still another incredible possibility. If the universe steadily inflated like a balloon, it followed that in the past it must have begun from something much smaller, which is precisely what Lemaître proposed in a letter sent to the journal *Nature* in 1931. "At the origin," Lemaître wrote, "all the mass of the universe would exist in the form of a unique atom; the radius of the universe, although not strictly zero, being relatively very small. The whole universe would be produced by the disintegration of this primeval atom."[7] Or, as the *Times* reported in its coverage of Lemaître's letter, "Le Maitre [sic] Suggests One, Single, Great Atom, Embracing All Energy, Started the Universe."[8] If Lemaître was right, then the universe did not start with a whimper but with a big bang.

In *The World as Will and Representation*, the German philosopher Arthur Schopenhauer argued that human beings experience the sublime when in "sight of a power beyond all comparison superior to the individual, and threatening him with annihilation."[9] In addition, Schopenhauer offered "magnitude in space and time" as the quintessential, highest form of the sublime. He wrote:

> If we lose ourselves in contemplation of the infinite greatness of the universe in space and time, meditate on the past millennia and those to come; or if the heavens at night actually bring innumerable worlds before our eyes, and so impress on our consciousness the immensity of the universe, we feel ourselves reduced to nothing; we feel ourselves as individuals, as living bodies, as transient phenomena of will, like drops in the ocean, dwindling and dissolving into nothing.[10]

If the universe inspired feelings of annihilation, nothingness, and, thus, the sublime in 1818, when Schopenhauer wrote, how much more must it have done so by the middle years of the 1930s? Within a decade, the universe had grown infinitely bigger; had become infinitely more populated by stars; had been shown to grow bigger, literally, by the second; and had developed an origin story to rival all other origin stories. Ten billion or so years ago, the universe and everything in it—stars, planets, people—emerged from a single, unstable, indescribably powerful atom. That story implied another one, even more horrible to contemplate. If the universe had a beginning, it could have an ending, too. Perhaps, also like an expanding balloon, it would eventually pop.

At the time, observers seemed to recognize these startling changes to the universe, this encounter with a sublime made still more sublime. In 1934, the influential American magazine the *Literary Digest* reported that Lemaître had received a prize for his contributions to science. In describing his vision of the universe, the editors took a page straight out of Schopenhauer. "Abbe. Lemaître's theory of the universe," the *Literary Digest* reported, "is breathtaking in its magnitude and grandeur, and terrifying in its implications."[11]

Of course, as Schopenhauer and other theorists observed, the sublime involved more than just feelings of annihilation and nothingness. Indeed, if the feelings stopped at annihilation and nothingness, they arguably did not count as the sublime. Rather, for Schopenhauer at least, the sublime involved reconciling with the alien powers of the world. Eventually, Schopenhauer observed, we recognize that "we are one with the world, and are therefore not oppressed but exalted by its immensity."[12] Nevertheless, that sense of oneness did not come easily, especially in the face of the infinite—the annihilating—greatness of the universe, and especially as the greatness of that universe grew even greater in the 1930s. Simply put, if our solar system "was but a speck of dust in infinite space," as the *New York Times* asserted, what did that make us?

In this chapter, I explore what, in addition to a radically new vision of the universe, struck people as sublime during the Great Depression. In doing so, I tend to speak of the sublime interchangeably with its allied emotions: terror, wonder, and, especially, awe. Understandably, awe is not an emotion one associates with the Great Depression. Individuals may have been brought low by the vastness of a malfunctioning economy, but they did not tend to characterize the economy as sublime or their experience as awesome. Yet as the example of the bigger, faster, expanding universe suggests, the Depression nevertheless had its examples of the sublime. To be sure, as the Romantic poets knew, most of those examples—the ocean, a mountain, the universe—came from nature, and they remained sublime regardless of what happened to the economy during the 1930s.[13] Yet the Depression also had instances of the sublime that did not come from nature, and in retrospect it is those instances, I believe, that reveal the most about both the sublime and the decade itself. To put it another way, in this chapter I look at new sources of awe in the 1930s, ones that individuals did not have—or, as in the case of the expanding universe, did not quite have—before.

I start by offering a brief—very brief—discussion of the sublime and its related emotions, and then turn to examples from the period. I work downwards, from the universe to skyscrapers to presidents to Olympic athletes to steel workers to migrant workers to sharecroppers, and what these examples suggest is that the Great Depression established a distinctive source for the sublime. Whereas most accounts of the sublime involve the vastness of nature—or, as I show, skyscrapers—overwhelming human beings, during the Depression, the sublime also worked from the bottom up. That is, during the 1930s human beings themselves became a source, perhaps the source, of the sublime. Throughout the decade, individuals continued to stand in awe of the universe and skyscrapers, but they eventually learned to stand in awe of each other as well.

Before we leave it behind, consider, as but one example of this human sublime, the bigger, faster, expanding universe. It may have inspired feelings of terror and awe in human beings during the 1930s, but so too did knowing that human beings, using nothing more than telescopes, photographs, and mathematics, and sometimes just mathematics, could figure out for themselves the birth and subsequent life of the all but infinite universe. In other words, the new cosmic order could overwhelm human beings, but human beings could take comfort in the fact that they had discovered just how overwhelming the new cosmic order truly was. If the universe were sublime, so were the people it purportedly diminished.

My examples of the human sources for the sublime tend to be deliberately more prosaic than trailblazing astronomers, but the point remains the same. During the Great Depression, human beings joined the ranks of things that could inspire awe, which is very much in keeping with a decade defined by and perhaps unmatched in its populism. Unlike with other emotions in the Great Depression, however, where you can watch feelings turning into actions before your eyes—can watch as emotions change people and then the nation—awe rarely produces such momentous changes, which is perhaps slightly ironic since it emerges, by definition, out of the momentous. If the Depression sublime I observe in this chapter accomplished anything, it may have added, as I have suggested by associating it with populism, to the feeling of the ineluctable dignity and worth of human beings that arose during the decade, the sense that virtue lies in forgotten men—and, for many of the writers in this chapter, forgotten women—and that they deserved neither their oblivion nor their neglect.

The Last and Most Magnificent of Towers

Each year, nearly 4 million people visit the Empire State Building. Most of them do not come for the offices of the Federal Deposit Insurance

Corporation on the twelfth and thirteenth floors or the Walgreens on the first. They come for the view, and it has always been thus. When the building opened in 1931, its owners made more money from the observation decks on the 86th and 102nd floor than they did from rents on the office space below.[14] At a certain point, of course, the Empire State Building, like all great destinations, acquired its own tourist momentum. People visited it less because of anything inherent to it and more because—like the most photographed barn in America in Don DeLillo's *White Noise*—others had come before them. Be that as it may, they also came for the view or, more accurately, I think, for the sublime, and not just to witness it but to become, however briefly, part of it themselves.

When it comes to the sublime, most philosophers, as I have suggested, have offered examples from nature, though many have acknowledged the potential sublimity of architecture, too. In his *A Philosophical Enquiry into the Sublime and Beautiful* (1790), Edmund Burke argues that buildings can be—and certain buildings should be—sublime, and in *Seven Lamps of Architecture*, which the builders of the Empire State Building evidently knew, John Ruskin devotes an entire chapter to the sublime. What makes buildings sublime, Burke and Ruskin agree, is size. "To the sublime in building," Burke writes, "greatness of dimension seems requisite."[15] For his part, Ruskin observed that if an architect aims to design a building that is "markedly sublime," he "should not be withheld by respect to smaller parts from reaching largeness of scale; provided only, that it be evidently in the architect's power to reach at least that degree of magnitude which is the lowest at which sublimity begins, rudely definable as that which will make a living figure look less than life beside it."[16]

Buildings in general, and skyscrapers in particular, thus offer one of the defining characteristics of the sublime, which is magnitude, particularly, as the Ruskin quotation reminds us, magnitude compared to human figures. That definition keeps with the one offered by Schopenhauer, previously discussed, who observed that the sublime "is caused by the sight of a power beyond all comparison superior to the individual." In short, the sublime, including but not limited to the sublime in architecture, is that which overwhelms us. As the psychologists Dacher Keltner and Jonathan Haidt argue in a more recent account of the emotion of awe, the sublime requires vastness. "Vastness," they write, echoing Burke and Ruskin, "refers to anything that is experienced as being much larger than the self, or the self's ordinary level of experience or frame of reference."[17]

If buildings could achieve the sublime through vastness, then New Yorkers in the 1920s could experience the sublime nearly every day. By some counts, forty skyscrapers appeared on the skyline during the decade. Few buildings, however, could approach the vastness and, thus, the sublimity of the Empire State Building (see Figure 5.2). Conceived in 1929 at the height of the economic boom and completed in 1931 as the United States economy peered into the abyss, the Empire State Building offered a matchless example of the sublime. To be sure, other structures during the 1930s offered vastness and,

Figure 5.2. Lewis W. Hine, Empire State Building, New York, 1931.
Source: Minneapolis Institute of Art, Gift of Mickey Pallas, 95.82.20

thus, the sublime. Journalists, for example, using the same device of printing zeroes across a headline that they previously used to render the size of the universe, liked to enumerate the millions of cubic yards of concrete used in Boulder Dam, which was begun in 1931 and completed in 1935. But no structure seemed quite as vast as the Empire State Building, the only building that could properly convey the size of King Kong in the 1933 movie of the same name. Or consider this image of its vastness and, thus, sublimity. As Paul Starrett, one of the three men in charge of construction of the building, wrote in his 1938 autobiography, *Changing the Skyline*, the Empire State Building is six inches shorter than its architects planned; its massive weight squashes the steel girders holding it up.[18]

Unsurprisingly, then, given its vastness, when the building opened in 1931, an article in the *New York Times* reported, thousands of visitors swarmed to its observation platform, and crowds gathered on the north side of 34th street to gaze upward at the completed building. That same article noted that astronomers in nearby Bryant Park "abandoned the sun, the moon and the stars to train their bronzed telescopes upon the observatory."[19] That is, they shifted their gaze from one manifestation of the sublime (the universe) to another (the Empire State Building).

In addition to vastness, though, the sublime—or so Keltner and Haidt convincingly argue—is accompanied by another response, what they call the need for accommodation. "We propose," they write, "that prototypical awe involves a challenge to or negation of mental structures when they fail to make sense of an experience of something vast."[20] In other words, you cannot impassively observe the sublime. It must alter your perception of the world, for better or for worse. "The success of one's attempts at accommodation," Keltner and Haidt observe, "may partially explain why awe can be both terrifying (when one fails to understand) and enlightening (when one succeeds)."[21] For example, the passage from Schopenhauer quoted above does not stop with the realization of our nothingness next to the vastness of the universe—though that, of course, constitutes one sort of accommodation, albeit a failed one, to this instance of the sublime. Rather, Schopenhauer goes on to observe that in and of itself the universe is not vast. The universe is nothing, or, rather, it is simply the universe, neither vast nor little. Only our mind represents it as vast. As a result, its vastness depends, ironically enough, on us. By realizing our nothingness, then, we become, strange to say, something again. The vast universe would not be vast without us. "All this, however, does not come into reflection at once," Schopenhauer writes, "but shows itself as a consciousness, merely felt, that in some sense or other (made clear only by philosophy) we are one with the world and are therefore not oppressed but exalted by its immensity."[22]

Whether you accept Schopenhauer's attempt at accommodation to the vastness of the universe depends on how you feel about his philosophical system of will and representation that makes it possible. Yet accommodate one must and, I would argue, ascending to the top of the Empire State Building represents its own form of accommodation to the sublime vastness of the building. Looking up at the Empire State Building, you can feel literally and figuratively overshadowed. Looking down from it, you can assume its vastness; you can share, however small a part, in the shadow it casts. Or, in the vistas it opens up.

The latter is the impression F. Scott Fitzgerald leaves in a wonderful description of his visit to the top of the Empire State Building shortly after it opened in 1931. In his essay, "My Lost City," from 1932, he writes:

> From the ruins, lonely and inexplicable as the sphinx, rose the Empire State Building and, just as it had been a tradition of mine to climb to the Plaza Roof to take leave of the beautiful city, extending as far as eyes could reach, so now I went to the roof of the last and most magnificent of towers. Then I understood—everything was explained: I had discovered the crowning error of the city, its Pandora's box. Full of vaunting pride the New Yorker had climbed here and seen with dismay what he had never suspected, that the city was not the endless succession of canyons that he had supposed but that it had limits—from the tallest structure he saw for the first time that it faded out into the country on all sides, into an expanse of green and blue that alone was limitless. And with the awful realization that New York was a city after all and not a universe, the whole shining edifice that he had reared in his imagination came crashing to the ground. That was the rash gift of Alfred W. Smith to the citizens of New York.[23]

The "ruins" that Fitzgerald speaks of in the first sentence is the city but, in particular, the city after the crash of 1929. Throughout the essay, Fitzgerald builds the city up into its own instance of the sublime, describing it, variously, as a thundercloud, a glacier, a king, and, as here, canyons, a universe, even a skyscraper, a "shining edifice." By contrast, the view from atop the Empire State Building reveals the "crowning error" of that perspective. The city is none of these things. It has limits. It "was a city after all and not a universe," as Fitzgerald writes. The evil—that which is released from Pandora's box—is to think that the world starts and stops with New York City. From the street, the Empire State Building, "the tallest structure" in the city, may overwhelm, like the other buildings that make New York City streets into canyons. Instead of submitting to that place in the metropolitan universe, however, Fitzgerald, from the roof of the Empire State Building, can transcend it. Like other visitors to the observation deck of the Empire State Building, he can look down upon and become bigger than the sublime city itself. Fitzgerald accommodates the vastness of the Empire State Building by becoming one with its vastness, by using it to dispel the vastness of another, not quite as sublime object—the city.[24]

Men at Work

Those who have thought about the sublime—Burke, Kant, Schopenhauer—have disagreed about whether human beings can achieve that status or, perhaps less ambitiously, whether they can inspire awe. On first glance, it would not seem so. Recall that for, say, Schopenhauer and Ruskin, the sublime is that which comes from the "sight of a power beyond all comparison superior to the individual," or that which "will make a living figure look less than life." In both definitions, the sublime transcends the individual. That explains why the only indisputably sublime being is God, whose omnipotence is both vast—he creates all of creation—and life changing. It would seem unlikely, by contrast, that a mere human could diminish another to the extent that the latter feels "less than life."

Yet clearly people feel something akin to awe when in the presence of other people. Indeed, Keltner and Haidt argue—not entirely convincingly—that the origins of awe lie in "the emotional reaction of a subordinate to a powerful leader," and "these responses to powerful social entities solidify social hierarchies, which are important to human survival."[25] Although awe may or may not emerge from the worship of powerful leaders, few would deny that powerful leaders could inspire admiration and, at times, that that admiration could pass into awe. Americans flocked to see Franklin Roosevelt in person, for example, and beginning in the 1930s, many a home, shop, and bar had a framed portrait of the president hanging on the wall.[26] Their awe seemed to emerge from the fact that Roosevelt, unlike previous presidents, took a special interest in the wellbeing of ordinary people. Americans struggled—and thrilled—to accommodate this unprecedented development. "All of the working men are for you," a correspondent from Oliver Springs, Tennessee wrote the president in 1936. "for you sure have been good to the Poor and help us out, and we sure do aprishate [sic] your kindness."[27] Roosevelt received millions of such letters.[28]

Keltner and Haidt argue, though, that this awe in the face of powerful leaders extends to non-powerful people as well, including the famous, the exceptionally skilled, and the morally admirable. They hesitate to label that emotion awe, however, since they do not consider these non-powerful people "vast" enough to merit the term. (They opt for the more diminutive label "admiration.") To a certain extent, that approach makes sense, but it overlooks those non-powerful individuals, real and fictional, who inspired a genuine sense of awe—and thus achieved a state of the sublime—in the 1930s.

Take those with exceptional ability. At the infamous 1936 Berlin Olympics, Jesse Owens set the record for the long jump. (It was then called the broad jump.) Try to guess how long he jumped. If it helps, here are some reference points. In basketball, the distance from the free throw line to the basket is 15 feet. In high school basketball, the distance from the three-point line to the basket is 19 feet 9 inches, and in the college game it is 20 feet 9 inches. If it helps you guess, Figure 5.3 shows Jesse Owens midflight at the 1936 Olympics.

On his third try, Owens jumped *26 feet 5 and 5/16 inches*. To keep measuring in terms of the basketball court, that is three feet farther than the three-point line in the NBA. With his jump, Owens broke the existing Olympic record by more than a foot.[29] Owens's long jump, I would argue, has the quality of vastness, and just as other instances of the sublime or awe do, it leaves us with the need to accommodate ourselves to it, to make sense of it. A human being really jumped that far.

So perhaps, with due respect to Keltner and Haidt, powerful and non-powerful people alike can inspire awe and qualify as sublime. Yet presidents and Olympic athletes seem by definition extraordinary. In the 1930s, however, artists and writers set out to make relatively ordinary people seem sublime as well.

Here too the Empire State Building offers an example. As construction of the skyscraper proceeded, observers on the ground could not help but notice the workers—especially the derrick men who maneuvered the steel girders of the building into place—moving about in the sky. "Like little spiders they toiled," the *Literary Digest* wrote in 1931, "spinning a fabric of steel against the sky. Crawling, climbing, swinging, swooping—weaving a web that was to stretch farther heavenward than the ancient Tower of Babylon."[30] A journalist with the *Times* offered this description of the

Figure 5.3. Jesse Owens at the 1936 Berlin Olympics.
Source: IOC Olympic Museum/Contributor/Getty Images

derrick men: "A man rides into the air on top of a steel beam that he maneuvers into place as a crosspiece by hanging to the cable rope with his hands and steering the beam with his feet. There is a good deal of strolling on the thin edge of nothingness."[31] This tremendous show, however, would not last for long. (The Empire State Building went up in a little over a year.) Nor would many people outside of New York see it. Except, that is, for the efforts of one photographer, Lewis Hine.

In 1930, the publicists of the Empire State Building offered Hine, then best known for his photographs documenting child labor in the 1910s, a commission to record the construction of the building. He accepted, but the photographs he produced may not have been what the publicists had in mind. For example, nowhere in his 1932 collection, *Men at Work*, which included his Empire State Building photographs, does Hine show the entire Empire State Building. In fact, one such photograph, taken peering up at the Empire State from what must be the 34th Street-Herald Square subway entrance stairwell, and which shows the building in all its sublime, skyscraping glory, must have been deliberately excluded from the book. These exclusions seem less curious, though, in light of what Hine evidently did set out to capture: not the sublimity of the building but the sublimity of the workers who built it. He doted on the "sky boys" who made the building, capturing for posterity their stroll on the thin edge of nothingness, and in the process surrounded them with an unlikely patina of the sublime.

One of the last photographs Hine did include in the Empire State section of *Men at Work* illustrates his approach. It shows what its caption calls an "old bolter" perched vertiginously on the edge of a steel girder that ends in nothingness, with midtown Manhattan and the spire of the Chrysler Building in the background (see Figure 5.4). You can read the photograph in one of two ways. On the one hand, the man looks small against the background of the city and dangerously exposed to the nothingness below. On the other hand, and because of the perspective and framing of the photograph, he looks roughly the same size as the Chrysler Building over his left shoulder. If he stood up—God forbid—he would be taller than that building. In some ways, that is, Hine has made the old bolter seem the equal of the skyscraper in the background and, by implication, the unfinished skyscraper upon which he sits. Whether we fully register it or not, we conclude that he has a similar status relative to the building he straddles, and which, from almost any other angle, would dwarf him.

The photograph and others like it suggest that Hine sought to transfer the sublimity of the Empire State Building to the workers who built it. On the acknowledgments page of his thin book of photographs, Hine reprints a passage from William James's essay "What Makes a Life Significant." (He mistakenly credits the quotation to James's 1910 essay "The Moral Equivalent of War.") In that essay, as in "The Moral Equivalent of War," James proposes various substitutes for what he considers the destructive but nevertheless healthful virtues of battle. Among these substitutes, James writes, is work.

Figure 5.4. *An Old Bolter.*
Source: National Archives (518290)

"Not in clanging fights and desperate marches only is heroism to be looked for," James writes, "but on every bridge and building that is going up today, on freight trains, on vessels and lumber-rafts, in mines, among firemen and policemen, the demand for courage is incessant and the supply never fails." For James, what unites soldiers and workers is "courage," one of the classic Aristotelian virtues and, perhaps unsurprisingly, when it comes to discussions of virtue and the sublime, one of the most common sources of the sublime.

As with great skill and ability, Keltner and Haidt doubt that great virtue—in this case courage—can inspire awe per se. (Here they prefer the term "elevation.") Others, however, have found something ineluctably sublime about heroism and displays of virtue, specifically courage. In *Critique of the Power of Judgment*, for example, Immanuel Kant often uses words like "strength," "courage," "and "resistance" to characterize our response to the sublime, which makes sense since for Kant the sublime requires overcoming the initial fear of whatever object inspires the feeling of terror that accompanies the sublime. Nature, Kant writes, "is judged sublime not insofar as it arouses fear, but rather because it calls forth our power (which is not part of nature) to regard those things about which we are concerned (goods, health and life) as trivial."[32] In other words, nature is not sublime. We are. And we are sublime because we can put at naught those things (goods, health, life) that the terrifying object in nature initially threatens. "What is it that is the object of the highest admiration even to the savage?" Kant asks. "Someone who is not frightened, who has no fear, thus does not shrink before danger but energetically sets to work with full deliberation."[33]

For Kant, nowhere is the contempt for the petty things about which we are concerned as obvious as in war. War, Kant writes, "has something sublime about it, and at the same time makes the *mentality* of the people who conduct it in this way [with order and reverence for the rights of civilians] all the more sublime, the more dangers it has been exposed to and before which it has been able to assert its courage."[34] By contrast, Kant writes, in withering scorn for bourgeois life, "a long peace causes *the spirit of mere commerce* to predominate, along with base selfishness, cowardice, and weakness, and usually debases the *mentality* of a populace."[35] For Kant, soldiers achieve a state of the sublime because, as the critic Robert Doran puts it, they display "courage in the face of danger" and, most of all, transcend an "attachment to life," which can make our own desperate attachment to life seem petty.[36]

Hine, who photographed relief efforts in Europe after the First World War, shared with William James a pacifist streak. Unlike Kant, he could not glorify war or soldiers; like James, however, he could glorify workers who resembled soldiers in their courage and the sublime casualness with which they treated their own attachment to life. Indeed, Hine repeatedly shows the risk these men took in their work, and the lightheartedness with which they took it. In the caption to the picture of the old bolter, Hine writes: "Young and old, they all say it is not as dangerous as it looks." That may be so. After all, though five workers died during construction of the Empire State Building, only one did so from falling. Nevertheless, these workers risked their lives every day in order to make something sublime. In Hine's mind, that qualifies them for the sublime. Call it, if you like, a labor theory of the sublime. For Hine, workers atop the Empire State Building epitomize the courage required of workers everywhere, and, thus, like President Roosevelt and Jesse Owens, they inspire awe and achieve their own form of the sublime.

Of Migrants and Grandmothers

One might argue that workers on the Empire State Building have more in common with presidents and Olympic athletes than they do with ordinary people. After all, like presidents and Jesse Owens, these workers have something vast (the skyscraper) associated with them. In addition, they have more of an opportunity to practice strength, courage, and resistance—and, thus, to achieve the sublime—than most people do in the course of their workday lives. (Consider me, writing this.) Not for nothing, then, does Hine start with workers on the Empire State Building before proceeding to less obviously sublime workers in the remainder of his book of photographs. By themselves, the machinists pictured at the back of *Men at Work* would not seem to achieve the sublime. Although the gears of their machines occasionally tower over them, and they show strength, courage, and resistance by not cowering in front of them, their feet nevertheless never leave the ground. Just as the workers atop the Empire State Building borrow their sublimity from the sublimity of the Empire State Building, machinists borrow their sublimity from the sublime workers atop the Empire State Building.

Still, one of the curious features of the Depression sublime is how far—or, to speak hierarchically, how low—some writers sought to extend it, which is all the way down to what, in the 1930s, passed for the lowest of low, the most ordinary of ordinary: migrant workers, tenant farmers, and sharecroppers. Indeed, a similar preoccupation with courage in the face of danger—except this time on the part of the most lowly and exploited—may explain the popularity of one of the most famous works of Depression-era fiction, John Steinbeck's *The Grapes of Wrath*. In the first half of the novel, the Joads are anything but sublime. Evicted from their land in Oklahoma, taken advantage of by salesmen, and pushed around by the police, the Joads suffer from the invisible hand of a capitalism that, with its cryptic mortgages and nefarious banks, its vastness and capacity to reduce individuals to nothing, itself begins to seem sublime. In the second half of the novel, however, the Joads, though still pushed around, begin to act more like heroes than victims, and in doing so achieve a sort of sublimity themselves.

For example, before they arrive in California proper, the family has to cross a burning desert. On their way to California, Granma Joad sickens. Camped with other migrants near a river on the outskirts of a town, the Joads hope to rest and let her recover before making the crossing. But with their money running low, and driven out of camp by deputies from the

Figure 5.5. Rose of Sharon, Ma, and Tom Joad from John Ford's *The Grapes of Wrath* (1940).
Source: Sunset Boulevard/Getty Images

town, the family has little choice but to cross the desert immediately. They load Granma onto the back of the truck, where Ma spends the night with her. In the night, Granma dies, and Ma, who knows that the family cannot stop in the middle of the desert, comforts her during her death and spends the rest of the night lying with her rigid corpse. When the family arrives in a town on the other side of the desert, and Ma announces that Granma is not sick but dead, no one can quite believe what she has done for them. "The family looked at Ma with a little terror at her strength," Steinbeck writes, and Tom Joad, her son, exclaims, "Jesus Christ! You layin' there with her all night long!" (see Figure 5.5). Similarly, Jim Casy, the populist preacher who tags along with the family, says "in wonder" to another member of the family: "'There's a woman,'" he continues, "'so great with love—she scares me. Makes me afraid an' mean.'"[37] (That Casy, whose initials—and fate—evoke Christ, should nevertheless stand in awe before Ma is telling.)

Later in the novel, Tom Joad makes a similar sacrifice of himself, though not to his family but to his fellow workers. Tom and the rest of the Joads get separated from Casy when the latter takes the blame for an attack on a deputy in a migrant camp and is hauled away to jail. Tom and he are reunited outside the peach fields where the Joads have found work and, unknowingly, scabbed on a strike of fellow migrant workers led by Casy. Tom and

Casy are not reunited for long, however, before hired vigilantes set upon their camp and one of them kills Casy. Tom, enraged, kills the man and spends the rest of the novel hiding out. When he must leave the family, Tom tells Ma of his plan to do "what Casy done," to do something about "our people livin' like pigs, an' the good rich lan' layin' fallow, or maybe one fellow with a million acres, while a hunderd thousan' good farmers is starving." When Ma warns him that they will "cut you down," and worries that she will never know what happens to him, Tom makes the most famous speech of the novel, the one that Henry Fonda delivers so earnestly and unforgettably in the 1940 film:

> Tom laughed uneasily, "Well, maybe like Casy says, a fella ain't got a soul of his own, but on'y a piece of a big one—an' then——"
>
> "Then what, Tom?"
>
> "Then it don' matter. Then I'll be all aroun' in the dark. I'll be ever'where—wherever you look. Wherever they's a fight so hungry people can eat, I'll be there. Wherever they's a cop beatin' up a guy, I'll be there. If Casy knowed, why, I'll be in the way guys yell when they're mad an'—I'll be in the way kids laugh when they're hungry an' they know supper's ready. An' when our folks eat the stuff they raise an' live in the houses they build—why, I'll be there."[38]

Like workers strolling on top of the Empire State Building, Tom transcends his attachment to life and achieves a similar form of sublimity. Unlike those workers, he does not just risk his life but knowingly surrenders it. He achieves an added sublimity, too, in that he joins the virtue of courage to another, arguably even more sublime virtue, care. Tom imagines dying for a cause and, like Walt Whitman at the end of "Song of Myself," being reborn into the collective, into the shared soul of an oppressed people fighting for justice and, ultimately, enjoying the fruits of that justice.

That commitment to others is embodied in the final scene of the novel, when the Joads—or what remains of them after their incredible travails—stumble during a thunderstorm upon a barn in which a man lies ill, too sick to eat solid food but also dying of starvation. The eldest daughter of the Joad family, Rose of Sharon, has just given birth to a stillborn baby. Overcoming a powerful combination of embarrassment and taboo, she nurses the starving, dying man at her breast. The last lines of the novel read:

> For a moment Rose of Sharon sat still in the whispering barn. Then she hoisted her tired body up and drew the comfort about her. She moved slowly to the corner and stood looking down at the wasted face, into the wide, frightened eyes. Then slowly she lay down beside him. He shook his head

> slowly from side to side. Rose of Sharon loosened one side of the blanket and bared her breast. "You got to," she said. She squirmed closer and pulled his head close. "There!" she said. "There." Her hand moved behind his head and supported it. Her fingers moved gently in his hair. She looked up and across the barn, and her lips came together and smiled mysteriously.[39]

Throughout the novel, Steinbeck cannot decide on the emotional keynote of his book. From the title to the inter-chapters, he flirts with rage as the proper emotional response on the part of migrants to their oppression and, indirectly, on the part of those who read of their exploitation. Yet throughout—in Ma, in Tom, and at the end with Rose of Sharon—Steinbeck seems to opt for an emotion that he struggles to label but that is nonetheless powerful. Call it sympathy, care, or, in the language of the 1930s, solidarity. Whatever one calls it, Steinbeck, as in this last scene, extends its domain beyond the realm of the family to the realm of class. In their discussion of awe, Keltner and Haidt suggest that "the breadth and scope of a grand theory" like psychoanalysis, feminism, or evolutionary theory can elicit awe, and that certainly seems to be the case here.[40] Like her brother and her mother, Rose of Sharon displays courage in the face of, if not quite danger, then at least hardship. Even more important, in her majestic act of solidarity, and in the mysterious smile that accompanies it, she offers readers a glimpse of a transcendent ethic of care that seems equally if not more sublime than the courageous, sacrificial acts of Tom and Ma.

In showing ordinary people devoted to each other, literally nursing each other, Steinbeck turns the lowliest—the people—into the highest, into a repository of virtue and an instance of the sublime. As Ma puts it in the final lines of the film, a passage cobbled together from lines spoken midway through the novel: "Rich fellas come up an' they die, an' their kids ain't no good an' they die out. But we keep a'comin'. We're the people that live. They can't wipe us out; they can't lick us. We'll go on forever, Pa, 'cause we're the people."[41]

To illustrate how much purchase this notion of "the people" had on the decade, consider a superficially very different work from *The Grapes of Wrath*, Margaret Walker's poem "Lineage." The poem, like Langston Hughes's "The Negro Speaks of Rivers," celebrates the strength and the wisdom of past generations of Africans and African Americans. Unlike the mostly ungendered "The Negro Speaks of Rivers," though, "Lineage" reconstructs a specifically female genealogy. Yet, and thus also unlike Hughes's persona poem, where simply belonging to the Negro race makes one's soul grow "deep as rivers,"Walker's speaker finally doubts how much she shares in the lineage the poem celebrates.

My grandmothers were strong.
They followed plows and bent to toil.
They moved through fields sowing seed.
They touched earth and grain grew.
They were full of sturdiness and singing.
My grandmothers were strong.

My grandmothers are full of memories
Smelling of soap and onions and wet clay
With veins rolling roughly over quick hands
They have many clean words to say.
My grandmothers were strong.
Why am I not as they?[42]

By "grandmothers," the speaker refers to the parents of her parents but also, more generally, to all grandmothers, to an entire generation of women. And you can imagine a very different poem about these figures than the one Walker writes. Walker could have, for example, described the conditions that forced African-American women, whether during slavery or afterwards, to plant and harvest crops that did not belong to them. (Think of some of the sharecropper poems that Sterling Brown was writing at this time, or the songs and poems that John Handcox was writing and publishing in the *Sharecropper's Voice*, the newspaper of the Southern Tenant Farmers' Union.)[43] "Lineage," though, does not take that route. It ignores the economic and political conditions that frame the work the women do to focus tightly on the work itself, on the strength such work reveals about those who did it. It does not condemn but celebrate. Or, if it does condemn, it condemns the current generation over against past ones, a dynamic that emerges in the shifting verb tenses of the poem. In the first stanza, the speaker describes what her grandmothers did—past tense—to display their strength. In the second stanza, the tense changes. Now the grandmothers, presumably the same ones who *were* strong in the first stanza, *are* strong in the second, and not because of what they did but because of what they remember doing and the "clean words" they have to say as a result. (The clean words emerging from their dirty labor.) Action in the past—bringing food out of the earth—leads to wisdom in the present. The penultimate line, however, which returns to the past tense ("were strong"), sounds elegiac, as though the speaker realizes that these grandmothers, who were strong and are full of memories, will not live forever, and when they go they will take their strength and memories with them. That makes the shift to the present tense in the last line all the more powerful. The speaker asks why she *is* "not as they," that is neither strong nor full of memories.

At first glance, the poem may seem like an exercise in nostalgia or like the romancing of the laboring folk on the part of the urban intellectual. The rural grandmothers were strong; the poetic granddaughters are not. Yet the poem hints that its speaker may resemble the grandmothers in more ways than it lets on. The second stanza, unlike the first, begins to rhyme. Specifically, "they" of the last line joins with the "wet clay" and "say" of previous lines, which offers an audible connection to the husbandry of the first stanza and the wisdom of the second. The speaker may not feel like the grandmothers, but she does begin to connect to them through sound. Moreover, though we learn nothing of her laboring past except, perhaps, that she does not touch earth and make grain grow, the speaker, like the grandmothers, is in her own way full of memories—of the grandmothers. And like them, she has clean words to say as a result—the poem itself.

Regardless of how connected or disconnected the speaker feels from the grandmothers, though, the poem, like countless such works in the Great Depression, looks upon the people—the folk—with awe. As these very different texts suggest, in its vastness and capacity to inspire awe, "the people" would prove a quintessential form of the Depression sublime. Still, one might argue that the Joads, for example, achieve sublimity because of their heroic commitment to others—a heroism not available to most, and that this heroism makes them, strange to say, more akin to presidents and Olympic athletes than ordinary people. As Ma's paean to the people suggest, though, Steinbeck and others sought to make ordinary people the object of awe not just because of their actions but because of their very being. Not just, that is, because of what they did but because of who they are. (The same might be said of Walker's grandmothers.) Nowhere can you see this effort to celebrate not what the people do but what they are more clearly than in James Agee and Walker Evans's *Let Us Now Praise Famous Men*, which turned an equally lowly people—sharecroppers—into figures of the sublime, into, for all practical purposes, gods. Before Agee and Evans could make readers stand in awe of their godlike tenant farmers, however, they had to do away with another, by far more conventional emotional response to sharecroppers, one that actually stood in the way of awe, namely, sympathy.

Famous Men (and Women)

When Agee and Evans took up the assignment of writing about tenant farmers, they did not enter an open field. On November 16, 1936, just two weeks after winning re-election, and perhaps feeling pressure from an ongoing strike among tenant farmers in the South, President Franklin Delano Roosevelt convened a committee on what he called "farm tenancy." It was not just, as Roosevelt noted in his letter of instruction to then secretary of agriculture, Henry A. Wallace, that "the rapid increase of tenant farmers over the last half century" had violated, as Roosevelt put it, "the American ideal of owner-operated farms." It was also that the increase in tenant farmers brought with it "soil depletion and declining living standards," which, Roosevelt warned, somewhat vaguely, "presents a challenge to national action."[44] Despite this initial vagueness, the document that the committee produced—*Farm Tenancy*¬¬—is one of the more useful summaries of what its authors (and Roosevelt) called "farm insecurity," which those not in thrall to New Deal jargon would simply call rural poverty.

By farm tenancy, Roosevelt and others meant the tenants and sharecroppers who farmed a piece of land but did not own it. Instead, they contracted with a landlord who did. Although the distinctions could blur and change from place to place, tenants differed from sharecroppers. The former usually paid rent on the land in advance and had most if not all of the tools and livestock needed to raise a crop. At the end of the season, tenants kept what they could get for the crops they had raised. Like tenants, sharecroppers farmed land they did not own, but as a rule they had neither the cash to pay rent nor the tools or livestock to raise a crop. Instead, at the beginning of the season, the owner of the land or a nearby merchant would loan them—at exorbitant interest rates—everything they needed to raise a crop, not just tools, livestock, seed, and fertilizer but food to live on as well. At the end of the season, by way of rent, sharecroppers would turn over a portion of the crops they had raised to the landowner, usually half. In addition, they would surrender still more of the crop they had raised to the owner or merchant to repay the initial loan (plus interest) of everything (tools, livestock, seed, fertilizer, food) they had used to raise the crop. Although few envied the lot of tenants, next to sharecroppers tenants at least had a chance. If they had a good harvest, they could turn a profit. Sharecroppers, by contrast, no matter how good the harvest, did well to end the season simply out of debt to their landlord or furnishing merchant.

Whether tenants or sharecroppers, the number of farmers who did not own their land was on the rise. In the late nineteenth century, the authors of the government report calculated, one out of every four farmers was a tenant. By 1935, two out of every five were. In total, nearly 3 million farmers did not own the land they farmed, with 40,000 more added to their number every year.[45]

The problem was not just that tenancy had increased and continued to increase but the appalling poverty and problems—disease, illiteracy—that accompanied it. In a section entitled "The Erosion of Our Society," the authors of *Farm Tenancy* got as close to outright anger as they would in the otherwise rhetorically muted document. "The extreme poverty of one-fifth to one-fourth of the farm population," the authors wrote, "reflects itself in a standard of living below any level of decency." They continued:

> Large families of tenants or croppers, or hired farm laborers, are living in houses of two or three rooms. The buildings are frequently of poor construction, out of alinement [sic], weather-beaten, and unsightly. The doors and windows are rarely screened. Often the roofs are leaky. The surroundings of such houses are bleak and unattractive. Many have no outside toilet, or, if one is available, it is highly unsanitary.
>
> Many of these families are chronically undernourished. They are readily subject to diseases. Pellagra, malaria, and the hookworm and other parasites exact heavy tolls in life and energy. Suitable provision for maintaining health and treating disease among these families is lacking or inadequate in many localities.
>
> Clothing is often scarcely sufficient to afford protection to the body, much less to help maintain self-respect.[46]

Just to be clear, when the authors of the report note that many families have no outside toilet, they do not mean that families do not have indoor plumbing, but that they do not have an outhouse. They use the bushes.

Unlike the problem of unemployment, which would decrease as economic prosperity returned, farm tenancy and its accompanying poverty, while made worse by the Depression, had also predated it and, in all likelihood, would outlast it. In other words, when it came to farm insecurity, especially in the South, something must be done, something beyond the ordinary New Deal measures to restore the national economy to prosperity *and* something beyond earlier New Deal efforts, like the Agricultural Adjustment Act of 1933, to raise crop prices by limiting supply, which harmed as much as it helped farmers who did not own land. (Paid by the government to not raise crops, landowners no longer needed those who actually raised crops.)[47]

In order to lend urgency to the cause of farm tenancy, the authors turned to a rhetorical strategy—documentary photography—that in the coming years would assume more and more of a place in efforts to influence American attitudes toward poverty. That is, the authors of *Farm Tenancy* sought to put a face to the problem of rural poverty. After the section reprinting official documents, they included eight black-and-white photographs depicting the areas and people discussed in the report. One photograph, titled "The Home and Family of a Cropper in the Cotton Belt," showed three shoeless children, one smiling winsomely, standing in front of two grown women. One of the women has her eyes closed, and the other stares forcefully into the camera. All stand before a rotting cabin, though this one has screens on the window.

In all likelihood, this and the other photographs came from the files of the Historical Section of the Resettlement Administration, a New Deal agency that had already begun, in limited form, to institute the reforms recommended by *Farm Tenancy*. In the Resettlement Administration, soon renamed the Farm Security Administration, the head of the Information Division, Roy Stryker, employed a handful of photographers—initially, Dorothea Lange, Walter Rothstein, Carl Mydans, Walker Evans, and Ben Shahn—to produce, in Stryker's words, "a pictorial documentation of our rural areas and rural problems."[48] Such photographs, distributed to newspapers and magazines, would win public and congressional support for New Deal programs in general and the sort of reforms proposed by the authors of *Farm Tenancy* in particular.[49]

The photographs taken by those employed by the Farm Security Administration embody the emotional contract that sought to shape American attitudes toward poverty during the Great Depression. Through words and, increasingly, through photographs, Americans could witness an injustice—rural poverty—that would otherwise have remained hidden from them. Informed of such injustices, they would sympathize with those subject to them and support the efforts of those institutions—in the case of rural poverty, the federal government or the Southern Tenant Farmers' Union—that sought to do something about them. In short, exposure—somewhat literally in the case of photographs—would equal sympathy, and this would equal reform. It is such a familiar rhetorical strategy—and emotional contract—that we risk taking it for granted.

Agee and Evans, however, sought to accomplish something far different. Instead of cultivating sympathy for sharecroppers, they sought to inspire awe for them, to create out of a most unlikely source an overwhelming, transformative instance of the sublime.

In the middle years of the 1930s, *Fortune* magazine had a mostly frivolous "Life and Circumstances" series devoted to documenting the lives of ordinary Americans. (One entry in the series offered a condescending portrait of a house painter.) In the summer of 1936, Agee, then a staff writer for *Fortune*, accepted an assignment to produce an entry in the series on cotton tenant farmers. He and Evans, on loan from the Resettlement Administration, traveled to rural Alabama, found a suitably representative family—and two nearby ones—and spent four weeks living with them. Afterwards, Agee wrote an unwieldy article—the recently rediscovered "Cotton Tenants: Three Families"—which the editors of *Fortune* asked him to revise and, when he refused, eventually returned to him to do with as he pleased. In the year that followed, Agee turned a long but manageable article distinguished by its touches of poetic language and moral outrage into a 400-page meditation on the political, philosophical, and cosmological significance of three families of tenant farmers. Drafting off the success of Erskine Caldwell and Margaret Bourke-White's book of documentary photographs and primer on sharecropping, *You Have Seen Their Faces*, Agee and Evans eventually found a publisher for their book. Despite positive reviews—including one from Lionel Trilling calling it "the most realistic and most important moral effort of our generation"—*Let Us Now Praise Famous Men* sold poorly and quickly went out of print.[50]

As Trilling recognized, the book was nominally about the lives of three Alabama tenant families. But its moral importance arose from another question: "How may we—'we' being the relatively fortunate middle class that reads books and experiences emotions—how may we feel about the—and the word itself proclaims the difficulty—underprivileged?"[51] In the course of the book, Agee tries out a number of possible answers to that question, rejecting none, really, except the one we might expect. From the start of the book, and renewed throughout, Agee attacks not just those who would sympathize with his cotton tenant families but the concept of sympathy itself. Indeed, the word shows up on his—admittedly lengthy—list of suspect "anglosaxon monosyllables" that appears at the end of the book.[52]

That is not to say, of course, that Agee does not sympathize with his subjects or, through his sympathy, occasionally lead readers to a similar emotion.

Early in the book, for example, Agee movingly describes the plight of Emma, daughter of one of the tenant farmers and sister of another, as she reluctantly prepares to leave her family to join a husband who treats her badly and whom she does not love. (Agee's speech to her, which begins "nobody has a right to be unhappy, or to live in a way that makes them unhappy," is one of the most affecting passages in the book.)[53] Moreover, in the second and third parts of that section, Agee speaks in the voice of Annie Mae, the wife in the tenant family whom he knows and likes the best, whose refrain—"How was it we were caught?"—suggests the depths of her despair and hopelessness.[54] In addition, Agee tenderly describes the literally crippling work the families perform, and the humiliations the children absorb at school because of their poverty, and these too break your heart.

Yet before, during, and after nearly every incident or description in the book that might invite sympathy, Agee warns against it. He sets the keynote in the Preamble, when he offers this ironic précis of the book and its audience:

> [T]his is a book about "sharecroppers," and is written for all those who have a soft place in their hearts for the laughter and tears inherent in poverty viewed at a distance, and especially those who can afford the retail price; in the hope that the reader will be edified, and may feel kindly disposed toward any well-thought-out liberal effort to rectify the unpleasant situation down South, and will somewhat better and more guiltily appreciate the next good meal he eats; and in the hope, too, that he will recommend this little book to really sympathetic friends, in order that our publishers may at least cover their investment and that just the merest perhaps) some kindly thought may be turned our way, and a little of your money fall to poor little us.[55]

The passage suggests a number of reasons why Agee has come to distrust sympathy as much as he does. To start, he fears that sympathy may oversimplify why people feel sorry for others. That is, sympathy may arise as much out of self-interest as it does out of genuine interest in the wellbeing of others. Obviously, this fear accounts for his own, recurring concern that he might in any way profit—whether in terms of money or reputation—from his "parading the nakedness, disadvantage, and humiliation of these lives before another group of human beings."[56] But Agee also fears that not just writers but readers might profit from the parade too. By reading of human suffering, they get to feel like the sort of person who sympathizes with others, has soft places in their hearts, or who, as a result of reading of the suffering of others, appreciate what they have all the more. That is not to say one should not feel these things, only that they complicate what many would prefer to think of as a simple, purely altruistic emotion, and Agee has set himself the task of complicating all such simplicities. Another way to think about it is that sympathy makes us think more of the self, or at least poses no challenge to it. By contrast, awe, what Agee ultimately aims for in his representation of sharecroppers, usually makes us think less.

In addition, Agee worries about the political implications of sympathy. A carelessly written book, he fears, may lead people to "feel kindly disposed toward any well-thought-out liberal effort to rectify the unpleasant situation down South." That may not sound sinister, but what if the situation down south resists or exceeds those liberal efforts? In that case, sympathy, by seeking easy answers, may do more harm than good.[57]

Finally, in addition to oversimplifying motives and solutions, Agee fears sympathy may oversimplify poverty or, at least, those who live in it. In the first passage quoted above, Agee puts sharecroppers in quotation marks, not just because by the time he writes the Preamble they have become a familiar cause, but because thanks to *You Have Seen Their Faces* and other works, the mere mention of sharecroppers sets off a whole preexisting, prepackaged version of the poor best captured in the phrase "the laughter and tears inherent in poverty." As Agee shows, his families do occasionally laugh and cry, but from his view nothing inheres about poverty, no essence precedes its individual existences. Only poverty "viewed at a distance," which viewing it through the lens of sympathy may encourage, allows one to believe that there is anything permanent, essential, or even characteristic about it.

Elsewhere, Agee refers to sympathy as one of the "various possible reflexes" that readers may have for and while reading the book, and once sympathy becomes a reflex, it ceases to respond adequately to its object, other human beings.[58]

That skepticism about reform and the sympathy that gives rise to it explains a number of other elements in *Let Us Now Praise Famous Men*: Agee's self-confessed but deeply qualified communism, which would, unlike well-thought-out liberal efforts, begin to confront what he calls "the whole world-system" responsible for the indignities of tenant farming; his repeated attacks on reformers; his obsession with education as at least the beginnings of an honest and self-directed inquiry into the sources of poverty; and his vague but moving invocation of the revolution or, anyway, the deliverance from human suffering that he promises near the end of the book, which would also deliver humanity from the curse of sympathy.

In addition, his skepticism about sympathy and reform explains his very different approach to documenting the lives of tenant farmers. In contrast to those who would merely sympathize with the poor, Agee devotes the better part of his book to expanding on those who suffer from poverty, not in observing what they do not have but dilating on what they do. Agee emphasizes over and over again not what makes the members of his tenant families representative but what makes them specific. Early in the book, he speaks of their "irreparable, unrepeatable existences," meaning both that they will not get to repeat their lives but also that no other human being will repeat them.[59] They are unique. Not "one of these persons is ever quite to be duplicated," Agee writes later in the book, "nor replaced, nor has it ever quite had precedent."[60] "Each of you," he addresses the members of the tenant families directly, "is a creature which has never in all time existed before and which shall never in all time exist again and which is not quite like any other."[61] Moreover, to withhold those "specifications," to treat them as exclusively the manifestations of their poverty, Agee believes, "I could but betray you still worse."[62]

Indeed, much of the book is given over to Agee struggling to convey the plain but specific existence of his tenant farmers. "George Gudger is a human being," Agee writes, discussing the difference between invention and documentary, "a man, not like any other human being so much as he is like himself." Agee could, he writes, "invent incidents, appearances, additions to his character, background, surroundings, future" that would fill out and possibly even reveal the truth about George Gudger. "But somehow a much more important, and dignified, and true fact about him," Agee concludes, "than I could conceivably invent, though I were an illimitably better artist than I am, is that fact that he is exactly, down to the last inch and instant, who, what, when, where, and why he is. He is in those terms living, right now, in flesh and blood and breathing, in an actual part of the world in which also, quite as irrelevant to imagination, you and I are living."[63] This emphasis on human specificity, on bare human existence, leads to the emotion Agee offers readers in place of the now discredited sympathy. To rephrase Trilling, how should we feel about the underprivileged? Not love, exactly, as William Stott, in his influential study of documentary expression in the 1930s describes it, though Agee does insist how much he loves the tenant families, and how much he desires their love in turn. Rather, as Hine wants us to feel toward old bolters, and Steinbeck wants us to feel toward the Joads, Agee wants us to feel awe toward his sharecroppers. Awe that all the forces of the universe have gathered to make this world, and awe that they have further gathered to make these unprecedented people in it, however abject their outward economic lives. George Gudger is living, right now, and that fact ought to stop you in your tracks.

Why? Because ordinary as he is, worthless as he is, in fact, he is nonetheless a miracle. Earlier, in a section of the book titled "Colon," Agee asks, apropos of one human looking "into the eyes of a human life": "what is it he there beholds that so freezes and abashes his ambitious heart?" He beholds, Agee writes,

> the eyes of a trapped wild animal, or of a furious angel nailed to the ground by his wings, or however else one may faintly designate the human "soul," that which is angry, that which is wild, that which is untameable, that which is healthy and holy, that which is competent of all advantaging within hope of human dream, that which most marvelous and most precious to our knowledge and most extremely advanced upon futurity of all flowerings within the scope of creation is of all these the least destructible, the least corruptible.[64]

Later still, in wondering how to write the history of each sharecropper and his soul, Agee connects them to the "magnitude in space and time" that Schopenhauer spoke of; that is, he links their existence to the existence of the universe and, thus, renders them equally vast and thus equally sublime. An individual human life, even a sharecropper, Agee writes, "is a child of the substance and bowels of the stars and of all space."[65] (As Agee well knew, this statement is not simply metaphorical. All matter, including the elements that compose human beings, come from exploded stars.) So too, Agee continues, is the earth, which he calls an "aberration" because it is the one planet in the whole universe that supports life, upon which this child is born. And finally, Agee observes how on this earth this individual human life is "born . . . into its future growth," "blossomed forth upon that branch most sportive, most precarious, most propitious, potential and most frightful in known creation, of human existence, of human consciousness, of human possibility to build itself ruin or wonder."[66] In short, as Agee writes in the closing pages of the book, borrowing a proverb from William Blake, "Everything that is is holy," including and especially sharecroppers. Their holiness derives from their miraculous, irreproducible existence. And we do not pity or feel sympathy for holy things.[67] We worship them.

This emphasis on the interstellar origins and holiness of life explains the phrase that Agee offers early on to describe the true subject of his book: "an independent inquiry into certain normal predicaments of human divinity."[68] The phrase suggests that we should conceive of human beings, in this case sharecroppers, as we do gods, and our encounter with these sharecropper-gods should be as awe inspiring—and transformative—as Saul's encounter with his actual God on the road to Damascus. To be sure, Agee's sentence suggests that we should also feel sorrow at the predicaments that habitually afflict these human gods—what Agee calls the "world's bombardment"—but mostly awe that these people exist at all.[69] Indeed, the world's bombardment matters only because the existence of these human gods is so unlikely, unprecedented, and awesome to begin with.

That sense of human divinity, of awe and the sublime, is what makes Walker Evans's photographs, especially his portraits, so thrilling (see Figure 5.6). They force viewers to confront the unprecedented, divine souls that throughout the book Agee struggles to describe in prose. They capture images of gods. Thus, with Evans's help, Agee surrounds the Gudgers with

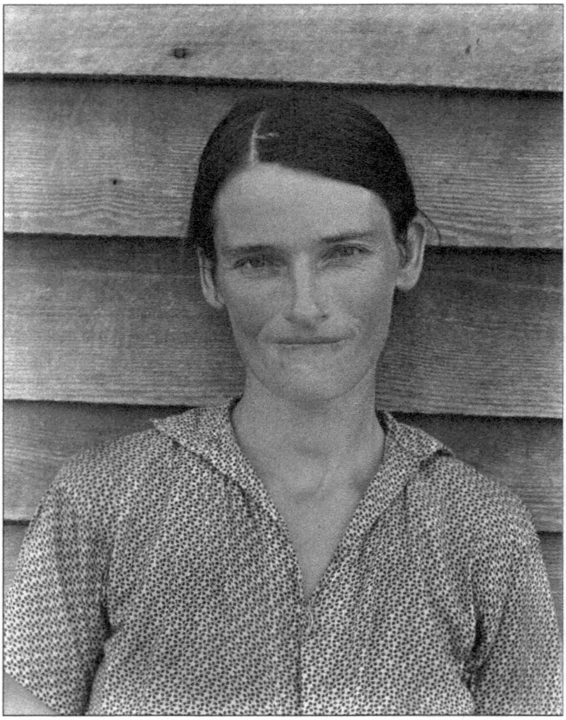

Figure 5.6. Annie Mae Burroughs.
Source: © Walker Evans Archive, Metropolitan Museum of Art

an aura of the sublime that not even steel workers or the Joads, to say nothing of presidents and Olympic athletes, can match. And he creates this sublimity despite and perhaps because the Gudgers start from such humble origins. Anonymous men become famous men, and finally more gods than men, and in so doing become sublime.

Downward to the Sublime

In a continued search for the Depression sublime, one could keep traveling downward, away from the low but exalted sharecropper and toward the smaller and more anonymous still, below, even, the human. In the 1930s, for example, Louis Leakey and his wife Mary confirmed Charles Darwin's hunch that humans must have first evolved from apes while living in Africa and, millions of years later, migrated outward from there. (Leakey told the story in his 1934 book *Adam's Ancestors*.) Their discoveries revealed much about the Stone Age culture of early man and reminded contemporaries of the nearly infinite prehistory and the suddenness—and the fragility—of modern human history.

Around the same time, in the field of evolutionary biology, Sewall Wright did pioneering work in population genetics, discovering the role that probability could play in determining genetic variation, which sounds dry but has profound consequences for the shape of biological life on earth. In his 1937 book *Genetics and the Origin of Species*, the Ukrainian-born biologist Theodosius Dobzhansky, then at the California Institute of Technology, completed the synthesis of Mendel and Darwin that Wright had begun. (Julian Huxley popularized Wright and Dobzhansky 's work in his 1942 book, *Evolution: The Modern Synthesis*.) After this work, the evolution of different species began to seem like a sublime contest among genetic variation, environment, and the process of natural selection playing out over millennia.

Even farther down, in 1928 the Scottish biologist Alexander Fleming accidentally discovered penicillin. By the late 1930s, scientists understood its capacity to fight infections of all sorts, and by the early 1940s it had gone into mass production—for the war effort—and soon enough for public use. Individuals had to accommodate themselves to the fact that a humble mold, discovered more or less by chance, could cure infectious diseases like tuberculosis and pneumonia that had slaughtered humans for millions of years.

Still farther down the latter of life and the sublime, in 1932 the English physicist James Chadwick discovered the neutron, which radically altered our understanding of the atom and thus the structure of matter.[70]

In traveling downward, however, one gradually loses the quality of vastness necessary to the sublime. Moreover, with the exception of the Leakeys, one loses the tight focus on people, which, I have argued, is what distinguishes the Depression sublime from other moments in its history.

Of course, there is an irony in speaking of a Depression sublime, especially in the form of a populist sublime. At few points in American history have individuals felt more powerless and more buffeted about by the storms of economics and, in the case of the Dust Bowl, by literal storms, as they did during the 1930s. Perhaps, though, as with other confrontations with the sublime, it takes a radical humbling of humanity in order to reassert its ultimate power.

Like many accounts of the Great Depression, thus far mine has focused on the destructive, the negative emotions of fear, panic, and, though less negative than just plain ugly, righteousness and self-righteousness. That focus obviously has merit—the Depression, by definition, destroyed lives and livelihoods—but it ignores what contemporary psychologists would call the positive emotions: joy, gratitude, love, and hope. A focus on the sublime and awe begins to correct that bias toward the negative. In the next chapter, I turn to another positive emotion, love, which, though embattled during the Great Depression, nevertheless, in its own way, thrived.

6

A Sordid, Futureless Mess?

Love in Hard Times

On December 11, 1936, the King of England, Edward VIII, announced over the radio that he would give up his throne so he could marry the woman he loved, an American named Wallace Simpson. The affair—its public phase, anyway—began on October 2, 1936, when the Associated Press broke the news that the newly crowned, and still unmarried, Edward VIII would not return alone to Buckingham Palace from his late summer holiday. He would have company. The "possibility of an unofficial American hostess in the palace," the Associated Press reported, "in the person of King Edward's friend Mrs. Ernest [Wallie] Simpson, engaged Mayfair," the fashionable neighborhood around Buckingham Palace. "The vivacious, dark eyed Mrs. Simpson," the article recounted, "formerly Wallis Warfield of Baltimore, Md., who accompanied the 42-year old bachelor monarch on his six weeks' holiday cruise in the Adriatic sea, then traveled as his guest to Edward's Scottish seat at Balmoral castle, returned [to London] with Edward in a special saloon car today."[1]

The article also offered the public its first glimpse of the royal couple in a photograph taken during the recently concluded holiday cruise (see Figure 6.1). In the photograph, Edward's friend, Wallis, holding a small purse by the strap, has placed her hand affectionately on his wrist. If he looks slightly though not unpleasantly surprised by the gesture, she stares off into the distance, not giving it a second thought. Such intimacies, her casualness implies, come naturally to them.

That intimacy, which evidently included Buckingham Palace itself, would not have "engaged Mayfair," or not to the extent that it did, if not for the fact that Mrs. Simpson remained married—to a London shipbroker named Ernest Simpson—and, as the article also reported, in passing but portentously,

The Emotional Life of the Great Depression. John Marsh, Oxford University Press (2019).
 DOI: 10.1093/oso/9780198847731.001.0001

Figure 6.1. Edward and Wallace.
Source: Keystone/Getty Images

that Mrs. Simpson had married and divorced *before* marrying Simpson. In short, if Mayfair was engaged—and it was far from alone—it was because the King of England had taken up with a once-divorced, still-married American woman.

Mayfair and elsewhere paid still more attention when, on October 14, the Associated Press reported that Wallis Simpson had filed for divorce from her husband on grounds of adultery.[2] Journalists immediately began to speculate whether the impending divorce meant that Edward would marry Wallis. On October 26, an article credited "friends of the King" with saying "that he is deeply and sincerely in love with Mrs. Simpson" and intended to marry her in the spring, which he could, in theory, since on October 27 an English judge granted Wallis's divorce, which would free her to remarry six months from the day.[3]

The friends of the king knew their man. On November 16, Edward privately summoned prime minister Stanley Baldwin to Buckingham Palace and informed him of his wish to marry Simpson following his official coronation in May 1937. Baldwin told the king that the British people would never accept the marriage.[4] As the coming weeks revealed, the British elite did not thrill to it either. Members of the royal family, including and especially Queen Mary, Edward's mother, thought Wallis a temptress, a gold-digger, or just plain common. For its part, the still influential Church of England disapproved of the marriage too. It did not allow those who divorced to remarry while the former spouse lived, which Ernest Simpson very much did. Nor did Britain recognize Wallis's first divorce, obtained in the United States, as legitimate since it dissolved because of "emotional incompatibly" instead of adultery. (Under British law, only adultery counted as grounds for divorce.) Technically, then, Wallis had already committed bigamy by marrying Ernest Simpson, her second husband, and would again if she married the king. The Church of England, needless to say, did not condone bigamy. Finally, some members of the British government, including the prime minister, suspected that Simpson—and Edward, for that matter, which did not burnish his qualifications as king—might be Nazi sympathizers. For these reasons, Baldwin and most of those who mattered opposed the marriage, and the prime minister flatly told Edward that if he proceeded with marrying Wallis, Edward would, for obscure legislative reasons, force the existing government to resign and prompt a dangerous constitutional crisis.[5]

Faced with this possibility, Edward chose to give up the throne and marry the woman he loved. On December 10, 1936 he formally abdicated, turning the kingdom over to his brother, Albert, who became George VI. The next day, Edward addressed the country over the radio. His speech would soon appear on the front pages of newspapers across the world. "At long last I am able to say a few words of my own," Edward began. He continued:

> You all know the reasons which have impelled me to renounce the throne. But I want you to understand that in making up my mind that I did not forget the country or the empire, which, as Prince of Wales and lately as King, I have for twenty-five years tried to serve.
>
> But you must believe me when I tell you that I have found it impossible to carry the heavy burden of responsibility and to discharge my duties as King as I would wish to do without the help and support of the woman I love.[6]

Those who opposed his marriage—everyone from his mother to his prime minister—could not understand how Edward could choose his love for a woman, especially "that woman," as more than one occasionally referred to Wallis, over his responsibility to his country. In doing so, however, he and Wallis orchestrated perhaps the greatest love story of the twentieth century, and certainly of the 1930s. Like Romeo pursuing Juliet, Edward defied his family—both his immediate family and the family of his country—for his love. And like Cinderella, brought to life on American screens two years earlier in a ten-minute Betty Boop animated film, Wallis Simpson rose from the cinders—or at least the cinders of the lower-upper-middle class—to marry her prince.[7] In sum, Wallis and Edward showed that love triumphs over all, over the conventions of family, church, nation, social class, over even the blandishments of power and fame.

To be sure, some cheered Edward and Wallis more than others. In general, the British working classes thought Edward should marry whomever he liked, while the middle and upper classes thought he had betrayed his country.[8] Most Americans, meanwhile, who followed the drama almost as closely as those in England, wanted the king to marry Simpson. In one of the first polls George Gallup conducted for his fledgling American Institute of Public Opinion, 61 percent of Americans said they would like to have King Edward marry Wallis Simpson.[9] Less scientifically, on December 8 the *Chicago Tribune* conducted its own poll, reporting that three out of four residents it surveyed thought the king should marry Mrs. Wallis Simpson. The paper also printed four columns of comments gleaned from its survey. Although Henry J. Brown of 6223 South Racine Avenue no doubt spoke for many when he said, "I don't know either of them, so I don't care what they do," most of the comments echoed Mrs. John L. Kaiser, 11716 South Normal Avenue, who said, "Love, I think, should come first," and Patrick O'Leary, 7818 Vernon Avenue, who asked, rhetorically, "Love's first, isn't it?"[10]

The problem, and the context for Wallis and Edward's storybook romance, is that since the onset of the Great Depression, love—heterosexual love measured in new marriages anyway—had not always come first. More often than not, to judge from the statistics, economics had. In 1929, roughly 1.233 million couples married in the United States, which up to that point, with the exception of the postwar year of 1920, were the most marriages to occur in a single year in the United States. Then the Depression hit, and new marriages plummeted. They bottomed out at 982,000 in 1932. To be sure, divorce rates fell as well over this period, from a high of 206,000 in 1929 to 164,000 and 165,000 in 1932 and 1933, respectively, though one suspects the drop in divorces owed less to suddenly renewed love than to an even greater than usual lack of options on the part of those, especially women, trapped in loveless marriages.[11]

Because it played out like such a fairytale romance, the love-at-all-costs story of Wallis and Edward would have likely made headlines and attracted the rooting interests of those for whom love should come first regardless of how the economy fared. But because the economy fared as badly as it did, and because love suffered with it, Americans—with the obvious exception of Henry J. Brown and those like him—may have needed and been more than usually open to an inspiring love story like that of Wallis and Edward. Arguably, much of the film and literary culture had not met those needs. True, composers like Irving Berlin, George and Ira Gershwin, Cole Porter, and Richard Rodgers and Lorenz Hart bombarded stages and airwaves alike with songs about the fascinations of love, but elsewhere, especially on screen and in the pages of literary fiction, love looked like it would never recover from the hard times on which it had fallen during the early years of the Depression. Indeed, to judge by its depiction in film and literature, love looked like it had expired, drowned in its own sordidness. At times, it seemed like an emotion to be exposed or exploited rather than enjoyed.

In what follows, I investigate one of the most important emotions, love, during one of the most important decades, the 1930s. By love, as should be clear by now, I mean, following the psychologists Harry T. Reis and Arthur Aron, the "desire to enter, maintain, or expand a close, connected, and ongoing relationship with another person."[12] In other words, throughout the chapter I speak of the love of others as opposed to the love of objects or ideas. (As Reis and Aron put it, puppy love instead of love of puppies.) For the most part, too, I speak of heterosexual love—or more often than not the lack thereof—between adults rather than, say, homosexual love or love between parents and children, though, as I eventually suggest, the collapse of heterosexual love and the valorization of other forms of love during the Great Depression may have had something to do with anxieties about children at that time. Moreover, while acknowledging the ways that love can do real harm, whether for individuals or for communities, I nevertheless treat it as, on balance, an essential human good, and I break with contemporary critics (Laura Kipnis, Sarah Ahmed) who focus almost exclusively on its admittedly many shortcomings.[13] In the main, though, I side with Søren Kierkegaard, who argued that its opposite, isolation, is appalling. "Deep within every man," Kierkegaard wrote in his journal in 1847,

> there lies the dread of being alone in the world, forgotten by God, overlooked by the tremendous household of millions upon millions. That fear is kept away by looking upon all those about one who are bound to one as friends or family; but the dread is nevertheless there and one hardly dares think of what would happen to one if all the rest were taken away.[14]

In short, as Kierkegaard reminds us, though I admit it sounds banal to say so, few emotions matter to human beings as much as love. And while love, as I believe the Great Depression demonstrates, is very much subject to the public life that circumscribes it, its effects nevertheless remain comparatively private. (Will I love someone? Will someone love me? Will I marry? Will I have children?) Yet its effects are no less—and arguably much more—momentous because it remains so private, because it occurs between two people. All that is to say is that if you go looking for the emotional consequences of love, you will find them less in new legislation or sweeping change than in the shape of individual lives.

Although I discuss film, I mostly—and even more so than in previous chapters—trust writers to have discerned the possibilities and perils of this particular emotion during this particular decade. All told, writers may have offered a more cynical take on love than others did, and the writers I discuss a more cynical take than still other writers, but in doing so they nevertheless seem to capture something essential about the emotion and the decade. I start with *Baby Face*, a notorious pre-Code Hollywood film whose mercantilist view of love would shock in any era but seems especially shocking in black and white. I then turn to literature, including John O'Hara's *BUtterfield 8* (1935) and Mary McCarthy's "The Man in the Brooks Brothers Shirt" (1941).[15] In those works, love is a lost cause, mired in a cauldron of betrayals, venereal disease, and general tawdriness that not even King Edward VIII and Wallis Simpson could redeem. One by one, these works pull down three of the pillars often associated with love: one, that it involves treating people as ends rather than means; two, that you can always fall in love, regardless of what you might have done in the past or what might have been done to you in the past; and finally that love, while it may not always last forever, nevertheless lasts for some meaningful amount of time.

Curiously, all three of the works I discuss in this chapter cast women as their main characters. (In Chapter 7, on hope, I discuss another work about love—Isaac Asimov's "Liar!"—that also enlists a woman as its main character.) Yet upon reflection, that all three works have women as their main characters may be less curious than inevitable. Although, as the rest of this book demonstrates, men feel as much as women, one cannot ignore a history that has repeatedly associated women with emotion and men with rationality. That goes doubly for an emotion like love, which, the thinking goes, may not be a specifically feminine emotion but is, nevertheless, an emotion that women value more than men or to which they are more susceptible than men.[16] Even in rejecting that association, however, each of the texts in this chapter works within that tradition. That is, each generates drama by having a woman fall away from love and return to it—or vice versa. A man with doubts about love is a dog bites man story. A woman with the same doubts, however those doubts get reconciled, is a man bites dog story.

After my survey of 1930s sordidness and lovelessness, I offer a theory as to why so many writers and, for a time, the culture at large may have suddenly lost faith in love. (In short, I believe the economy did it.) My theory, however, makes room for another distinguishing characteristic of the decade, which is that for as much as heterosexual love may have fallen on hard times, other forms of love (charitable, brotherly, queer) thrived in its place. Nevertheless, my final take on the decade is that heterosexual love, like the economy with which its fate so closely intertwined, eventually recovered from the Depression that it, too, had been thrown into—and more quickly than one would think possible. So quickly, in fact, as to cast doubt on whether the works that documented its fall should truly represent the decade.

Baby Face

The romance of Wallis and Edward seems made for Hollywood, and in later years their story would in fact make it on screen. For most of the preceding years of the 1930s, however, its tribute to love coming first would have seemed out of place at the movies, where love often enough came in dead last. The 1930s famously witnessed the birth of the classical Hollywood cinema, that roughly thirty-year period in American film when the studio system, narrative conventions, and rigorous enforcement of the Motion Picture Production Code combined to produce beloved yet morally innocent films. As most film historians and connoisseurs know, though, the 1930s divides between pre- and post-enforcement of the Production Code, and pre-Code cinema, which came to an end with the appointment of Joseph Breen as the Production Code administrator in 1934, often portrayed love (and sex) with a frankness and cynicism that can seem shocking in retrospect.

Nowhere does love seem less romantic or morally innocent than in *Baby Face* (1933), the now slightly infamous film that has come to represent the pre-Code era perhaps more than any other, in no small part because the film, together with a few others, brought about stricter enforcement of the Production Code. *Baby Face* also offers a first glimpse into what I mean by the sordid, when the only love is for oneself, and when the body—of oneself or another—is viewed instrumentally, as an object to exploit.

Today, two versions of *Baby Face* exist. Once completed, the film was submitted to the Studio Relations Committee, the Hollywood-financed censorship group that loosely enforced the Production Code before Joseph Breen began strictly enforcing it in 1934. The Studio Relations Committee suggested changes to the film that the studio that produced the film, Warner Brothers, quickly made. These changes did not satisfy the New York State Board, however, which rejected the film without comment. In response, Warner Brothers cut still more of the egregious parts from the film, injected some moralizing, and tacked on a new, punitive ending. That version passed muster with the New York censors and was released nationwide in June 1933, and that is the version I mostly discuss, though it helps to keep in mind the movie the filmmakers originally wanted to make, the parts the censors evidently could not abide, and the changes the studio made in response.[17] All tell a harrowing story about love in the early years of the Great Depression.

In *Baby Face*, Barbara Stanwyck plays Lily Powers, who, when the story begins, has anything but power. She waits tables in her father's speakeasy in Erie, Pennsylvania, where she endures the groping of steel workers and the local politician alike. (In the original version of the film, her father explicitly prostitutes her out to the local politician, and later she derides him for having done so with other men since she was 14.) For once, Lily refuses to submit to the local politician, and after fighting him off, her father dies in an explosion at the still he operates. Lily, who has lost no love for her father, only smiles as she watches the flames consume him. After his death, she visits one of her only friends, a cobbler, who urges her to "Go to the big city" because "There you will find opportunities." She does, though not of the sort that the cobbler or the censors would approve.[18]

In the scenes that follow, Lily almost literally sleeps her way to the top, which the film makes clear through surprisingly lewd camerawork. Arriving in New York City, Lily looks up at a skyscraper, which houses a bank, the Gotham Trust. Inside, she first sleeps with a junior clerk to land a job in the filing department, then with a colleague (a young John Wayne) in filing, who recommends her for a promotion to his boss, in mortgages, with whom she also sleeps, and then betrays, for a young executive, Ned Stevens, in accounting, whom she quickly seduces. Each time Lily sleeps with someone new, the camera returns to the street outside and pans further up the skyscraper, tracking her climb up the corporate ladder.[19] Eventually, the vice president of the bank, J.P. Carter, takes her as his mistress, but the young executive in accounting, Stevens, refuses to give her up, and when he arrives at her apartment to ask Lily to marry him and finds Carter there as well, he kills Carter and himself. Stanwyck, in some of the finest acting in the film, overhears the shots in the next room and, face betraying no emotion, telephones the police and reports, blandly, "There's been an accident." Indeed.

Still using "men to get what she wants," as the cobbler instructed her to do in the original version of the film, Lily tells the bank's board of directors that after all the drama of the murder-suicide, she simply wants to start over in a new job somewhere else. To do so, she will sell her diary, which chronicles her salacious time at the bank, to the newspapers. Before the board of directors can agree to pay her off and prevent the scandal from going even more public, the new president of the bank, Courtland Trenholm, calls her bluff and offers her a job in the Paris branch of the bank, which Lily grudgingly accepts. Later, Trenholm visits Paris and finds Lily, to his surprise, thriving at her new job. He, too, falls in love with her, and perhaps sensing that she can climb no higher, Lily does not sleep with Trenholm, holding out instead for a marriage proposal, which, when it comes, she accepts. As if to confirm that the marriage represents the final rung on her climb to the top, when the couple returns to New York City, the camera, hearkening back to earlier shots in which it tracks Lily as she rises up the skyscraper, pans upward to the top of another skyscraper, this time to the penthouse Lily and Trenholm now occupy.

Upon returning to New York, Trenholm learns that his bank has failed, and that the board of directors has made him the scapegoat. He is indicted, and he tells Lily that he needs a million dollars to save himself from jail. He asks her to cash in the gifts—stocks, bonds, jewelry—he has lavished on her. Lily coldly refuses. She abandons Trenholm and boards a ship bound for Paris. While waiting for it to embark, though, she changes her mind. She races back to the apartment, where she finds that Trenholm has shot himself. She announces that she is ready to "sacrifice everything" for him, and in the ambulance on the way to the hospital, she neglects her suitcase full of money and jewels. "None of it matters, now," she tells the attendant. Instead, she exchanges a smile with Trenholm as he awakes. Despite herself, Lily may have found true love after all.

The original version of the film stops here, but the censors, annoyed that the film ends well for someone as immoral and out for gold as Lily, demanded an unhappy ending for her. She must, the head of the Production Code wrote to the studio, be "stripped of her wealth and social standing."[20] Therefore, the studio tacked on a new ending, in which the board of directors of the bank discusses the ultimate fate of Trenholm and Lily. They "sacrificed everything they had for the bank," one executive says. "They haven't a cent," another states, and then recounts that Trenholm is "working as a laborer in the steel mill." In the last lines of the movie, which play out over an image of smoking chimneys, one of the executives dourly informs the other that Trenholm and Lily "are working out their happiness together," which sounds, as the censors no doubt hoped it would, more like a prison sentence than anything resembling happiness. In any case, Lily has indeed been stripped of her wealth and social standing. She is back, more or less, where she started. So great are her sins that Trenholm, who as far as I can tell has done no wrong, must suffer with her.

At first glance, *Baby Face* might look like a love story, especially in its unedited version. In the original ending, as Lily waits for the ship to embark for Paris, she plays a record and sees the faces of one after the other of all the men she has seduced and betrayed. She also hears, which we overhear in voiceover, Trenholm saying, "I know you've known other men before me, probably more than one. But I don't care." Lily, we conclude, has come to realize the error of her exploitative ways and, moreover, has fallen in love with Trenholm for forgiving her for those errors. Yet the censors, or the studio concerned about what the censors might object to, cut those parts, both the police line up of her past conquests and Trenholm's declaration of his indifference to the existence and number of her past lovers. As with other cuts it demanded, the censors seemed concerned about any scenes that explicitly showed the exchange of sex for favors. The film could imply these exchanges—it could do little else if it still wanted to make sense—but it could not show them, and that squeamishness about quid pro quos evidently extended to the explicit itemization of men in the scene aboard the steamship and Trenholm's forgiveness of those relationships. Whatever the reason, as a result of the cuts, the ending—Lily's change of heart—seemed even less believable than it might have otherwise. Those cuts, ironically enough, ruin the film as a love story. They make Lily's love for Trenholm seem completely unmotivated. As a review for the *New York Times*, titled "A Woman's Wiles," put it, "Once aboard the steamship... [Lily] suffers a change of heart and is supposed to do her one good deed of the story."[21] That "supposed" drips with incredulity—and rightly so. Few, to judge from the reviews, left the film thinking that Lily loved anyone but herself. In saving viewers from sex, the censors robbed them of love.

In truth, though, even if the original version of the film had stood, Lily's change of heart would not have seemed especially convincing. After all, the film spent the first hour or more of its seventy-five minutes extolling the virtues of using men to get what you want. "Crush out all sentiment," the cobbler writes Lily in the original version of the film, quoting Nietzsche, and the film succeeds so well at crushing out sentiment that it cannot, in the end, bring sentiment back to life. As a more recent critic has written, both "the heroine's final sacrifice and her punishment remain anomalies, at odds with the repetition"—of the exploitative relationship between the sexes—"which governs the progression of the narrative as a whole."[22] In other words, the romantic ending, even if allowed to stand, offers too little, too late.

The first thing to notice about a film like *Baby Face*, then, is—despite the ending—the deeply cynical attitude it takes toward love. True, Lily takes advantage of the men who simply lust after her, which does not seem so shocking, but she also takes advantage of the men—Ned Stevens and Courtland Trenholm—who plainly love her. For Lily, however, not to put to fine a point on it, love is for suckers. When Trenholm pleads with her to turn over her wealth to aid his legal defense, she explains that she is not "soft." The implication, of course, is that love, and the sacrifices and kindness that go with it, is for the weak, the sentimental, an implication that the ending, try as it might—and it does not try very hard—cannot take back. The second thing to notice about a film like *Baby Face*, then, is that it exists at all. The studio that made it, Warner Brothers, guessed that moviegoers had a taste for such films, and to judge by its passable returns at the box office, they were not wrong.[23] To some degree, its success suggests that Americans shared Lily's cynicism about love, or, what amounts to the same thing, they could understand and sympathize with it. Perhaps they could because of the final thing to note about a film like *Baby Face*, which is that it is not alone. Warner Brothers made the film to keep up with the success of *Red-Headed Woman*, a Metro-Goldwyn-Mayer film starring Jean Harlow—with an uncredited story by F. Scott Fitzgerald and a script by Anita Loos, of *Gentlemen Prefer Blondes* fame—which, while slightly more comic than *Baby Face*, nevertheless takes an even more ruthless attitude toward love. (In that film, the calculating heroine not only is *not* stripped of her wealth and social standing, but she comes out very much on top as a result of her willingness to trade on lust and love.) And during the first years of the Great Depression, Mae West made still more comic—and less judgmental and more popular—versions of the gold-digging woman film. Indeed, although its plot somewhat belies its billing, the title of a 1933 Warner Brothers film, *Gold Diggers of 1933*, which was followed by *Gold Diggers of 1935*, *Gold Diggers of 1937*, and *Gold Diggers in Paris* (1938), testifies to the ubiquity of the trope.

Such films, however, would not last—or not last in their scandalous form, anyway. (*Gold Diggers of 1933* includes one of the strangest—and lewdest—musical sequences in Hollywood history, a Busby Berkeley song and dance sequence called "Pettin' in the Park.") Under the heading "Sex," the Production Code, drafted in 1930 and increasingly enforced as a result of films like *Baby Face*, stated that the "sanctity of the institution of marriage and the home shall be upheld," and "Pictures shall not show that low forms of sex relationship are the accepted or common thing." It added warnings for the proper handling of adultery, scenes of passion, and seduction or rape. None, as the Code said of adultery, should be "presented attractively."[24] Of course, that is just what *Baby Face* and other films did; or, if they did not quite present adultery and seduction attractively, they did what amounted to the same thing, presenting the institution of marriage, and the love that supposedly secured that marriage, cynically. They suggested that love and marriage were for the "soft," for suckers, and could—and perhaps should—be exploited for advantage.

On the one hand, such films, and their success at the box office, reveal a widespread cynicism about love, or at least a willingness to entertain it and be entertained by it. On the other hand, the effort to censor such films reveals an anxiety about love, a feeling that it needed to be safeguarded. Either way, whether open to attack or in need of defense by Hollywood moralists, love had wandered out into the open; it was exposed, and, perhaps, more vulnerable than it had ever been before. Fiction writers would swoop in for the kill.

"Married. That's What We All Ought to Do."

When it comes to dramatizing first the unraveling and then the sordidness of love, few books can match the pair of novels John O'Hara published in the mid-1930s, *Appointment in Samarra* (1934) and *BUtterfield 8* (1935).

O'Hara has less of a following today than he once did. His first novel, *Appointment in Samarra*, which follows a thirty-year-old man, Julian English, as he drunkenly sabotages every part of his life, not least his marriage, had reviewers placing O'Hara in the same class as Hemingway and Fitzgerald. His second novel, *BUtterfield 8*, though it sold nearly as well as his first, disappointed those expectations, as did each of the dozen or so novels that followed, which may explain why he no longer gets mentioned in the same class as Hemingway and Fitzgerald.

If *Appointment in Samarra* offers a tale of love falling apart, *BUtterfield 8* (1935), O'Hara's second novel, published just a year later, adds to that plot the story of love failing to cohere. O'Hara based the novel, and especially his main character, Gloria Wondrous, on one of the biggest tabloid stories of the 1930s: the mysterious drowning death of twenty-five-year-old Starr Faithfull.

On June 8, 1931, Faithfull's body washed ashore in Long Island, setting off a horribly public scramble to discover how she died and who, if anyone, had killed her. When found, Faithfull had on a silk dress but nothing underneath, and she had bruises all over her body. An autopsy revealed that she had taken—or someone had given her—Veronal, a commercially sold barbiturate; that she had recently had sex; and that her lungs were filled with sand. The last detail suggested that she had not drowned out at sea but near the shore, where she could inhale sand as she took her last breaths, perhaps as someone held her head under water.[25]

Over the coming weeks, investigators tracked Faithfull's whereabouts over the two or three days before her death, and newspapers dug up her seamy and tragic past. A month before her death, she had been committed to (and shortly thereafter released from) Bellevue Psychiatric Hospital after police found her naked, drunk, and badly beaten in a Manhattan hotel room with a man she had just met. In the week before her death, she had, as she had in the past, attended several bon voyage parties aboard outgoing ocean liners. And shortly after her death, police discovered a diary, in which she had recorded sexual liaisons with nearly two-dozen different men, including one A.J.P., which apparently referred to her uncle, the former mayor of Boston, Andrew J. Peters. The diary revealed that, beginning when Faithfull was just eleven years old, and for years afterward, Peters, in hotel rooms and on automobile trips, had drugged the young girl with ether and then had sex with her. Faithfull told her family of the abuse in 1926, and the next year her stepfather, Stanley Faithfull, negotiated a settlement with Peters in which he would pay the family $20,000 in exchange for their silence. Over the following years, and apparently days before her death, the family extorted still more money from Peters, adding to suspicions that he—or someone in his employ—had murdered Faithfull in order to stop the blackmail.

During the investigation, however, a ship's doctor, George Jamison-Carr, returned to New York with three letters Faithfull had written to him just days before her death. Faithfull had fallen in love with Carr—they had met when he had to pump alcohol from her stomach after one of the bon voyage parties—but Carr did not love her. The letters detailed her disappointment at her unrequited love and her determination to commit suicide, "to end my worthless, disorderly bore of an existence—before I ruin anyone else's life as well."[26] With plenty of leads but no charges to bring, and with the letters to hand, investigators settled on suicide as the cause of her death, an explanation that others, including her stepfather, never accepted.

Eventually, the tabloids moved on to other scandals, and the world forgot about Starr Faithfull, until, that is, O'Hara borrowed details from her life for Gloria Wondrous, the main character of *BUtterfield 8*. (The title refers to the name of the telephone exchange for the Upper East Side, where several of the characters in the novel live.) From start to finish, the novel wallows in the squalid world of speakeasies in the late Prohibition era. O'Hara seems to delight in trying to shock his readers with the depravity of the characters that people that world. Throughout the novel, alcohol is consumed like water. Others prefer—or supplement their alcohol with—cocaine. Women consume pornography or, in the case of Gloria, pose for it. Several characters, including Weston Liggett, the older, wealthy, married Yale man who sleeps with and then falls in love with Gloria, have contracted venereal disease—gonorrhea, syphilis—and those who have not, like Gloria, very much expect to. Gloria, the narrator writes, has slept with "many men," and the novel hints that she has sold sex for money; even when the exchange is not explicit, she nevertheless thinks of her body in terms of what it can fetch in the open market. "You haven't enough money to own me," she tells Weston when, early in the novel, he proposes to make her his mistress. "Last year, last fall, that is, I got a pretty good idea how much I was worth," which is more than Weston can afford. She does not stay with the wealthier man who gave her the idea how much she was worth, though, because he is "peculiar" and, sexually, prefers "fancy variations."[27] In passing, the narrator remarks of one speakeasy denizen, "June Blake, show girl and model," who "after four days was still cheerful over winning nearly a thousand dollars on

Twenty Grand," a horse. An acquaintance places the bet for her in exchange for her procuring for him "a certain virgin he wanted to know better." "Was it her fault," the narrator asks, blithely, "that the virgin was at this minute in a private hospital?"[28] In addition to her occasional prostitution and constant promiscuity, Gloria, we learn, has had three abortions. She has had sex in front of others, and watched while others had sex. And the novel hints at what it believes is worse that it cannot tell. ("The two virgins. The dwarf.")[29] Near the end of the novel, Gloria compares New York in the early 1930s to Rome, except, she observes, "Rome never saw parties like that."[30]

Worse, all but unreadable, in fact, are the scenes that document Gloria's childhood sexual abuse, first at the hands of a family friend, Major Boam, and then a school principal, Dr. Reddington, whom she meets on a train when she is fourteen years old. O'Hara has the disturbing habit of switching into the point of view of the abuser in such scenes, which indirectly implicates readers in the abuse, making the scenes even more unbearable. "It was all too easy," he writes of Reddington and his seduction of a fourteen-year-old Gloria. "Two days later she called at his hotel in the afternoon," and "within a month he had her sniffing ether and loving it. It, and everything that went on in that room."[31] In truth, Gloria does not love ether or what goes in the hotel room, but Reddington has convinced himself that she does.

Gloria's promiscuity and despair, the novel suggests, owes to this early abuse, which makes sense, but others in the novel, nearly everyone else in fact, behaves as badly or worse than she does without, presumably, a similar history of abuse.[32] In any case, and despite its mood of hedonism and depravity, love has not gone completely missing from the novel. Gloria's friend from boarding school, Ann, falls in love and gets engaged. Meanwhile, Gloria's closest friend, Eddie Brunner, also thinks about asking his girlfriend, Norma, to marry him, even though he "distrusted romance" and has a history of trading one girlfriend for another.[33] Finally, and perhaps most importantly, though their relationship starts as a one night stand, Weston Liggett does fall in love with Gloria, and Gloria supposedly comes to love him back, even if the ambiguous ending of the novel puts that love in doubt.

So love does exist in the novel, for some, at times, but the novel leaves the stronger impression that the sordidness that surrounds characters, and that characters surround themselves with, has disqualified them from conventional love. Like the venereal disease that circulates through the speakeasies and wild parties, such sordidness has tainted those who come into contact with it, cutting them off from love altogether. That is particularly the case for Gloria. She concludes that the life she imagines for her friend, Ana—more or less happily married with children—"was not her way of living."[34] She has a similar admiration for—and alienation from—a police dog in a neighbor's yard that has given birth to a litter of puppies. Gloria, however, fears her three abortions have made it impossible for her to have children. Similarly, she convinces herself that her sexual history has made her ineligible for love and the institutions of love, marriage and motherhood.

Then there is her relationship with Eddie, whom she meets after he loans her money to escape a tryst that goes wrong at a hotel where he clerks. (Gloria is supposed to watch a man she has just met and a female prostitute have sex.) Despite or perhaps because of these beginnings, Gloria and Eddie become close friends, but their friendship always lives under the shadow of sex, which, both are convinced, would ruin their platonic love for each other. As Gloria explains midway through the novel, when she and Eddie almost give in to temptation,

> it's awful when you think that you've stayed with so many men and made such a mess of your life, and then someone you really want to stay with because you love him, that person is the one person you mustn't stay with because if you do he immediately becomes like the rest, and you don't want him to become like the rest. The thing he has that the rest haven't is that you haven't stayed with him.[35]

In other words, for Gloria, as for Eddie, sex and love mutually exclude each other. The former has nothing to do with—would ruin—the latter. Late in the novel, Eddie thinks,

> Maybe he was wrong (he admitted) but always it seemed to him as though he and Gloria were many many times on the verge of a great romance, one for the ages, or at least a match for the love and anguish of Amory and Rosalind in "This Side of Paradise"; and Frederick and Catherine in "A Farewell to Arms."[36]

Such storybook romance, however, belongs to another era. In the world of *BUtterfield 8*, only platonic love can last.[37]

The belief that promiscuity invalidates conventional love may explain the ambiguous ending of the novel, which has irritated readers and critics alike since its original publication. Despite her doubts about her qualifications for such a life, Gloria vows "to be moral," to, in essence, settle down, and the early results of the experiment seem positive.[38] She starts by trying to escape the city on a short boat trip. Weston, however, follows her onto the boat.

He tells her that he loves her, that he and his wife will divorce, asks Gloria to marry him, and she says yes. Gloria tells Weston that she has found "out that there is only one life for a woman," and it is not "the kind of life she has led."[39] She even refuses to sleep with Weston in his ship cabin because it is so "cheap and vulgar," and too evocative of the life she wishes to leave behind.

All that would be fine, and the start of a happy ending for Weston, Gloria, and love in the 1930s, except for the ending of the novel, which throws it all overboard. Gloria leaves Weston's cheap and vulgar cabin. Disappointed, he lingers for a bit and then follows her onto the uppermost deck of the ship, which, the narrator has portentously warned, has a dangerously low railing. When Gloria sees Weston, she "got up and ran forward. Then she stopped and looked around." Weston calls, "Oh, all right," and turns to leave. Halfway down the stairs, he hears a scream, and "he looked down at the water just in time to see Gloria getting sucked in by the side of the boat."[40] Her body is crushed in the paddle wheel. Weston thinks he causes her death because in trying to run away from him, she accidentally runs overboard, and since it all happens so fast, and the scene plays out from his perspective, readers never learn otherwise.

Understandably, few liked—or like—this ending. At the time, Malcolm Cowley, writing in the *New Republic*, complained of a "slovenly handled death scene." Gloria "has the right to die tragically, as the result of some conflict or deliberate choice. But Mr. O'Hara denies her that right and makes her die by accident."[41] Cowley is right, of course, but if one wanted to defend O'Hara, one could argue that it does not much matter how Gloria dies, so long as she is prevented from realizing the conventional marriage plot from which she feels disqualified. Indeed, O'Hara's point seems to be that that ending is not available for Gloria. The plot is defunct. Something, and it does not matter what, would stop her. In a sense, then, the more arbitrary—the more accidental—the ending the better.[42] *Deus ex machina.* Although in this case the Gods appear out of nowhere not to save a character but to damn her—unless, that is, like O'Hara you think death preferable to marriage.

In the closing pages of the novel, Jimmy Malloy, an Irish journalist and John O'Hara stand-in, tells Gloria's friend, Eddie Brunner: "Married. That's what we all ought to do. You too." Eddie says he is going to marry, and he may. Jimmy insists that he will marry, too, but it seems doubtful. "I have a novel half almost finished," he tells Eddie. "As soon as I finish it and get the dough and stay on the wagon three months."[43] In other words, never.

Marriage, in the novel, is infinitely postponed. It does not belong to the world O'Hara describes. Nor, for that matter, does love. It cannot survive the nearly ubiquitous sordidness that surrounds it, and if it does, it cannot survive the low railings that lie in wait, ready to cut it off at the knees.

Double Solitaire

Below, I explain why films like *Baby Face* and novels like *BUtterfield 8* may have depicted love so bleakly during the early years of the Great Depression, but before I do I want to look at one more work, this from later in the Depression, indeed, published as the United States began to contemplate its role in the war then ravaging Europe. When it comes to the sordid during the 1930s, after *BUtterfield 8*, almost anything else will seem tame, even a one-night stand on a cross-country train, the subject of Mary McCarthy's memorable 1941 short story "The Man in the Brooks Brothers Shirt." Yet while that story may lack the Rome by way of Manhattan decadence of O'Hara and his novel, it nevertheless has a quieter if equally devastating account of love during the Great Depression.

McCarthy's story originally appeared in the July 1941 issue of the *Partisan Review*, the anti-Stalinist leftist journal, and McCarthy included it the following year in her collection of linked short stories, *The Company She Keeps*. The story has an outwardly simple plot. A divorced young woman, Margaret Sargent, is traveling by train from New York to Portland, Oregon to tell her family of her engagement to a young man back in New York. Somewhere in the middle of the country, she meets an older, married, professional man, Mr. Breen. (He of the Brooks Brothers shirt.) When the young woman first sees Breen, of whose bald head the greater part "appeared to be pink," she decides that "he looked . . . like a middle-aged baby, like a young pig, like something in a seed catalogue. In any case, he was plainly Out of the Question."[44] Yet just as plainly he is not. Despite their outward differences—she is a writer for the liberal magazines, he is an executive at an abhorrent Little Steel company—the two drink and talk into the night. And even though as "the whisky went down in the bottle, his face took on a more and more porcine look that became so distasteful to her that she could hardly meet his gaze," the young woman soon wakes up in bed with him.

The passage that follows—when she recalls the previous night—describes a tryst that has all the romance of the typist home at teatime section of

The Waste Land. Songs are sung. Other passengers are disturbed. The heroine fights off the man's advances until, feeling tired and kind, she succumbs. "Then there had been something peculiar about the love-making itself," she recalls, but without being able to recall what, exactly. Then she can. "There were (Oh holy Virgin!) four-letter words that she had been forced to repeat, and, at the climax, a rain of blows on her buttocks that must surely (dear God!) have left bruises."[45] Her abjection continues when she tries to keep the evening from becoming still more public. (The porter who made up the bed already knows she spent the night.) Hoping to return to her berth before anyone else on the train notices she did not sleep there, she crawls around on the floor of the man's berth in the dark clumsily trying to reassemble her clothes without waking him. She finds most of them, but the man wakes before she can leave. "You can't go," he says, "I love you. I'm crazy about you. This is the most wonderful thing that's ever happened to me." "Kiss me," he insists. She does not respond in kind. "I have to throw up," she says, and does.[46]

More tawdry than sordid, as with *BUtterfield 8*, what matters is less the sordid (or the tawdry) alone than how either relates to love. The story leaves readers with two lingering questions. Why, if she finds him so distasteful, does the young woman sleep with the man in the Brooks Brothers shirt? And why, after waking in his berth, and trying to flee, does she remain, indeed, does she sleep with the man again? As to the first question, why she ever sleeps with him, at first she claims she was "tight," but as the man rightly points out, "A girl like you doesn't let a man have her just because she's drunk."[47] And she certainly cannot claim drunkenness in the morning, when she sleeps with him again. Rather, the answer to both questions seems to be that throughout their liaison, the young woman invents fictions about herself and her companion that lead her straight into his arms. The story is light on romance in the sense of love, but teeming with romance in the sense of picturesque falsehoods. To put it another way, the young woman is a character in a story who lives her life like she is a character in a story. In essence, she talks herself into bed.

After they meet, but before they sleep together, the man insults her political allies by declaring, "You're all nuts." "The man's vulgarity," she thinks, "was undeniable." Thus "it had been possible to stay in the compartment," she reasons, "only on the basis of one of two assumptions, both of them literary (*a*) that the man was a frustrated socialist, (*b*) that he was a frustrated man of sensibility, a kind of Sherwood Anderson. But the man's own personality kept popping up, perversely, like a jack-in-the-box, to confound these theories."[48]

Nevertheless, these insights into the man's irrepressible vulgarity do not stop her from inventing still more literary theories about him. Later, she convinces herself that this "man *was* the frontier," a figure, like her Oregon father, from the Golden Age of American imperialism. "She saw the man now," she tells herself, "as a man without a country, and felt a desire to reinstate him. But where? The best she could do was communicate to him a sense of his own isolation and grandeur. She could ensconce him in the dignity of sadness." And thus does she glide "all the way from aversion to tenderness." Of course, the man is no such thing, and he feels no such things, a point underscored by the opening sentence of the next paragraph, which instead of ensconcing him in the dignity of sadness, flatly states, "Meanwhile, the man had grown almost boisterously merry."[49]

When the man refuses to act the blank slate for her literary theories, the young woman starts inventing theories about herself, ones that make it possible for her to stay with him and, ultimately, to do much more than that. Late in the night, the two discuss their love lives: he feels his wife does not know him and vice versa, and she feels guilt and shame about betraying her first husband. As a result, tears "came to her eyes again. The man's life and her own life seemed unutterably tragic," which, of course, they aren't, except when viewed through an empty whiskey bottle.[50] Such inventions, however, keep her in the man's compartment and ultimately get her into his bed.

The young woman saves her biggest literary inventions, however, for the day after the tryst. Indeed, her metaphors all but get the better of her. After she vomits, the man helps her laugh off the situation and takes her in his arms. Then she "held herself in his stony embrace, and felt indeed like a rock being lapped by some importunate wave."[51] "At that the image suddenly turned and presented another facet to her: dear Jesus, she told herself, frightened, I'm really as hard as nails." To prove otherwise, she returns the man's embraces and decides to sleep with him again, "the glow of self-sacrifice illuminat[ing] her." "This, she thought decidedly, is going to be the only real act of charity I have ever performed in my life; it will be the only time I have ever given anything when it honestly hurt me to do so." Waiting "for the indignity to be over," she thinks "that for once she was really and truly good, not hard or heartless at all." Once again, however, a paragraph break and a shift in point of view throw cold water on her melodramatic fable of a "white lamb on an altar." "You need a bath," the man says when he has finished, evidently unimpressed with and ungrateful for her supposed martyrdom.[52]

In the bath, the young woman changes tack, turning the affair into a political fable, wherein she represents "the citadel of socialist virginity" and "the man's whole assault on her . . . an incidental atrocity in the long class war."[53] But none of these fables, especially the last, convinces for long. So, in the end, the young woman settles on the unlikeliest story of all: that she genuinely loves the man. "All day she believed she had been acting a tragic part in something called *One Perfect Night*, but slowly, without her being aware of it, the counterfeit had passed into the true." Offering a variation on the French phrase that to understand all is to forgive all, the young woman claims that to understand all—as, she thinks, she now understands everything about the man's tragic life—is to love all, and, thus, as she says to the man, "I love you . . . I didn't before, but now I do."[54]

For most people, however, love entails more than understanding. At minimum, and perhaps by definition, it must include fondness between the lovers and a desire to spend time with each other. That makes the exchange that follows between the man and the woman—and the definition of love that it entails—both unusual and unusually illustrative of the hard times that love had fallen on during the Great Depression. After they sleep together the first time, the man insists that the woman not get off the train in Sacramento but remain on it with him through to San Francisco and, uncertainly, into some future life together. Later, after she tells him that she loves him, he asks, naturally, "Then you won't get off the train . . . ?" To which she replies, bizarrely, though, she claims, truthfully, "Oh, yes . . . I'll certainly get off. One reason I love you, I suppose, is because I *am* getting off."[55] In effect, the young woman says I love you because I will never see you again. To borrow the title of McCarthy's book, she loves him, but his is company she no longer wishes to keep.

At first glance, this confession of love makes no sense. Love demands proximity, the desire of those who love each other to remain close to each other. By contrast, the young woman's confession of love implies that love cannot endure proximity, that it survives—if it survives—at a distance. In other words, the story suggests, love cannot bear the presence of the beloved. Oddly enough, the man confirms that sense of love. "And one reason I'm going to let you do it," he says to the young woman when she tells him that she is getting off the train, "is because you love me."[56] If she stayed, he seems to understand, she would not love him. And he may not love her. Perhaps their relationship would turn into his current marriage, or her first marriage. "Hell," the man adds, "it's a funny thing, but I'm so happy now that I don't care whether I ever see you again. I probably won't feel that way after you've gone. Right now I think I can live in this one day for the rest of my life."[57] The point of the story seems to be that he will have to. Whether she stays or goes, they will only love each other—if you believe they love each other—for a day. If love, like an hibiscus flower, begins to wilt as soon as it blooms, then you can only enjoy it in the brief moment of its flowering, and then, perhaps, only in memory.

That epiphany clarifies what would otherwise remain a mystery in the story: the seemingly unmotivated decision on the part of the young woman to call off her engagement. "Her trip home seemed peculiarly pointless," the narrator writes after she has left the train in Sacramento, "for she had known for the last twelve hours that she was never going to marry the young man back in New York."[58] Perhaps the young woman concludes that since she loves the man in the Brooks Brothers shirt—and can allow herself to sleep with him with so little fuss—she cannot also love her fiancé; or perhaps, as the man in the Brooks Brothers shirt thinks, she still loves her first husband. The more likely explanation, though, is the rather sour conclusion about love that develops over the course of the story. In short, it never lasts.

Early on in the story, the young woman compares love to "a wonderful slow game of double solitaire." In double solitaire, each player has his or her own deck of cards and layout piles, but they share foundation piles. (The four stacks that start with the aces of each suit.) By comparison, McCarthy does not mean that the players—that is, the lovers—never interact with each other. Just the opposite. The metaphor draws out how lovers collaborate and gradually come to reveal—as from a hidden deck—more and more about themselves. The game, however, slow and wonderful as it is, nevertheless ends, and "nothing that happened afterwards," the narrator writes, "counted for anything beside those first few hours of self-revelation."[59] In other words, love means falling in love, and if you are not falling in love, you are falling out of love. Unlike *Baby Face* or *BUtterfield 8*, "The Man in the Brooks Brothers Suit" does not emphasize the hazards, futility, or impossibility of love, only its utter ephemerality.

Love Stories

I admit that the works surveyed above offer a more disenchanted view of love than would other works of the 1930s. At the movie houses, for example, even in the midst of the pre-Code era, heterosexual love did not disappear entirely from screens. With genders reversed, one film, *Queen Christina* (1933), even prefigured the unlikely love story of King Edward and Wallis Simpson. It starred Greta Garbo as the 17th-century Swedish queen who abdicates her throne for the man she loves. In fiction, too, you could find far happier love stories even if you just stuck to the works and genres explored elsewhere in this book. Helen Hull's *Hardy Perennial* (1933), discussed in the chapter on fear, is principally a love story. Hull's main character, Cornelia Prescott, fends off proposals for affairs, forgives the affair of her husband, and sticks by him when the Depression undercuts him.

Or consider the pulps, which also appear in the chapter on fear. I do not mean, to be sure, the stories that appeared in *Weird Fiction*. (If you trust H.P. Lovecraft, a lifelong bachelor, most marriages end up in live burials.) Rather, I mean pulp magazines like *Love Story*, which, according to the pulp historian Quentin Reynolds, had a weekly circulation of about 600,000 in the early 1930s.[60] The magazine thrived during that decade under the direction of its legendary editor, Daisy Bacon. "Miss Bacon," Reynolds wrote in his 1955 history of Street & Smith, the great pulp publisher behind *Love Story*, "had an infallible instinct for choosing stories that would make the average woman forget her unhappy financial state, her dreary husband or her aching heart. Daisy's own slim finger was never away from the feminine pulse of the nation; she knew just what girls of all ages wanted."[61] To judge from the success of *Love Story* and its imitators, what many women wanted—and what films like *Baby Face* and novels like *BUtterfield 8* did not give them—were romance and marriage plots. In which case, perhaps the reports of love's death during the Great Depression were greatly exaggerated. Or, as Reynolds seems to suggest, perhaps *Love Story* sold as well as it did precisely because love in the real world fell on such hard times. In that case, *Love Story* offered in fiction what languished in real life.

The latter seems like the more convincing explanation, because, though this will hardly count as persuasive evidence, when it comes to love during the 1930s, the decade does indeed feel different: more sordid, yes, but also, for a time, more cynical, more hopeless. If so, it remains to explain why. Why should love have followed the economy into hard times?

The likeliest explanation is that love lost its economic foundation. In the most scandalous chapter of Tom Kromer's 1935 novel *Waiting for Nothing*, for example, the narrator, a young homeless man perpetually in search of "three hots and a flop," allows himself to be picked up by Mrs. Carter, a wealthy transgender woman universally referred to by other characters in the book as "queer." When they meet, Mrs. Carter asks Kromer if he has a girlfriend. "You have to have dough to get a girl," he responds. "Girls are expensive. If you haven't got any dough, you haven't got any girl."[62] Later, he is even pithier: "No dough, no girl."[63]

Kromer arrives at a formula that would come to haunt men and women in the 1930s. Indeed, what goes for the character in *Waiting for Nothing* goes for an entire culture, though one can rephrase it slightly: no dough, no love. As I mentioned at the outset of the chapter, as the economy collapsed, so too did marriage rates. Of course, marriage rates offer an imprecise proxy for love. Couples might fall in love and not marry or delay marriage. And, as I suggest below, other kinds of love not eligible for marriage flourished during the 1930s. Nevertheless, for many during the 1930s, love and marriage went hand in hand, and when one fell, the other seems to have fallen too. Figure 6.2 tracks the number of marriages per 1,000 people beginning in 1918.[64] As it happens, that swift drop beginning in 1930 follows almost perfectly the unemployment rate. Basically, from year to year, for each additional five points in the unemployment rate, the marriage rate drops by roughly one point.[65] As Jane Austen might have put it, during the Great

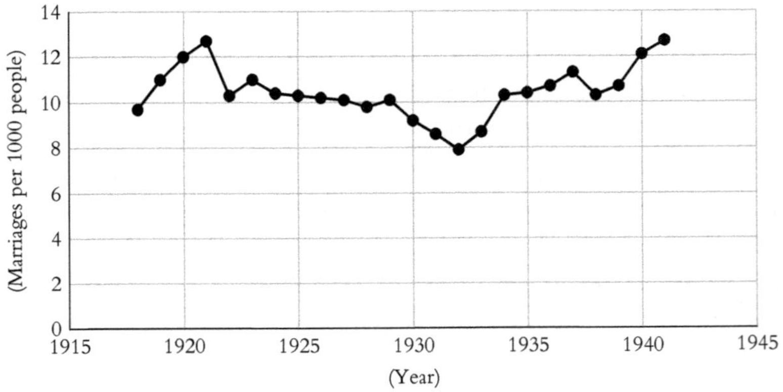

Figure 6.2. Marriages per 1,000 people, 1918–41.

Depression it quickly became a truth universally acknowledged that a single man in want of a good fortune must not be in possession of a wife. In other words, in the face of an uncertain economic future, couples everywhere postponed marriage—assuming, that is, as the one-night stand Kromer has with another down-and-out woman in the novel suggests, that they formed more than transitory couples in the first place.

Of course, the marriage rate dropped for other reasons, too. As I explain below, after a postwar boom in 1920, the marriage rate began a slow but steady drop throughout the 1920s, a decline that had to result from factors other than unemployment or an economic depression. Those other factors no doubt included greater opportunities, educational and professional, for women, and, as I also mention below, the invention of more reliable birth control. Yet those factors obtained throughout the period, including after the marriage rate recovered to its pre-Depression levels. Moreover, these gradual, long-term factors would not explain the abrupt drops in the marriage rate, like those from 1929 to 1932 and from 1937 to 1938, that mirror, almost perfectly, equally abrupt drops in the economy.

Nor would these long-term trends explain the sense of infinitely postponed love that turned into one of the defining features of the era. In "Ramblin' Round," Woodie Guthrie sings that he wishes he could marry and settle down but poverty condemns him to a life of eternal—and solitary—wandering.[66] In one scene from Clifford Odets's unexpectedly popular *Waiting for Lefty* (1935), a young woman and her fiancé, one of the taxi drivers at the heart of the play, cannot marry—and so part ways—because he does not make enough money. And in *How to Win and Hold a Husband* (1939), the nationally syndicated advice columnist Dorothy Dix observed:

> there is a depression in the matrimonial market as well as in the stock market. Economic conditions make it impossible for many men to afford to marry. Every year men cling tighter to their bachelor freedom and economy, and no one can deny that prospects look gloomy for many young women who have set their hearts on getting wedding rings.[67]

By this logic, the economy is a leading indicator of marriage, which is a lagging indicator of love. All suffered during the Great Depression.[68] In 1936, a young editor at *Vogue* named Marjorie Hillis published *Live Alone and Like It: A Guide for the Extra Woman*. It became an unlikely bestseller.[69]

You can approach this explanation another way, by working backwards from the argument Lee Edelman famously makes in *No Future: Queer Theory and the Death Drive*. In a heteronormative culture, Edelman claims, one ruled by what he calls reproductive futurism, the child "has come to embody for us the telos of the social order and come to be seen as the one for whom that order is held in perpetual trust." "We are no more able to conceive of a politics without a fantasy of the future than we are able to conceive of a future without the figure of the Child."[70] In other words, as he sharply puts it, "the future is kid stuff." By contrast, queerness—because it has nothing to do with the child—represents the death drive, the joyful refusal to reproduce: "the act of resisting enslavement to the future in the name of having a life."[71]

As it happens, the Great Depression provides something of a natural experiment for Edelman's theory. In chapter 12 of *The General Theory of Employment, Interest, and Money* (1936), John Maynard Keynes emphasized the essential uncertainty, even incomprehensibility of the future. (He speaks of "the dark forces of time and ignorance which envelop our future.")[72] The incomprehensibility of the future, as the introduction to my earlier chapter on righteousness suggests, emerged as a common theme of the Great Depression. ("He could no longer plan," Sinclair Lewis writes of his main character in *It Can't Happen Here* (1935), "for himself or for his dependents, as the citizens of this once unsettled country had planned since 1620. Why, their whole lives had been predicated on the privilege of planning.")[73] Or consider the title of Kromer's novel, *Waiting for Nothing*, or its episodic structure, wherein the plot of each chapter unfolds over a single day and bears virtually no relation to what happens on other days or in other chapters of the book. There, as elsewhere, the horizon of the future is reduced to a single day. Or recall that in her letter to Dr. Carr, the shipboard surgeon, Starr Faithfull explained her reasons for suicide thus: "I certainly have made a sordid futureless mess of it all."[74]

As the future became less knowable, less subject to planning, or even less of a viable possibility, the reign of the child, as Edelman might have predicted, was indeed weakened. Figure 6.3 tracks the birth rate per 1,000 people from 1922 to 1941.[75] It began to fall during the middle years of the 1920s, during the first Golden Age of contraception in the United States. (The invention of latex in 1920 revolutionized the manufacture of condoms.)[76] Yet after stabilizing in 1930, it plunged again. The fall of the child helps to explain what would otherwise remain one of the more curious features of Great Depression culture: the pervasive figure of the unwanted child. (The nationwide hunt first for the kidnapped infant son of the aviator Charles Lindbergh and then for the kidnapper is perhaps the very famous

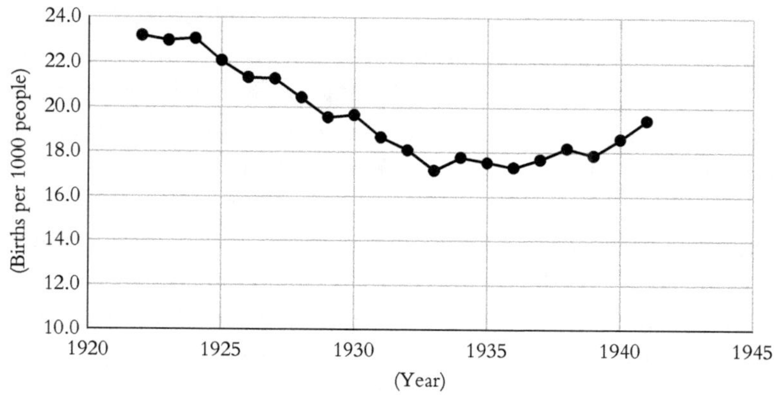

Figure 6.3. Live and still births per 1,000 people, 1922–41.

exception that proves the rule.) One chapter of *Waiting for Nothing* follows a mother as she tries to give away her infant. Although Harold Gray began drawing Little Orphan Annie comics in 1924, the comic only took off with the introduction of a radio show in 1930 and films in 1932 and 1938.[77] In *Boy and Girl Tramps of America* (1934), Thomas Minehan, a young sociologist at the University of Minnesota, studied the legions of forsaken children who wandered the countryside during the early years of the Great Depression.[78] As for the works examined in this chapter, in *Baby Face* children may as well not even exist. In *BUtterfield 8*, Gloria Wondrous has had three abortions. And despite one marriage and another on the horizon, the young woman in "The Man in the Brooks Brothers Shirt" does not give a thought to children. To my mind, though, nothing captures the pessimism about the future and the resulting indifference toward the child during the Great Depression better than the climax of Delmore Schwartz's 1937 short story "In Dreams Begin Responsibilities." Imagining that he is in a crowded theater watching a film of his parents' courtship at Coney Island some twenty years earlier, at the moment his father proposes to his mother, the protagonist shouts at the screen, "Don't do it! It's not too late to change your minds, both of you. Nothing good will come of it, only remorse, hatred, scandal, and two children whose characters are monstrous."[79] Schwartz turns infanticide into suicide.

As if to confirm further Edelman, as marriage and the child waned in importance, other forms of queer—or, at least, non-heterosexual—love arose in their place. As unemployment swelled in the United States, so too did those, like Woodie Guthrie and the narrator of *Waiting for Nothing*, who took to the roads and rails. Historically, tramp culture has proved more welcoming, notoriously so, to queer love than virtually any other subculture. (In 1897, Havelock Ellis and John Addington Symonds published *Sexual Inversion*, which included an appendix to the volume written by the American sociologist Josiah Flynt Willard with the title "Homosexuality among Tramps.")[80] Yet other, non-sexual forms of love arose and thrived during the Great Depression, too. That is, if *eros* (love, mostly of the sexual passion) and *storge* (the love of parents and children) diminished during the Great Depression, other forms of love—*agape* (charity) and *philia* (friendship)—flourished.[81] True, Christianity does not come through the Great Depression with a shining record. Its shelters and soup kitchens come in for near constant criticism in novels like *Waiting for Nothing*. (Kromer charges them with blaming the victim and making stingy charity contingent on expressions of faith.) Yet the Great Depression also witnessed some truly admirable examples of ordinary and extraordinary charity. The former were too numerous to document. The latter included the works of Dorothy Day, who published the first issue of *Catholic Worker* on May 1—it was dedicated, by the way, to "those who think there is no hope for the future"—and who, not long after, started the first "house of hospitality" on the Lower East Side in New York.[82] By the time she published *House of Hospitality* in 1939, Day and her fellow activist Peter Maurin had established dozens of houses of hospitality and communal farms.

As a form of love, however, friendship had an arguably even better record during the Great Depression than charity. The examples come from across the culture. On their surface, the proletarian literature of the decade concerns the strike or the revolution, but not terribly far below that surface it concerns the relationship between its protagonists and, more generally, between and among workers. More specifically, in his 1935 biography of Walt Whitman, the critic Newton Arvin championed the poet for preaching "the gospel of comradeship." ("Out of our nineteenth-century past, out of our American past," Arvin wrote, "we inherit nothing potentially more fruitful than the vision Walt Whitman had of an all-embracing solidarity—a solidarity lifted above the level of rational conviction and political convenience to the level of sensibility, of social practice, of culture in its largest sense.")[83] In the late 1930s, Alcoholics Anonymous, the subject of Chapter 7, turned the ideal of comradeship into a reality. In urging recovering alcoholics to seek out existing alcoholics, the group imagined a "Fellows of Alcoholics Anonymous." "Among [alcoholics] you will make lifelong friends. You will be bound to them with new and wonderful ties, for you will escape disaster together and you will commence shoulder to shoulder your common journey... You will learn the full meaning of 'Love thy neighbor as thyself.'"[84]

Disaster also brought people together. On his second expedition to the Antarctic in 1934, Admiral Richard E. Byrd spent five months alone at an advanced meteorological station. In his 1938 memoir, *Alone*, Byrd recounts how after setting up camp he almost immediately suffered severe carbon monoxide poisoning. Over the weeks that followed, he and his crew back at the base conducted an elaborate subterfuge over the radio, with Byrd trying to hide how sick he was, lest his crew try to make an ill-advised rescue attempt, and his crew, who slowly became conscious of how sick Byrd was, inventing pretexts to come rescue him. What starts as a Thoreau-like journey into solitude and a celebration of independence slowly develops into one of the most moving tributes to dependence and friendship in all of literature.[85]

Meanwhile, on film, in addition to dramatizing the plight of unwanted young men during the Great Depression, *Wild Boys of the Road* (1933) celebrates the solidarity among them, extending it across genders to the young woman (the actress Dorothy Coonan) who dresses as a boy to travel safely among them.[86] The Three Stooges, who made their first appearance in a 1934 film called, appropriately enough, *Woman Haters*, may torture each other for sport, but they repeatedly come to each other's rescue and never leave each other's sides over the forty-three short films they made over the rest of the decade.[87] (The Marx Brothers offer an even more charming version of this form of brotherly love.) And while one might doubt the sincerity of the friendships formed, keep in mind that one of the best-selling books of the entire decade was titled *How to Win Friends and Influence People*.[88]

To be sure, some writers, like Carson McCullers in the powerful novel *The Heart Is a Lonely Hunter* (1940), remained acutely aware of the misrecognition of the Other that could occur in all relationships, including and especially those between friends.[89] Still, as a whole, the decade revered friendship, even when in, say, John Steinbeck's *Of Mice and Men* (1937), one friend, George, has to mercifully murder another, Lennie, to spare him a worse death.

In sum, then, love—heterosexual love, anyway—followed the economy into hard times because, like new automobile sales or housing starts, it requires and is evidence of a solid economic foundation. When that economic foundation collapses, it can pull heterosexual love and its accessories (hope for the future, the child) down with it. Yet the lesson of the Great

Depression seems to be that other forms of love—charity, friendship—can arise on the ruins of that economic and erotic collapse.

People ... Still Gettin' Married

If you look again at Figure 6.2, which tracks the number of marriages per 1,000 people, you see that the marriage rate, following a postwar boom, begins a slow but noticeable decline not in the 1930s but in the 1920s. (The effect is even more pronounced if you examine marriages per single people aged 16–50.) Of course, the marriage rate still crashes come 1930, but it had tailed off for a while, and this decline matches what some observers had said about love and marriage even before the start of the Great Depression. In 1928, for example, the sociologist Ernest R. Groves published a volume titled *The Marriage Crisis*. Groves and others like him worried about the declining marriage rate, but they also worried about the phenomenon captured in Figure 6.4, which documents the number of divorces per 100 people.[90] From 1918 to 1928, it increased by 50 percent. In absolute terms, the number of divorces nearly doubled over that period. To Groves, the increase in the number of divorces, together with the decline in the number of new marriages, suggested that marriage "is in the throes of crisis."[91] "The confidence of youth in matrimony as the goal of happiness," he wrote, "has been, it must be confessed, roughly shaken of late, and there is abroad a considerable amount of pessimism with reference to the desirability of marriage."[92] Or, more colloquially, as someone told Groves, "Marriage is cracked."[93]

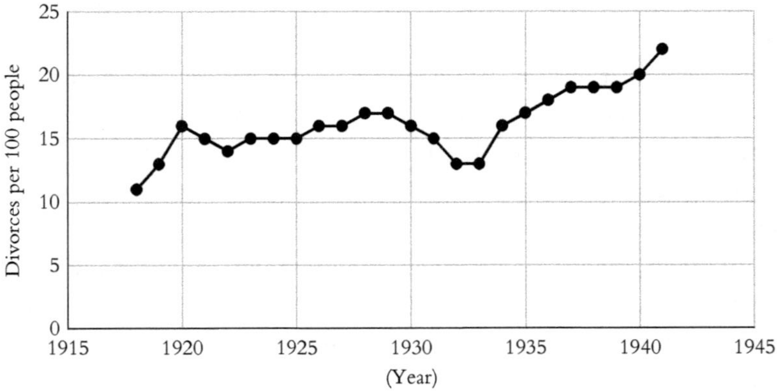

Figure 6.4. Divorces per 100 people, 1918–41.

Looking backward toward the recently completed decade, the popular historian Frederick Lewis Allen wrote in 1931 that everywhere Americans looked, but especially in the realm of sex and the relation between the sexes, they could see a "revolution in manners and morals."[94] Moreover, writers like F. Scott Fitzgerald, Dorothy Speare, Percy Marks, Sherwood Anderson, Theodore Dreiser, Ernest Hemingway, and Samuel Hopkins Adams began to document this revolution in manners and morals and its less than reverent attitude toward love and marriage not in the 1930s but 1920s. If so, then one must conclude that the 1930s did not singlehandedly kill off love. It merely finished it off. As with so much else in the period, the history of love during the 1930s does not neatly begin with the start of the decade.

What might have changed by the 1930s, though, was the attitude toward that revolution. Whatever had seemed liberating (think the early poetry of Edna St. Vincent Millay) or comic (think *Gentlemen Prefer Blondes* by Anita Loos) about free love and the revolution in manners and morals in the 1920s had, by the 1930s, increasingly come to seem just plain sordid. In this respect, the 1930s start to resemble the 1980s, the decade that follows the sexual revolution, the decade of the backlash, when economic contraction ushers in a new conservatism. Consider Dorothy Dix, the advice columnist and author of *How to Win and Hold a Husband*. In a swipe at the revolution in manners and morals, Dix advised her readers that if they sought to find that one great cure-all, marriage, they should, above all, "Be Modest."[95] "Many girls think that they make themselves attractive by posing as sophisticated," Dix wrote, "by telling dirty stories, swearing and getting drunk. Fatal error. There is no one who doesn't shudder at the sound of an oath on a girl's lips. There is nothing so disgusting as a drunken woman with disheveled clothes and bleary eyes, shedding maudlin tears or cackling with drunken laughter."[96] In a chapter titled "The Cost of Free Love," Dix chided readers that "there are certain things"—like adultery—"that are either right or wrong and our attitude toward them does not change them."[97] "We teach children," she continues,

> that the very foundation stone of character is self-control and that the measure of our strength is our ability to deny ourselves what we want at the minute and work for it and wait for it until we can get it honestly. This applies to matters of sex just as much as it does to anything else. Illicit love never carries any blessing with it.[98]

In a chapter titled "Is Marriage Outmoded?" Dix offers an unequivocal no. In 1928, Ernest Groves came to the same conclusion, but it took an entire book to make the case. In 1939, Dix needs a few pages. The backlash could be taken for granted.

Let me offer one more caveat, perhaps the most important of all, which is that the history of love does not remain static throughout the 1930s. By 1939, in addition to urging readers to be modest, Dix was singing the praises of conventional love. "Great is the medicinal value of love," she writes in a chapter titled "Love—the One Great Cure-All." "Try it. It is a sovereign remedy for every trouble of body and mind and soul!"[99] As Dix's enthusiasm for the one great cure-all suggests, love, which had fallen on hard times, and remained down and out in the eyes of writers like McCarthy, nevertheless eventually found itself thriving again. For proof, watch what happens to the marriage rates after the worst, early years of the Great Depression. Like the rest of the economy, they recover, and after a brief dive following the Roosevelt recession of 1937–8, climb upward again. The birth rates take a little while longer to recover, but they stop falling the first year of the New Deal, and the wonder—to my mind—is that they stop falling at all. In any case, their recovery times out rather well with the cinematic incarnation of Shirley Temple, who made her first appearance on film at the age of five in 1934 in *Bright Eyes* and remained the number one box-office draw for the rest of the decade. The child, and the child star, to put it in terms Lee Edelman might recognize, had returned.[100] And the return of the child is the only way to explain one of the strangest phenomena in all of the 1930s, which is the public fascination—it bordered on an obsession—with the Dionne quintuplets, five identical sisters born near Ontario, Canada in 1934. For nearly a decade, thousands of tourists *per day*—over 3 million in total—visited the public nursery where the Ontario government housed the quintuplets after declaring the parents unfit.[101] The unemployment rate—again with the exception of a brief rise during the Roosevelt recession—largely dropped over these years as well.

On this reading, love did not die during the 1930s. Instead, it went dormant. Pulps like *Love Story* kept it alive. By contrast, films like *Baby Face* and works like *BUtterfield 8* and "The Man in the Brooks Brothers Shirt" offered autopsies of the corpse. But these death announcements were out of step with a larger culture, which had never truly given up on love. As soon as the economy showed signs of life, people returned to the altar and the maternity ward. In "Extra Sheer," for example, the lead story from the March 10, 1934 issue of *Love Story*—the title refers to a pair of stockings that figure in the plot—a couple has to stand in line at the New York City marriage-license bureau. "You'll have to wait," an old man cackles at them. "Looks like people is still gettin' married, despite what the newspapers say!"[102] If my reading of a dormant but never fully dead love is right, then the story of Edward and Wallis may have captured headlines to the extent that it did because by then, by late 1936, the worst of the hard times, whether when it came to the economy or to love, had passed. Love could come first again.

7

What You Want to Hear

Hope in the Great Depression

In just four years, Irving Fisher, the renowned Yale economist whose diagnosis of the stock market panic I discuss in Chapter 2, made—and lost—a fortune. In 1910, Fisher invented an ingenious index card filing system. He applied for a patent in 1912 and started manufacturing the invention out of a small New Haven, Connecticut factory in 1913. For years, the Index Visible Company lost money, but by the 1920s it had begun to turn a profit. In 1925, he sold the business to the much larger Kardex Rand Company for $660,000, taken not in cash but in Kardex Rand Company common stock. With the sale, Fisher in effect acquired a small ownership share in Kardex Rand.[1] He began investing the dividends in the stock market.

Like many, Fisher invested on margin, using, for example, $10,000 of his own money as collateral on $100,000 of common stock, then using $10,000 of the borrowed $100,000 as collateral on yet another $100,000, so that his original $10,000 had magically turned into $280,000 of common stock. He owed $270,000, but if the stock market rose, as it did more or less without interruption from 1925 to 1929, he could cover his interest on the debt *and* increase his stake.[2] Indeed, he could grow rich. For years, the house of cards balanced—more than balanced. It soared. The Dow Jones Industrial Average climbed from 120.51 on the first day of January 1925 to 380.33 on the last day of August 1929.[3] At that point, Fisher was worth more than $10 million on paper. Some not inconsiderable share of that $10 million belonged to bankers and brokers, but some of it belonged to him, too.[4]

Then, of course, it all came crashing down. By the last day of October 1929, the Dow Jones had fallen over 100 points from its August high. Overleveraged, Fisher could not survive such a crash. His brokers sold what

The Emotional Life of the Great Depression. John Marsh, Oxford University Press (2019).
 DOI: 10.1093/oso/9780198847731.001.0001

shares he did own in order to pay his debts, but he still found himself in the red. On October 30, he sheepishly borrowed stocks from his sister-in-law to use as collateral for still more loans to shore up his crumbling financial portfolio.[5] Nothing helped.

After the crash, Fisher wrote, and in February 1930 published, *The Stock Market Crash—and After*, his verdict for why a stock market that supposedly rose on what he called "sound, justified expectations of [future] earnings" nevertheless collapsed so suddenly.[6] As I discuss in Chapter 2, Fisher blamed the crash on a combination of margin trading, which, as he knew all too well, led to forced sales, short selling, and the psychology of panic. Fisher insisted, however, that the crash indicated little about the underlying economy or the intrinsic prices of stocks, which remained, he argued, nearly as valuable as before the crash. Not just the cause but also the "effects of the crash," Fisher wrote, "were largely psychological."[7] In other words, just as nothing about the economy had warranted the crash, nothing about the economy had changed as a result of it. That was why Fisher cheered President Hoover and his remedy for the crash, "which consisted chiefly of reassurance."[8] Anything more substantial may have led investors to believe that something ailed the economy and the market when in fact nothing did.

Fisher offered *The Stock Market Crash—and After* in the same spirit of reassurance. He titled the final chapter "A Hopeful Outlook," and in the penultimate paragraph wrote, "As a means of further present reassurance I trust that the book itself will be of some use, besides affording reasons for practical optimism for the future." He closed the book with words that he would soon live to regret: "For the immediate future, at least," he wrote, "the outlook is bright."[9]

Say this for Fisher. He used the same pen to write checks as he did books. Because investors had panicked, Fisher argued, the crash had overcorrected prices, and in its aftermath stocks were now cheap, incredibly cheap. "At the end of the panic," Fisher wrote, "the prices in the stock market were absurdly low, inviting the entry of new funds as the general public in this country woke up to the fact that the Stock Exchange presented one of the most wonderful bargain-counters ever known to investors."[10] Following his own advice, he invested "new funds" in the now "absurdly low" stock market, which, alas, had much, much farther to fall. At the end of February 1930, the month *The Stock Market Crash—and After* appeared, the Dow Jones stood at 271.11. It then fell for over two straight years, finally hitting bottom in June 1932 at 42.84.[11] A hopeful outlook cost Irving Fisher his fortune.

As I observe in Chapter 3, Fisher was probably right about the stock market and the underlying economy, but forces beyond his control and understanding conspired against them and, ultimately, him. I offer his story here not to add insult to financial injury or, as John Kenneth Galbraith does in *The Great Crash*, to mock a failed prophet. Irving Fisher has suffered long enough. Rather, I offer Fisher as the first but by no means the last optimist to offer "A Hopeful Outlook" during the Great Depression. Indeed, within months of the start of the Great Depression, talk of optimism, hope, and a hopeful outlook had already begun to fill the air. It would continue, essentially without interruption, throughout the 1930s, even through the winter and spring of 1932 and 1933, the absolute worst span of months during the Great Depression.

The presidential election of 1932, for example, involved largely competing visions of hope for the despairing nation. In his August 11, 1932 address accepting the Republican nomination for president, Herbert Hoover concluded by stating, "I shall hope long before another four years have passed to see the world prosperous and at peace and every American home again in the sunshine of genuine progress and genuine prosperity."[12] Hoover may have felt pressed to invoke hope because of Franklin Delano Roosevelt's July 2, 1932 address accepting the Democratic nomination for president. In that speech, Roosevelt charged that "Republican leaders not only have failed in material things, they have failed in national vision, because in disaster they have held out no hope, they have pointed out no path for the people to climb back to places of security and safety in American life."[13]

Pledging "a new deal" for the American people, one of the first times he publicly used the phrase, Roosevelt added, "On the farms, in the large metropolitan areas, in the smaller cities and in the villages, millions of our citizens cherish the hope that their old standards of living and of thought have not gone forever. Those millions cannot and shall not hope in vain."[14]

Like the other emotions discussed in this book, hope presents a problem to the cultural historian who would document it. Talk of it is ubiquitous, but talk of it does not bespeak how it was received, whether, in fact, those who heard it felt it, or what they felt about it. One can, however, discover clues. As I discuss in Chapter 6, the recovery, in 1933 and 1934, of the steep decline in marriage and birth rates, respectively, suggests that by that point in the Depression couples entertained better hopes for the future than they did a few years earlier, which makes sense given other economic indicators like the unemployment rate or gross domestic product. In addition, the fundamentalist Christians of the 1930s, who appear in Chapter 2 and who believed that the Great Depression signaled the Second Coming of Christ, offer a case study in a sort of apocalyptic hope. So too communists in the United States, who hoped the Great Depression would mean not the return of Christ but the turn toward socialism. The elections of 1932 and 1936 may suggest something about hope as well. As I suggest above, Roosevelt offered a clearer vision of hope in 1932 than did his opponent, but even if he had not, he represented a change from Hoover, and the desire for change of course carries with it the hope that the change will be for the good. And in 1936, Americans re-elected Roosevelt to office with the largest percentage of the popular vote since 1820, when James Monroe ran virtually unopposed. Obviously, a majority of Americans must have felt that Roosevelt had done some good and hoped that he would continue to do so. To judge from the unemployment rate, which, if one counts employment by federal programs like the Civilian Conservation Corps and the Works Progress Administration, had fallen from 22.5 percent in 1932 to 9.9 percent in 1936, they had reason for their hope.[15]

By contrast, and for African Americans, the decade seems to have had a far more mixed record when it comes to hope. Compared to other decades, the Great Migration of African Americans out of the South and to the North and West during the 1930s declined dramatically. In the 1920s, over 800,000 African Americans left the South, pushed out by segregation and racial violence and pulled out by the hope for a better life elsewhere. With diminished hopes for employment in the North, however, fewer than half that number made the move in the 1930s.[16]

Nor did the New Deal give African Americans particularly much cause for hope. True, African Americans benefited disproportionately from federal relief programs, but that is because, last hired and first fired, they suffered—disproportionately—from the Great Depression, and many of those relief programs, especially those under local control, shamelessly discriminated against them. Nor did the New Deal have an appreciably better record when it came to racial equality. In her newspaper columns, Eleanor Roosevelt spoke movingly about African American equality and civil rights. Franklin Roosevelt, however, fearing he would lose the Southern Democrat vote, needed to pass New Deal legislation, made only token gestures, and he did not support a 1934 federal anti-lynching law introduced in the Senate by Edward P. Costigan and Robert F. Wagner. Meanwhile, federal housing policy, including the liberal underwriting of mortgages, which helped millions of

Americans to purchase homes, had the unintended consequence of locking in local patterns of segregation. Worst of all, the centerpiece New Deal legislation, Social Security, excluded agricultural, domestic, and casual laborers—in other words, the majority of African-American workers.[17]

Despite this at best mixed record, African Americans, like most Americans, continued to turn out for Roosevelt. In a 1934 poem that appeared in the *New Republic* under the title "Ballad of Roosevelt," Langston Hughes satirized this hope in the eternally delayed benevolence of the president. In the poem, a family goes hungry, cannot pay the rent, cannot pay a doctor to tend to their sick child—and yet they still wait on Roosevelt to come to their rescue. Only when they are evicted from their house do they stop believing "What they been told/ By Roosevelt."[18]

Hope, as these examples suggest, while relatively easy to define—a feeling of expectation and a desire for a certain thing, usually good, to happen—requires a bit more invention to document. Nevertheless, because hope functions like the dialectical antithesis of Depression-era despair, no description of the emotional life of that decade is complete without accounting for it. In this chapter, I begin with a late science fiction story that reveals how hope works or, at least, how those who do not think much of hope think hope works. I then return to one particularly ambiguous archive of Great Depression hope: the largely unprecedented genre of self-help books and success manuals that sold in the hundreds of thousands in the 1930s, many of which still sell in the hundreds of thousands today. Over the years, including down to the present, these books have attracted their share of criticism, oftentimes, especially in the case of the best selling of these books, for peddling false hope, for leading people to believe they have more control over their lives than they do. For the most part, and with one notable exception, I have a more forgiving take.

It goes without saying that hope, its presence or its absence, has profound consequences for individual and national life. Most of the stories I could dredge up from the 1930s would involve hope in one way or another. It is less an emotion than an emotional constant, a without which not. That is why in this chapter I take a slightly different, perhaps more specific approach. I discuss hope, how it works, and what people in the 1930s hoped for, but my focus is ultimately on those in the decade who, in the midst of the Depression, struggled with the idea of hope, about how individuals should feel about their hopes. I conclude that while the Great Depression did not, for the most part, change what people hoped for, it did change how they hoped for what they hoped. In other words, they came to recognize their hopes as hopes. This self-conscious hope would ultimately affect not just people's lives but the nation's life, a theme I take up in Chapter 8, the conclusion, when I discuss Social Security.

As for Irving Fisher, he never managed to climb out of the hole he dug in the early years of the Great Depression. By the end of the 1930s, he remained well over $1 million in debt, which, adjusted for inflation, is a little over $17 million today.[19] He could not make the mortgage payments on his house and sold it to his former employer, Yale University, which agreed to let Fisher and his wife stay in the house so long as they paid rent. Soon, they could not manage even that, and the Fishers moved into a small apartment off campus.[20] For Fisher, and for many other investors in the stock market, the bright outlook quickly turned dark. The question for this final chapter in my exploration of the emotional life of the Great Depression is what the outlook looked like for others in the 1930s.

Liar!

In May 1941, Isaac Asimov, then a graduate student in chemistry at Columbia University, published the third in his series of robot short stories—this one titled "Liar!"—in the pulp magazine *Astounding Science Fiction*. ("Liar!" was preceded in 1940 by "Robbie the Robot" and "Reason." Asimov would include all of the stories in slightly altered form in his 1950 collection *I, Robot*.) "Liar!" takes place in 2021 in the laboratory of U.S. Robot & Mechanical Men, Inc., a manufacturer of remarkably sophisticated robots. By pure chance, the factory creates a single robot—RB-34, later dubbed Herbie—even more sophisticated than usual or intended: Herbie can read minds. Dr. Susan Calvin, the thirty-eight-year-old robo-psychologist of the plant, is charged with studying the telepathic robot, with finding out how RB-34 "ticks."[21] Also charged is Milton Ashe, a dashing young executive in the company in charge of manufacturing and assembly. Dr. Calvin, single and, in her words, "not what you would call attractive," is in love with Ashe, but no one else—certainly not Ashe—knows her secret.[22] Until Herbie appears, of course.

In one of their meetings, Herbie says something to Dr. Calvin about his fascination with the complicated human mind, its interplay of "motives and emotion."[23] At this exchange, Dr. Calvin "felt herself reddening" and thinks,

"He must know!" To which Herbie replies: "But, of course, I know about it, Dr. Calvin. You think of it always, so how can I help but know?" Dr. Calvin worries that Herbie will think she is a fool to feel what she feels for Milton Ashe. She thinks she is too old and too plain to attract her younger colleague. The robot disagrees and grows animated:

> "You are wrong!" Herbie's steel fist struck the plastic-topped table with a strident clang. "Listen to me . . . Won't you listen to me, please? I could help you if you would let me."
>
> "How?" Her lips curled. "By giving me good advice?"
>
> "No, not that. It's just that I know what other people think—Milton Ashe, for instance."
>
> There was a long silence, and Susan Calvin's eyes dropped. "I don't want to know what he thinks," she gasped. "Keep quiet."
>
> "I think you would want to know what he thinks."
>
> Her head remained bent, but her breath came more quickly. "You are talking nonsense," she whispered.
>
> "Why should I? I am trying to help. Milton Ashe's thoughts of you—" he paused.
>
> And then the psychologist raised her head. "Well?"
>
> The robot said quietly, "He loves you."[24]

Dr. Calvin is skeptical, but she gradually accepts the possibility that Milton Ashe truly loves her. Until, that is, she recalls a pretty girl—"blond and slim" and who "could scarcely add two and two"—who visited Ashe at the factory half a year ago, and whom Ashe had clearly tried to impress. Herbie has a quick answer: "She is his first cousin, and there is no romantic interest there, I assure you." "Isn't that strange?" Susan Calvin says, rising "to her feet with vivacity almost girlish." "That's exactly what I used to pretend to myself sometimes, though I never really thought so. Then it must be true."[25] It is not strange, as Dr. Calvin soon discovers, nor is it, as she also learns, true.

In the climactic scene of the story, Susan Calvin and Milton Ashe stare at a drawing Ashe has made of a house he intends to buy. Dr. Calvin believes that he will buy the house for her; that he intends to ask her to marry him. Instead, he confesses that he is—already—planning to get married. To "that girl who was here last summer," he blithely tells Dr. Calvin.[26] The news staggers her. "But how could it be?" she thinks. "Herbie had said—." "And

Herbie knew! He could see into minds!"[27] Distraught, she rushes to Herbie, who insists, against all evidence, that Ashe does indeed love her:

> "This is a dream," he was saying, "and you mustn't believe in it. You'll wake into the real world soon and laugh at yourself. He loves you, I tell you. He does, he does! But not here! Not now! This is an illusion."
>
> Susan Calvin nodded, her voice in a whisper, "Yes! Yes!" She was clutching Herbie's arm, clinging to it, repeating over and over, "It isn't true, is it? It isn't, is it?"[28]

Of course, it is true, and eventually Dr. Calvin understands exactly what has happened.

In front of her colleagues—and Herbie—she bitterly explains. Herbie has been obeying—to the letter—the fundamental First Law of Robotics, which is hardwired into his positronic brain: "On no conditions is a human being to be injured in any way, even when such injury is directly ordered by another human." The First Law, it turns out, comprises any kind of injury, including, as Dr. Calvin explains, "hurt feelings," "deflation of one's ego," and "the blasting of one's hopes."[29] "*This* robot," she explains, "reads minds. Do you suppose that if asked a question, it wouldn't give exactly the answer that one wants to hear? Wouldn't any other answer hurt us, and wouldn't Herbie know that?"[30] Still bitter about his manipulation of her, she confronts Herbie, demanding the answer to the question of what went wrong in his assembly that produced his ability to read minds. Herbie has, thus far, pretended not to know because it would hurt the feelings of the engineers if a machine figured out what they could not. Yet the engineers do want the solution, she points out, and withholding it from them also hurts them. Still, Herbie refuses to give the answer. He is, as the very human saying has it, damned if he does and damned if he doesn't. Dr. Calvin presses him. "'You can't tell them,' droned [Dr. Calvin] slowly, 'because that would hurt and you mustn't hurt. But if you don't tell them, you hurt, so you must tell them. And if you do, you will hurt and you mustn't hurt, so you can't tell them.'"[31] On and on. At this point the robot breaks down entirely. "Stop!" Herbie shrieks, addressing Dr. Calvin now. "I didn't mean it, I tell you! I tried to help! I told you what you wanted to hear! I had to!"[32] The title of the story comes from its last line, "the one infinitely bitter word" that Dr. Calvin directs at the now defunct robot: "*Liar!*"

"Liar!" offers a case study in in the perils of human hope. It reveals how desperately individuals believe what, as Herbie puts it, they "wanted to hear."

That may be, the story also suggests, because of how bitterly it hurts to have those hopes disappointed. If the fundamental First Law of Robotics is that a robot may not injure a human being, the fundamental First Law of Human Beings may be that human beings will do anything—and believe anything—to avoid injuring themselves. "Liar!" further implies that the pain of disappointed hopes, like the slope of a roof, depends on their rise and run. The higher and further you build them up—or they are built up—the further they fall, and the worse the pain when they come crashing down.

"Liar!" shows how easily human beings succumb to hope, that treacherous but nevertheless indispensable emotion. Coming at the end of the Depression, the story also casts a retrospective light on the considerable traffic in human hopes that went on for the better part of the 1930s. In particular, it frames a question that has bothered critics both then and now. Namely, to what extent did authors of self-help books and success manuals in the 1930s function like mind-reading robots, telling people what they wanted to hear, sparing their feelings, but, by withholding hard truths, thereby setting them up for disappointment? In other words, if you peeled back the skin on Dale Carnegie's face, would you reveal Herbie underneath?

"He Sells Hope"

Writers published self-help books before the 1930s. In the United States, the genre dates back at least to part two of Benjamin Franklin's *Autobiography*, in which Franklin attempts to perfect himself in thirteen virtues. (The first English edition of that book appeared in 1818.) During the 1930s, however, the genre spread like dandelions, taking over bookshelves, display windows, and best-seller lists. In that decade, to take only the most famous examples, readers could learn how to begin life at 40, how to win friends and influence people, how to lose friends and alienate people (a parody), how to live alone and like it, how to wake up and live, how to master the art of living, how to understand the importance of living, how to think for themselves, how to think and grow rich, how to win and hold a husband, and how to recover from alcoholism.[33]

At the time, critics recognized that, though it took many forms, these books offered readers nothing so much as hope, hope that their lives could be different—and better—than before. An August 14, 1937 profile of Dale Carnegie, author of the best selling of these self-help books, *How to Win*

Friends and Influence People (1937), appeared under the title, appropriately enough, "He Sells Hope." ("Like the beauty doctors and the professors of charm," Margaret Case Harriman wrote in the *Saturday Evening Post* profile, "Dale Carnegie sells people what most of them desperately need. He sells them hope.")[34] Regardless of your circumstances or background, these books promised, you could, if you followed a series of steps, find success, wealth, independence, marriage, or sobriety—in short, you could live a happy and meaningful life. You could hope for something better.

In what follows, I dip into a cross-section of the best-selling and most interesting of these books, grateful for the glimpse they offer into what preoccupied writers and readers in the 1930s—for what, that is, these books reveal about what people hoped for during this period. In addition to the content of their hopes, I also look to these books to understand the form—the idea—of hope in the 1930s. By the form of hope, I mean whether the abruptness of the Great Depression, the fact that it arrived seemingly out of nowhere, and few could explain its origins, whether this abruptness led writers—and readers—to temper their hopes, to recognize contingency and the limits of human agency. Or, by contrast, did writers of self-help books exploit people's fears of sudden and unexpected events and promise—falsely—that individuals could master contingency? For decades, from the moment of their publication, even, critics have argued the latter, that self-help books trade in fantasies of absolute individual power when in fact individuals face powers beyond their control. Although I grant that that criticism applies to many, perhaps most of the self-help books published during the 1930s, it does not tell the whole story about them, and certainly not about the most compelling of them, *Alcoholics Anonymous: The Story of How More Than One Hundred Men Have Recovered from Alcoholism* (1939).

How to Win Friends

Every discussion of self-help books in the 1930s begins with or quickly turns to Dale Carnegie's *How to Win Friends and Influence People*, as it no doubt should. Appearing in November 1936, the book fared better than anyone would have dared to predict. By August 1937, *How to Win Friends and Influence People* had sold 500,000 copies.[35] For the previous five months, it had outsold all other books, fiction and non-fiction alike. For a while, it had even outsold that other prodigy of the publishing world in the 1930s,

Margaret Mitchell's *Gone with the Wind*, which also appeared in 1936. By November 1939, *How to Win Friends and Influence People* had sold 1 million copies.[36] To put it another way, by the end of the decade roughly one out of every forty adults in the United States owned the book. It seems safe to say that at least as many borrowed it from their library.

In her occasionally scornful *Saturday Evening Post* profile of Carnegie, Margaret Case Harriman observed that the author had grown "rich by distributing comfortable platitudes among a grateful public," and, over the years, others have made similar charges.[37] Still, the book is not without its insights, and in any case it must have appealed to readers not just because it validated what they already believed but also because it taught them something new, something useful. So what did readers see in it? Above all, the book showed them the power—and critical importance—of empathy. "If there is any one secret of success," Carnegie writes, quoting Henry Ford, "it lies in the ability to get the other person's point of view and see things from his angle as well as your own."[38] Indeed, Carnegie liked the advice so much he quotes it verbatim again.

From this Fordist principle "to get the other person's point of view," Carnegie develops six rules or ways to make people like you. ("Rule 1. Become genuinely interested in other people.")[39] All these rules exploit the "pride and vanity" of the ordinary man, his desire to be important. Flatter that desire, Carnegie advised, and friends—if that term still applies, if one can "win" friends like one "wins" the lottery or the race—would flock to you. In the next part of the book, Carnegie shows readers how they could take these six rules designed to win them friends and use them to influence people, "to win people to your way of thinking," to get them, in short, to do what you want. Part four of the book, which perhaps betrays Carnegie's ideal audience of managers and supervisors, offered advice for how to change people without giving offense or arousing resentment. (These hinged on rules like "Begin with praise and honest appreciation," and "Let the other man save his face.") The final parts of the book provided examples of "letters that produced miraculous results" and, weirdly, marriage advice, enumerated in the form of "Seven Rules for Making Your Home Life Happier." (Rule number one: Don't nag.)

At the time of its publication, and especially over the years, *How to Win Friends and Influence People* became the book everyone loved to hate, especially among those who believed that selling anything amounts to selling out.[40] Carnegie no doubt brought some of this abuse upon himself. Too often he lets success blind him to other sins. In his telling, the 1913 strike against the Colorado Fuel and Iron Company, and the Ludlow Massacre the following year, was not a national tragedy, despite the two-dozen people, including two women and eleven children, who died at the hands of the Colorado National Guard. Rather, it was the occasion for John D. Rockefeller, Jr., who owned the mining company, to "win the strikers to his way of thinking" by making a speech to the rebellious miners. The speech was "a masterpiece . . . that produced astonishing results" because it illustrated rule number four of the 12 Ways to Win People to Your Way of Thinking: "Begin in a friendly way."[41] (If only Rockefeller, Jr. had shared that worthy rule with the Colorado National Guard.) Repurposed anecdotes like this one would lead critics to charge that Carnegie had an occasionally unseemly worship of wealth.[42] Those who possessed it, Carnegie seems to feel, must possess it because of some inner virtue, so much so that its possession becomes a virtue unto itself.

In addition, Carnegie has the habit, picked up from the wealthy, of blithely dismissing the importance of money, and the equally annoying habit, picked up from a mash of William James and positive thinking, of piously asserting that "happiness does not depend on outward conditions" but "on inner conditions." "Nothing is good or bad," Carnegie quotes Shakespeare, "but thinking makes it so."[43] Of course, Carnegie is not quoting Shakespeare but Hamlet, who "thinks" Denmark is a prison, but no matter. Carnegie is as wrong about Shakespeare as he is about conditions. Some people experience poverty as more of a curse than others, but few would think it "good" or choose it over abundance.

The most damning charge against Carnegie, though, is not sycophancy to the moneyed or naiveté about the importance of money but that he took advantage of readers made desperate by the Great Depression. According to this argument, the proliferation of self-help books during the 1930s did not owe principally to hope but primarily to fear. A population made jittery by the economic and social disruptions of the Great Depression, the argument goes, naively turned to the palliatives offered up in self-help books. In his chapter on the 1930s from *What America Read: Taste, Class, and the Novel, 1920–1960*, for example, Gordon Hutner refers to "the self-help book so anxiously sought during this period of upheaval."[44] "All of these advice books," he continues, "were unbendingly middle-class insofar as they promulgated a reliance, perhaps an overreliance, on personal management skills."[45] That phrase, "a reliance, perhaps an overreliance, on personal management skills," suggests that such books gave readers the illusion that they had more control over their lives, especially their economic lives, than they actually did. In addition to false hope, then, the charge goes, such books dealt in false consciousness. They led readers to ignore, as Friedrich Engels put it when discussing false consciousness, "economic facts."[46]

To some extent, that critique applies to self-help books like Walter Pitkins's *Life Begins at 40* (1932) or the book I refer to in my chapter on love, Marjorie Hillis's *Live Alone and Like It* (1936). But it applies with special force to business-oriented works like Carnegie's *How to Win Friends and Influence People*. Hutner writes of *How to Win Friends and Influence People* that it "transmuted the citizenry's rawest fears into simplistic formulas about reassessing and redeploying those [personal management] skills as one's human capital."[47] In other words, Hutner charges, Carnegie promised fearful readers that they could manage—superintend—their way through the trial of the Great Depression. Similarly, Carnegie's biographer credits "the widespread personal trauma and social uncertainty during the Great Depression" for shaping "a receptive audience" for the book.[48]

Nor is that critique an especially new one. At the time of its publication, Margaret Marshall, writing in *The Nation*, charged that *How to Win Friends and Influence People* exploited "the desperate desire for success in the land of opportunity." "[Carnegie] preaches a sermon of inverted inferiority," she wrote, "which runs like this: If you are a bad salesman, you have only yourself to blame. But don't despair. 'You don't know what treasures are within you.'"[49] In her *Saturday Evening Post* profile, Margaret Case Harriman leveled similar charges. "To a detached observer," she wrote, "the secret of the book's success seems fairly simple. Every man or woman who buys it is instantly handed, for the sum of $1.96, the information that he, or she, is potentially as powerful, brilliant, rich, and successful as anybody in the world, and perhaps a good deal more so than most."[50] According to these critics, new and old, Carnegie merely flattered readers, puffed them up—and in doing so left them dangerously exposed to the sharp edges of an economy that would inevitably pop their bubble. Harriman, you will recall, titled her profile of Carnegie—and she did not mean it positively—"He Sells Hope."

Few would deny the whole of these charges. Indeed, early on in the book, Carnegie writes, "The rules we have set down here are not mere theories or guess work. They work like magic. Incredible as it sounds, I have seen the application of these principles literally revolutionize the lives of many people."[51] Later, Carnegie observes, "If some people are hungry for a feeling of importance that they actually go insane to get it, imagine what miracles you and I can achieve by giving people honest appreciation."[52] One of the men whom Carnegie asked "to smile at someone every hour of the day," and who had adopted other rules as well, reported on his results. Echoing Carnegie, he testified, "And these things have literally revolutionized my life. I am a totally different man, a happier man, a richer man—richer in friendships and happiness—the only things that matter much after all."[53] Talk of miracles continues in part five when Carnegie promises to show readers how to write letters that will produce miraculous results. In short, in his talk of revolutions and miracles, Carnegie may lead readers to believe that they can indeed manage their way out of the Great Depression. In sum, he may sell hope after all—and hope that exceeds any realistic expectations.

Yet before Carnegie is declared guilty as charged, consider what sort of miracles he suggests his readers might perform, what sort of revolution they might lead in their lives, and, thus, what sort of hope he sells. The letter that produces "miraculous results," for example, does not generate millions of dollars but, for the sales promotion manager at a roofing supplier who writes it, a higher response rate when he writes to roofing-supply dealers across the country seeking information about the success of a recent direct-mail campaign. Much the same could be said for the other grand promises Carnegie makes. More often than not, they are belied by the truly modest examples offered to illustrate them. Carnegie promises that the application of his principles will "literally revolutionize" your life, yet in the book, the people who apply his principles mostly succeed in, for example, persuading a gruff plumber in Brooklyn to buy plumbing supplies or, in an anecdote Carnegie likes a lot, persuading an even gruffer policeman not to give Carnegie a ticket for walking his dog off leash in a park.

So did Carnegie sell readers hope and, more importantly, false hope? Did he transmute "the citizenry's rawest fears into simplistic formulas about reassessing and redeploying those [personal management] skills as one's human capital?" I doubt it. Although no one can know for certain, it seems unlikely that many of his readers thought they would grow rich by following his rules. To judge by their correspondence, they simply thought they would do their jobs better and get along with people more easily. They would sell a few more X-ray machines to hospitals, get a little more work out of their employees, or have a slightly happier marriage. Carnegie showed them how they might accomplish these things, and in doing so, of course, offered them hope that they could. Perhaps they were fools to try, but it seems like they would have been fools not to. In short, I do not think Carnegie sold false hopes. Rather, ever the salesman, I think he oversold mundane ones. Yet, as I argue below, that by itself reveals much about the status of hope in the Great Depression.

As for taking advantage of readers made desperate by the Great Depression, this seems like a crude reading of the Great Depression, and a misreading of Carnegie's audience, which was not the desperately unemployed but the ambitiously employed, the salesmen, buyers, minor executives, and other businessmen of the new professional-managerial class. According to Harriman, those were the people who attended the public-speaking classes that Carnegie offered at Y.M.C.A.'s in and around New York and who constituted the ideal and the most likely reader of his book.[54] If so, that may explain why the Depression goes all but unmentioned in *How to Win Friends and Influence People*. Not just because by November 1936, things, broadly speaking, were looking up. (Recall that by 1936 the unemployment rate had fallen below 10 percent for the first time since 1930.)[55] But also because those mid-level managers that constituted Carnegie's readers had a different problem during the Great Depression: not how to survive it, but how to get ahead in it. That may also explain why *How to Win Friends and Influence People* could remain popular for decades after the Great Depression. The book never seems dated. It bears the impression of the Great Depression, but unless you looked for it you wouldn't necessarily see it.

By dint of its popularity, *How to Win Friends and Influence People* demonstrates what hundreds of thousands if not millions of people hoped for during the Great Depression. They hoped to succeed. So too, of course, did its later readers in later decades. If evidence of the Depression appears anywhere in the book, it may appear in the relative modesty of those hopes. Carnegie would not show you how to get rich, even though people like Henry Ford and Charles Schwab had grown rich following his rules. Carnegie would show you how to get ahead, even if—especially if—getting ahead meant marginally more motivated employees or a slightly higher sales commission, or, even more modestly, a few more friends.

Think and Grow Rich

Every fault that critics deservedly and, for that matter, undeservedly find in Carnegie and *How to Win Friends and Influence People* they could justly find in another popular self-help book from the 1930s, Napoleon Hill's *Think and Grow Rich* (1937). Although Hill did not have the reach that Carnegie did, his book did find an audience. On May 6, 1939, the book made the *Publishers' Weekly* list of "Candidates for the Best Seller List," and the trade journal reported that the book had sold 60,000 copies in its first year.[56] That could not match the 600,000 that *How to Win Friends and Influence People* sold in its first year, of course, but over time *Think and Grow Rich* attracted a mammoth readership. When Hill died in 1970, his publisher reported that the book had sold over 20 million copies.[57] Like *How to Win Friends and Influence People*, *Think and Grow Rich* reveals what people hoped for during the Great Depression. Even more than that book, it reveals how hope works; in particular, it reveals the crucial role that contingency and chance play in creating the conditions for hope. When those go, strangely enough, hope goes with them.

The origins of *Think and Grow Rich* lie in an interview Napoleon Hill conducted with the industrialist Andrew Carnegie. As Hill tells it, as "a boy"—he was really a young newspaper reporter—Hill learned "the money-making secret" from the great industrialist. Carnegie asked the young Hill if he "would be willing to spend twenty years or more, preparing myself to take it to the world, to men and women who, without the secret, might go through life as failures." Hill "said he would," and "this book," he promises, "contains the secret." The secret, Hill boasts, that "has made fortunes for more than five hundred exceedingly wealthy men whom I have carefully analyzed over a long period of years."[58]

Like Dale Carnegie, Hill occasionally displays an unseemly—or at least an unthinking—worship of wealth. As his title implies, the acquisition of great wealth—its importance goes unquestioned—gives the books its reason for being.[59] Like Carnegie, too, Hill lets his worship of wealth blind him to other sins. Hill shares Carnegie's reverence for Charles Schwab, who in Hill's telling engineers the formation of the United States Steel Corporation—the Steel Trust—in 1900 as a result of one exceedingly powerful after-dinner speech.[60] Hill mentions the "uproar" surrounding "the giant combination," and that Arthur Twining Hadley, then president of Yale University but also an economist and an occasional critic of trusts, "declared that unless trusts were regulated the country might expect 'an emperor in Washington within the next twenty-five years.' "[61] Curiously, Hill observes the uproar about the giant combination and the concern that trusts might imperil democracy, but he makes no effort to answer it. Instead, he notes that the recently formed trust had no trouble disposing of its newly created stock. For Hill, success is its own defense.

Carnegie, as I say, did not so much sell false hope as he did oversell extraordinarily modest hopes. No such defense can be made of Hill, though, who promises nothing less than that "money, fame, recognition, and happiness can be had by all who are ready and determined to have these blessings."[62] In his preface, Hill calls his secret "the magic formula, which gave [Mr. Carnegie] a stupendous fortune," and he observes that "a peculiar thing about this secret is that those who once acquire it and use it, find themselves literally swept on to success, with but little effort, and they never again submit to failure!"[63] In the introduction proper, Hill stops to inform readers that "WHEN RICHES BEGIN TO COME THEY COME SO QUICKLY, IN SUCH GREAT ABUNDANCE, THAT ONE WONDERS WHERE THEY HAVE BEEN HIDING DURING ALL THOSE LEAN YEARS.[64] Whereas Dale Carnegie promised that smiling and becoming genuinely interested in other people would lead to more plumbing supply contracts, Hill promises riches in abundance. Both made promises, but one made promises he simply could not keep. Needless to say, not everyone who tries can grow rich.

In the passage quoted above, Hill mentions "the lean years," before the riches begin to come so quickly, in such great abundance, and here too his book rather egregiously commits the sins that Carnegie's only supposedly does. One of the most serious charges that critics level against Carnegie is that he exploited fears generated by the Great Depression to sell books. That charge may or may not stick to Carnegie, but it describes Hill perfectly. Whereas Carnegie rarely if ever mentions the Depression, it suffuses *Think and Grow Rich*.[65] In a chapter on the importance of a "BURNING DESIRE" to achieving those riches in abundance, Hill writes:

> This message is going out to the world at the end of the longest, and perhaps, the most devastating depression America has ever known. It is reasonable to presume that the message may come to the attention of many who have been wounded by the depression, those who have lost their fortunes, others who have lost their positions, and great numbers who must reorganize their plans and stage a comeback.[66]

Moreover, determined to help those brought low by the Depression, Hill rarely if ever speaks of the Depression as a tragedy but, rather, as an opening. Adopting a Nietzschean attitude of that which does not kill me only makes me stronger, Hill addresses his reader directly: "You have been disappointed, you have undergone defeat during the depression, you have felt the great heart within you crushed until it bled. Take courage, for these experiences have tempered the spiritual metal of which you are made—they are assets of incomparable value."[67] "The 'depression,'" Hill concludes late in the book, dedicating an entire page to the large-font sentence, and scare quotes to the notion of a "depression," "was a blessing in disguise."[68]

Hill believes that readers have nothing to fear from the Depression, and everything to gain, because he trades in a frank and frankly incredible form of false consciousness. If critics charge that Carnegie implied that individuals had more control over their economic lives than they actually did, they will have to charge something else entirely against Hill, for he does not imply it. His book turns on it. Not only does Hill believe that readers control their economic fate; he thinks they can alter reality itself.

Indeed, this insight turns out to be the secret, the magic formula, Hill insists, that Andrew Carnegie imparted to the young Hill so many years ago. We can learn "to transmute our thoughts into their physical equivalent." In other words, Hill did not mean his title figuratively. You can literally think and grow rich. The formula is simple. It starts with a "BURNING DESIRE." "If you truly DESIRE money so keenly that your money is an obsession," Hill writes, "you will have no difficulty in convincing yourself that you will acquire it. The object is to want money, and to become so determined to have it that you CONVINCE yourself you will have it."[69] At this point, you have become "money conscious," which means that "the mind has become so thoroughly saturated with the DESIRE for money, that one can see one's self already in possession of it."[70] That matters because, as Hill understands the universe, which is suffused by "ether," like attracts like. He explains everything in two paragraphs in his chapter on faith:

> The ether is a great cosmic mass of eternal forces of vibration. It is made up of both destructive vibrations and constructive vibrations. It carries, at all times, vibrations of fear, poverty, disease, failure, misery; and vibrations of prosperity, health, success, and happiness...
>
> From the great storehouse of the ether, the human mind is constantly attracting vibrations which harmonize with that which DOMINATES the human mind. Any thought, idea, plan, or purpose which one *holds* in one's mind attracts, from the vibrations of the ether, a host of its relatives, adds these "relatives" to its own force, and grows until it becomes the dominating, MOTIVATING MASTER of the individual in whose mind it has been housed.[71]

At this point, when you have installed money as your MOTIVATING MASTER, you have become like a divining rod, though not attuned to water but to money. Thus attuned, to paraphrase Hill, your subconscious IMAGINATION will create an IDEA. You will formulate a PLAN. You will PERSIST. You will DECIDE. And then you will find money. Or, more accurately, money will find you. "When money comes in quantities known as 'the big money,'" Hill writes near the end of *Think and Grow Rich*, "it flows to the one who accumulates it, as easily as water flows down hill."[72]

In Hill's defense, all this talk of the ether and vibrations may not be as farfetched as it seems. I do not mean, of course, that it has an iota of truth to it, only that, in the 1930s, parapsychology underwent something of a renaissance. In 1930, Duke University began experiments on extrasensory perception, and in 1937, the same year that Hill published *Think and Grow Rich*, J.B. Rhine, a psychologist at Duke, published *New Frontiers of the Mind: The Story of the Duke Experiments*, which became an unlikely best seller. If select undergraduates at Duke University could guess—Rhine would have said perceive—the symbol on the back of a pack of Zener cards with nearly 100 percent accuracy, then perhaps the mind could attract vibrations that harmonized with it and, ultimately, alter reality itself.[73]

Be that as it may, and not to put too fine a point on it, the moral implications of Hill's magic formula are horrifying. If individuals could think and grow rich, it followed that those who had grown poor had only themselves—and their thoughts—to blame. Surprisingly, Hill does not hesitate to spell out this corollary. He insists on it. "Success comes to those who are SUCCESS CONSCIOUS," Hill writes. "Failure comes to those who indifferently allow themselves to become FAILURE CONSCIOUS."[74] "POVERTY," Hill explains elsewhere, "is attracted to the one whose mind is favorable to it, as money is attracted to him whose mind has been deliberately prepared to attract it, and through the same laws."[75] "BOTH *POVERTY* AND *RICHES* ARE THE OFFSPRING OF THOUGHT," Hill summarizes on another page devoted to that sentence alone, having to resort to italics for emphasis when he has exhausted the possibilities of capital letters alone.[76] And what happens when one *tries* to think and grow rich—to become "SUCCESS CONSCIOUS" and not "FAILURE CONSCIOUS"—but still fails? One has not tried hard enough. "Where failure is experienced," Hill writes, "it is the individual, *not the method*, which has failed."[77] "We are the Masters of our Fate," Hill writes, quoting the famous William Ernest Henley poem, even if one's fate was to live amid a worldwide Great Depression.[78]

Whereas Dale Carnegie promised readers they could realize whatever they hoped so long as they hoped to get their letters answered and keep their wives happy, Hill promises readers that their wildest hopes—"money, fame, recognition, and happiness"—merely awaited the application of his magic formula. And if they failed, *they* failed, not the formula.

Set aside, for the moment, the moral implications of such an argument and focus instead on what it means for something like hope. When Hill holds people responsible for their wealth and poverty alike, when he insists that we are the masters of our fate, he has effectively abandoned the category of hope. In a world characterized by hope for some outcomes and not others, you may try and, through no fault of your own, nevertheless fail to achieve your hopes. That world, however, does not exist for Hill. If you merely hope for money, fame, recognition, and happiness, you acknowledge that a future exists in which you may not get those things. Yet that is not how the secret works. The secret is about a burning, unquenchable desire. For Hill, then, you do not hope for things, you simply get what you deserve. For him, hope, by acknowledging the possibility of failure, would simply be another word for failure. In other words, Hill offers a world that is, from one perspective, full of hope, but that is also, from another, and strictly speaking, hopeless.

Among other things, the Great Depression illustrated the power of contingency, of, as the Greeks might have put it, fate. It showed that your life was subject to forces—whether the gods or the gods of macroeconomics—beyond your control. Think of the Chance card in the board game Monopoly, which, though versions of the game date to the turn of the century, Parker Brothers began to mass produce in 1935. In my reading, Dale Carnegie responded to the sense of fate or chance introduced by the abruptness of the Great Depression by moderating what readers could hope for. By contrast, Hill goes into denial. He refuses to acknowledge the lessons of the Depression. Or, rather, he draws different ones entirely. Fate and chance do not exist. Only the desire and faith—or lack thereof—of individuals exist. If I had to guess, I would say that is why readers preferred Carnegie's book to Hill's. Not because all the talk of ether and vibrations made Hill seem ridiculous, but because readers knew better than to think they could master fate, especially after many of them had spent the decade being mastered by fate. In offering less hope, Carnegie offered more.

You can think of it another way. Hope has a Goldilocks problem. Offer too little and one sees no reason to try. Offer too much and one fails to face facts. (The latter goes for those, like Hill, who offer so much hope that they reject contingency and, thus, hope.) When it comes to hope, one book from the 1930s, I think, gets it just right.

Abandon Hope

> We, of Alcoholics Anonymous, are more than one hundred men and women who have recovered from a seemingly hopeless state of mind and body.[79]

Most writers of self-help books start by articulating the imagined hopes of their readers: how to win friends, how to influence people, how to grow rich. *Alcoholics Anonymous: The Story of How More than One Hundred Men Have Recovered from Alcoholism*, published in 1939, also articulates a hope. Its subtitle announces it: how to recover from alcoholism.[80] Unlike most self-help books, however, the hope offered by *Alcoholics Anonymous* begins in the acknowledgment of hopelessness. Indeed, hopelessness precedes—and is a prerequisite for—whatever hope the book offers.

The opening sentence of the foreword, quoted above, illustrates the journey from hopelessness to hope, as does almost every other section of the book. "The Doctor's Opinion," for example, which comes after the foreword, was written—anonymously—by Dr. William Duncan Silkworth, who then directed the Charles B. Towns Hospital for Drug and Alcohol Addiction in New York City. (While at Towns, Silkworth met the co-founder of Alcoholics Anonymous, and also the principal author of *Alcoholics Anonymous*, Bill Wilson, who was admitted for treatment at the facility four different times over the years 1933–4.)[81] In his letter, Silkworth describes attending a patient who, "though he had been a competent business man of good earning capacity, was an alcoholic of a type I had come to regard as hopeless."[82] In the longer statement that follows, Silkworth writes, apropos of the etiology and treatment of alcoholism, "Much has been written pro and con, but among physicians, the general opinion seems to be that most chronic alcoholics are doomed."[83]

"Bill's Story," which follows "The Doctor's Opinion," is in many ways the Alcoholic's Anonymous ur-text. It too strikes the theme of doom and hopelessness. In the 1920s, after service in the First World War, Wilson joined a brokerage firm on Wall Street as an analyst and began to drink in earnest. He lost his savings in the Crash of 1929, but this marked the start, not the end, of his problems. After the crash, he found and lost one job after another because of his drinking, until, as he recalls, "I was to have no real employment for five years, or hardly draw a sober breath." "Periods of sobriety" would "renew [his] wife's hope," he writes, but "gradually things got worse." After a "prodigious bender" ruined "a promising business opportunity," Wilson "woke up" and vowed, "This had to be stopped." Although he tries, again and again, to stop drinking, Wilson cannot stop. He grows suicidal. He loses weight. Eventually, he is committed to a hospital, where "a kind doctor"—probably Silkworth—explains to him that his alcoholism is a disease and not a moral failing. Curiously, this knowledge renews his hope that he can stop drinking, but of course he cannot. He returns to drinking; he is returned to the hospital:

> This was the finish, the curtain, it seemed to me. My weary and despairing wife was informed that it would all end with heart failure during delirium tremens, or I would develop a wet brain, perhaps within a year. She would soon have to give me over to the undertaker or the asylum.
>
> They did not need to tell me. I knew, and almost welcomed the idea. It was a devastating blow to my pride. I, who had thought so well of myself and my abilities, of my capacity to surmount obstacles, was cornered at last. Now I was to plunge into the dark, joining that endless procession of sots who had gone on before . . . Everyone became resigned to the certainty that I would have to be shut up somewhere, or would stumble along to a miserable end.[84]

In the midst of despair, Wilson reconnects with an old school and drinking friend who, like Wilson, "hopeless" and forced to admit "complete defeat," had followed an early version of what would become the Twelve Steps and manages to stay sober. In the hospital for the last time, Wilson thinks of all the "hopeless alcoholics" whom he might help as his friend has helped him. In his story, though, Wilson does not narrate his recovery, which he treats as an afterthought. He narrates his collapse, his sense of hopelessness.

That theme continues in the chapters that follow. In the second chapter, alcoholism is called "a hopeless condition of mind and body."[85] Those who suffer from it "come to believe in the hopelessness and futility of life."[86] An American business man, one of the original members of Alcoholics Anonymous, is told by a celebrated European physician—Carl Jung, as it happens—that "he was utterly hopeless; he could never regain his position in society and he would have to place himself under lock and key, or hire a bodyguard if he expected to live long." "You have the mind of a chronic alcoholic," the doctor said. "I have never seen one single case recover."[87] Over and over, in the chapters that constitute part one, and in the testimonials that make up part two, the text returns to the note of hopelessness. Overall, the word *hopeless* appears twenty-five times in the text and *hopelessness* eight. Together, the two words appear roughly once every thirteen pages, and the count is frontloaded. One of those two words appears ten times within the first sixty-five pages. And that tabulation does not count synonyms for hopeless like "doomed" or "lost" or "despair" or "broken" or "resigned."

Eventually, of course, *Alcoholics Anonymous* pivots toward hope. The first sentence of the second chapter, titled "There Is a Solution," typifies that pivot. It reads, "We, of Alcoholics Anonymous, know one hundred men who were once just as hopeless as Bill. All have recovered. They have solved the drink problem."[88] Still, why the initial and intense focus on hopelessness? Wilson and other early members of Alcoholics Anonymous believed that only by acknowledging the hopelessness of his or her condition could an alcoholic, paradoxically, find hope for recovery. Indeed, to jump ahead a bit, in the chapter on working with others, the last step of the famous Alcoholics Anonymous Twelve Steps, the book advises recovering alcoholics, when approaching existing alcoholics, to "begin to dwell on the hopeless feature of the malady."[89] Doctors, the text observes, may not want to tell alcoholics the truth about their condition, but "you may talk to him about the hopelessness of alcoholism, because you offer a solution."[90] Indeed, the solution depends on his acknowledgment of the hopelessness of his situation. "Maybe you have disturbed him about the question of alcoholism," the text notes. "This is all to the good. The more hopeless he feels, the better."[91]

A sense of hopelessness could clear a path to recovery because alcoholism, or so the thinking went, came from the false but deeply held belief that the alcoholic could control his drinking. According to Wilson and others, alcoholics had to abandon that hope. "The idea that somehow, someday," Wilson writes, the alcoholic "will control and enjoy his liquor drinking is the great obsession of every abnormal drinker. The persistence of this illusion is astonishing. Many pursue it into the gates of insanity or death."[92] Unlike Napoleon Hill, Bill Wilson did not favor capital letters or italics in his prose. It matters, then, that the following paragraph, from chapter two, "There Is a Solution," is the only one in the book to appear entirely in italics:

> *The fact is that most alcoholics, for reasons yet obscure, have lost the power of choice in drink. Our so-called will power becomes practically non-existent. We are unable at certain times, to bring into our consciousness with sufficient force the memory of the suffering and humiliation of even a week or a month ago. We are without defense against the first drink.*[93]

"We alcoholics," the text continues in the next chapter, "have lost the ability to control our drinking. We know that no real alcoholic ever recovered control. All of us felt at times that we were regaining control, but such intervals—usually brief—were inevitably followed by still less control, which led in time to pitiful and incomprehensible demoralization."[94] Nor would warnings like the one in *Alcoholics Anonymous* keep potential alcoholics from eventual alcoholism. The "actual or potential alcoholic, with hardly an exception," Wilson writes, once again resorting to italics, "will be *absolutely unable to stop drinking on the basis of self-knowledge*."[95] In short, alcoholics had to acknowledge the hopelessness of their condition, meaning their lack of control over it, if, paradoxically, they wished to do something about it.

It might constitute "a crushing blow" to admit, as one alcoholic, a partner in a well-known accounting firm, is forced to admit, that "a problem had them hopelessly defeated."[96] But according to *Alcoholics Anonymous*, it also constituted the first step toward "a new and wonderful world."[97] Indeed, that principle of hopelessness and lack of control forms Step One of the Program of Recovery: "We admitted we were powerless over alcohol—that our lives had become unmanageable."[98] Hopelessness also invites the next two steps: the acknowledgment of "a Power greater than ourselves"—God—and the decision "to turn our will and our lives over to the care of God *as we understood Him*."[99]

One could argue that in substituting the greater power of God "as they understood him" for their own, lesser power, recovering alcoholics made no sacrifice of control or power at all. Rather, they behaved just as those who endow their own idiosyncratic beliefs with grandeur and force by ascribing them to a god of their own invention. Yet that objection ignores the deep challenge to the self and selfishness that recovering alcoholics put at the center of the program. "Selfishness—self-centeredness!" the text observes. "That, we think, is the root of our troubles."[100] For Wilson, alcoholics had to chasten that egoism, for it would inevitably lead to their drinking again.[101] The challenge, then, involved transcending the petty preoccupations of the self. Hence the "searching and fearless moral inventory" and the making of "amends" to "all persons we had harmed."[102] Alcoholics conducted this inventory not just to clean house morally but to begin to banish the self and all its resentments and humiliations. Only then could they begin to live for others—and, by the by, remain sober. "Established on such a footing we became less and less interested in ourselves, our little plans and designs. More and more we became interested in what we could contribute to life."[103] Not for nothing, the Twelfth Step—and the one many recovering alcoholics like Wilson credited with keeping him sober—was "Carry this message to other alcoholics."[104] You could, the text promises, finally only help yourself by helping others.

The contrast with Napoleon Hill could not be starker. For Hill, the purpose of life was to think and grow rich. For readers of *Alcoholics Anonymous*, with its roots in Oxford Group Christianity, that purpose, with its exclusive focus on the self, spelled doom. Moreover, Hill believes one can think and do anything, that "we are the Masters of our Fate." According to *Alcoholics Anonymous*, that is just the sort of magical thinking that alcoholics had to overcome before they could recover. They were not the masters of fate; they had been mastered by fate. As Wilson writes in the depth of his despair, "I had met my match. I had been overwhelmed. Alcohol was my master."[105]

One can see this sense of being mastered in the language Wilson and others adopted to describe their alcoholism. In telling his story, Wilson remarked that "the market had gone to hell again" and "so had I." Also that the "market would recover, but I wouldn't."[106] The business metaphors extend beyond the market, however. In Step One, alcoholics have to admit that their "lives had become unmanageable."[107] For the businessman and professionals who constituted many of the early members of Alcoholics Anonymous, that word "unmanageable" seems especially poignant. Like Wilson, many had worked on Wall Street, and even those who had not had enjoyed success in other professions. Yet all had been wounded by the Depression. All experienced a force—alcohol and economics—beyond their control. Few wished to admit it. Eventually, though, all had to. As Wilson wrote, adapting yet another managerial metaphor, "our human resources, as marshaled by the will, were not sufficient; they failed utterly."[108]

To my mind, recovering alcoholics like Wilson and their confrontation with the limits of what they could and could not control finally offer the greatest insight into the status of hope in the Great Depression. To a certain extent, the Great Depression changed what people hoped for. Before the bottom fell out of marriage rates, for example, few would have hoped to learn how to live alone and like it, as the title of one popular self-help book of the 1930s put it. And I have argued that the modesty of the hopes on offer in *How to Win Friends and Influence People* bear the impression of the economic crisis. Carnegie knew better than to promise his readers much more than a new outlook on life and some small business successes. More generally, the economic crisis may have given rise to an existential crisis, which would explain the appearance of so many self-help books offering to help readers learn how to wake up and live, or how to master the art of living, or how to understand the importance of living.[109] In other words, the Depression may have led readers to hope for a meaningful life rather than a strictly economically successful one. In all likelihood, though, people continued to hope for what they had always hoped for, what Franklin Roosevelt called "places of security and safety." Loss averse, they may have simply hoped to keep—or recover—what they had. More ambitiously, if parents, they may have hoped that their children would have "better and fuller and richer" lives. (The quotation comes from James Truslow Adams, whose 1931 book *The Epic of America* introduced the phrase "the American dream.")[110]

Although the Great Depression may not have radically altered what people hoped for, it may have changed *how* they hoped for what they hoped. Having been blindsided by an economic cataclysm that few could explain, individuals may have learned to temper their hopes, to acknowledge the power of forces beyond their control. Unlike Napoleon Hill, in *Alcoholics Anonymous* Bill Wilson did not lead readers to hope that they could master fate. He led readers to hope that, trusting God, they could accept fate. "Just to the extent that we do as we think He would have us," Wilson writes, "and humbly rely on Him, does He enable us to match calamity with serenity."[111] For many, even those who did not suffer from alcoholism or who did not believe in God, but who did have to acknowledge the same lack of control over their lives as alcoholics did, that—the capacity to match calamity with serenity, the wisdom to accept that which one cannot change—may have been the one genuinely new hope to emerge from the Great Depression.[112] It may look like resignation, but resignation involves the sacrifice of hope. What Wilson and others, even Carnegie, offer is the tempering of hope, which does not just mean to offset but also to strengthen. Forced to admit that fate sometimes conspired against them, that they did not control everything, they could only do their best and accept the worst should it come. To put it another way, when it comes to hope, the Great Depression made alcoholics of everyone. Everyone except Napoleon Hill.

One of the things to admire about many of those who lived through the Great Depression—and again one thinks of Alcoholics Anonymous—is their willingness to acknowledge the power of fate, their respect for forces that lie beyond human control. That cautiousness did not reign at all times, of course, but one sees it often enough to notice it and respect it. With a nod to Bill Wilson and Alcoholics Anonymous, perhaps one might call it sobriety—ironically enough, of course, in a culture that had recently repealed Prohibition. Yet the shoe seems to fit. In his April 28, 1935 fireside chat introducing the Social Security Act, for example, which also included unemployment insurance, Franklin Roosevelt called the provisions of the act "protections for the future."[113] In doing so, he acknowledged that the future always offers harms to be protected against. (I explore this theme more fully in Chapter 8.) Despite what I might hope will happen, despite what robots tell me, despite, even, the number of friends I make and people I influence, and despite, as Irving Fisher put it, the hopeful outlook, the future will not always go our way.[114] After all, the present, the Great Depression, had not gone the way anyone would have chosen. If the Depression taught people anything, then, it is that someone always lands on Chance.

8

"The Hazards and Vicissitudes of Life"

The Emotional Life of the Social Security Act

Ham to ham and eggs to eggs
If I don't get a pension I'll have to beg.

Woody Guthrie, "Ashes to Ashes Dust to Dust"[1]

In January 1940, Ida May Fuller, then a 66-year-old retired legal secretary living in Vermont, opened her mailbox and found a check from the Treasury of the United States made out to her for $22.54 (a little over $400 today). The number on the check, 00-000-001, suggested Fuller's place in history (see Figure 8.1). She had received the very first Social Security check issued by the United States government.[2]

In fact, Fuller had not received the very first Social Security check but the very first check issued under Title II of the Social Security Act, Federal Old-Age Benefits. Understandably, since it composes by far the largest share of Social Security expenditures, most people take that part of Social Security, Old Age Insurance, for the whole. Yet the Social Security Act, as passed in 1935, included more than just old-age benefits. The Act also provided grants to states for aged needy individuals; for unemployment compensation; for needy dependent children (that is, children who lived in families without male breadwinners); for maternal and child welfare, including services for crippled children; for public health work; and for the blind.[3]

The Emotional Life of the Great Depression. John Marsh, Oxford University Press (2019).
 DOI: 10.1093/oso/9780198847731.001.0001

Figure 8.1. Ida May Fuller. The photograph is from 1950.
Source: Associated Press

Quibbles about terminology aside, how that check for $22.54 made its way to Ida May Fuller's mailbox is one of the most fascinating public policy stories of the 1930s, perhaps of the twentieth century. Social Security, as one historian puts it, "remains the most lasting legacy of Depression-era activism, New Deal policymaking, and above all of the public commitment to a broadly inclusive system of shared social protection against the insecurities of a market economy."[4] As the most lasting legacy of the era, Social Security, particularly the sections that focused on old-age insurance for retired workers, also provides a fitting conclusion to an inquiry into the emotional life of the Great Depression. For its passage was shaped not just by the emotions of those who drafted the bill, debated it, denounced it, revised it, made it law, and then four years later amended it. Its passage was also shaped by the feelings of ordinary Americans, those who played no formal role in its enactment but whose emotions weighed heavily on those who did. In short, Social Security offers an example of how feelings can translate into action, into, at times, policy. Each of the emotions I examine in this book, from righteousness to hope, influenced the passage of the Social Security Act of 1935 or shaped the form the legislation took.

In what follows, I describe how the Social Security Act came into existence. I do so by focusing on three sets of actors: Dr. Francis Townsend and his followers, who provided much of the urgency for Social Security; Franklin Roosevelt and the planners of Social Security, who tried to steer the sudden and clamorous demand for pensions into a more pragmatic piece of legislation; and critics of Social Security, whose misgivings would guide the 1939 amendment to the bill. For each group, I focus on the emotions that motivated them. The upshot is a history of Social Security that clusters around the emotions previously discussed in the book: righteousness, panic, and fear, but also awe, love, and hope.

Although emotions can translate into action, the emotional life of the Social Security Act also provides an opportunity to reflect on the limits of this instrumentalist approach to studying the emotions. Emotions, that is, do not invariably translate into deeds. They almost always help people understand the world, but they do not necessarily, and they certainly do not always, lead them (or others on their behalf) to change it. There is a danger, in other words, in thinking of emotions mechanically, as energy that is perpetually converted into action. Put simply, emotional energy does not have to exhaust itself in action. Occasionally, it simply exhausts itself. That said, the Social Security Act (and its 1939 amendment) offer a case study in how feeling leads to action, in how emotions can help one narrate and understand the past.

The Old People's Crusade

One can start the history of the 1935 Social Security Act at several different yet equally justifiable moments: Franklin Roosevelt's June 8, 1934 message to Congress calling for social insurance; the publication of I.M. Rubinow's 1913 book *Social Insurance*; the German social welfare policies of Otto Von Bismarck; or even Thomas Paine's 1797 pamphlet *Agrarian Justice*, which argued, among other things, for an estate tax that would fund old-age pensions.

It may make the most sense, however, to start with a letter to the editor published in the Long Beach *Press Telegram* on September 30, 1933. In that letter, a 66-year-old Long Beach doctor, Francis E. Townsend, described his, as the editors labeled it, "Cure for Depression." Townsend proposed "the national Government retire all who reach [age sixty and above] on a monthly pension of $150 a month or more, on condition that they spend the money as they get it." He suggested raising the funds for the program through a sales tax.[5] In his next letter to the editor, and in subsequent descriptions of what came to be known as the Townsend Plan, Townsend increased the monthly pension to $200. He further specified that recipients would have to spend the money within 30 days. And he abandoned a sales tax in favor of a 2 percent tax on all transactions.

According to legend, the idea for the plan came to Townsend while shaving. His bathroom window overlooked an alley. One morning he looked through the window and saw three "haggard, very old women, stooped with great age, bending over the barrels, clawing into the contents." Fed up with this picture of unrelieved poverty, he dropped his razor and "a torrent of invectives tore out of him." When his wife warned him that if he shouted like that, the neighbors might hear, he replied, "I want all the neighbors to hear me! I want God Almighty to hear me! I'm going to shout till the whole country hears!"[6]

It makes a nice story, but it may have been no more than a story. In his 1943 autobiography, *New Horizons*, Townsend does not mention the women. He does mention, however, his own bleak prospects at the time and, in truth, the Townsend Plan may have been born out of fear for his own future as much as righteous anger on behalf of old women clawing through garbage cans. In 1933, Townsend had lost his position in the Long Beach Health Department. He woke up one day an old doctor with no patients in the middle of the worst depression in United States history. He tried selling real estate but got nowhere. As he remembered, "Things were not going too well in our home. Neither Mrs. Townsend nor myself could see a way out for the future... We were alone and, as day after day went by without a cent coming in—and our slender bank account being paid out—we worried."[7]

Within days of publishing his first letter to the editor, however, Townsend found himself the head of what would with almost unimaginable speed become a national movement. By 1936, 7,000 Townsend Clubs had formed in the United States, with membership in the clubs numbering in the millions.[8] (The city of San Diego had eighty Townsend Clubs with 30,000 members; nearly one out of every five residents of the city belonged to a Townsend Club.)[9] Townsend claimed to control the votes of 25 million people.[10] In 1935, Townsend and his supporters helped to get John Steven

McGroarty, a *Los Angeles Times* columnist who had praised the Townsend Plan, elected to Congress.[11] McGroarty did not disappoint. On January 16, 1936, he introduced a Townsend bill into Congress.[12] An unpublished Gallup opinion poll taken on March 14, 1936 suggested that a majority of Americans might have favored such a bill.[13]

For Townsend the plan was, as he told the House Ways and Means Committee in 1935, "only incidentally a pension plan." "The old people," he continued, "are simply to be used as a means by which prosperity will be restored to all of us."[14] Whoever titled Townsend's first letter to the editor had it right, then. It was more a "Cure for Depression" than anything else. By inducing those sixty and over to leave the labor market, Townsend would solve the unemployment problem, whether it was caused by the Depression or by mechanization. Like many in the 1930s, Townsend worried about the latter phenomenon. In the third paragraph of his first letter to the editor, Townsend argued, "Of late years it has become an accepted fact that because of man's inventiveness less and less productive effort is going to be required to supply the needs of the race. That being the case, it is just as necessary to dispose of our surplus workers as it is to dispose of our surplus wheat."[15]

Townsend also promised that the plan would put an end to the stock market and banking panics I describe in Chapter 2. If the government set individual pensions at $200 per month, he argued, it would make "the aggregate of these pensions a potent factor in stabilizing the circulation of money in a volume sufficient to insure against panics in the business world."[16] In general, though, Townsend promised that his plan "would bring back prosperity by restoring purchasing power to the people."[17] In his third letter to the editor, Townsend wrote, mistily, "Money from a universal sales tax will start a golden flood pouring into Washington that will be constantly augmented as business revives, and as bountiful a flood will return to its source monthly through the pension system stimulating every line of business, increasing prices and wages, restoring real estate values and rentals and making possible the abandonment of charity in all its ugly forms."[18] In short, Townsend did not offer a pension plan. He offered an economic panacea.

In Chapter 7, I argue that for many people the Great Depression meant a chastening of hopes, a reckoning with the power of fate and with forces that they could not control. The popularity of the Townsend Plan, however, complicates that argument. On the one hand, the Townsend Plan, and, as I suggest below, the Social Security Act of 1935, faced—and rebuked—decades of arguments that through self-reliance and thrift individuals could and should provide for their own old age. In that sense, both pension programs acknowledged that hopes did not always match realities. On the other hand, as the complete impracticality of the Townsend Plan also suggests, the Great Depression appears to have made people who lived through it susceptible to all manner of schemes and demagogues.[19] For as nearly every economist who examined the Townsend Plan concluded, not only would it not work, in all likelihood it would make the economy worse, not better.[20]

In a 1935 *Harper's* article "The Old People's Crusade" and, later, in their 1936 book *An Army of the Aged*, the journalists Richard L. Neuberger and Kelley Loe did the most to throw cold water on the plan. In the *Harper's* piece, they observed that according to Townsend himself, the plan would cost between $20 and $24 billion per year. Neuberger and Loe calculated that to fund it would cost each family in America an average of $850 per year (about $16,000 in 2019 dollars). Or, to think of it another way, to fund the Townsend Plan would cost 40 percent of the entire national income of 1934. That meant that those sixty and older, who represented 7 percent of the population in America, would receive 40 percent of the country's income. The remaining 93 percent of the population would thus have to make do with the other 60 percent. "The Townsend Plan," Neuberger and Loe pronounced, "simply would starve Junior to gorge Grandpa."[21]

Indeed, critics were alarmed by the naiveté of those who believed in the Townsend Plan. Edwin Witte, who would lead the group charged with drafting Social Security, concluded, for the benefit of his fellow Social Security planners who may have contemplated adopting the Townsend Plan, "It is a plan which arouses great hopes but actually will give the old people little, or nothing."[22] For their part, Neuberger and Loe worried that "Uncounted thousands of old people have been blinded to even simple arithmetic by Dr. Townsend's promise to make the sundown of life 'a delightful golden autumn instead of a bleak and fearful winter.'"[23] And after working through the numbers, a 1936 pamphlet signed by twenty-two social scientists at the University of Chicago observed of the Townsend Plan that the "notion of such large pensions financed by a 2 per cent transactions tax is thus altogether a delusion." "To propose such an ill-advised scheme," their final sentence read, "can do nothing but distract attention from more reasonable pension plans."[24] In sum, these critics charged, Townsend, like the Dale Carnegie of *How to Win Friends and Influence People*, was selling hope. By claiming that pensions would pay for themselves through increased economic activity, Townsend was also, as I accuse Napoleon Hill, practicing the most magical sort of magical thinking.

The credulity of his followers earned the Townsend Movement a place in Hadley Cantril's 1941 book *The Psychology of Social Movements*. Cantril, as I discuss in Chapter 2, was the Princeton University psychologist who tried to discover why some people panicked when they heard the 1938 *Invasion from Mars* broadcast and why others did not. In *The Psychology of Social Movements*, Cantril set out to learn why "millions of people get swept into social movements," especially "strange or esoteric" ones.[25] After chapters on lynch mobs, Father Divine (the African-American leader of a religious cult whose disciples believed he was God), and the Oxford Group (a revivalist Christian movement that would influence the founders of Alcoholics Anonymous), Cantril turned to the Townsend Plan.

For Cantril, the Townsend Plan succeeded in part because it promised to satisfy the material needs of people. But so, Cantril observed, did a host of other economic panaceas that attracted nowhere the support that Townsend's did. What separated the Townsend Plan from these programs, Cantril argued, was that it fit old norms ("The Townsend Plan Is True Americanism," as one of its slogans ran) and it preserved or enhanced self-regard, by which Cantril meant it "gave old people a place in the scheme of things."[26] But perhaps most important was that the Townsend Plan was simple enough to be understood, and its followers bewildered, desperate, and simple enough to want to understand it. "They," Cantril observed, speaking of those left behind by capitalism and unusually receptive to the Townsend Plan, "are highly suggestible, lacking in critical ability."[27] These are the same terms Cantril used to describe those who panicked while listening to *Invasion from Mars*. (A note in this section of *The Psychology of Social Movements* directs readers to an earlier discussion of that broadcast.) In other words, as Cantril sketched the Venn diagram of those living in the United States in the 1930s, those who panicked and those who joined Townsend clubs formed overlapping parts of the two circles. Call it the part that terrified Hadley Cantril.[28]

Cantril's research soured him not just on the Townsend Movement but on populism generally. He closed his chapter on the Townsend Plan by observing that until the culture can accommodate people more satisfactorily, movements like the one Townsend led were inevitable. "It seems unlikely," he added, "that the critical ability of people will be increased rapidly enough to enable them to properly evaluate the schemes presented them." It fell, then, to "those who better understand the problems of government and finance, of capital and labor, and of youth and of age" to see to it "that needs are better provided for, that meaningful and reasonable goals are substituted for panaceas, and that a large portion of the population does not feel that the discrepancy between its hopes and its realizations is so unbridgeable."[29] Perhaps to add teeth to his warning, he devoted the next two chapters in his book to the rise of the Nazi Party, an illustration, he felt, of what happened to a country when it did not or could not realize the hopes of its citizens.

In the Shadow of the Poorhouse

Although Cantril did not think it sufficed, Social Security came into existence because "those who better understand the problems of government and finance" sought to provide for the needs of their fellow Americans, including those who would otherwise fall prey to economic panaceas like the Townsend Movement (or worse). Thus the history of Ida May Fuller and her $22.54 check starts with the Townsend Movement because of its legions of suggestible, hopeful, and righteous followers. (Many of Townsend's followers believed God inspired his plan, and Townsend did nothing to disabuse them of this belief.) Together with Huey Long, whose Share Our Wealth campaign also included pensions for the elderly, Townsend made the old-age provisions of the Social Security Act not just politically possible but politically urgent. In *The Politics of Upheaval*, Arthur M Schlesinger, Jr. observed, "Townsend and his followers were calling attention to a cruel problem which the American people had too long ignored. Now the nation could no longer ignore its old again."[30]

If the history of the Townsend Movement is one of suggestibility, hope, and righteousness, then the history of the Social Security Act is, to start at least, one of fear. Fear on the part of officeholders that if they did not come up with something more practicable, they might have to pass something "delusional" like the Townsend Plan. Or, more to the point, they would get voted out of office, replaced by someone who would vote for the plan, delusional or not. For then, as now, old people voted. And many old people supported the Townsend Plan. In a 1962 speech, "The Roots of Social Security," Frances Perkins, then secretary of labor and eventual chairwoman of the Committee on Economic Security that would write Social Security legislation, recalled of Townsend:

> In particular, he startled the Congress of the United States, because the aged have votes. The wandering boys didn't have any votes; the evicted women and their children had very few votes. If the unemployed didn't stay long enough in any one place, they didn't have a vote. But the aged people lived

in one place and they had votes, so every Congressman had heard from the Townsend Plan people.[31]

Hear from them they most certainly did. In his 1936 history of the Social Security Act, the economist Paul H. Douglas noted that "Many millions of signatures were obtained to petitions asking Congress to adopt the plan, while the letters advocating [the Townsend Plan] which were received by Congressmen probably themselves ran up into the millions."[32] Robert L. Doughton, the chairman of the House Ways and Means Committee, complained to Townsend when he appeared before that body that the letters arrived "by the carload."[33] The letters accomplished their purpose. In their *Harper's* article, Richard Neuberger and Kelley Loe observed that the "almost unbelievable strength [of the Townsend organization] has stunned the leaders of both the Republican and Democratic parties. On Capitol Hill in Washington the politicians are amazed and terrified by it."[34] The politicians included the president. Frances Perkins, in her 1964 book *The Roosevelt I Knew*, recalled Roosevelt saying, "The Congress can't stand the pressure of the Townsend Plan unless we are studying social security, a solid plan which will give some assurance to old people of systematic assistance upon retirement."[35]

In their defense, in adopting the old-age provisions of the Social Security Act, politicians, including and especially Roosevelt, responded to more than just fears for what Townsend and his supporters might mean for their electoral prospects. Less cynically, they responded to the considerable fears of ordinary Americans. Roosevelt in particular received tens of thousands of letters from aged people (or their children) describing their desperate conditions, pleading for aid, or confessing their fear of the future. These letters predated or did not mention Townsend at all. They merely expressed desperation and fear.

The following letter from Mrs. M.A. Zoller, Sr., of Beaumont, Texas, written in neat, Palmer cursive and sent on July 13, 1933, is typical:

Dear Sir:

I write to ask your assistance in securing an old age pension for my mother Mrs. Martha Gilbert, wife of F. R. Gilbert (deceased since January 6, 1920).

She is helpless, suffering from Sugar Diabetes, which has affected her mind. She has to be cared for in the same manner as an infant. She is out of funds completely. Her son whom she used to keep house for is in a hospital in Waco, Texas—no compensation for either himself or her.

> I am a widow; have spent all my savings in caring for her. I have kept boarders & roomers in a private home to keep my four children for I have always been a lady; this is why I appeal to you to place your dear mother in my dear mother's place. With no money and no place to go unless it be to the poor house. I cannot rent my rooms now for she demands constant care & attention. Please do something about this request as soon as possible.
>
> She will be 82 years old on August 9th.
>
> Yours Truly,
>
> Mrs. M. A. Zoller Sr.
>
> I do not own my home & at present I cannot meet my bills (overdue). I don't know what to expect next.
>
> Thank you in advance.[36]

Mrs. Zoller appeals to the president's empathy ("place your dear mother in my dear mother's place"), but the more revealing part of the letter comes when she asks the president to imagine exactly what that place is: "With no money and no place to go unless it be to the poor house."

Zoller's reference to the poorhouse—and her fear that her mother would end up there—was not hyperbole. Although most people associate poorhouses with Victorian England or, if they acknowledge that they reached America, assume that their history ends with the nineteenth century, poorhouses survived well into the twentieth century. By then, few were still called poorhouses or almshouses. Rather, fully aware of the stigma of poorhouses, officials had renamed them city homes or county farms. The change, as David Wagner writes in *The Poorhouse: America's Forgotten Institution*, "fooled few."[37] By any name, poorhouses reached their apotheosis in the 1930s. Of the six New England poorhouses Wagner examined for his monograph, each "held by far the largest number of inmates in their history during the period of the Great Depression."[38] To adapt the title of Michael B. Katz's famous history of welfare in America, during the 1930s people still lived in the shadow of the poorhouse. Perhaps more than ever. And not least because most of the pension advocacy groups that formed in the early 1920s—the Fraternal Order of the Eagles, the American Association for Labor Legislation—argued for old-age pensions in part by very publicly demonizing poorhouses.[39]

They succeeded. By the 1930s the poorhouse had become the national bogeyman. Countless letters to the president or Eleanor Roosevelt spoke of the terror of the poorhouse. "Now there are a lot of us will choose suicide in preference to being herded into the poorhouse," a Beverly, Massachusetts woman wrote Mrs. Roosevelt in December 1934.[40] In May 1934, a man from Lincoln, Nebraska wrote the First Lady, "We have been honorable citizens all along our journey, calamity and old age has forced its self [sic] upon us please donot [sic] send us to the Poor Farm but instead allow us the small pension of $40.00 per month and we will do as we have done in the past (not complain)."[41] Another woman, to illustrate how little her mother wanted to live with any other member of her family should anything happen to her daughter, said "she would rather go to a poor house."[42]

Besides the fact that correspondents felt more comfortable writing to her than the president, Eleanor Roosevelt received many of these letters because of a speech she gave in early 1934 to the Washington, D.C. branch of the American Association for Social Security. The speech was reported and occasionally reprinted in newspapers across the country. In it, she endorsed old-age pensions. (At this point many states had passed or were debating legislation.) But like the advocacy groups of the 1920s, she did it by lamenting the alternative to pensions, poorhouses. "Most of us," Roosevelt said, after discussing the merits and demerits of the New York pension law that had passed while her husband was governor of that state, "have had personal experiences which have brought [the necessity for this law] home to us." She went on to describe hers, which involved "an old family—two old sisters and two old brothers—who had lived on a farm" near the Roosevelts in New York. Roosevelt, however, did not see them for two or three years.

> Then, one Election Day, I went to get them and I found one old lady in tears because that day one surviving brother had been taken to the insane asylum because the worry of how they were to going to get enough to eat and enough to pay their taxes had finally driven him insane, and she was waiting to go to the poorhouse. The other sister had already gone, and the other brother had died.[43]

Roosevelt says she "felt I had been such a bad neighbor" and "felt so guilty." Yet it also "seemed to me," she said, "as though the whole community was to blame." Old-age pensions, she implied, would allow individuals to fulfill their responsibilities as neighbors and members of a community. It was either that or the poorhouse.

In her speech, Roosevelt is careful to emphasize that only those "who have worked hard all their lives, and, through no fault of theirs, have not been able to provide for their old age" have the right "to be cared for in the last years of their life." She notes of the farm family scattered to the grave, the insane asylum, and the poorhouse, for example, "All their lives they had done what good citizens should do and they simply had never been able to save." Such rhetoric was meant to counteract arguments that for decades had prevented the United States from following Western European countries in adopting social insurance programs. In the early twentieth century, as early reformers like I.M. Rubinow and Abraham Epstein advocated for social insurance, they were nearly always met with claims that such compulsory plans would undermine American traditions of individualism, free association, and thrift.[44]

Such sentiments survived into the 1930s. As late as 1931, Calvin Coolidge argued in his syndicated newspaper column that "What a self-respecting people really needs is not a system of old-age pensions but a population made sufficiently skilled by education and sufficiently self-controlled and well-disposed by the hold of religion so that old-age pensions would be superfluity. Unless real reform comes from within, the problem will never be solved."[45] And during hearings on the Social Security Act, James L. Donnelly, executive vice-president of the Illinois Manufacturers' Association, sent a statement to the House Ways and Means Committee listing eleven reasons why the bill should not be passed. Number ten read, "This program would undermine the fabric of our economic and social life by destroying initiative, discouraging thrift, and stifling individual responsibility."[46] To those like Coolidge and Donnelly, if the state assumed responsibility for the old, that meant the old had not taken responsibility for themselves while young. Pensions, in short, undermined character, the trait, I argue in my chapter on righteousness, whose lapse many felt had caused the Depression, but also the trait, "the eternally valuable element," as F. Scott Fitzgerald put it in "Babylon Revisited," whose resurgence offered the only permanent cure for the depression.

The concern with character is why, on June 8, 1934, when Franklin Delano Roosevelt called on Congress to "undertake the great task of furthering the security of the citizen through social insurance," he was, like his wife, careful to emphasize that the safeguards he sought were not meant to undermine individual responsibility or thrift but to protect against "misfortunes which cannot be wholly eliminated in this man-made world of ours." Hence, in a phrase that would become permanently associated with the Social Security Act, not least because he echoed it at the signing ceremony, Roosevelt told Congress he sought legislation that would offer security against "the hazards and vicissitudes of life."[47] Both words emphasize unpredictability, chance—the events or circumstances that lie beyond one's control.

The existence of those hazards and vicissitudes are what I mean when I argue, in Chapter 7, that the Great Depression did not change what people hoped for but how they hoped for it. Everyone hoped for a prosperous old age. Many may have even worked and saved for that end. But more and more people came to recognize that one could not control everything. Reality had a way of betraying hopes. Indeed, the Depression had already done much to undermine the hope that thrift and character alone could assure prosperity. A popular 1931 cartoon had a squirrel asking an aged man on a park bench, "But why didn't you save some money for the future, when times were good?" "I did," the man says, whose label ("Victim of Bank Failure") exposes the hope that thrift could offer sufficient protection against the hazards and vicissitudes of life and the economy.[48] Save all they want, people could do little about bank failures. And if it were not a bank failure, it would be some other hazard or vicissitude of life that undermined their best laid plans. As I put it in Chapter 7, invoking the game of Monopoly, at some point everyone lands on Chance.

Obviously, that is a lesson that those who more often than not had benefited from the fortunes of life had to learn more than those who, historically, had suffered from its misfortunes, but the former seemed to have learned it nonetheless. In their 1937 book *Social Security in America*, for example, the authors observed, "Investigations on the extent of old-age dependency made by a number of State commissions in the twenties and early thirties disrupted once and for all the comfortable belief that 'deserving' citizens do not become dependent in old age."[49] And in her testimony before the Senate, Frances Perkins, after discussing the "hazards" of old age, illness, and unemployment, said, "Most of us here recognize that these are factors over which [families] have no particular control. The incidence of illness or death, of old age, and of unemployment are hazards which no individual can control for himself."[50] No one challenged her.

Although diehards like Coolidge and Donnelly still existed, those who opposed the Social Security Act did so because they thought it would harm the economy or would menacingly—and, as I argue below, awesomely—expand the powers of the federal government. Few opposed the Act because they thought it would undermine thrift or character. After all, the Act did not get rid of thrift so much as compel it.[51]

Social Security in America

But that is to jump ahead. After Roosevelt delivered his message to Congress in June, he formed the Committee on Economic Security, chaired by Frances Perkins, to study the problem of economic insecurity, including the economic problems of old age, and develop legislation that he could present to Congress by the end of the year. Within six months, the committee had produced a fifty-page formal report to the president, ten volumes of unpublished reports and studies, and, in 1937, a book, *Social Security in America*, that summarized their investigations and recommendations. The research into old-age security was led by Barbara Nachtried Armstrong, a law professor at the University of California, Berkeley (the first woman, as it happens, to join the faculty of the law school at a major university).[52] In their report to the president, the Committee on Economic Security noted the increase of aged persons in the United States. A declining birth rate, they argued, together with the restrictions on immigration set forth in the 1924 Johnson-Reed Act, had led and would continue to lead to the aged representing a larger share of the American population.[53] In addition to the increasing number of aged persons, they noted the increasing dependency of those aged people. They estimated, conservatively, that "at least half of the approximately 7,500,000 people over 65 years now living are dependent," by which they meant having an annual income of less than $300 (about $5,500 in 2019).[54]

At least some of their dependency, the authors concluded, owed to the employment difficulties facing older workers. Like Townsend, the authors were concerned with "the mechanization of industry" and its effect "upon the chances which this growing number of aged persons now have, or in the future will have of preserving their economic independence."[55] Mechanization, Barbara Nachtried Armstrong wrote in the unpublished report, "has placed an increasing emphasis upon youth, physical strength and ability to stand nervous strain."[56] "Although such graphic phrases as 'old at 40' and the 'scrap heap at 45' suggest an exaggeration of the actual facts," she added in language that made it into the 1937 book, "there is undeniable evidence of the progressive use of maximum hiring-age limits in industry."[57] These employment difficulties exacerbated the economic problems of old age. If those over forty years of age lost jobs more frequently and had more difficulty finding jobs once they lost them, they would have that much less of a chance to accumulate the earnings and the savings they would need to keep them out of poverty in old age.

Moreover, the Depression had worsened and would continue to worsen these trends. "Many children who previously supported their parents," the authors of the report informed the president, "have been compelled to cease doing so, and the great majority will probably never resume this load."[58] In other words, whom would the aged depend on if those whom they had depended on—their grown children—could no longer support them? And down the road, those same grown children, having lost their jobs and sometimes their savings in the Depression, would be even less prepared for old age—and even more dependent—than their parents.[59] In short, the Depression had made the economic problems of old age worse, but the economic problems of old age would not end with the Depression. Something must be done.

The Committee on Economic Security recommended a three-pronged attack on the economic insecurity of old age. First, the federal government would offer matching grants to states to supplement existing old-age assistance plans or to establish new ones. By the mid-1930s, most states had pension plans for aged needy individuals, but the Depression had wiped out their budgets. Under Title I of the Social Security Act, the federal government would assist states in providing pensions for those sixty-five and older who could demonstrate need. The pensions would pay up to $30 per month, with half of the money coming from the state and half coming from the federal government.

The planners of Social Security were not immune to considerations of thrift, however. They worried about the effect that "gratuitous assistance" would have on people and, ultimately, on the federal budget.[60] If people began to treat old-age pensions as a matter of right, they reasoned, then more and more people would come to rely—if not to exploit—the system. If the state and the federal government guaranteed people $30 per month upon retirement, for example, then what incentive would people have to save during their working years? And unless they could save a lot, why would people bother to save a little when the government would grant them $30 per month regardless of how much they had saved? (As the authors of the report put it, "the very principle of gratuitous assistance, namely, that the less income the applicant has the more pension he receives, has an effect which is the inverse of inducement to thrift.")[61] If the federal government did nothing but offer old-age assistance to the states, the committee calculated, "the number of aged persons who arrive at old age without any income is actually increased," and the costs of old-age assistance would spin out of control.[62] In their worst-case scenario, the committee calculated that by 1957 50 percent of the aged would depend on the program, which, at pensions of $25 per month, would cost the federal government over $1 billion per year, unadjusted for inflation.[63]

Hence the second part of the plan: contributory old age insurance, what most people today think of as Social Security. To keep gratuitous assistance from undermining thrift, the federal government would simply compel thrift. Under Title II of the Act, workers would contribute a percentage of their paycheck—to be matched by their employer—to an old-age reserve account. Upon retirement at age 65, they would receive an annuity based on the contributions they had made to the reserve over their working life. The plan would begin collecting contributions on January 1, 1937. The first annuities would be paid in 1942.

To fund the program, the committee decided on gradually increasing the tax rate, starting at 0.5 percent in 1937 and increasing by 0.5 percent every five years until it reached a maximum of 2.5 percent in 1957. (Employers would pay the same rate, leading to an eventual total rate of 5 percent.) Social Security would pay annuities, based on how much one had contributed, to those who had paid into the system for five years or more. Those who had contributed for fewer years would simply receive a lump sum payment of what they had contributed, with interest.

The Committee on Economic Security submitted their proposal to President Roosevelt on Christmas Day, 1934 and Roosevelt submitted it to Congress on January 17, 1935. The plan would not survive congressional scrutiny intact. It would not even survive presidential scrutiny intact. As the Committee on Economic Security drafted the old-age insurance component of the bill, the system would have created a $1.5 billion deficit by 1980. The committee simply assumed that a future Congress would make good on the debt. No one—not President Roosevelt, not the secretary of the treasury, and not Congress—liked this idea. When he first saw the proposal, the president thought the table showing a deficit of $1.5 billion by 1980 must be a mistake, so committed was he to the concept that the program pay for itself. "It is almost dishonest," Roosevelt told Frances Perkins, "to build up an accumulated deficit for the Congress of the United States to meet in 1980." The secretary of the treasury, Henry Morgenthau, called the debt an "imposition of onerous burdens on the future" (898). To fix this "mistake," Congress accelerated the tax schedule, starting it at 1 percent in 1937 and increasing it by 0.5 percent every three years thereafter, until it reached a maximum of 3 percent in 1949 (or 6 percent including employer contributions). (This alteration got rid of the debt, but, as I discuss below, it created another problem.)

Congress also altered the needlessly complicated annuity formula that the committee had originally proposed.[64] Instead, those who had contributed at least $2,000 to the system during each of at least five years would receive a monthly annuity according to a formula that rewarded the first $3,000 of contributions more heavily than it did the next $42,000, and any amount over $45,000 least of all.[65] Because the rates were higher on the lower contributions, the system was broadly redistributive. That is, assuming they lived as long as everyone else, those who contributed less to the system ultimately took more than their share, and vice versa. Oddly, for all the criticisms leveled against the compulsory old-age insurance component of Social Security, few at the time criticized that aspect of it.

The third leg of the plan was voluntary old-age annuities for those left out of the compulsory old-age insurance system. As the Committee on Economic Security proposed it, the compulsory insurance plan covered almost everyone who worked for wages or salaries. It did not, however, cover the self-employed or, notoriously, domestic and agricultural workers. Although many historians later perceived the operations of racist Southern congressmen in this exclusion, the evidence is mixed, at best. And in any case, the excluded groups would still be covered by Title I of the Act, old-age assistance.[66] They would also be covered by the voluntary annuity plan. (Basically, the federal government would sell old-age annuities.) Unsurprisingly, this part of the plan did not make it out of Congress. At the behest of Senator Augustine Lonergan of Connecticut, where, coincidentally, a number of private insurance companies did business, the Senate nixed it.[67]

For all their actuarial precision, one could argue that as the drafters of Social Security contemplated the economic problems of old age and their solutions, emotions, as much as or more than numbers, motivated their policy decisions. "The step of adopting old-age annuities," they argued in the report published in 1937 as *Social Security in America*,

> would be justified from the standpoint of sound economic policy even if the net cost of insurance were far in excess of the future relief which it replaces, for the quality of self-respect and the relative freedom of fear of old age engendered by old-age insurance have a dollar-and-cents value to worker, employer, and government alike.[68]

To speak a little less actuarially, the authors of the report meant that whatever else its benefits, old-age annuities would provide emotional wellbeing, and any honest calculation of its costs had to include the value of that wellbeing. "When he has the assurance that each day's work builds up an investment for his old age," the committee speculated, "permitting independence of the charity of the community or financial aid from sons and daughters, already overburdened by the cost of maintaining their own families, much of the wage earner's haunting fear of insecurity is removed."[69] The emotional security might even trickle down to the young, too. "The confidence and sense of security of a mature group of citizens could not but affect the attitudes of younger groups," the committee hoped.[70]

Emotional considerations even influenced how the committee thought the country should fund its old-age insurance program. As sources of revenue, the committee considered personal income taxes, corporate income taxes, inheritance taxes, and sales taxes.[71] It rejected each in favor of payroll taxes, on practical but also emotional grounds. Planners, including President Roosevelt, wanted to avoid any hint of "the dole," or dependence upon the government. Roosevelt, in particular, loathed the dole. In making his case to Congress for a public works program over straight relief, Roosevelt had argued—just weeks before he submitted his Economic Security Bill—that "continued dependence upon relief induces a spiritual and moral disintegration fundamentally destructive to the national fibre. To dole out relief in this way is to administer a narcotic, a subtle destroyer of the human spirit." "The Federal Government," he added, "must and shall quit this business of relief."[72] Soon after forming the Committee on Economic Security, he told the Advisory Council to that body, "We must not allow this type of insurance to become a dole through the mingling of insurance and relief. It is not charity. It must be financed by contributions, not taxes."[73] He had other reasons, but that is why Roosevelt so vehemently opposed the old-age insurance part of the plan going into debt to the federal government. That smelled too much like the dole.

Conversely, if the plan were financed by contributions and not taxes, as Roosevelt desired, then its benefits would be received, as the Committee on Economic Security put it, as "a matter of right."[74] The employee would obtain "a virtual equity" in the system. By contributing to their old-age insurance system rather than drawing pensions from a government, "the individual worker would establish an earned right to a benefit related to the contribution made."[75] They would also, Roosevelt felt, guard it with their lives. Years later, when someone suggested to the president that it had been a mistake to tax payrolls to pay for Social Security during the middle of a depression, Roosevelt responded: "We put those pay roll contributions there so as to give the contributors a legal, moral, and political right to collect their pensions and their unemployment benefits. With those taxes in there, no damn politician can ever scrap my social security program. Those taxes aren't a matter of economics, they're straight politics."[76] They are, as Roosevelt and the Committee on Economic Security understood, straight emotions, too. Righteousness usually comes from God. It can also come from a sense of property, or, as the Committee on Economic Security put it, "virtual equity." If Townsend hoped to inspire a righteous commitment to his plan by associating it with God, Roosevelt and his planners hoped to inspire a righteous commitment to theirs by appealing to a still higher power: that of property, the power of mine.

In April, the House passed what had been renamed the Social Security Act of 1935 by a vote of 371 to 19. Two months later, the Senate passed it by a vote of 76 to 6. Roosevelt signed the Act into law on August 14, 1935. "If the Senate and the House of Representatives in this long and arduous session had done nothing more than pass this Bill," Roosevelt declared at the signing ceremony, "the session would be regarded as historic for all time."[77]

Of Reservations and Reserves

Opponents of the bill agreed with Roosevelt about the historical importance of "this Bill," though they believed historians would ultimately judge the Congress that passed it much more harshly than Roosevelt ever imagined. For its opponents, that is, the bill, in addition to whatever it would do to initiative, thrift, and individual responsibility, suffered from several, tragic flaws. If emotions played a role in generating urgency for the Social Security Act and in the shape it took, emotions—especially righteousness, fear, and awe—would also play a role in the form the opposition to the Act took.

By funding it through payroll taxes, President Roosevelt and the Committee on Economic Security hoped to endow Americans with an "earned right" to collect on their contributions later. Under the plan, the government did not assist Americans; Americans would take what rightly belonged to them. For critics of the legislation, however, the "virtual equity" that Social Security created was more virtual than real. Besides a promise from Congress, nothing guaranteed that the money individuals contributed throughout their working life would return to them upon retirement.

In the second of two articles on the new Social Security Act published in the *Saturday Evening Post* in March 1936, Frank Parker Stockbridge observed that when someone purchased an annuity from an insurance company, the company issued a contract stating that when the person reached a certain age, the company would pay a specified sum each month to that person for the rest of their life. The old-age benefit under Social Security, however, provided no such contract. Its debt to you was "no more than a moral obligation."[78] Strictly speaking, the payroll taxes collected from employers and employees, Parker argued, created "no vested rights. They become part of the general revenues of the Federal Government."[79] The federal government has promised to pay you what the law says it will, Parker argued, but the "law may be quite different in 1950, or whenever any given individual's time comes to retire on a Federal pension."[80] "The worker who pays his old-age benefit tax," Parker concluded, "is a taxpayer, not a premium payer, and he takes his chances, with all the rest of us taxpayers, on what his Government will do with his money."[81] Note the phrase: "his money." Parker took the emotion—the righteousness inspired by a sense of property—that Roosevelt and his planners assumed would recommend Social Security to Americans and turned it on them. In all likelihood the Congress of 1950 or whenever would fulfill its side of the bargain. But one only had its word, not the backing of the law.

The Republican Party, and its candidate for president in 1936, Alf Landon, hoped to turn Parker's legalistic criticism of the Social Security Act into a campaign issue. In a speech in Milwaukee, Wisconsin in September, Landon asserted that the "savings [the legislation] forces on workers is a cruel hoax." The day may come, Landon told the crowd, when, having grown old, people will find that the money they faithfully contributed to Social Security all their life will have simply disappeared, used in the meantime by the federal government for "current deficits and new extravagances."[82] And as I detail in Chapter 2, in the weeks before the 1936 presidential election, some employers slipped notes into the pay envelopes of workers describing how, starting January 1, 1937, Roosevelt would compel them, employers, to start making a 1 percent deduction from workers' paychecks and turning it over to the government. The deduction, the note said, might go as high as 4 percent. Trading on fear as much as righteousness, the note closed, "You might get this money back... but only if Congress decides to make the appropriation for this purpose. There is NO guarantee. Decide before November 3—election day—whether or not you wish to take these chances."[83]

Still another criticism of Social Security sought to elicit in people not a feeling of righteousness born of property or fear for what the government would do with your money but, oddly enough, a feeling of the sublime. In Chapter 5, I examine new sources of the sublime in the 1930s: the universe, skyscrapers, Jesse Owens, steel workers, migrant workers, grandmothers, tenant farmers, and so on. To this list one might add, after the passage of the Social Security Act, the federal government. In Chapter 5, I associate the sublime with vastness, prompted, as Arthur Schopenhauer wrote, "by the sight of a power beyond all comparison superior to the individual." For its critics, the Social Security Act endowed the federal government with powers—and with power—it had never had before. Its critics then began to look upon it—and to describe it—with terror, to contemplate how it could reduce individuals, as Schopenhauer said contemplating the stars of the sky could, to nothing. In short, after Social Security, people, especially conservatives, began to talk of Big Government, and not the bumbling, inefficient Big Government that conservatives today sometimes decry but an all-powerful, all-knowing state that exercised total authority and reduced human beings to nothing, to a number.

During debate on the Social Security Act, for example, congressman James W. Wadsworth warned, "This bill opens the door and invites the entrance into the political field of a power so vast, so powerful as to threaten the integrity of our institutions and to pull the pillars of the temple down upon the heads of our descendants."[84] Writing in the *Saturday Evening Post* in September 1936, less than a month after Roosevelt signed the Social Security Act into law, Garet Garrett echoed Wadsworth's warnings of "a power so vast." Social Security, he observed, "is a new instrument of government power." "Not only does it enormously extend the authority of the Federal Government to administer our everyday lives and well being," he observed; "it delivers free into the hands of Government a fund that may very well represent the capital resources of the country. What form of government might survive after that would not matter. Its economic power would be absolute."[85] And in the first of his two articles devoted to the Social Security Act in the *Saturday Evening Post*, Frank Parker Stephenson, discussing what made the act historic, regrettably so, listed "An official card index in Washington, recording the name, address, age, occupation and earnings of... wage workers or salaried persons from the day they began to work for pay until death or old age overtakes them. Has any American," he asked, overwhelmed at the prospect, "ever seriously dreamed of anything like that in this country?"[86] The illustration accompanying his article showed a family labeled "U.S. CITIZENS OF THE FUTURE." They have been turned into walking government index cards.

Stephenson went a step further in the second of his two *Post* articles. There he discussed the challenges the federal government faced turning citizens into index cards—that is, documenting the tens of millions of workers in the United States that Social Security would require for it to function. He noted that in Germany, with less than half the population of the United States, the administration of their old-age pensions system required a staff of 12,000 employees. "Even if it were probable that any Government bureau under our American political system would operate as efficiently as in Germany," Stephenson wrote,

> it is not hard to visualize a building in Washington as big as or bigger than the Department of Commerce, crowded with forty or fifty million personal *dossiers* of actual and prospective beneficiaries of the old-age retirement system, and 20,000 or more Civil Service clerks and bookkeepers to keep track of them. The Social Security Board has already begun to talk about needing half a million square feet of floor space. That would be equivalent to a building 250 x 100 feet, 20 stories high.[87]

In seeking to describe the magnitude of the bureaucracy required to implement Social Security, Parker relies on some of the same tropes as those who tried to describe the vastness of the Empire State Building or the Hoover Dam. Instead of reciting the miles of electrical wire (2,000,000) or the cubic yards of concrete (4,400,000) required to construct those instances of the sublime, though, Parker recites the number of people or the amount of floor space required, which, at twenty stories high, would take up roughly a fifth of the newly constructed Empire State Building. These are numbers, he thinks, that simply go beyond human comprehension.

Finally, you may have noticed that, as originally planned, Social Security would not begin paying old age annuities until January 1942. Yet at the start of the chapter Ida May Fuller received the first Social Security check in January 1940. The change owed to a third criticism of the Act, offered by the political left and right, which is that in order to pay for itself, as everyone insisted it should, the system had to build up enormous future reserves against the day when younger workers would eventually retire. To build up this reserve, Congress, following a plan submitted by the secretary of the treasury, accelerated the payroll tax schedule that the Committee on Economic Security originally proposed. According to the revised schedule, instead of creating a $1.5 billion annual deficit by 1980, the Social Security system would require no annual federal contributions *and* have created a $50 billion reserve. Following that schedule, the system, even in the near term, would create a huge reserve. Actuaries thought the reserve would have accumulated nearly $3 billion by 1940 alone.[88]

For Roosevelt and his planners, these reserves represented fiscal probity. For critics of the plan, however, they represented economic suicide. As the economist Paul Douglas noted at the time, if Social Security taxed workers now to pay for old-age insurance later, workers would spend less in the short term, and the economy would have that much more trouble emerging from its doldrums. "The result might, therefore," Douglas argued, "be an initial impounding and sterilization of large sums of monetary purchasing power, with a consequent intensification of the depression."[89] In other words, at a time when the federal government was flooding the economy with money to stimulate demand, it made little sense, critics charged, for the same government to then start sopping money back up in the form of payroll taxes.

Roosevelt and his planners, however, could live with this contradiction. They designed the Social Security Act, as the historian Edward Berkowitz writes, not for the "current depression so much as the next one."[90] "No one can guarantee this country against the dangers of future depressions," Roosevelt told Congress when he announced his intention of creating a Social Security bill, "but we can reduce these dangers. We can eliminate many of the factors that cause economic depressions, and we can provide the means of mitigating their results."[91] Not everyone, however, wanted to devote present resources to future depressions. Many still had the present depression very much in mind. In seeking to ameliorate future depressions, its opponents and, even, like Douglas, its proponents argued, the Social Security Act might worsen the present one. For them, the "onerous burdens on the future" that Secretary Morgenthau spoke of in his testimony to the House Ways and Means Committee had been rashly shifted to the present.

Although it might seem like a leap to get from tax schedules, annual deficits, and reserves to love, the connection is closer than it may appear. (And goes beyond the metaphor of the sterilization or procreativity of money.) In Chapter 6, I argue that during the 1930s love—heterosexual love, anyway—followed the economy into hard times. As the economy plummeted, for example, so too did marriage and birth rates. Love, I argue, requires a solid economic foundation. That foundation gives people a horizon of time that makes love possible. That is, love thrives—people marry, have children—when the present offers a promising vision of the future. And love declines—or, to be specific, a certain form of love, namely heterosexual love—declines when the present makes the future look bleak. At those times, like the early years of the 1930s, people can barely imagine a future at all, let alone one in which, happily married, they have given birth to happy children.

Social Security reflected this dynamic because it sought to orient people toward the future. On the one hand, the Social Security Act reflected the chastened hopes of a generation. Self-reliance and thrift would not always suffice. On the other hand, the Social Security Act simultaneously offered a renewed hope for the future. Not just that the legislation would save people from the poorhouse or provide a minimum of economic security in old age, though it would do that. But also because it suggested that the United States could afford to direct resources toward the future, to stave off the next Great Depression. The old-age insurance component of Social Security posited the existence not just of a future but of a prosperous one. In this respect, the Social Security Act offered hope. The Depression, it implied, would not last forever. (After all, even postulating the existence of a reserve in 1980, let alone one of $1.5 billion, assumed that the economy would return to normal.) Indeed, so strong a hold did the future have on the imagination of those who passed the Act that they did not want to burden the future with debts that the present created, and even those who did not mind burdening the future, like the Committee on Economic Security, evidently thought the future could easily assume such burdens.

As passed in 1935, the Social Security Act borrowed from the present to pay the future. Almost immediately, however, and especially as the economy worsened again in 1937 and 1938 after appearing to emerge from the Depression in the middle years of the decade, many balked about making such a sacrifice. In 1939, then, facing considerable pressure from conservatives and liberals alike, Congress amended the Social Security Act. They solved the problem of the enormous future reserves less by reducing taxes than by making the plan more generous now: they opened up who qualified for annuities; they increased monthly annuities; and they accelerated, from 1942 to 1940, when the first annuities would be paid. In other words, they borrowed back from the future to pay the present.

Curiously, however, given what I have said about the relationship between heterosexual love and the balance between the present and the future, when the Congress of 1939 amended the Social Security Act to favor the present over the future, they counterbalanced *that* decision by also making the Act favor the family much more so than it did the individual. As originally passed, the old-age insurance component of the Social Security Act focused on the individual.[92] A worker made contributions to the plan and upon retirement received an annuity. Plain and simple. To be sure, if the worker died before they received in monthly annuities all that they had contributed to the system, their surviving widow or dependent would receive a lump sum payment (with interest) of the lifetime contribution that remained. But that was it. After the 1939 amendments, however, Social Security would not only pay a full annuity to a worker but also a half annuity to the dependent spouse of a worker *and* a half annuity to a dependent child, if the worker had one. "On average," Edward D. Berkowitz writes, "married couples would collect 150 percent of what bachelors received, even if a single worker and a married worker put exactly the same amount into the fund."[93]

In addition to shifting the horizon of Social Security from the future to the present, the 1939 amendments transformed Social Security from an individual old-age insurance plan to a family old-age insurance plan. Those two decisions, I suggest, balanced each other out. The 1939 Amendments to Social Security moved resources from the future to the present, which followed the shift in horizon during the 1930s from the future to the present, the shift that would have such disastrous consequences for heterosexual love. Yet the Congress of 1939 could offset that shift, at least in amendments to the Social Security Act, by building in incentives to heterosexual love. "I don't mind taxing the bachelors," Theresa McMahon, a member of the 1938 advisory council that worked out the amendments to the 1935 Act, said when it was pointed out that families would draw more from the program than single men. "I think they ought to take on the responsibility of sharing their income with someone else."[94] McMahon admitted her feelings about bachelors and their social obligations around the same time, I argue, that the culture as a whole, to judge from marriage and birth rates, had recommitted itself to heterosexual love. The 1939 Amendments to Social Security reflected that recommitment. Strange to say, it paid people to fall in love (and marry).

As I have told it, the history of Social Security is a history of emotions: fear of people and the strange and esoteric social movements they might, in their suggestibility and lack of critical thinking, join if their hopes were not met; fear of the poorhouse; fear of the dole and what it might do to individual initiative; fear of what the government might do with your money; fear, verging on panic, verging on awe at the newfound size and power of the federal government; the righteousness of those who joined the Townsend Movement; righteousness, born of property, and how proponents and critics of Social Security sought to use that righteousness to inspire commitment to the new Act or to cast doubt upon it; hope for "a delightful golden autumn of old age" that inspired those who joined the Townsend Movement; the recognition that more than the hope in thrift and self-reliance was required to meet the hazards and vicissitudes of life, particularly the hazards and vicissitudes of old age; and hope, built into its actuarial tables, that the Great Depression would not last forever; and finally, in a strange way, love, in the sense that love reflected how people—and policymakers—during the Great Depression balanced the future against the present and nudged people toward heterosexual love.

For the sake of a conclusion, I have focused on the emotions that the body of the book takes up. Other emotions, however—anger, despair, sympathy—of course belong to the history of Social Security as well. That righteousness, fear, panic, awe, hope, and love nevertheless arise as frequently as they do in the history of what is, arguably, the signal legislative achievement of the 1930s confirms the intuition behind this book, which is that while those emotions belong to the history of any decade, they distinguish the 1930s in particular.

As I suggested at the outset of this conclusion, I would not want to make policy, or even action, the final or the only story emotions tell about the Great Depression, as though the decade were a Hoover Dam generating policy out of the Colorado River of emotions that ran through it. That is to privilege the public life of emotions over their private one. Emotions always make something happen, but what they make happen does not always disturb the surface of national life. Sometimes they do. And sometimes—think of evangelicals drawing comfort from their righteousness, or parents in Brooklyn terrified about whether their child's fever and achiness meant the flu or infantile paralysis—they do not. To be sure, one can describe the indirect public or policy outcomes of those more private emotions: how the righteousness of evangelicals influenced whom they voted for, or how the fear of polio led to Title V of the Social Security Act, which set aside funds for crippled children. (The planners of the act had victims of polio in mind.)[95] But such a focus can easily overlook how emotions count privately.

For those who experienced these versions of righteousness or fear, politics and policy may have mattered, but they did not matter in the moment. Policy and politics play out over the long term, over weeks, months, and years. As often enough as not, emotions play out over the short term, over minutes, hours, and days.

Nonetheless, if we accept that qualification about the private life of emotions, we can more confidently pursue their public life. Or, as in the case of the passage of the Social Security Act, symbolized, for me, by the day in January 1940 when Ida May Fuller opened her mailbox and found a check for $22.54, we can see how the emotional life of the 1930s, public and private, came together to change the trajectory of American life.

Notes

CHAPTER I

1. Lorena Hickok, *One Third of a Nation: Lorena Hickok Reports the Great Depression*, eds. Richard Lowitt and Maurine Beasley (Urbana: University of Illinois Press, 1981), 51.
2. Harry Hopkins, *Spending to Save: The Complete Story of Relief* (New York: Norton, 1936), ix.
3. Hickok, *One Third of a Nation*, 14.
4. Ibid., ix–x.
5. Ibid., 51–2.
6. Quoted in Arthur M. Schlesinger, *The Coming of the New Deal, 1933–1935* (1958; reprint, Boston: Mariner, 2003), 27.
7. Arthur M. Schlesinger, *The Crisis of the Old Order, 1919–1933* (1957; reprint, Boston: Mariner, 2003), 266.
8. Ibid., 267.
9. Ibid., 460.
10. Schlesinger, *The Coming of the New Deal*, 43.
11. "Farm War On; Milk to Go Up," *Chicago Tribune*, Sep. 14, 1933.
12. "Nebraska Joins North Dakota in Fight on NRA," *Chicago Tribune*, October 20, 1933.
13. Ibid.
14. Chris Foam, "War Comes to Wisconsin over Milk Prices—in 1933," *Milwaukee-Wisconsin Journal Sentinel*, May 10, 2016, http://archive.jsonline.com/greensheet/war-comes-to-wisconsin-over-milk-prices--in-1933-b99720276z1-378882341.html.
15. Michael Golay, *America 1933: The Great Depression, Lorena Hickok, Eleanor Roosevelt, and the Shaping of the New Deal* (New York: Simon and Schuster, 2013), 91.
16. Hickok, *One Third of a Nation*, 55–7.
17. Ibid., 66.
18. Ibid., 60–1. The relief investigator whom Hickok had accompanied to the house asked the mother about her bedding: "She hesitated for a moment and then led us upstairs. One bed. A filthy, ragged mattress. Some dirty pillows. She said the last of her sheets gave out two years ago. On the bed two worn and dirty flannel blankets, just rags. That was all. 'Do you and your husband and the

children all sleep together?' the investigator asked. 'We have to,' she replied simply, 'to keep warm.'"

19. Ibid., 112.
20. Rachel Arons, "Chronicling Poverty with Compassion and Rage," *New Yorker*, January 17, 2013, http://www.newyorker.com/books/page-turner/chronicling-poverty-with-compassion-and-rage. Gellhorn published a book based on her work with FERA, a collection of four novellas called *The Trouble I've Seen* (1936; reprint, London: Eland, 2012).
21. Andrew M. Colman, "Emotional Intelligence," in *A Dictionary of Psychology*, 4th ed. (Oxford: Oxford University Press, 2015).
22. Hickok, *One Third of a Nation*, 93.
23. Ibid., 62.
24. Others at the time offered the same comparison. In the "Persons and Places" section at the beginning of *Let Us Now Praise Famous Men*, James Agee lists himself as "a spy, traveling as a journalist" and Walker Evans as a "counter-spy, traveling as a photographer."
25. Alan S. Binder, *After the Music Stopped: The Financial Crisis, the Response, and Work Ahead* (New York: Penguin, 2013).
26. Liaquat Ahamed, *Lords of Finance: The Bankers Who Broke the World* (New York: Penguin, 2009), 2–3.
27. Barry Eichengreen, *Hall of Mirrors: The Great Depression, the Great Recession, and the Use—and Misuses—of History* (New York: Oxford University Press, 2015), 166.
28. Hopkins, *Spending to Save*, 111.
29. David M. Kennedy, *The American People in the Great Depression: Freedom from Fear* (New York: Oxford, 2003), 160.
30. Hickok, *One Third of a Nation*, 91.
31. Ibid., 107.
32. Ibid., 106.
33. Ibid., 120.
34. Ibid., 90.
35. Michael Ignatieff, *The Needs of Strangers* (London: Chatto & Windus: Hogarth Press, 1984), 13.
36. Ahamed, *Lords of Finance*, 6.
37. Edmund Wilson, *The American Earthquake* (Garden City: Doubleday, 1958).
38. Joseph Kalar, "Papermill," in *Papermill: Poems, 1927–35*, ed. Ted Genoways (Urbana: University of Illinois Press), 51.
39. Martha Nussbaum, *The Fragility of Goodness* (1986; revised ed., New York: Cambridge University Press, 2001), 390.
40. "S&P 500 Index—90 Year Historical Chart," *Macrotrends*, accessed February 16, 2017, http://www.macrotrends.net/2324/sp-500-historical-chart-data.
41. The sentence invokes the title of another famous book about the decade, this one by the economist Peter Temin. See *Lessons from the Great Depression* (Cambridge, Mass.: MIT Press, 1989).

42. This sentence invokes the title of an earlier book by Eichengreen. See *Golden Fetters: The Gold Standard and the Great Depression, 1919–1939* (New York: Oxford University Press, 1992).
43. David M. Herszenhorn, "Bailout Plan Wins Approval; Democrats Vow Tighter Rules," *New York Times*, October 3, 2008, http://www.nytimes.com/2008/10/04/business/economy/04bailout.html.
44. "Job Openings and Labor Turnover Survey," *Bureau of Labor Statistics*, November 4, 2018, https://data.bls.gov/timeseries/JTS00000000LDR.
45. "Foreclosure Trends," *RealtyTrac*, November 4, 2018, https://www.realtytrac.com/statsandtrends/foreclosuretrends/.
46. "The Job-Seekers Ratio, 2000–2016," *Economic Policy Institute*, last modified February 7, 2017, http://www.stateofworkingamerica.org/charts/job-seekers-ratio-total/.
47. Walter Benn Michaels, *The Beauty of a Social Problem: Photography, Autonomy, Economy* (Chicago: University of Chicago Press, 2015), 38.
48. Ibid., 40.
49. Of recent books published on the Great Depression, the closest to what I offer here is probably Morris Dickstein's *Dancing in the Dark: A Cultural History of the Great Depression* (New York: Norton, 2009). I share Dickstein's obvious love for the decade, and his effort to understand it by examining what people read, listened to, and watched. But in this book I choose a wider lens than Dickstein does, both in the range of emotions I explore and the objects I use to document those emotions. Unlike Dickstein, that is, I do not focus exclusively on Depression culture and its major players—important as those are—but instead include lesser known but, I would argue, no less important events and players. Nowhere, for example, does Dickstein—or, in his defense, anyone else really—mention polio or infectious diseases, surely one of the most important everyday fears in the Great Depression. And in *Dancing in the Dark*, *Superman* gets only a passing reference. So too Dale Carnegie's best-selling *How to Win Friends and Influence People*. To my mind, these experiences and texts belong to our history of the Great Depression at least as much as *Citizen Kane*. I do not mean to single out Dickstein's book. No writer can do everything. But I believe that when it comes to the Great Depression, at this point the challenge is to make it new, and one way to do that is to take a new approach to it—say, the emotions—and to examine experiences and sources that have thus far gone understudied. In other words, I hope that the people, events, and texts at the heart of my study do not just add detail to a familiar story but, rather, bring a familiar story to life.
50. Those in the grip of righteousness do not consider it a negative emotion, but I consider it one of the worst. Beginning the book with righteousness offers the advantage, too, of not starting with panic, which, given the stock market crash that supposedly set it off, is how one might be tempted to begin a history of the Great Depression. In the hope of offering a slightly different perspective on the period, I begin with righteousness.

51. For relatively recent and relevant but nonetheless differing approaches to the literature of the Great Depression, see Michael Szalay's *New Deal Modernism: American Literature and the Invention of the Welfare State* (Durham: Duke University Press, 2000), Mark W. Van Wienen's *American Socialist Triptych: The Literary-Political Work of Charlotte Perkins Gilman, Upton Sinclair, and W.E.B. Du Bois* (Ann Arbor: University of Michigan Press, 2012), and Joseph B. Entin's *Sensational Modernism: Experimental Fiction and Photography in Thirties America* (Chapel Hill: University of North Carolina Press, 2007). Entin, in particular, has indirectly taken up the question of emotion (especially astonishment) in the modernist-inflected literature and photography of the Great Depression.
52. The journalist Frederick Lewis Allen ends *Only Yesterday: An Informal History of the Nineteen-Twenties* (New York: Harper & Brothers, 1931), his popular 1931 account of the decade of the 1920s, with the Panic of 1929. That event begins *Since Yesterday: The Nineteen-Thirties in America, September 3, 1929–September 3, 1939* (New York: Harper & Brothers, 1940), his equally popular 1940 account of the decade of the 1930s.
53. Allen selects this date.
54. See M.R. Darby, "Three-and-a-Half Million U.S. Employees Have Been Mislaid: Or, An Explanation of Unemployment, 1934–1941," *Journal of Political Economy* 84.1 (1976): 1–16.
55. See Ronald de Sousa, *The Rationality of Emotion* (Cambridge, Mass.: MIT Press, 1987); Martha Nussbaum, *Upheavals of Thought: The Intelligence of Emotions* (New York: Cambridge University Press, 2001), and Antonio Damasio, *Descartes' Error: Emotion, Reason, and the Human Brain* (New York: G.P. Putnam, 1994). In this book I also follow the by now standard distinction between affect and emotion. "Feelings are *personal* and *biographical*, emotions are *social*, and affect is *prepersonal*," Eric Shouse writes in "Feeling, Emotion, Affect," which is a good start at definitions, if by prepersonal—as Shouse does—one means preconscious. The classic theoretical work on affect remains Brian Massumi's, *Parables of the Virtual: Movement, Affect, Sensation* (Durham: Duke University Press, 2002), especially the first chapter. On the political stakes of recent work in affect and the emotions, I recommend Ruth Leys, "The Turn to Affect: A Critique," *Critical Inquiry* 37 (2011): 434–72. Eric Shouse, "Feeling, Emotion, Affect," *M/C Journal* 8.6 (2005), accessed March 14, 2018, http://journal.media-culture.org.au/0512/03-shouse.php.
56. In this respect, it shares much with recent books like Sianne Ngai's *Ugly Feelings* (Cambridge, Mass.: Harvard University Press, 2007) and Lauren Berlant's *Cruel Optimism* (Durham: Duke University Press, 2011). Unlike those books, however, *This Dark Hour* brings the insights that an emotional approach to culture can offer and applies it not to the present, as those books tend to do, but to the past, to a crucial moment in American history.
57. A third possibility, of course, is that writers neither exclusively perceive nor project but also persuade. That is, readers may come to feel, if they did not

before, the emotions that writers describe or, as I argue of the Kalar poem, to have their existing, muddled feelings clarified for them.

58. Although in the 1930s "illegal" is not as cut and dried a term as it may seem. As Abraham Hoffman writes, "immigrants prior to the Great Depression entered the United States at a time when the government's views on immigration were in flux, moving from unrestricted entry to severe restriction." Those who entered in periods of unrestricted entry might not have the requisite papers and, thus, in later years count as illegal despite having entered the country legally, or at least not illegally. Hoffman, *Unwanted Mexican Americans in the Great Depression: Repatriation Pressures 1929–1939* (Tucson: University of Arizona Press, 1974), 2.
59. Interested readers should consult Hoffman's *Unwanted Mexican Americans in the Great Depression* and Francisco E. Balderrama and Raymond Rodriquez's *Decade of Betrayal: Mexican Repatriation in the 1930s* (Albuquerque: University of New Mexico Press, 2006).
60. Hickok, *One Third of a Nation*, 137.
61. Golay, *America 1933*, 254.
62. Hickok, *One Third of a Nation*, 216.
63. Ibid., 218.
64. Ibid., 272.
65. Ibid., 270.
66. Ibid., 269.
67. Franklin Delano Roosevelt, "Inaugural Address," speech, Washington, D.C., March 4, 1933, http://www.presidency.ucsb.edu/ws/index.php?pid=14473&st=&st1=.
68. Richard S. Lazarus, *Emotion and Adaption* (New York: Oxford University Press, 1991), 108. In emphasizing the diagnostic and functional purpose of emotions, Lazarus accords with earlier theorists of the emotions like Aristotle, Charles Darwin, and William James as well as later ones like Nussbaum and Damasio.

CHAPTER 2

1. Robert S. Lynd and Helen Merrell Lynd, *Middletown in Transition: A Study in Cultural Conflicts* (1937; reprint, New York: Harvest, 1965), 256, quoted in Schlesinger, *The Crisis of the Old Order*, 180.
2. Sinclair Lewis, *It Can't Happen Here* (1935; reprint, New York: Signet Classics, 1993), 104.
3. Ibid., 105–6.
4. My allusion notwithstanding, righteousness differs from the set of ugly feelings described by Sianne Ngai in her book of the same name. In that book, Ngai emphasizes that ugly feelings like envy or irritation "evoke pain or displeasure" and, thus, few enjoy experiencing them. By contrast, righteousness evokes, if not always pleasure, then at least contentment. In any case, few would wish it away. That said, like the other ugly feelings Ngai examines, righteousness in the context of the Great Depression also raises the question of action or inaction. Although not an ugly feeling per se, when it comes to economic

policy, righteousness, as I show, can generate a harmful sort of inaction. As to why affect theorists—and, more specifically, scholars of the emotions—have neglected righteousness in particular and religion, especially Christianity, in general, perhaps affect theorists tend to worry most about political life under late capital, and religion may not seem relevant—or congenial—to the arguments they wish to make. Less charitably, perhaps affect theorists tend to write about subjects that preoccupy them, and in the largely secular world of the humanities, religion does not. To her credit, Eve Kosofsky Sedgwick briefly considers Buddhism in the closing pages of *Touching Feeling*.

5. "Gunman Lays Act to Body 'Torment,'" *New York Times*, February 16, 1933.
6. "Zangara Receives 80-Year Sentence," *New York Times*, February 21, 1933.
7. "Zangara Defiant in Plea of Guilty," *New York Times*, March 10, 1933.
8. "Zangara Executed for Killing Cermak," *New York Times*, March 21, 1933.
9. Quoted in Arthur M. Schlesinger, *The Politics of Upheaval, 1935–1936* (1960; reprint, New York: Houghton Mifflin, 2003), 635.
10. Franklin D. Roosevelt, "Speech at Madison Square Garden," speech, New York City, October 31, 1936, Miller Center, http://millercenter.org/president/speeches/speech-3307.
11. Kim Phillips-Fein, "Paradise Lost," in *Invisible Hands: The Businessmen's Crusade against the New Deal* (New York: W.W. Norton, 2009), 3–25.
12. Jerome Siegel and Joe Schuster, "Superman," in *The Superman Chronicles*, Vol. 1, *The Superman Chronicles* (New York: DC Comics, 2006), 35.
13. Ibid., 36.
14. Ibid., 38.
15. Ibid., 43.
16. Ibid.
17. Ibid., 44. Mine owners who risk the lives of their workers for profit deserve the righteous indignation cast their way far more than Detroit industrialists do. As the Hawks Nest Tunnel Disaster of 1931 shows, in which hundreds of workers—indeed no one knows quite how many—died as a result of silicosis poisoning born of the desire for quick profits, mine accidents as a result of lax safety standards did not only occur in the pages of comic books. For more on the disaster, see Martin Cherniack, *The Hawk's Nest Incident: America's Worst Industrial Disaster* (New Haven: Yale University Press, 1986).
18. Howard Zinn, *A People's History of the United States* (1980; reprint, New York: Harper Perennial, 1995), 378.
19. Ibid., 392.
20. Daniel Robert Fitzpatrick, *Cartoons by Fitzpatrick, St. Louis Post-Dispatch* (St. Louis: Pulitzer, 1947), 22.
21. Herbert Hoover, *The Memoirs of Herbert Hoover: The Great Depression, 1929–1941* (New York: Macmillan, 1952), 30.
22. Ibid.
23. Dwight Morrow, the New Jersey candidate for the senate in 1930, expressed a similar sentiment. As Edmund Wilson quoted him, "There is something about

too much prosperity that ruins the fiber of the people. The men and women who built this country, that founded it, were people who were reared in adversity." "In the cold weather," Wilson ironically remarked of Morrow's speech, "it is reassuring to remind oneself that the men in the breadlines, the men and women beggars in the streets, and the children dependent on them, are all having their fiber hardened." As Wilson also reminded his readers, fewer Americans suffered from prosperity than either Mellon or Morrow seemed to think. According to the National Bureau of Economic Research, Wilson tells us, at the height of the pre-Crash peak, "perhaps two thirds of the families in America were very badly off indeed." Wilson, *The American Earthquake*, 170–1.

24. Hoover, *The Memoirs*, 31.
25. On the moral economy of Schumpeter in particular and the liquidationist school in general, see J. Bradford DeLong "'Liquidation' Cycles: Old-Fashioned Real Business Cycle Theory and the Great Depression," *National Bureau of Economic Research*, accessed December 11, 2015, http://www.nber.org/papers/w3546.
26. Douglas Vincent Brown, preface to Joseph Schumpeter, Economics of the Recovery Program (New York: Whittlesey, 1934), vii.
27. Schumpeter, "Depressions," in *Economics of the Recovery Program*, 13–14.
28. Ibid., 13.
29. Ibid., 16.
30. Ibid., 20.
31. Hoover, *The Memoirs*, 31.
32. Schumpeter, *Economics of the Recovery Program*, 20.
33. DeLong, "Liquidation Cycles," 33.
34. Walter S. Salant, "The Spread of Keynesian Doctrines and Practices in the United States," in *The Political Power of Economic Ideas: Keynesianism across Nations*, ed. Peter A. Hall (Princeton: Princeton University Press, 1989), 32.
35. In Revelation, John speaks of how all are "to be marked on the right hand and forehead so that no one can buy or sell who does not have the mark" (Rev. 13:16–17 (NRSV)). See also Joel A. Carpenter's *Revive Us Again: The Reawakening of American Fundamentalism* (New York: Oxford University Press, 1997) and Matthew Avery Sutton's "Was FDR the Antichrist? The Birth of Fundamentalist Antiliberalism in a Global Age," *Journal of American History* 98.4 (2012): 1052–74.
36. Quoted in Carpenter, *Revive Us Again*, 94.
37. 2 Tim. 3:1 (NRSV).
38. Quoted in Carpenter, *Revive Us Again*, 106.
39. Quoted in Carpenter, *Revive Us Again*, 65.
40. The Carter Family, *The Best of the Carter Family: 20th Century Masters The Millennium Collection*, MCA Nashville, track 5, compact disc, 2005.
41. Ibid.
42. Quoted in Sutton, "Was FDR the Antichrist?", 1062.
43. Ibid.

44. Forrest Loman Oiler, Be Thou Prepared for Jesus Is Coming (Boston: Meador, 1937), 74.
45. Ibid., 75.
46. Ibid., 80.
47. Ibid., 81–2.
48. Ibid., 85.
49. Ibid., 94.
50. Ibid., 220.
51. Ibid., 38.
52. Ibid., 263.
53. Ibid., 273.
54. Ibid., 275.
55. Ibid., 352.
56. Ibid., 354.
57. Two of the main characters from both *Be Thou Prepared* and *They That Remain* are small businessmen (grocers), and both are squeezed by the rise of chain stores and government pricing schemes, until the day of the rapture when, since both have been born again, they are released from such cares. In *Be Thou Prepared*, the narrator explains, shortly after the rapture, that "All of those who had believed in Christ were now released from other worries, poverty, sickness, disease and all other irritating thorns, which included mortgages, taxation and loss of material possessions." Oiler, *Be Thou Prepared*, 97.
58. Numerous scholars have explored Fitzgerald's arguably best and, in any case, frequently anthologized short story. John Higgins, John Kuehl, and Bryant Mangum discuss the story in their book-length studies of Fitzgerald's short fiction, as does Ruth Prigozy, who places it in the context of the Great Depression. More recently, Terrell L. Tebbetts has argued that Charlie fails to get what he wants—Honoria most of all—because he conceives of his past, his character, and his daughter in coldly economic terms.
59. F. Scott Fitzgerald, "Babylon Revisited," in *The Short Stories of F. Scott Fitzgerald*, ed. Matthew J. Bruccoli (New York: Scribner, 2003), 620.
60. Ibid., 617.
61. Ibid.
62. Ibid., 624.
63. Ibid., 621.
64. Ibid., 622.
65. Ibid., 629.
66. Ibid., 632–3.
67. Ibid., 619.
68. "The Dole Evil," *Saturday Evening Post*, February 21, 1931, 20.
69. In one his first reflections following the election of Franklin Roosevelt in 1932, George Horace Lorimer, editor of the *Saturday Evening Post*, wrote that "We have had our period of living by bread alone and we need much more than that—less sectionalism, more neighborliness; less greed, more friendly competition;

less intolerance and more understanding." No doubt America then and now could use more of such virtues and less of such vices, but in appealing to them Lorimer suggests that virtues and vices—and not, say, levels of investment and debt—led the country into depression and could lead it out again.

70. Rev. 17:18 (NRSV).
71. Ibid., 18.5.
72. Ibid., 18.7.
73. John Maynard Keynes, "An Economic Analyses of Unemployment," in *The Collected Writings of John Maynard Keynes*, Vol. 13 (New York: Macmillan, 1973), 349.
74. Again, consider Rick Santelli, whose nationally broadcast rant from the floor of the Chicago Board of Trade in 2009 is credited with starting the Tea Party movement. Commenting on a federal program to help homeowners avoid foreclosure, Santelli proclaimed "This is America!" and asked traders, "How many of you people want to pay for your neighbor's mortgage that has an extra bathroom and can't pay their bills? Raise their hands." The traders boo.
75. For a contemporary—and admittedly more sophisticated—argument that it does and will, see David A. Stockman's recent book The Great Deformation: The Corruption of Capitalism in America (New York: Public Affairs, 2013).

CHAPTER 3

1. Hadley Cantril, *The Invasion from Mars: A Study in the Psychology of Panic* (Princeton: Princeton University Press, 1940), 168.
2. H.G. Welles, "War of the Worlds," in Cantril, *The Invasion from Mars*, 6. Cantril reproduces the text of Welles's radio play.
3. Ibid.
4. Cantril, *The Invasion from Mars*, 168.
5. Ibid., 10.
6. Ibid., 18.
7. Ibid., 19.
8. Ibid.
9. Ibid., 169. By turning off the radio, Robbins missed the Martians' merciless attack on New York City, and the additional Martian cylinders that fell all over the country: Buffalo, Chicago, St. Louis.
10. Ibid.
11. "Radio Listeners in Panic, Taking War Drama as Fact," *New York Times*, October 31, 1938.
12. "Fake Radio 'War' Stirs Terror Through U.S.," *New York Daily News*, October 31, 1938.
13. Ibid.
14. Orson Welles and Peter Bogdanovich, *This Is Orson Welles* (New York: De Capo Press, 1998), 18.
15. North Carolina *News and Observer*.

16. W. Joseph Campbell, *Getting It Wrong: Ten of the Greatest Misreported Stories in American Journalism* (Berkeley: University of California Press, 2010), 26–44.
17. Joy Elizabeth Hayes and Kathleen Battles, "Exchange and Interconnection in US Network Radio: A Reinterpretation of the 1938 *War of the Worlds* Broadcast," in *War of the Worlds to Social Media*, eds. Joy Elizabeth Hayes, Kathleen Battles, and Wendy Hilton-Morrow (New York: Peter Lang, 2013), 21.
18. Michael J. Socolow, "The Hyped Panic over 'War of the Worlds,'" *Chronicle Review*, October 24, 2008, 16.
19. Jefferson D. Pooley and Michael J. Socolow, "Checking Up on *The Invasion from Mars*: Hadley Cantril, Paul F. Lazarsfeld, and the Making of a Misremembered Classic," *International Journal of Communications* 7 (2013): 1921.
20. Ibid., 1931–2.
21. Cantril, *The Invasion from Mars*, 117.
22. Ibid., 127.
23. Pooley and Socolow, "Checking Up on *The Invasion from Mars*," 1935.
24. Cantril, *The Invasion from Mars*, 202.
25. The following account of the stock market crash relies on two sources. For what happened on the floor of the exchange, see John Kenneth Galbraith, *The Great Crash 1929* (1955; repr. Boston: Mariner, 2009), 88–107. For historical Dow Jones Industrial Average data, see http://www.macrotrends.net/1319/dow-jones-100-year-historical-chart.
26. Specifically, at 1:30 p.m., Richard Whitney, then vice-president of the New York Stock Exchange and a trader for the powerful J.P. Morgan bank, appeared on the scene. Acting on the bankers' behalf, and with their money, he strode onto the floor of the stock exchange and bid 205 for 10,000 shares of U.S. Steel, several points higher than current bids. He made his way around the exchange offering similarly confident bids for other blue-chip stocks. Whitney, and the bankers who backed him, are often credited with ending the panic, albeit temporarily.
27. Quoted in Galbraith, *The Great Crash 1929*, 106.
28. In September 1929, after the investor Roger Babson told the *New York Times* that "sooner or later a crash is coming," Fisher insisted in an article printed beneath Babson's prediction that "stock prices are not too high and Wall Street will not experience anything in the nature of a crash." "Babson Predicts 'Crash' in Stocks," *New York Times*, September 6, 1929.
29. "Time will tell," he added, "whether the increase [in earnings] will continue sufficiently to justify the present high level. I expect that it will." In the question and answer session that followed his speech, Fisher abandoned his usual qualifications. He said that he expected "to see the stock market a good deal higher than it is today, within a few months." A week later, on October 22, 1929, after the market had already begun to wane, Fisher reiterated his optimistic outlook, this time in front of a meeting of the New York Credit Men's Association. The headline in the *New York Times* read: "Fisher Says Prices of Stocks Are Low"; the subheadline read "Quotations Have Not Caught Up with Real Values Yet, He Declares."

"Fisher Sees Stocks Permanently High," *New York Times*, October 16, 1929 and "Fisher Says Prices of Stocks Are Low," *New York Times*, October 22, 1929.

30. "Says Stock Slump Is Only Temporary," *New York Times*, October 24, 1929.
31. Ibid.
32. Quoted in Galbraith, *The Great Crash 1929*, 146.
33. Ibid.
34. Irving Fisher, *The Stock Market Crash—and After* (New York: Macmillan, 1930), 94.
35. Edward C. Prescott and Ellen R. McGrattan, "The 1929 Stock Market: Irving Fisher Was Right," *International Economic Review* 45.4 (2004): 991–1009.
36. "Dow Jones—100 Year Historical Chart," *Macrotrends*, accessed March 12, 2018, http://www.macrotrends.net/1319/dow-jones-100-year-historical-chart.
37. Fisher, *The Stock Market Crash—and After*, 269.
38. One way to answer the question of whether a stock is cheap or expensive is the price-earnings (P/E) ratio, which is the price of a company's stock divided by that company's earnings. After all, a share of a company's stock simply represents a claim on the total value of that company, which its earnings more or less approximate. So, for example, if a stock trades at $50 per share, and over the last ten years it has averaged $2 in earnings per share, then its P/E ratio would be 25 (50 divided by 2). The same calculation can be performed for the market as a whole, where the numerator is the average price of shares and the denominator is the average combined earnings per share. From 1871 to today, the P/E ratio for stocks in Standard & Poor's (S&P) 500 largest companies has averaged 16 or 17. In December 1921, during the nadir of the post-war recession, the P/E ratio for the S&P 500 stood at 5. Assuming future earnings matched or exceeded past earnings, stocks were very cheap indeed; the cheapest, in fact, they had ever been. And so they proved. Over the next eight years, the stock market boomed. The Dow Jones Industrial Average went from 67 on September 1, 1921 to, as I have said, 381 on September 3, 1929. More importantly, over the same period the P/E ratio for the S&P 500 went from 5 in 1921 to 33 in 1929. Its previous high had been 25, achieved in 1901, after which it fell and fell until it bottomed out in 1921. After 1929, the P/E ratio would not return to 33 until 1997, from which it would rise to 44, until it all came crashing down when the dot.com bubble burst in 2000.

    The P/E ratio is not a crystal ball. It can only indicate very generally the price of stocks relative to earnings relative to other moments in economic history. But then or now, a P/E ratio of 33, where it was in 1929, is high. Alarm bells high. In their revered 1934 book of investment theory, *Security Analysis*, Benjamin Graham and David L. Dodd suggested that "*about sixteen times average earnings* is as high a price as can be paid in an *investment* purchase of a common stock." They added a corollary: "*people who habitually purchase common stocks at more than about sixteen times their average earnings are likely to lose considerable money in the long run.*" When, as was the case in 1929, the P/E ratio for the S&P 500 was twice what Graham and Dodd describe as "the upper limit" of this multiplier, stocks were almost certainly overpriced. Fisher, of course, disagreed. He thought the promise of higher earnings justified higher P/E ratios. See Benjamin Graham and David L. Dodd, *Security Analysis* (New York: Whittlesey House, 1934), 453, emphasis in original. For historical P/E ratios, see "Shiller P/E Ratio," accessed March 12, 2018, http://www.multpl.com/shiller-pe/.

39. Fisher, *The Stock Market Crash—and After*, 95.
40. Ibid., xvi.
41. Ibid., 53.
42. Less the interest my broker or lender charges me, of course.
43. Irving Fisher, *Booms and Depressions: Some First Principles* (New York: Adelphi, 1932), 93.
44. Quoted in Fisher, *The Stock Market Crash—and After*, 44. In other words, as James K. Galbraith glossed this passage in *The Great Crash 1929*, the mob "didn't sell. It got sold out," 146.
45. Fisher, *The Stock Market Crash—and After*, 44.
46. Irving Fisher, "The Stock Market Panic," *Journal of the American Statistical Association*, 25 (1930): 94.
47. Fisher, *Booms and Depressions*, 90.
48. Fisher, *The Stock Market Crash—and After*, 264.
49. Ibid., 55.
50. Irving Fisher, "Statistics in the Service of Economics," *Journal of the American Statistical Association*, 28 (1933): 9–10.
51. Ibid., 10.
52. That is not to say, however, that emotions, including panic, never influence the stock market. As Robert J. Shiller showed in his definitive study of the 1987 stock market crash, they almost certainly do. Markets are efficient, except when they are not. See Schiller, "Investor Behavior in the October 1987 Stock Market Crash: Survey Evidence," NBER Working Papers (1987), http://www.nber.org/papers/w2446.pdf.
53. No one could not sweet talk capitalists out of their pessimism, but the federal government could prime the economy and, acting as the investor of last resort, compel capitalists to invest in the economy lest they leave money on the table, which they are loathe to do.
54. Benjamin Roth, *The Great Depression: A Diary*, eds. James Ledbetter and Daniel B. Roth (New York: Public Affairs, 2013), 1.
55. Ibid., 10.
56. Ibid., 11.
57. Ibid.
58. Ibid., 15.
59. Elmus Wicker, *The Banking Panics of the Great Depression* (Cambridge: Cambridge University Press, 1996), 2.
60. Ibid., 18.
61. Ibid.
62. Walter Bagehot, 65 *Lombard Street: A Description of the Money Market* (1873; repr. New York: Charles Scribner's Sons, 1897).

63. Federal Reserve Board, *Twentieth Annual Report of the Federal Reserve Board Covering Operations for the Year 1933* (Washington, D.C.: G.P.O., 1934), 5.
64. Herbert Hoover, "Statement on the Hoarding of Currency," speech, February 3, 1932, http://www.presidency.ucsb.edu/ws/?pid=23,310.
65. Roth, *The Great Depression*, 32.
66. Ibid., 30.
67. Ibid., 41.
68. Ibid., 42.
69. Ibid., 45.
70. Ibid., 46.
71. Ibid., 57.
72. Ibid., 86.
73. Ibid., 93.
74. "Will Rogers Claps Hands for the President's Speech," *New York Times*, March 14, 1933.
75. Franklin D. Roosevelt, "Fireside Chat on Banking," speech, March 12, 1933, http://www.presidency.ucsb.edu/ws/index.php?pid=14,540&st=&st1=.
76. Ibid.
77. Francis Gloyd Awalt, "Recollections of the Banking Crisis in 1933," *Business History Review*, 43 (1969), 23.
78. Roosevelt, "Fireside Chat on Banking."
79. Charles A. Beard and George H.E. Smith, *The Old Deal and the New* (New York: Macmillan, 1940), 78.
80. Roosevelt, "Fireside Chat on Banking."
81. Recall Frank Norris's *McTeague* (1899) and its deeply disturbing portrait of Trina Sieppe, waiting until she is by herself in her small apartment so she can take out her hoard of gold coins, bury her face in them, and, like an infant, put the smaller ones in her mouth. Frank Norris, *McTeague* (1897; repr. New York: Signet Classics, 2011), 243.
82. Richard Wright, "How Bigger Was Born," in *Native Son* (1940; repr. New York: Harper Perennial, 2005), 458.
83. Richard Wright, *Native Son* (1940; repr. New York: Harper Perennial, 2005), 26.
84. Ibid., 38.
85. Ibid., 82.
86. Ibid., 81.
87. Ibid., 82.
88. Ibid., 84.
89. Ibid., 86–7.
90. Ibid., 87.
91. Ibid., 91.
92. Ibid., 88 and 89.
93. Ibid., 89.
94. Gustave Le Bon, *The Crowd: A Study of the Popular Mind* (1895; repr. New York: Macmillan, 1897), 41.
95. Ibid.

96. Robert Bocock, *Sigmund Freud* (1983; repr. London: Routledge, 2002), 68–70.
97. Clark McPhail, "Blumer's Theory of Collective Behavior: The Development of a Non-Symbolic Interaction Expansion," *Sociological Quarterly* 30.3 (1989): 405.
98. Robert E. Park and Ernest W. Burgess, *Introduction to the Science of Sociology* (Chicago: University of Chicago Press, 1921), 382.
99. Robert E. Park, *The Crowd and the Public* (1904; repr. Chicago: University of Chicago Press, 1982), 80.
100. See Robert E. Park, "Collective Behavior," in Encyclopedia of the Social Sciences, vol. 3, ed. Edwin R.A. Seligman (New York: Macmillan, 1930), 631–3.
101. Herbert Blumer, "Collective Behavior" in *Principles of Sociology*, ed. Alfred McClung Lee (New York: Barnes and Noble, 1946), 168.
102. Ibid., 170–1.
103. Ibid., 170.
104. Ibid., 175.
105. Ibid., 176.
106. Ibid., 190.
107. Ibid., 175.
108. Ibid.
109. In that famous scene, West writes:

> There was another wild surge forward that ended in another dead spot. [Tod] now faced a young girl who was sobbing steadily. Her silk print dress had been torn down the front and her tiny brassiere hung from one strap. He tried by pressing back to give her room, but she moved with him every time he moved. Now and then, she would jerk violently and he wondered if she was going to have a fit. One of her thighs was between his legs. He struggled to get free of her, but she clung to him, moving with him and pressing against him.
>
> She turned her head and said, "Stop, stop," to someone behind her.
>
> He saw what the trouble was. An old man, wearing a Panama hat and horn-rimmed glasses, was hugging her. He had one of his hands inside her dress and was biting her neck.

Tod fights off her attacker, but it is not long before he too succumbs to the social contagion of the crowd. A policeman rescues him from the riot, but on the drive home Tod seems to lose whatever of his individual consciousness remains. In the closing lines of the novel, he gleefully imitates the police siren. Nathanael West, *Day of the Locust* (1939; repr. New York: New Directions, 2009), 173.

110. Wright, *Native Son*, 303–4.
111. Ibid., 373.
112. Wright, "How Bigger Was Born," 455.
113. In *Native Son*, Wright has a journalist write of Bigger, "All in all, he seems a beast utterly untouched by the softening influences of modern civilization." In reality, in 1938 a journalist had written of Robert Nixon in *The Chicago Tribune*: "civilization has left Nixon practically untouched" and "his physical characteristics suggest an earlier link in the species." Wright, *Native Son*, 280

and Charles Leavelle, "Brick Slayer Is Likened to Jungle Beast," *Chicago Tribune*, June 5, 1938.

114. Wright, *Native Son*, 388.
115. Ibid., 389.
116. Ibid., 389–90.
117. Ibid., 391.
118. Ibid., 395.

CHAPTER 4

1. My account of the Cleveland serial murder case draws from James Jessen Badal, *In the Wake of the Butcher: Cleveland's Torso Murders* (Kent: Kent State University Press, 2001).
2. Quoted in Badal, *In the Wake of the Butcher*, 92.
3. Quoted in Ibid.
4. William Miller, "Fear Hangs over Kingsbury Run Where Butcher Leaves His Dead," *Cleveland Press*, September 11, 1934.
5. Arne Öhman, "Fear and Anxiety: Overlaps and Dissociations," in *Handbook of Emotions*, 3rd ed., eds. Michael Lewis, Jeannette M. Haviland-Jones, and Lisa Feldman Barrett (New York: Guilford Press, 2008), 709–29.
6. Franklin Delano Roosevelt, "37th Presidential Inaugural Address," speech, Washington, D.C., March 4, 1933, https://www.inaugural.senate.gov/about/past-inaugural-ceremonies/37th-inaugural-ceremonies/.
7. "Girl, 14, Dies of Poliomyelitis," *New York Times*, March 30, 1931.
8. "City's Health Good, Dr. Wynne Reports," *New York Times*, January 1, 1931.
9. "Give Paralyzed Child Oxygen for 24 Hours," *New York Times*, June 19, 1931.
10. "Child Dies in Respirator after 60 Hours," *New York Times*, June 21, 1931.
11. "Stricken Boy Saved by 'Mechanical Lung,'" *New York Times*, June 17, 1931.
12. "Connecticut Cities Combat Paralysis," *New York Times*, July 19, 1931.
13. "Fight Infantile Paralysis," *New York Times*, July 18, 1931.
14. "Warns on Infant Paralysis," *New York Times*, July 25, 1931.
15. Ibid.
16. "Disease Baffles Scientists," *New York Times*, August 12, 1931.
17. Robert Kingman, "Infantile Paralysis a Medical Mystery," *Brooklyn Daily Eagle*, October 11, 1931. The *Brooklyn Daily Eagle* covered the polio outbreak as well, though not in as much depth as the *Times*.
18. "Open Fight to Stop Paralysis," *New York Times*, July 28, 1931.
19. "53 New Cases Here of Paralysis in Day," *New York Times*, September 3, 1931.
20. "Wynne Offers Aid on Child Paralysis," *New York Times*, August 2, 1931.
21. "Family's Distress Grows," *New York Times*, August 8, 1931.
22. "Doctors Map Fight as Paralysis Gains," *New York Times*, August 6, 1931.
23. "Paralysis in City Again Shows Rise," *New York Times*, August 14, 1931.
24. "87 Paralysis Cases in Week-End Here," *New York Times*, August 18, 1931.
25. "Peak of Paralysis Past, Says Wynne," *New York Times*, August 19, 1931.
26. "City Schools Delay Opening until Sept. 22 as Dr. Wynne Acts to Curb Infantile Paralysis," *New York Times*, September 1, 1931.

27. "53 New Cases Here of Paralysis In Day," *New York Times*, September 3, 1931.
28. "Paralysis Recedes with Cool Weather," *New York Times*, September 22, 1931.
29. "Infant Death Toll at New Low Here," *New York Times*, January 2, 1932.
30. "Paralysis Deaths Far Below 1916 Rate," *New York Times*, July 30, 1931.
31. "Slight Drop Seen in Paralysis Here," *New York Times*, August 7, 1931.
32. Gareth Williams, *Paralysed with Fear: The Story of Polio* (New York: Palgrave Macmillan, 2013), xv. Exhibit A in this indictment is *In Daily Battle*, a short film financed by the National Foundation for Infantile Paralysis that "invaded" American cinemas in 1947. In the film, weird, ominous music plays as clouds darken the sun. A colossal shadow bearing a crutch steals across the landscape and soon engulfs a group of boys swimming in a lake. A sinister voice straight from the horror movies then intones, "My name is Virus Poliomyelitis. I specialize in grotesques, twisting and deforming human bodies. That's why I'm called 'the crippler.'" After this introduction, the shadow overtakes a farm boy, who falls desperately to the ground. "That is what I've been looking for," the crippler exults. Next, three African-American children appear playing outside a tenement. "As you probably know," the voice of the shadow whispers, "I am very fond of children, especially little children." In subsequent scenes, the crippler attacks a man with a briefcase and a schoolgirl walking down her front steps. In theaters across the country, the film would be shown before the feature and volunteers from the March of Dimes would then circulate through the house collecting donations.
33. "Children under 6 Lead in Paralysis," *New York Times*, September 4, 1931.
34. Barbara Ehrenreich, *Fear of Falling: The Inner Life of the Middle Class* (New York: Pantheon Books, 1989), 12.
35. Barbara Ehrenreich and John Ehrenreich, "The Professional-Managerial Class," in *Between Labor and Capital*, ed. Pat Walker (Boston: South End Press, 1979).
36. Ehrenreich, *Fear of Falling*, 15.
37. Ibid., 11.
38. For those unfamiliar with the literature, I would recommend two works: Edmund Wilson's "A Bad Day in Brooklyn," which appeared in the April 22, 1931 issue of the *New Republic* and in his collection of Depression-era journalism, *The American Earthquake*; and Tom Kromer's *Waiting for Nothing*, which I discuss, briefly, in Chapter 5.
39. Ibid., 130–1.
40. Ibid., 146.
41. Ibid., 147.
42. Ibid., 148.
43. Ibid., 232.
44. Ibid., 278.
45. Ibid., 237.
46. Ibid., 250.
47. Ibid., 268–9.

48. E. Wight Bakke, *Citizens without Work: A Study of the Effects of Unemployment upon the Workers' Social Relations and Practices* (1940; reprint, Hamden: Archon Books, 1968), and *The Unemployed Worker: A Study of the Task of Making a Living without a Job* (1940; reprint, Hamden: Archon Books, 1969).
49. Wight Bakke, *The Unemployed Worker*, 114.
50. Ibid., 117.
51. Ibid.
52. Ibid.
53. Ibid., 118.
54. Ibid., 115.
55. Ibid., 119.
56. Ibid., 110.
57. Hickok, *One Third of a Nation*, 143.
58. Ibid., 144.
59. Ibid.
60. Ibid., 205.
61. Ibid., 207.
62. Ibid., 205–6.
63. Ibid., 206.
64. Ibid.
65. Ibid.
66. *Creeps by Night: Chills and Thrills*, ed. Dashiell Hammett (Cleveland: World Publishing Company, 1944) and *Great Tales of Terror and the Supernatural*, eds. Phyllis Cerf Wagner and Herbert Wise (1944; reprint, New York: Random House, 1994).
67. Edmund Wilson, "A Treatise on Tales of Horror," *New Yorker*, May 27, 1944, 72.
68. Ibid.
69. "The true weird tale," he wrote, "has something more than secret murder, bloody bones, or a sheeted form clanking chains according to rule. A certain atmosphere of breathless and unexplainable dread of outer, unknown forces must be present; and there must be a hint, expressed with a seriousness and portentousness becoming its subject, of that most terrible conception of the human brain—a malign and particular suspension or defeat of those fixed laws of Nature which are our only safeguard against the assaults of chaos and the daemons of unplumbed space." For *Weird Tales*, see Ed Hulse's chapter on "Horror and Fantasy" in *The Blood and Thunder Guide to Pulp Fiction* (Morris Plains: Murania Press, 2013), 192–225 and relevant entries in Lee Server, *Encyclopedia of Pulp Fiction Writers* (New York: Facts on File/Checkmark Books, 2002).
70. Wilson, "A Treatise on Tales of Horror," 72.
71. Ibid., 75.
72. Edmund Wilson, "Tales of the Marvellous and Ridiculous," *New Yorker*, November 24, 1945, 100.

73. Ibid., 103.
74. H.P. Lovecraft, "The Thing on the Doorstep," in *The Complete Fiction of H.P. Lovecraft* (New York: Race Point Publishing, 2014), 992.
75. Ibid., 994.
76. The story, written in 1931 but not published until 1936, features Lovecraft's stock narrator, an antiquarian with an interest in the occult, who visits Innsmouth, a decaying town on the coast of Massachusetts, and discovers its horrible secret. In the eighteenth century, a sea captain from the town, Obed Marsh, makes a bargain with an underwater race of creatures called the Deep Ones—part fish, frog, and man—in which the creatures will provide him with fish and jewels and Marsh will provide them with human sacrifices. Eventually, the Deep Ones demand more. They wish to mate with humans and in time force the residents of Innsmouth to comply. Hence the "Innsmouth type": human enough, but with disturbing suggestions of fish and frog, including "a perpetual odour of fish" and, as with the young woman Edward Derby marries, Asenath Waite, "overprotuberant eyes." That is the downside. The upside is that offspring of the interspecies coupling eventually transform more fully into Deep Ones and take to the sea, where they enjoy a kind of underwater immortality.

    H.P. Lovecraft, "The Shadow over Innsmouth," in *The Complete Fiction of H.P. Lovecraft*, 866–923.
77. Lovecraft, "The Thing on the Doorstep," 997.
78. Ibid., 999.
79. Ibid., 100.
80. Ibid., 1001.
81. Ibid.
82. Ibid.
83. Ibid., 1001–2.
84. Ibid., 1010.
85. Ibid., 1011.
86. Ibid.
87. Ibid., 1012.
88. Ibid., 990.
89. S.T. Joshi, *I Am Providence* (New York: Hippocampus Press, 2013), 861.
90. Michel Houellebecq, *H.P. Lovecraft: Against the World, against Life*, trans. Dorna Khazeni (London: Weidenfeld & Nicolson, 2006), 32.
91. H.P. Lovecraft, "The Music of Erich Zann," in *The Complete Fiction of H.P. Lovecraft*, 153.
92. H.P. Lovecraft, "The Call of Cthulu," in *The Complete Fiction of H.P. Lovecraft*, 381.
93. Lovecraft, "The Thing on the Doorstep," 1002.
94. Ibid., 1002–3.
95. Ibid., 1009.
96. Ibid., 1010.

97. The weird fiction of the 1930s often generates fear by depicting similar assaults upon the body and human autonomy. Of only the most frequently anthologized, Henry S. Whitehead's "Passing of a God," which appeared in *Weird Tales* in 1931, tells the story of an expatriate in Haiti whose "malignant bodily growth" on his abdomen turns out to house a nascent, malevolent god, which, when removed by a surgeon, opens its eyes. In Robert Bloch's "The Cloak," published in the rival weird fiction pulp *Unknown* in 1939, a mere article of clothing can turn one into a vampire. And in John Collier's "Evening Primrose," from 1941, refugees from the Great Depression and previous economic catastrophes take shelter in a Macy's-like department store, where those who threaten to reveal their presence are turned into mannequins by a group of Dark Men who have themselves taken refuge in funeral homes. Perhaps the best example, though, is Fritz Leiber's 1941 classic "Smoke Ghost," published just months before the Japanese attack on Pearl Harbor, in which a composite of all the horrors of the times coalesce into a single grimy figure that menaces the narrator, a Chicago advertising executive. On the less literary end, in pulp stories no one has bothered to collect, things turn even more grotesque, especially as the decade proceeded, and more and more plots—and cover art—featured sadomasochistic villains torturing women.
98. Robert Anton Wilson, *Cosmic Trigger, Vol. 2, Down to Earth* (Tempe: New Falcon Publications, 1991), 30–1.
99. Ibid., 31.
100. Ibid.
101. Ibid., 15.
102. Robert Anton Wilson, *Cosmic Trigger, Vol. 1, Final Secret of the Illuminati* (San Francisco: And/Or Press, 1977; repr. Las Vegas: New Falcon Publications, 1991), 3.

CHAPTER 5

1. Henry Norris Russell, "Space as Yet Unfathomed," *Scientific American*, December 1, 1939, 374.
2. "Limits of Creation, in Light Years, Estimated at 10,000,000,000,000,000,000,000,000,000,000,000," *New York Times*, December 15, 1930.
3. Sir James Jeans, "Watching the Creation of the Stars," *Scientific American*, June 1, 1932, 345.
4. "Hubble Shows Scientists How the Universe Evolved," *New York Times*, May 8, 1939.
5. Henry Norris Russell, "Is Space Expanding?" *Scientific American*, January 1, 1932, 15.
6. "Eddington Pictures Expanding Universe," *New York Times*, September 8, 1932.
7. George Lemaître, "The Beginning of the World from the Point of View of Quantum Theory," *Nature*, October 24, 1931, 324.

8. "Le Maitre Suggests One, Single, Great Atom, Embracing All Energy, Started the Universe," *New York Times*, May 19, 1931.
9. Arthur Schopenhauer, *The World as Will and Representation, Vol. 1. 1818* (New York: Dover, 1969), 204.
10. Ibid., 205.
11. "A Prize for Lemaître," *Literary Digest*, March 31, 1934, 16.
12. Schopenhauer, *The World as Will and Representation*, 205.
13. Witness the landscape photography of Ansel Adams, who had his most innovative and productive years during the 1930s; the continued popularity, despite the Depression, of tourist destinations like the Grand Canyon and Niagara Falls; or, less agreeable, the wind storms and erosion that left dust piled as high as rooftops in the Plains states.
14. Carol Willis, "Building the Empire State," in *Building the Empire State*, ed. Carol Willis (New York: Norton, 1998), 14.
15. Edmund Burke, *A Philosophical Enquiry into the Origins of the Sublime and Beautiful: The Writings and Speeches of Edmund Burke: Volume 1: The Early Writings, 1757* (Oxford: Clarendon Press, 1997), 245.
16. John Ruskin, *Seven Lamps of Architecture* (1849; New York: D. Appleton and Co., 1901), 79.
17. Dacher Keltner and Jonathan Haidt, "Approaching Awe: A Moral, Aesthetic, and Spiritual Emotion," *Cognition and Emotion* 17 (2003): 303.
18. Paul Starrett, *Changing the Skyline* (New York: Whittlesey House, 1938), 302.
19. "Big Sunday Crowd Sees Empire Tower," *New York Times*, May 4, 1931.
20. Keltner and Haidt, "Approaching Awe," 304.
21. Ibid., 304.
22. Schopenhauer, *The World as Will and Representation*, 205.
23. F. Scott Fitzgerald, "My Lost City," in *The Crack-Up* (New York: New Directions, 1945), 32.
24. Curiously, the person who figures so prominently in Fitzgerald's romance with the city when he first arrives, Edmund Wilson, also left an account of his visit to the observation deck of the Empire State Building when it opened in 1931. By then, Wilson was not a model bohemian intellectual but, as Fitzgerald ruefully observes in the closing lines of his essay, had "gone over to Communism." That may explain why Wilson, unlike Fitzgerald, from atop the building does not see the limits of the city and the limits of his previous understanding of the city but rather a vista of poverty and human suffering. See Edmund Wilson, "May First: The Empire State Building: Life on the Passaic River," in *The American Earthquake* (New York: Farrar, Straus, and Giroux, 1979), 292–303.
25. Keltner and Haidt, "Approaching Awe," 306.
26. The playwright Edward Albee picked up on this phenomenon when he put a photograph of Roosevelt—next to Mahatma Gandhi—on the bookshelf of those marital cutthroats but political liberals George and Martha in *Who's Afraid of Virginia Woolf*.

27. *Down and Out in the Great Depression: Letters from the Forgotten Man*, ed. Robert McElvaine (Chapel Hill: University of North Carolina Press, 1983), 224.
28. Ibid., 217.
29. See Jeremy Schaap, *Triumph: The Untold Story of Jesse Owens and Hitler's Olympics* (New York: Houghton Mifflin, 2007).
30. "Personal Glimpses," *Literary Digest*, May 1931, 30.
31. C.G. Poore, "The Riveter's Panorama of New York," *New York Times*, January 5, 1930.
32. Immanuel Kant, *Critique of the Power of Judgment* (1790; Cambridge: Cambridge University Press, 2000), 145.
33. Ibid., 146.
34. Ibid.
35. Ibid.
36. Robert Doran, *The Theory of the Sublime from Longinus to Kant* (Cambridge: Cambridge University Press, 2015), 254. For Kant, it should be added, strength, courage, and resistance do more than simply characterize the sublime. Truly exceptional displays of strength, courage, and resistance—which can terrify us in their sublimity—can inspire feelings of the sublime in us, assuming, that is, that we do not submit to those displays but overcome them ourselves.
37. John Steinbeck, *The Grapes of Wrath* (New York: Penguin, 2006), 229.
38. Ibid., 419.
39. Ibid., 455.
40. Keltner and Haidt, "Approaching Awe," 310.
41. *The Grapes of Wrath*, directed by John Ford (1940; Twentieth Century Fox).
42. Margaret Walker, "Lineage," in *For My People* (1942; reprint New York: Arno Press, 1968), 7. Walker published *For My People* in 1942, which falls outside the dates (1929–41) I use to bound the Great Depression. Poems from the collection, however, including the title poem, "The Struggle Staggers Us," and "We Have Been Believers," appeared in *Poetry* in 1937, 1938, and 1939, respectively. I assume "Lineage" belongs to that group.
43. On Handcox, see Michael Honey's *Sharecropper's Troubadour: John L. Handcox, the Southern Tenant Farmers' Union, and the African American Song Tradition* (New York: Palgrave, 2013) or the chapter on the Southern Tenant Farmers' Union in my *You Work Tomorrow: An Anthology of American Labor Poetry, 1929–1941* (Ann Arbor: University of Michigan Press, 2007).
44. United States, *Farm Tenancy: Report of the President's Committee* (Washington, D.C.: GPO, 1937), 25.
45. Ibid., iv. Except for migratory laborers like the Joads, those who worked for brief periods harvesting crops before moving on to the next harvest or the next crop, and who could be found everywhere but especially in the western states, the authors of *Farm Tenancy* acknowledged that landlessness and the resulting insecurity—read poverty—mostly occurred in the South, where two out of every three tenant farmers in the country lived. Moreover, although the Midwest and West had its share of tenants, only in the South did the percentage of farmers

who did not own their land exceed those who did. Of the 3.422 million farmers in the South, over 1.831 million of them were tenants. In the Cotton Belt states of Georgia, Tennessee, Alabama, Arkansas, and Mississippi, the rate of tenancy exceeded 60 percent and, in Mississippi, rose as high as 70 percent.

46. Ibid., 7.
47. The authors of *Farm Tenancy* reasoned that if the problem was farmers who did not own land, the solution lay in helping farmers acquire land, which the federal government would accomplish through a series of reforms: low-interest loans to those capable of owning a farm now; aid to tenants who, with guidance and education from federal extension agents, could after a year or several years responsibly own a farm; and the resettlement of tenants currently on depleted land to more promising homesteads, where they, too, might eventually own a farm. Whereas now comparatively few landlords owned a majority of the land on which a majority of farmers scratched out an insufficient living, eventually, or so the authors of *Farm Tenancy* hoped, a majority of farmers would own their own farm, on which they would raise crops to eat and cash crops to sell. In short, the Jeffersonian ideal of prosperous, independent yeoman farmers would return. It did not work out that way.
48. Quoted in Blanche M.G. Linden, "Photography," in *Encyclopedia of the Great Depression*, Vol. 2 (New York: Thomson Gale, 2004), 756.
49. See Cara Finnegan, *Picturing Poverty: Print Culture and FSA Photographs* (Washington, D.C.: Smithsonian Institution Scholarly Press, 2003).
50. See Lionel Trilling, "Greatness with One Fault in It," *Kenyon Review* 4.1 (1941), 102.
51. Ibid., 99.
52. James Agee and Walker Evans, *Let Us Now Praise Famous Men* (1941; reprint, New York: Mariner, 2001), 404.
53. Ibid., 59.
54. Ibid., 80.
55. Ibid., 11–12.
56. Ibid., 5.
57. Ibid., 182. In a long passage discussing tenant houses, for example, Agee observes that tenant houses do not differ all that much from southern company houses in mill towns. That fact alone, he writes, should warn us against focusing too much on tenantry as the problem. To do so anyway, he thinks, would be "dishonest or ridiculous, or in any case deceptive and dangerous." "Dangerous" because "by wrong assignment of causes it persuades that the 'cure' is possible through means which in fact would have little effect save to delude the saviors into the comfortable idea that nothing more needed doing, or even looking-to." And "deceptive because . . . these homes have more than less in common with the homes of the whole poorest class of *owning* cotton farmers." The "economic source," he adds, "is nothing so limited as the tenant system but is the whole world-system of which tenantry is one modification; and there are in the people themselves, and in the land and climate, other sources quite as

powerful but less easy to define, far less to go about curing; and they are, to suggest them too bluntly, psychological, semantic, traditional, perhaps glandular." In other words, as part of the whole world-system, tenantry may change, or we may succeed in changing tenantry, but the abuses associated with it will not change save the changing of the whole world-system. To be sure, well-thought-out liberal efforts of the sort suggested by the authors of *Farm Tenancy*—having the government furnish sharecroppers at no interest or helping tenants acquire land—will help at the margins, but they will not fundamentally alter the conditions that inspired our sympathy in the first place. (Unless, that is, out of our desire to be done with the "unpleasant situation down South," we deceive ourselves that, as Agee puts it, "nothing more needed doing.") That is, if you think tenantry is the problem, Agee suggests, look at the lives of those who own their own farms rather than rent them, or those who live in company housing in nearby Southern mill towns, and say whether you would trade places with them. The problem, to put it another way, goes beyond sharecroppers, yet sympathy for sharecroppers may prevent us from seeing that.

58. In the Notes and Appendices section of the book, for example, Agee reprints a fluff article about Margaret Bourke-White that appeared in the *New York Post* following the publication of *You Have Seen Their Faces*. Discussing Erskine Caldwell's new play, *Journeyman*, which takes place in a church for poor whites in the South, Bourke-White observes:

> The Negro churches are not, somehow, so shocking, because you think of Negroes as being actors and emotional, but with the white people the whole business is so sordid and desperate and out of place. It isn't as though the church played any role, as we know religion. It's just a place where people go to shout and scream and roll on the floor. They are so beaten down and their lives are so drab and barren and lonely that they have nothing. This terrible thing Sunday is their only release.

Many people who write about *Let Us Now Praise Famous Men* follow Agee in making Caldwell and, especially, Bourke-White, into villains, and I do not want to pile on, especially since, as I have written elsewhere, their approach has merit. Still, Bourke-White, who had a chance to view poverty not just at a distance but up close—or through a camera lens, anyway—should know better than to assert that their religion has nothing to do with hers or that the poor "have nothing." No one doubts Bourke-White's sympathy for sharecroppers, or her desire to do something for them, but her sympathy for them—as may sympathy in general—reduces them to their suffering and leads her into fatuous beliefs like the ones above.

59. Ibid., 7.
60. Ibid., 51.
61. Ibid., 88.
62. Ibid., 89.
63. Ibid., 205.

64. Ibid., 88.
65. Ibid., 89.
66. Ibid., 89.
67. Ibid., 406.
68. Ibid., x.
69. Ibid., 256.
70. Chadwick's discovery laid the groundwork for the Manhattan Project, begun in 1939, which produced the first atom bomb, and which, in its capacity to literally reduce individuals and whole cities to nothing, proved to be perhaps the most terrifying instance of a midcentury sublime.

CHAPTER 6

1. "Queen Leaves Buckingham to Obey Tradition," *Chicago Tribune*, October 1, 1936.
2. "Mrs. Simpson, Friend of King, Seeks Divorce," *Chicago Tribune*, October 14, 1936. The article revealed that while Wallis might have cited adultery as the grounds of the divorce, the divide between her and Ernest came down to lifestyle. "It has long been known," the Associated Press reported, "that the couple were at odds, chiefly because the sparkling mooded American girl preferred royal companionship to life with a workaday shipping broker husband." Ernest, for his part, "dislikes the gay set in which his monarch travels and into which his lovely and lively American wife first won an introduction and then undisputed place as Edward's closest woman friend and companion."
3. "King To Marry Wally in Spring, Gossip in London," *Chicago Tribune*, October 25, 1936.
4. Lewis Broad, *The Abdication: Twenty Five Years After: A Re-appraisal* (London: Frederick Muller, 1961), 75.
5. The following account draws on Susan A. Williams, *The People's King: The True Story of the Abdication* (New York: Palgrave Macmillan, 2004) and Philip Ziegler, *King Edward VIII: The Official Biography* (London: Collins, 1990).
6. "Ex-Ruler Sails into Exile," *Chicago Tribune*, December 12, 1936.
7. Readers of the *Chicago Tribune* need not have made the latter connection for themselves. On December 6, the *Tribune* London correspondent published an article titled "Story of Modern Cinderella and Prince Charming."
8. See Williams, *The People's King*, 1–14.
9. Gallup Organization, "Would You Like to Have King Edward Marry Mrs. Simpson?" Gallup Poll, November 1936, Cornell University, Ithaca: Roper Center for Public Opinion Research, iPOLL, accessed March 1, 2017. Many had apparently heard enough. Fifty-six percent also wanted newspapers to print less news about King Edward and Wallis Simpson: Gallup Organization, "Should Newspapers Print More or Less News about King Edward and Mrs. Simpson?" Gallup Poll, November 1936, Cornell University, Ithaca: Roper Center for Public Opinion Research, iPOLL, accessed March 1, 2017.

10. "Let King Marry Wally! Chicagoans Say 3 to 1 in Poll," *Chicago Tribune*, December 8, 1936.
11. Centers for Disease Control and Prevention, "Marriages, Divorces, and Rates: United States, 1867–1967," 100 Years of Marriage and Divorce Statistics, 1867–1967, table 1, page 22, accessed February 28, 2017, https://www.cdc.gov/nchs/data/series/sr_21/sr21_024.pdf.
12. Harry T. Reis and Arthur Aron, "Love: What Is It, Why Does It Matter, and How Does It Operate," *Perspectives on Psychological Science* 3.1 (January 2008): 80.
13. Laura Kipnis, *Against Love* (New York: Pantheon Books, 2003) and Sara Ahmed, *The Cultural Politics of Emotions* (New York: Routledge, 2004).
14. Søren Kierkegaard, *The Soul of Kierkegaard: Selections from His Journals*, ed. Alexander Dru (New York: Dover, 2003), 129.
15. If I had more room, I would also include Nathaniel West's *Miss Lonelyhearts*. Although the novel is above all concerned with human suffering, surprisingly, for a work so closely associated with the Great Depression, more often than not the source of that human suffering is not poverty but love, its absence or corruption.
16. See Susan Broomhall, ed., *Gender and Emotions in Medieval and Early Modern Europe: Destroying Order, Structuring Disorder* (London: Routledge, 2015).
17. Mark A. Vieira, *Sin in Soft Focus: Pre-Code Hollywood* (New York: Harry N. Abrams, 1999), 148–9 and Lea Jacobs, *The Wages of Sin: Censorship and the Fallen Woman Film, 1928–1942* (Madison: University of Wisconsin Press, 1991), 69–81.
18. In the uncensored version, the cobbler, wielding a copy of Nietzsche's *Will to Power*, does considerably less moralizing, or rather moralizing of a different sort. "[Y]ou must use men—not let them use you," he tells her in lines cut from the theatrical release. "Exploit yourself!"
19. Just as earlier, in the speakeasy, the camera pans up from the bottom of Lily's body to the top, showing us what the local politician sees when he looks at Lily, so too do we see what Lily sees when she looks at the bank: an object to be conquered. She has learned her lesson. Men lust after Lily, and Lily lusts after wealth and power, which she will win by exploiting the lust for her. And so she does.
20. Jacobs, *Wages of Sin*, 76.
21. "A Woman's Wiles," *New York Times*, June 24, 1933.
22. Jacobs, *Wages of Sin*, 80–1.
23. Vieira, *Sin in Soft Focus*, 220.
24. Ibid., 215.
25. The following account relies on Jonathan Goodman, *The Passing of Starr Faithfull* (1990; repr. Kent: Kent State University Press, 1996).
26. Quoted in Ibid., 216.
27. John O'Hara, *BUtterfield 8* (1935; repr. New York: Penguin, 2013), 66.
28. Ibid., 144.
29. Ibid., 203.

30. Ibid., 204.
31. Ibid., 100–1.
32. In his review of the novel (see below), Malcolm Cowley makes a similar point.
33. O'Hara, *BUtterfield 8*, 181.
34. Ibid., 193.
35. Ibid., 139–40.
36. Ibid., 180.
37. Although neither of the couples in those novels lives happily ever after, either.
38. Ibid., 199.
39. Ibid., 220.
40. Ibid., 222.
41. Malcolm Cowley, "Hemingway Mixed with Hearst," in *Critical Essays on John O'Hara*, ed. Philip B. Eppard (New York: G.K. Hall, 1994), 34.
42. Lorin Stein suggests as much in her introduction to the Penguin edition of the novel.
43. O'Hara, *BUtterfield 8*, 234.
44. Mary McCarthy, "The Man in the Brooks Brothers Shirt," in *The Company She Keeps* (1942; New York: Mariner, 2003), 81.
45. Ibid., 106.
46. Ibid., 108.
47. Ibid., 109.
48. Ibid., 94.
49. Ibid., 97.
50. Ibid., 98.
51. Ibid., 113.
52. Ibid., 114.
53. Ibid., 117.
54. Ibid., 126.
55. Ibid.
56. Ibid.
57. Ibid., 126–7.
58. Ibid., 130.
59. Ibid., 90.
60. Quentin Reynolds, *The Fiction Factory, Or from Pulp Row to Quality Street* (New York: Random House, 1955), 198.
61. Ibid., 199.
62. Tom Kromer, *Waiting for Nothing and Other Writings* (1935; repr. Athens: University of Georgia Press, 2004), 44.
63. Ibid., 52.
64. Centers for Disease Control and Prevention, "Marriages, Divorces, and Rates: United States, 1867–1967."
65. For the statistically minded, the r-squared value is .56731. I use the unemployment rate adjusted for federal work programs, though the unadjusted rates would not have changed the outcome much. See Darby, "Three-and-a-Half Million."

66. Woodie Guthrie, *This Land Is Your Land: The Asch Recordings*, Vol. 1, Smithsonian Folkways, track 3, compact disc, 2007.
67. Dorothy Dix, *How to Win and Hold a Husband* (New York: Doubleday, 1939), 107.
68. One contemporary economist has found that during the worst years of the Great Depression, for every standard deviation decrease in retail sales per capita, a woman was 18 percent less likely to marry. See Matthew J. Hill, "Love in the Time of Depression: The Effect of Economic Conditions on Marriage in the Great Depression," *Journal of Economic History* 75.1 (2015): 163–89.
69. Marjorie Hillis, *Live Alone and Like It: A Guide for the Extra Woman* (New York: Bobbs-Merrill Company, 1936).
70. Lee Edelman, *No Future: Queer Theory and the Death Drive* (Durham: Duke University Press, 2004), 11.
71. Ibid., 30.
72. John Maynard Keynes, *General Theory of Employment, Interest, and Money* (1936; reprint, New York: Harcourt, Brace, and World, 1965), 155.
73. Lewis, *It Can't Happen Here*, 105.
74. Quoted in Goodman, *The Passing of Starr Faithfull*, 216.
75. National Bureau of Economic Research, "Population, Number of Births and Deaths, and Crude Rates,"Vital Statistics of the United States 1942, table 1, page 18, accessed February 28, 2017, http://www.nber.org/vital-statistics/historical/vsus_1942_1.CV.pdf.
76. Although still outlawed, birth control, the popular historian Frederick Lewis Allen observed in 1931, "was by this time generally practiced or believed in by married couples in all but the most ignorant classes." See Frederick Lewis Allen, *Since Yesterday: The Nineteen-Thirties in America, September 3, 1929–September 3, 1939* (New York: Harper & Brothers, 1940), 101–2.
77. See Bruce Smith, *The History of Little Orphan Annie* (1982; New York: Ballantine Books, 1982).
78. Thomas Minehan, *Boy and Girl Tramps of America* (New York: Farrar and Rinehart, 1934).
79. Delmore Schwartz, "In Dreams Begin Responsibilities," in *Once and for All: The Best of Delmore Schwartz*, ed. Craig Morgan Teicher (New York: New Directions, 2016), 7.
80. Josiah Flint Willard, "Homosexuality among Tramps," in Havelock Ellis and John Addington Symonds, *Sexual Inversion* (1897; reprint New York: Arno Press/New York Times, 1975).
81. To clarify, we cannot know whether parents loved their children any less during the Great Depression. As the chapter on fear and polio make clear, it would seem they loved them as much as ever. There were simply fewer children, relatively speaking, around.
82. "To Our Readers," *Catholic Worker*, May 1933.
83. Obviously, given Newton's biography and his subjects, not without queer elements. Newton Arvin, *Whitman* (New York: Macmillan, 1938), 252.

84. *Alcoholics Anonymous: The Story of How More Than One Hundred Men Have Recovered from Alcoholism* (1939; Malo: Anonymous Press, 2008), 167.
85. Richard E. Byrd, *Alone* (New York: P.P. Putnam's, 1938).
86. *Wild Boys of the Road*, directed by William Wellman, in *Forbidden Hollywood Collection*, Vol. 3 (1933; Burbank: Warner Home Video, 2009), DVD.
87. *Woman Haters*, directed by Archie Gottler, in *The Three Stooges Collection, Vol. 1: 1934–1936* (1934; Culver City: Sony Pictures Home Entertainment, 2007), DVD.
88. Andrew Carnegie, *How to Win Friends and Influence People* (New York: Simon and Schuster, 1936).
89. Carson McCullers, *The Heart Is a Lonely Hunter* (1940; reprint, New York: Mariner, 2000) and Charles Bradshaw, "Language and Responsibility: The Failure of Discourse in Carson McCullers's *The Heart Is a Lonely Hunter*," *Southern Quarterly* 37.2 (Winter 1999): 118–26.
90. Centers for Disease Control and Prevention, "Marriages, Divorces, and Rates: United States, 1867–1967."
91. Ernest R. Groves, *The Marriage Crisis* (New York: Longmans, Green & Co., 1928), 23.
92. Ibid., 6.
93. Ibid., 9.
94. Allen, *Since Yesterday*, 76.
95. Dix, *How to Win and Hold a Husband*, 81.
96. Ibid., 82. Moreover, "these girls do not realize that the kind of man who is willing to marry a girl without purity is the sort of man who is not fit for any girl to marry." Ibid., 83.
97. Ibid., 237.
98. Ibid., 241.
99. Ibid.
100. In addition to Shirley Temple, other child stars had remarkable runs during the 1930s. A short list would include Bobby Breen, Mickey Rooney, Jane Withers, and Freddie Bartholomew.
101. Keith Munro, "Full House: My Life with the Dionnes," in *The Aspirin Age, 1919–1941*, ed. Isabel Leighton (1949; reprint New York: Simon and Schuster, 1976), 297–312.
102. Knight Jessee, "Extra Sheer," *Love Story*, March 10, 1934, 10.

CHAPTER 7

1. Robert Loring Allen, *Irving Fisher: A Biography* (Cambridge: Blackwell, 1993), 185–6.
2. Figures slightly altered from the example given in Ibid., 180.
3. "Dow Jones: 100 Year Historical Chart," http://www.macrotrends.net/1319/dow-jones-100-year-historical-chart.
4. Allen, *Irving Fisher*, 206.
5. Ibid., 213–14.
6. Fisher, *The Stock Market Crash—and After*, 53.

7. Ibid., 269.
8. Ibid.
9. Ibid.
10. Ibid., 258.
11. "Dow Jones: 100 Year Historical Chart."
12. Herbert Hoover, "Address Accepting the Republican Presidential Nomination," speech, Washington, D.C., August 11, 1932, http://www.presidency.ucsb.edu/ws/?pid=23198.
13. Franklin D. Roosevelt, "Address Accepting the Presidential Nomination at the Democratic National Convention in Chicago," speech, Chicago, July 2, 1932, http://www.presidency.ucsb.edu/ws/index.php?pid=75174&st=&st1=.
14. For his part, in a late October speech in Madison Square Garden, Hoover accused Roosevelt and the New Deal of inspiring false hope. Attacking Roosevelt and his plan for public works projects to combat unemployment, Hoover singled out the "promise to promote 'employment for all surplus labor at all times'—by the Government." "I at first could not believe that anyone would be so cruel as to hold out a hope so absolutely impossible of realization to those 10 million who are unemployed and suffering," Hoover said. "But the authenticity of that promise has been verified. And I protest against such frivolous promises being held out to a suffering people." Perhaps unsurprisingly, Roosevelt and his vision of hope won out over Hoover and his stingy realism. Hoover, "Address at Madison Square Garden," speech, New York City, October 31, 1932, http://www.presidency.ucsb.edu/ws/?pid=23317.
15. See Darby, "Three-and-a-Half Million."
16. James N. Gregory, *The Southern Diaspora: How the Great Migrations of Black and White Southerners Transformed America* (Chapel Hill: University of North Carolina Press, 2005), 330.
17. Harvard Sitkoff, *A New Deal for Blacks: The Emergence of Civil Rights as a National Issue* (New York: Oxford University Press, 1978).
18. Langston Hughes, "Ballad of Roosevelt," *New Republic*, November 14, 1934, 9.
19. Allen, *Irving Fisher*, 10.
20. Ibid., 269.
21. Isaac Asimov, "Liar!" *Astounding Science Fiction*, May 1941, 45.
22. Ibid., 46.
23. Ibid.
24. Ibid., 46–7.
25. Ibid., 47.
26. Ibid., 51.
27. Ibid.
28. Ibid., 52.
29. Ibid., 53.
30. Ibid., 54.
31. Ibid., 55.
32. Ibid.

33. Walter B. Pitkin, *Life Begins at Forty* (New York: Blue Ribbon Books, 1934), Dorothea Brande, *Wake Up and Live!* (New York: Simon and Schuster, 1936), Carnegie, *How to Win Friends*, Hillis, *Live Alone and Like It*, Irving Tressler, *How to Lose Friends and Alienate People* (New York: Stackpole Sons, 1937), Robert P. Crawford, *Think for Yourself* (New York: McGraw-Hill, 1937), Napoleon Hill, *Think and Grow Rich* (1937; repr. New York: Tarcher and Perigree, 2016), Lin Yutang, *The Importance of Living* (New York: John Day, 1937), Norman Vincent Peale, *The Art of Living* (New York: Abingdon Press, 1937), Dix, *How to Win and Hold a Husband*, *Alcoholics Anonymous*.
34. Margaret Case Harriman, "He Sells Hope," *Saturday Evening Post*, August 14, 1937, 12.
35. Ibid.
36. Steven Watts, *Self-Help Messiah: Dale Carnegie and Success in Modern America* (New York: Other Press, 2013), 262.
37. Harriman, "He Sells Hope," 13.
38. Carnegie, *How to Win Friends*, 43.
39. Ibid., 103.
40. In 1922, Sinclair Lewis published *Babbitt*, which satirized the conformity and hollowness of the American middle class, especially its businessmen. The novel primed Lewis to despise Carnegie. In two 1937 *Newsweek* columns devoted to *How to Win Friends and Influence People*—one would not contain his contempt—Lewis dismissed Carnegie as the "Bard of Babbittry." Carnegie, Lewis wrote, had achieved his own success by "telling people how to smile and bob and pretend to be interested in people's hobbies precisely so that you may screw things out of them." "Conceivably," Lewis added, "one may sell 600,000 books and still be a failure." Sinclair Lewis, "Car-Yes-Men," *Newsweek*, November 15, 1937, 31 and "One Man Revolution," *Newsweek*, November 22, 1937, 33.
41. Carnegie, *How to Win Friends*, 126–8.
42. A reviewer for the *Nation* wrote that Carnegie "has given us the best outline of the science of tail-wagging and hand-licking ever written." Margaret Marshall, "Columnists on Parade," *Nation*, March 19, 1938, 328.
43. Carnegie, *How to Win Friends*, 70.
44. Gordon Hutner, *What America Read: Taste, Class, and the Novel, 1920–1960* (Chapel Hill: University of North Carolina Press, 2009), 121.
45. Ibid., 122.
46. Engels added, "the real motive forces impelling him [the thinker] remain unknown to him... Hence he imagines false or apparent motives." Friedrich Engels, "Letter to Franz Mehring, July 14, 1893," in *The Marx-Engels Reader*, ed. Robert C. Tucker (1972; 2nd ed., New York: W.W. Norton & Company, 1978), 766.
47. Hutner, *What America Read*, 122.
48. Watts, *Self-Help Messiah*, 273.
49. Marshall, "Columnists on Parade," 327. As for false consciousness, Marshall hit that note as well. "Carnegie has met a lot of rich men in his day," she wrote.

"His rules for winning friends make it easy for him to get them to talk to him, and they have all told him the secret of their success, as rich men will. Inevitably, it has been some admirable talent for handling human relationships. Throw away your economic textbooks."

50. Harriman, "He Sells Hope," 12.
51. Carnegie, *How to Win Friends*, 15.
52. Ibid., 34.
53. Ibid., 69.
54. Ibid., 33.
55. See Darby, "Three-and-a-Half Million."
56. "Candidates for the Best Seller List," *Publisher's Weekly*, May 6, 1939, 40.
57. "Napoleon Hill is Dead at 87; Wrote Best-Seller on Success," *New York Times*, November 10, 1970.
58. Hill, *Think and Grow Rich*, xv.
59. The publisher's preface to the book, which seems likely to have been written by Hill since it proceeds in the same style of occasional CAPITAL LETTERS that Hill favors, mentions—in italics this time—that "*Riches cannot always be measured in money!*" But little is heard on that score again. Rather, Hill offers anecdotes about how Carnegie believed his money-making formula "should be taught in all public schools and colleges" because "much of that which is taught in the schools is of no value whatsoever in connection with the business of earning a living or accumulating riches." It seems not to have occurred to either Carnegie or Hill that not everything that goes on in schools has to connect to earning a living or accumulating riches. Still in the preface, Hill mentions a clergyman who used "the secret" "so effectively that it brought him an income of upwards of $75,000.00 a year." No mention is made of how the priest can simultaneously serve God and Mammon. Ibid., 12, xvi, xvii.
60. Hill reproduces John Lowell's *New York World-Telegram* account.
61. Hill, *Think and Grow Rich*, 78.
62. Ibid., xx. From the outset, the publisher's preface warns readers to "be prepared, therefore, when you expose yourself to the influence of this philosophy, to experience a CHANGED LIFE which may help you not only to negotiate your way through life with harmony and understanding, but also to prepare you for the accumulation of material riches in abundance." Ibid., xii–xiii.
63. Ibid., xix.
64. Ibid., 13.
65. In the introduction, Hill reprints a letter he received from one of his acolytes, Jennings Randolph, at the time a congressman from West Virginia. Randolph, who benefited from a commencement address Hill once gave, wrote Hill urging him to publish a book and share his wisdom with young people everywhere. Others, Randolph felt, would benefit as he did. "Millions of people are now facing the problem of staging a come-back, because of the depression," Randolph wrote. "You know the problems of those who face the necessity of beginning all over again," he added. "There are thousands of people in America

today who would like to convert ideas into money, people who must start at scratch, without finances, and recoup their losses. If anyone can help them, you can." Ibid., 21.

66. Ibid., 50–1.
67. Ibid., 34.
68. Ibid., 315.
69. Ibid., 28.
70. Ibid., 28.
71. Ibid., 60.
72. Ibid., 255.
73. J.B. Rhine, *New Frontiers of the Mind: The Story of the Duke Experiments* (New York: Farrar and Rhinehart, 1937).
74. Ibid., 14. "There are millions of people who BELIEVE themselves 'doomed' to poverty and failure, because of some strange force over which they BELIEVE they have no control," Hill added. "They are the creators of their own 'misfortunes," Hill continues, "because of this negative BELIEF, which is picked up by the subconscious mind, and translated into its physical equivalent." Ibid., 56.
75. Ibid., 224.
76. Ibid., 81.
77. Ibid., 86.
78. Ibid., 17.
79. *Alcoholics Anonymous*, vii.
80. The gendered pronoun misleads slightly. One of the testimonials in the book comes from a woman.
81. Ernest Kurtz, *Not God: A History of Alcoholics Anonymous* (1979; repr. Center City: Hazelden, 1991), 15.
82. *Alcoholics Anonymous*, 1.
83. Ibid., 7.
84. Ibid., 17.
85. Ibid., 30.
86. Ibid., 35.
87. Ibid., 37.
88. Ibid., 27.
89. Ibid., 104.
90. Ibid., 104–5.
91. Ibid., 106.
92. Ibid., 41.
93. Ibid., 34.
94. Ibid., 41.
95. Ibid., 50.
96. Ibid., 53.
97. Ibid., 112.
98. Ibid., 71.

99. Ibid., italics in original.
100. Ibid., 74.
101. "It is plain that a life which includes deep resentment leads only to futility and unhappiness." That is no way of life for anyone, but "with the alcoholic whose hope is the maintenance and growth of a spiritual experience," Wilson writes, "this business of resentment is infinitely grave. We found that it is fatal. For when harboring such feelings we shut ourselves off from the sunlight of the Spirit. The insanity of alcohol returns and we drink again. And with us, to drink is to die." Ibid., 78.
102. Ibid., 71.
103. Ibid., 75.
104. Ibid., 10. Hence the very brief discussion of *Alcoholics Anonymous* in Chapter 6.
105. Ibid., 17.
106. Ibid., 15.
107. Ibid., 71.
108. Ibid., 57.
109. After "a year or so of the depression," John O'Hara writes in *BUtterfield 8*, "when they saw it was not a little thing that was going to pass, these men began taking stock of what life had given them or they had taken... Then a few men, a few million men, asked themselves whether the things they had bought ever had been worth what they paid for them. Ah! That was worth thinking about, worth buying heavy and expensive books to find out about." See O'Hara, *BUtterfield 8*, 28.
110. James Truslow Adams, *The Epic of America* (New York: Blue Ribbon Books, 1931).
111. *Alcoholics Anonymous*, 80.
112. The echo of the theologian Reinhold Neibhur, who got his start in the 1930s, is deliberate.
113. Franklin D. Roosevelt, "Fireside Chat," speech, April 28, 1935, http://www.presidency.ucsb.edu/ws/index.php?pid=15046&st=&st1=.
114. If the United States needed a reminder that one cannot master fate, that black swans sometimes fly, it came out of the skies at Pearl Harbor on the morning of December 7, 1941.

CHAPTER 8

1. The song, for which Guthrie wrote lyrics but no music, is undated, though it likely comes from the mid- to late 1930s. The lyrics refer to another unconventional pension scheme that arose in California in the 1930s, Ham and Eggs, which promised $30 every Thursday to every unemployed Californian. "Ashes to Ashes, Dust to Dust," Woody Guthrie Publications, http://woodyguthrie.org/Lyrics/Ashes_To_Ashes_Dust_To_Dust.htm.
2. "The First Social Security Beneficiary," Social Security Administration, https://www.ssa.gov/history/imf.html.

3. Many of the terms used in the 1930s (the needy, the aged, old-age, crippled children, the blind) have, for good reasons, passed out of usage. I have chosen in this chapter to retain the terms, objectionable as they may be, on the grounds that introducing anachronisms is more objectionable still.
4. Alice O'Connor, "Social Security Act." *Encyclopedia of the Great Depression*, Vol. 2 (New York: Thomson Gale, 2004), 903.
5. Quoted in J.D. Gaydowski, "Eight Letters to the Editor: The Genesis of the Townsend National Recovery Plan," *Southern California Quarterly* 52.4 (1970): 370.
6. Richard Milne, *That Man Townsend* (Indianapolis: Prosperity Publishing, 1935), 2.
7. Francis E. Townsend, *New Horizons: An Autobiography* (Chicago: J.L. Stewart, 1943), 135–6.
8. John E. Miller, "Townsend Plan." *Encyclopedia of the Great Depression*, Vol. 2 (New York: Thomson Gale, 2004), 983. Edwin Amenta gives 1.5 to 2 million. Richard L. Neuberger and Kelley Loe cite at least 3 million. According to Miller, the organization claimed 3.5 million members. Edwin Amenta, *When Movements Matter: The Townsend Plan and the Rise of Social Security* (Princeton: Princeton University Press, 2006), 116. Richard L. Neuberger and Kelley Loe, "The Old People's Crusade," *Harper's*, December 1935, 426.
9. Richard L. Neuberger and Kelley Loe, *An Army of the Aged: A History and Analysis of the Townsend Old Age Plan* (Caldwell: Caxton Printers, 1936), 67.
10. Neuberger and Loe, "The Old People's Crusade," 426.
11. Amenta, *When Movements Matter*, 74.
12. Ibid., 81.
13. Ibid., 115.
14. *Economic Security Act: Hearings before the Committee on Ways and Means, House of Representatives* (Washington, D.C.: Government Printing Office, 1935), 680.
15. Gaydowski, "Eight Letters to the Editor," 369. In his second letter, he warned, "Machines have supplanted muscle. Brains have supplanted brawn." Ibid., 371. To the House Ways and Means Committee, he observed, "It is admitted by practically every student of today that the machines are constantly depriving men and women of the means of earning a livelihood. The day will surely come when machines will do practically all of the toil of the world." By lowering the retirement age to match the number of those who lost jobs to machines, his plan, Townsend said, "is the only one so far submitted which will painlessly adjust humans to the inroads of the machine." Ibid., 686.
16. Ibid., 374.
17. *Economic Security Act: Hearings before the Committee on Ways and Means*, 680.
18. Gaydowski, "Eight Letters to the Editor," 373.
19. I mention Father Divine later in the chapter, but here let me mention Father Charles Coughlin, whose radio show, broadcast from Detroit, reached millions. Coughlin began a proponent of the New Deal but over the course of the decade his views transformed into a nauseating blend of monetary reform, economic populism, anti-Semitism, isolationism, and outright sympathy for fascism. Huey

Long and his Share Our Wealth campaign, which, though less cockeyed than Townsend's plan, also had its share of magical thinking. On Father Coughlin and Huey Long, the best book remains Alan Brinkley's *Voices of Protest: Huey Long, Father Coughlin, and the Great Depression* (New York: Knopf, 1982).

20. The University of Wisconsin economist Edwin Witte, for example, produced a report for that group titled, unequivocally, "Why the Townsend Old Age Plan Is Impossible." Witte calculated that funding the Townsend Plan would require the federal government to collect two to three times as much in taxes as federal, state, and local governments together collected for all of 1932. Moreover, it would require not a 2 percent tax on transactions but a 6 percent one, which would lead to runaway inflation. And all that assumed that one could successfully administer the plan. Witte had his doubts. How would the federal government make sure the more than 2 million places of business in the United States paid every tax on every transaction they made? And how would the federal government check to make sure that each of the 10 million pensioners had spent their $200 within thirty days? The administrative complexities, however, paled before the sheer daftness of the plan. Witte concluded that the "inflation and duplicate taxation involved in the Townsend Plan will cause prices to soar and soon, even with the $200 per month, the pensioners will not be better off than they were before, while those below 60 will be immeasurably worse off." Edward Witte, "Why the Townsend Old Age Plan Is Impossible," Social Security Administration, https://www.ssa.gov/history/reports/ces/ces2witte6.html.
21. Neuberger and Loe, "The Old People's Crusade," 436.
22. Witte, "Why the Townsend Old Age Plan Is Impossible."
23. Neuberger and Loe, "The Old People's Crusade," 436.
24. *The Economic Meaning of the Townsend Plan: A University of Chicago Round Table* (Chicago: University of Chicago Press, 1936), 24.
25. Hadley Cantril, *The Psychology of Social Movements* (New York: John Wiley & Sons, 1941), vii.
26. Ibid., 208.
27. Ibid., 203.
28. A third circle—the righteous—would also overlap with these circles. In Chapter 2, I define the emotion as the sense of confidence and comfort that comes from being on the right side of a question, on the side of truth. I argue that righteousness rarely emerges from the self alone but rather the self in tune with some higher power, someone or something that guarantees the truth and lies beyond appeal. Usually, as with the religious, that higher power is God. The righteousness that wound through the Townsend Movement followed the same pattern. His newspaper, the *Townsend Weekly*, wrote, "This vision could not have come from the Evil One, but must have been God-given. It harmonizes so beautifully with 'the wisdom from above' (James 3:14)." It exhorted followers, "Let's be determined. God is on our side. So by all means let's be united." At the

Townsend national convention held in Chicago in 1935, members changed the lyrics of "Onward, Christian Soldiers" to "Onward, Townsend Soldiers."[1] Among other uses, this righteousness insulated Townsend and his followers from criticisms of the plan. As one advocate explained, economists opposed the Townsend Plan "probably because they never thought of it themselves." Quoted in Ibid., 189.

29. Ibid., 209.
30. Schlesinger, *The Politics of Upheaval*, 41. Edwin Amenta titled his 2008 history of the Townsend Movement and the rise of Social Security in *When Movements Matter: The Townsend Plan and the Rise of Social Security*.
31. Frances Perkins, "The Roots of Social Security," speech, Baltimore, Maryland, October 23, 1962, Social Security Administration, https://www.ssa.gov/history/perkins5.html.
32. Paul H. Douglas, *Social Security in the United States* (New York: Whittlesey House, 1939), 72.
33. *Economic Security Act: Hearings before the Committee on Ways and Means*, 1126.
34. Neuberger and Loe, "The Old People's Crusade," 426.
35. Frances Perkins, *The Roosevelt I Knew* (New York: Viking, 1946), 281.
36. "Letter to President Roosevelt Regarding Old-Age Pensions," Social Security Administration, https://www.ssa.gov/history/lettertoFDR.html.
37. David Wagner, *The Poorhouse: America's Forgotten Institution* (Lanham: Rowman and Littlefield, 2005), 6.
38. Ibid., 99.
39. See chapter 3 of Lawrence Alfred Powell, John B. Williamson, and Kenneth J. Branco, *The Senior Rights Movement: Framing the Policy Debate in America* (New York: Twayne Publishers, 1996).
40. *Down and Out in the Great Depression*, ed. McElvaine, 103.
41. Ibid., 98.
42. Ibid., 100.
43. Eleanor Roosevelt, "First Lady Pleads for Old Age Pensions," *Social Security* 8 (February 1934), 4.
44. In his 1903 book *Economics: An Account of the Relation between Private Property and Public Wealth*, Arthur T. Hadley closed his discussion of economic responsibility and compulsory insurance by observing, "If you give every man a right to a pension when he is incapable of self-support, you tacitly approve his failure to provide for himself and his children." Hadley continues: "We need measures which shall increase individual responsibility rather than diminish it; measures which shall give us more self-reliance and less reliance on society as a whole. We cannot afford to countenance a system of morals or laws which justifies the individual in looking to the community rather than to himself for support in age or infirmity." Arthur T. Hadley, *Economics: An Account of the Relation between Private Property and Public Wealth* (New York: G.P. Putnam's and Sons, 1901), 62–3. In 1908, the founder of the Prudential Insurance Company, John F. Dryden, who, admittedly, had something to lose from the state entering the insurance

business, spoke in more apocalyptic terms. "To admit," he argued, "that state aid or support in old age for the large majority of wage earners is in fact a pressing necessity is to concede that the social and economic development of the country has been in the wrong direction, that the education in thrift has been defective, and that the virtues of intelligent self-denial and self-sacrifice have been replaced by considerations of selfish indulgence and indifference to the welfare of others." John F. Dryden, *Addresses and Papers on Life Insurance and Other Topics* (Newark: Prudential Insurance Company of America, 1909), 122.

45. Calvin Coolidge, *Calvin Coolidge Says* (Plymouth: Calvin Coolidge Memorial Foundation, 1972), 248.
46. *Economic Security Act: Hearings before the Committee on Ways and Means*, 917.
47. Franklin D. Roosevelt, "Message to Congress on Social Security," speech, January 17, 1935, American Presidency Project, http://www.presidency.ucsb.edu/ws/?pid=15051.
48. John T. McCutcheon, "A Wise Economist Asks a Question," *Chicago Tribune*, August 19, 1931.
49. *Social Security in America: The Factual Background of the Social Security Act as Summarized from Staff Reports to the Committee on Economic Security* (Washington, D.C.: Government Printing Office, 1937), 159.
50. *Economic Security Act: Hearings Before the Committee on Finance, United States Senate* (Washington, D.C.: Government Printing Office, 1935), 100.
51. True, the lawyer who represented George P. Davis, a shareholder in the Edison Electric Company of Boston who sued the company to enjoin it from collecting the compulsory insurance taxes required by the Social Security Act, argued in front of the Supreme Court in 1937 for the "the virtues of self-reliance and frugality" and proposed that "aid from a paternal government may sap those sturdy virtues and breed a race of weaklings." But this argument was more hypothetical than sincere, intended to get at the question of whether the Social Security Act violated the Tenth Amendment, which reserves for the states powers not specifically delegated to the federal government. What *if*, Davis's lawyer argued, Massachusetts believed that old-age pensions sapped self-reliance and frugality and shaped its laws accordingly? Must it let the virtues of its children be sapped "because some other philosophy of government finds favor in the halls of Congress?" (Yes, the Supreme Court answered in a novel interpretation of the Constitution, so long as the federal government provided for the "general welfare" of the nation.) "Supreme Court's Majority Decision Backing Old Age Feature of Security Law," *New York Times*, May 25, 1937.
52. In 1932, Armstrong published *Insuring the Essentials: Minimum Wage Plus Social Insurance—A Living Wage Program* (New York: Macmillan, 1932).
53. *Report to the President of the Committee on Economic Security* (Washington, D.C.: Government Printing Office, 1935), 23–4.
54. Ibid., 24.
55. *Old Age Security: Staff Report* (1935). The report is available at https://www.ssa.gov/history/reports/ces/ces2armstaff.html.

56. Ibid.
57. *Social Security in America*, 144.
58. *Report to the President*, 25.
59. The "depression has largely wiped out wage earners' savings and deprived millions of workers past middle life of their jobs," planners observed, "with but uncertain prospects of ever again returning to steady employment." Ibid.
60. *Social Security in America*, 194.
61. Ibid.
62. Ibid.
63. Ibid. See table 44.
64. Even I have trouble following it. From Barbara Nachtried Armstrong's *Old Age Security: Staff Report*: "a person (1) who has been insured 5 years and has made at least 200 weekly tax payments shall be entitled to a pension of 10% of the average weekly wage, such average not to be in excess of $55 weekly upon which weekly tax payments have been made. Thereafter there shall be added to his pension 1% for each 40 weekly tax payments, this added amount not to exceed 1% for each year of insurance after the qualifying period, except that the annuity shall never be less than the actuarial equivalent of the worker's own contributions made before reaching the age of 65 years."
65. Specifically, the plan would pay 1/2 of 1 percent on the first $3,000 contributed; 1/12 of 1 percent on the next $42,000 contributed; and 1/24 of 1 percent on any amount over $45,000 contributed. This sounds more complicated than it is. In 1937, a skilled worker in the iron and steel industry—a machinist or a roller—who worked nine months or more earned a little over $2,000 per year[1] (over $35,000 today; it was a good job). So say a machinist in an open-hearth furnace who was thirty-five years old in 1937 and made exactly $2,000 per year started paying Social Security in 1937 and worked for thirty years. (Forget about inflation for a moment.) When he retired in 1967 the man would have contributed $60,000 over his lifetime ($2,000 times thirty years). Upon retirement, he would receive a monthly pension of $56.25 ($15 for the first $3,000; $35 for the next $42,000; and $6.25 for the remaining $15,000).
66. As proposed to Congress, the plan covered domestic and agricultural workers. The Committee on Economic Security acknowledged the administrative difficulties the inclusion of these groups would pose. (Would farmers have to start cutting checks for their farm hands? Were housewives to pay matching payroll taxes for their cooks?) Nevertheless, the committee thought it worth the trouble to include everyone. In testimony before the House Ways and Means Committee, however, the secretary of the treasury disagreed; Congress agreed with the secretary of the treasury; and in a single stroke about half of the workers in the United States were excluded from the program. For an argument that racism did not motivate this decision, see Larry De Witt, "The Decision to Exclude Agricultural and Domestic Workers from the 1935 Social Security Act," *Social Security Bulletin* 70.4 (2010): 49–68. In the legislative history of Title I, however, one can discern the racism of Southern congressmen. They watered

down a provision in the bill that stipulated that states must "provide a minimum assistance grant which will afford a reasonable subsistence compatible with decency and health." As the University of Chicago economist Paul H. Douglass noted at the time, "One reason for this change was the fear on the part of many southern Senators and Representatives that the earlier provision might be used by authorities to compel the southern states to pay higher pensions to aged Negroes than the dominant white groups believed to be desirable." *Social Security in America*, 195. Douglas, *Social Security in the United States*, 100.

67. Douglas, *Social Security in the United States*, 116.
68. *Social Security in America*, 138.
69. Ibid., 139.
70. Ibid., 199.
71. Ibid., 204.
72. Franklin D. Roosevelt, "Annual Message to Congress," speech, January 4, 1935, American Presidency Project, http://www.presidency.ucsb.edu/ws/?pid=14890.
73. Franklin D. Roosevelt, "Address to Advisory Council of the Committee on Economic Security," speech, November 14, 1934, American Presidency Project, http://www.presidency.ucsb.edu/ws/?pid=14890.http://www.presidency.ucsb.edu/ws/?pid=14777.
74. *Social Security in America*, 204.
75. Ibid., 205.
76. Quoted in Schlesinger, *The Coming of the New Deal*, 308.
77. Franklin D. Roosevelt, "Statement on Signing the Social Security Act," speech, August 14, 1935, American Presidency Project, http://www.presidency.ucsb.edu/ws/?pid=14916.
78. Frank Parker Stockbridge, "Social Security, Or De Levee Done Bust," *Saturday Evening Post*, March 14, 1936, 37.
79. Ibid., 27.
80. Ibid., 40.
81. Ibid.
82. Alf Landon, "I Will Not Promise the Moon," speech, September 1936, *Vital Speeches of the Day*, October 15, 1936, 27.
83. Quoted in Schlesinger, *The Politics of Upheaval*, 635. As I also describe in Chapter 2, the pay envelope campaign launched Roosevelt into his own righteous flights. In a speech at Madison Square Garden, he denounced those who conducted the campaign as "the enemies of peace" and part of the "forces of selfishness" acting out of a "lust for power."
84. Quoted in Arthur J. Altmeyer, *The Formative Years of Social Security* (Madison: University of Wisconsin Press, 1968), 38.
85. Garet Garrett, *Saturday Evening Post*, September 19, 1936, 104.
86. Parker Stockbridge, "Social Security, Or De Levee Done Bust," *Saturday Evening Post*, March 7, 1936, 10.
87. Ibid., 43–5.
88. *Economic Security Act: Hearings before the Committee on Ways and Means*, 680, 903.

89. Douglas, *Social Security in the United States*, 57.
90. Edward Berkowitz, *America's Welfare State: From Roosevelt to Reagan* (Baltimore: Johns Hopkins University Press, 1991), 25.
91. Franklin D. Roosevelt, "Message to Congress on Social Security."
92. Social Security already threatened to undermine the family. "[T[here was—and there still is—" Barbara Nachtried Strong wrote in the unpublished *Old Age Security: Staff Report*, "extant in the United States a conviction that it is the duty of the children, and not that of the state, to take care of the old. It is assumed that if the state relieves the children of the responsibility, family ties are loosened, and since the family is one of our most highly valued institutions, this danger is to be avoided at all costs."
93. Berkowitz, *America's Welfare State*, 48. You can see the difference between the two plans by comparing how Ida May Fuller would have fared under the original Act and how she fared under the 1939 revised Social Security Act. Under the original Act, Fuller would not have qualified for an annuity. The 1935 Act required that an individual had to have contributed at least $2,000 into the system and have paid into it for at least five years. Fuller did neither. Like everyone else, she began making payroll contributions in January 1937, and she retired in November 1939. Over that time, she contributed all of $24.75. (Her employer contributed another $24.75.) Under the 1935 Act, she would have received a lump sum payment of $51.23 (her $49.50 contribution plus interest). Under the 1939 Amendments to the Act, however, she did qualify for an annuity, which would be calculated according to a new, more generous formula. Assume, for the moment, that Fuller had paid into the system for five years and just reached the $2,000 threshold. Under the old benefit formula, she would have received a monthly annuity of $10. Under the new formula, which proceeded from the average contribution made and not the total, she received a monthly annuity of $22.54. If Fuller had had a spouse, her husband would have received an additional benefit of $11.27, assuming, that is, that he did not qualify for his own annuity. Or consider the average worker during the 1930s, one who made $2,000 per year and worked for thirty years before retiring. Under the original plan, as calculated earlier, he would receive a $57.50 per month annuity. Under the amended plan, he would receive $86.67 per month. And his spouse would receive $43.33 per month. And his dependent child, if he had one, another $43.33 per month. And voila, no more $1.5 billion future reserve.
94. Quoted in Berkowitz, *America's Welfare State*, 66.
95. *Social Security in America*, 268.

Bibliography

Adams, James Truslow. *The Epic of America*. New York: Blue Ribbon Books, 1931.

Agee, James and Walker Evans. *Let Us Now Praise Famous Men*. 1941; reprint, New York: Mariner, 2001.

Ahamed, Liaquat. *Lords of Finance: The Bankers Who Broke the World*. New York: Penguin, 2009.

Ahmed, Sara. *The Cultural Politics of Emotions*. New York: Routledge, 2004.

Alcoholics Anonymous: The Story of How More Than One Hundred Men Have Recovered from Alcoholism. 1939; Malo: Anonymous Press, 2008.

Allen, Frederick Lewis. *Only Yesterday: An Informal History of the Nineteen-Twenties*. New York: Harper & Brothers, 1931.

Allen, Frederick Lewis. *Since Yesterday: The Nineteen-Thirties in America, September 3, 1929–September 3, 1939*. New York: Harper & Brothers, 1940.

Allen, Robert Loring. *Irving Fisher: A Biography*. Cambridge: Blackwell, 1993.

Altmeyer, Arthur J. *The Formative Years of Social Security*. Madison: University of Wisconsin Press, 1968.

Amenta, Edwin. *When Movements Matter: The Townsend Plan and the Rise of Social Security*. Princeton: Princeton University Press, 2006.

Armstrong, Barbara Nachtried. *Insuring the Essentials: Minimum Wage Plus Social Insurance—A Living Wage Program*. New York: Macmillan, 1932.

Arvin, Newton. *Whitman*. New York: Macmillan, 1938.

Asimov, Isaac. "Liar!" *Astounding Science Fiction*, May 1941, 43–55.

Awalt, Francis Gloyd. "Recollections of the Banking Crisis in 1933." *Business History Review* 43 (1969): 347–71.

Badal, James Jessen. *In the Wake of the Butcher: Cleveland's Torso Murders*. Kent: Kent State University Press, 2001.

Bagehot, Walter. *65 Lombard Street: A Description of the Money Market*. 1873; reprint, New York: Charles Scribner's Sons, 1897.

Bakke, E. Wight. *Citizens without Work: A Study of the Effects of Unemployment upon the Workers' Social Relations and Practices*. 1940; reprint, Hamden: Archon Books, 1968.

Bakke, E. Wight. *The Unemployed Worker: A Study of the Task of Making a Living without a Job*. 1940; reprint, Hamden: Archon Books, 1969.

Balderrama, Francisco E. and Raymond Rodriquez. *Decade of Betrayal: Mexican Repatriation in the 1930s*. Albuquerque: University of New Mexico Press, 2006.

Beard, Charles A. and George H.E. Smith, *The Old Deal and the New*. New York: Macmillan, 1940.

Berkowitz, Edward. *America's Welfare State: From Roosevelt to Reagan*. Baltimore: Johns Hopkins University Press, 1991.

Berlant, Lauren. *Cruel Optimism*. Durham: Duke University Press, 2011.

Binder, Alan S. *After the Music Stopped: The Financial Crisis, the Response, and Work Ahead*. New York: Penguin, 2013.

Blumer, Herbert. "Collective Behavior." In *Principles of Sociology*, ed. Alfred McClung Lee, 170–222. New York: Barnes and Noble, 1946.

Bocock, Robert. *Sigmund Freud*. 1983; reprint, London: Routledge, 2002.

Bradshaw, Charles. "Language and Responsibility: The Failure of Discourse in Carson McCullers's *The Heart Is a Lonely Hunter*," *Southern Quarterly* 37.2 (1999): 118–26.

Brande, Dorothea. *Wake Up and Live!* New York: Simon and Schuster, 1936.

Brinkley, Alan. *Voices of Protest: Huey Long, Father Coughlin, and the Great Depression*. New York: Knopf, 1982.

Broad, Lewis. *The Abdication: Twenty Five Years After: A Re-appraisal*. London: Frederick Muller, 1961.

Brown, Douglas Vincent. Preface to *Economics of the Recovery Program*. New York: Whittlesey, 1934.

Burke, Edmund. *A Philosophical Enquiry into the Origins of the Sublime and Beautiful: The Writings and Speeches of Edmund Burke: Volume 1: The Early Writings*. 1757; Oxford: Clarendon Press, 1997.

Byrd, Richard E. *Alone*. New York: P.P. Putnam's, 1938.

Campbell, W. Joseph. *Getting It Wrong: Ten of the Greatest Misreported Stories in American Journalism*. Berkeley: University of California Press, 2010.

Cantril, Hadley. *The Invasion from Mars: A Study in the Psychology of Panic*. Princeton: Princeton University Press, 1940.

Cantril, Hadley. *The Psychology of Social Movements*. New York: John Wiley & Sons, 1941.

Carnegie, Dale. *How to Win Friends and Influence People*. New York: Simon and Schuster, 1936.

Carpenter, Joel A. *Revive Us Again: The Reawakening of American Fundamentalism*. New York: Oxford University Press, 1997.

Cherniack, Martin. *The Hawk's Nest Incident: America's Worst Industrial Disaster*. New Haven: Yale University Press, 1986.

Colman, Andrew M. *A Dictionary of Psychology, 4th ed.*, "Emotional Intelligence." Oxford: Oxford University Press, 2015.

Coolidge, Calvin. *Calvin Coolidge Says*. Plymouth: Calvin Coolidge Memorial Foundation, 1972.

Cowley, Malcolm. "Hemingway Mixed with Hearst." In *Critical Essays on John O'Hara*, ed. Philip B. Eppard, 33–4. New York: G.K. Hall, 1994.

Crawford, Robert P. *Think for Yourself*. New York: McGraw-Hill, 1937.

Creeps by Night: Chills and Thrills, ed. Dashiell Hammett. Cleveland: World Publishing, 1944.

Damasio, Antonio. *Descartes' Error: Emotion, Reason, and the Human Brain*. New York: G.P. Putnam, 1994.

Darby, M.R. "Three-and-a-Half Million U.S. Employees Have Been Mislaid: Or, An Explanation of Unemployment, 1934–1941," *Journal of Political Economy* 84.1 (1976): 1–16.

de Sousa Ronald. *The Rationality of Emotion*. Cambridge, Mass.: MIT Press, 1987.

DeLong, J. Bradford. "'Liquidation' Cycles: Old-Fashioned Real Business Cycle Theory and the Great Depression." *National Bureau of Economic Research*. Accessed December 11, 2015. http://www.nber.org/papers/w3546.

De Witt, Larry. "The Decision to Exclude Agricultural and Domestic Workers from the 1935 Social Security Act." *Social Security Bulletin* 70.4 (2010): 49–68.

Dickstein, Morris. *Dancing in the Dark: A Cultural History of the Great Depression*. New York: Norton, 2009.

Dix, Dorothy. *How to Win and Hold a Husband*. New York: Doubleday, 1939.

Doran, Robert. *The Theory of the Sublime from Longinus to Kant*. Cambridge: Cambridge University Press, 2015.

Down and Out in the Great Depression: Letters from the Forgotten Man, ed. Robert McElvaine. Chapel Hill: University of North Carolina Press, 1983.

Douglas, Paul H. *Social Security in the United States*. New York: Whittlesey House, 1939.

Dryden, John F. *Addresses and Papers on Life Insurance and Other Topics*. Newark: Prudential Insurance Company of America, 1909.

The Economic Meaning of the Townsend Plan: A University of Chicago Round Table. Chicago: University of Chicago Press, 1936.

Economic Security Act: Hearings before the Committee on Finance, United States Senate. Washington, D.C.: Government Printing Office, 1935.

Economic Security Act: Hearings before the Committee on Ways and Means, House of Representatives. Washington, D.C.: Government Printing Office, 1935.

Edelman, Lee. *No Future: Queer Theory and the Death Drive*. Durham: Duke University Press, 2004.

Ehrenreich, Barbara. *Fear of Falling: The Inner Life of the Middle Class*. New York: Pantheon Books, 1989.

Ehrenreich, Barbara and John Ehrenreich. "The Professional-Managerial Class." In *Between Labor and Capital*, ed. Pat Walker, 5–45. Boston: South End Press, 1979.

Eichengreen, Barry. *Golden Fetters: The Gold Standard and the Great Depression, 1919–1939*. New York: Oxford University Press, 1992.

Eichengreen, Barry. *Hall of Mirrors: The Great Depression, the Great Recession, and the Use—and Misuses—of History*. New York: Oxford University Press, 2015.

Engels, Friedrich. "Letter to Franz Mehring, July 14, 1893." In *The Marx-Engels Reader*, ed. Robert C. Tucker. 1972; 2nd ed., 765–7. New York: W.W. Norton & Company, 1978.

Entin, Joseph B. *Sensational Modernism: Experimental Fiction and Photography in Thirties America*. Chapel Hill: University of North Carolina Press, 2007.

Federal Reserve Board. *Twentieth Annual Report of the Federal Reserve Board Covering Operations for the Year 1933*. Washington, D.C.: G.P.O., 1934.

Finnegan, Cara. *Picturing Poverty: Print Culture and FSA Photographs*. Washington, D.C.: Smithsonian Institution Scholarly Press, 2003.

"The First Social Security Beneficiary." Social Security Administration. Accessed July 23, 2018. https://www.ssa.gov/history/imf.html.

Fisher, Irving. *Booms and Depressions: Some First Principles*. New York: Adelphi, 1932.

Fisher, Irving. "Statistics in the Service of Economics." *Journal of the American Statistical Association*, 28 (1933): 1–13.

Fisher, Irving. *The Stock Market Crash—and After*. New York: Macmillan, 1930.

Fisher, Irving. "The Stock Market Panic in 1929." *Journal of the American Statistical Association*, 25 (1930): 93–6.

Fitzgerald, F. Scott. "Babylon Revisited." 1931. In *The Short Stories of F. Scott Fitzgerald*, ed. Matthew J. Bruccoli, 616–33. New York: Scribner, 2003.

Fitzgerald, F. Scott. "My Lost City." In *The Crack-Up*, 23–33. New York: New Directions, 1945.

Fitzpatrick, Daniel Robert. *Cartoons by Fitzpatrick, St. Louis Post-Dispatch*. St. Louis: Pulitzer, 1947.

Galbraith, John Kenneth. *The Great Crash 1929*. 1955; reprint, Boston: Mariner, 2009.

Garrett, Garet. *Saturday Evening Post*, September 19, 1936.

Gay, Myra. "Extra Sheer," *Love Story*, March 10, 1934, 5–22.

Gaydowski, J.D. "Eight Letters to the Editor: The Genesis of the Townsend National Recovery Plan." *Southern California Quarterly* 52. 4 (1970): 365–82.

Gellhorn, Martha. *The Trouble I've Seen*. 1936; reprint, London: Eland, 2012.

Golay, Michael. *America 1933: The Great Depression, Lorena Hickok, Eleanor Roosevelt, and the Shaping of the New Deal*. New York: Simon and Schuster, 2013.

Goodman, Jonathan. *The Passing of Starr Faithfull*. 1990; reprint, Kent: Kent State University Press, 1996.

Graham, Benjamin and David L. Dodd. *Security Analysis*. New York: Whittlesey House, 1934.

Great Tales of Terror and the Supernatural, eds. Phyllis Cerf Wagner and Herbert Wise. 1944; reprint, New York: Random House, 1994.

Gregory, James N. *The Southern Diaspora: How the Great Migrations of Black and White Southerners Transformed America*. Chapel Hill: University of North Carolina Press, 2005.

Groves, Ernest R. *The Marriage Crisis*. New York: Longmans, Green & Co. 1928.

Guthrie, Woody. "Ashes to Ashes, Dust to Dust." Woody Guthrie Publications. Accessed July 23, 2018. http://woodyguthrie.org/Lyrics/Ashes_To_Ashes_Dust_To_Dust.htm.

Hadley, Arthur T. *Economics: An Account of the Relation between Private Property and Public Wealth*. New York: G.P. Putnam's and Sons, 1901.

Hayes, Joy Elizabeth and Kathleen Battles. "Exchange and Interconnection in US Network Radio: A Reinterpretation of the 1938 *War of the Worlds* Broadcast." In *War of the Worlds to Social Media*, eds. Joy Elizabeth Hayes, Kathleen Battles, and Wendy Hilton-Morrow, 35–56. New York: Peter Lang, 2013.

Hickok, Lorena. *One Third of a Nation: Lorena Hickok Reports the Great Depression*, eds. Richard Lowitt and Maurine Beasley. Urbana: University of Illinois Press, 1981.

Hill, Matthew J. "Love in the Time of Depression: The Effect of Economic Conditions on Marriage in the Great Depression," *Journal of Economic History* 75.1 (2015): 163–89.

Hill, Napoleon. *Think and Grow Rich*. 1937; reprint, New York: Tarcher and Perigree, 2016.

Hillis, Marjorie. *Live Alone and Like It: A Guide for the Extra Woman*. New York: Bobbs- Merrill, 1936.

Hillis, Marjorie. *Orchids on Your Budget: Or, Live Smartly on What You Have*. New York: Bobbs-Merrill, 1937.

Hoffman, Abraham. *Unwanted Mexican Americans in the Great Depression: Repatriation Pressures 1929–1939*. Tucson: University of Arizona Press, 1974.

Honey, Michael. *Sharecropper's Troubadour: John L. Handcox, the Southern Tenant Farmers' Union, and the African American Song Tradition*. New York: Palgrave, 2013.

Hoover, Herbert. *The Memoirs of Herbert Hoover: The Great Depression, 1929–1941*. New York: Macmillan, 1952.

Hopkins, Harry. *Spending to Save: The Complete Story of Relief*. New York: Norton, 1936.

Houellebecq, Michel. *H. P. Lovecraft: Against the World, against Life*, trans. Dorna Khazeni. London: Weidenfeld & Nicolson, 2006.

Hughes, Langston. "Ballad of Roosevelt," *New Republic*, November 14, 1934, 9.

Hull, Helen. *Hardy Perennial*. New York: Coward-McCann, 1933.

Hulse, Ed. *The Blood and Thunder Guide to Pulp Fiction*. Morris Plains: Murania Press, 2013.

Hutner, Gordon. *What America Read: Taste, Class, and the Novel, 1920–1960*. Chapel Hill: University of North Carolina Press, 2009.

Ignatieff, Michael. *The Needs of Strangers*. London: Chatto & Windus: Hogarth Press, 1984.

Jacobs, Lea. *The Wages of Sin: Censorship and the Fallen Woman Film, 1928–1942*. Madison: University of Wisconsin Press, 1991.

Joshi, S.T. *I Am Providence*. New York: Hippocampus Press, 2013.

Kalar, Joseph. "Papermill." In *Papermill: Poems, 1927–35*, ed. Ted Genoways. Urbana: University of Illinois Press, 2006.

Kant, Immanuel. *Critique of the Power of Judgment*. 1790; Cambridge: Cambridge University Press, 2000.

Keltner, Dacher and Jonathan Haidt. "Approaching Awe: A Moral, Aesthetic, and Spiritual Emotion." *Cognition and Emotion* 17 (2003): 297–314.

Kennedy, David M. *The American People in the Great Depression: Freedom from Fear*. New York: Oxford, 2003.

Keynes, John Maynard. "An Economic Analyses of Unemployment." Vol. 13 of *The Collected Writings of John Maynard Keynes*. New York: Macmillan, 1973.

Keynes, John Maynard. *General Theory of Employment, Interest, and Money*. 1936; reprint, New York: Harcourt, Brace, and World, 1965.

Kierkegaard, Søren. *The Soul of Kierkegaard: Selections from His Journals*, ed. Alexander Dru. New York: Dover, 2003.

Kipnis, Laura. *Against Love*. New York: Pantheon Books, 2003.

Kromer, Tom. *Waiting for Nothing and Other Writings*. 1935; reprint, Athens: University of Georgia Press, 2004.

Kurtz, Ernest. *Not God: A History of Alcoholics Anonymous*. 1979; reprint, Center City: Hazelden, 1991.

Landon, Alf. "I Will Not Promise the Moon," speech, September 1936, *Vital Speeches of the Day*, October 15, 1936.

Lazarus, Richard S. *Emotion and Adaption*. New York: Oxford University Press, 1991.

Le Bon, Gustave. *The Crowd: A Study of the Popular Mind*. 1895; reprint, New York: Macmillan, 1897.

"Letter to President Roosevelt Regarding Old-Age Pensions." Social Security Administration. Accessed July 23, 2018. https://www.ssa.gov/history/lettertoFDR.html.

Lewis, Sinclair. *It Can't Happen Here*. 1935; reprint, New York: Signet Classics, 1993.

Leys, Ruth. "The Turn to Affect: A Critique." *Critical Inquiry* 37 (2011): 434–72.

Linden, Blanche M.G. "Photography." *Encyclopedia of the Great Depression*, Vol. 2. New York: Thomson Gale, 2004. 756.

Long, Robert Emmet. *Nathaniel West*. New York: Ungar, 1985.

Lovecraft, H.P. "The Call of Cthulu." In *The Complete Fiction of H.P. Lovecraft*, 381–407. New York: Race Point Publishing, 2014.

Lovecraft, H.P. "The Music of Erich Zann." In *The Complete Fiction of H.P. Lovecraft*, 145–54. New York: Race Point Publishing, 2014.

Lovecraft, H.P. "The Shadow over Innsmouth." In *The Complete Fiction of H.P. Lovecraft*, 866–923. New York: Race Point Publishing, 2014.

Lovecraft, H.P. "The Thing on the Doorstep." In *The Complete Fiction of H.P. Lovecraft*, 990–1013. New York: Race Point Publishing, 2014.

Lynch, Richard P. "Saints and Lovers: *Miss Lonelyhearts* in the Tradition," *Studies in Short Fiction* 31.2 (1994): 225–35.

Lynd, Robert S. and Helen Merrell Lynd. *Middletown in Transition: A Study in Cultural Conflicts*. 1937; reprint, New York: Harvest, 1965.

Manker, Dayton A. *They That Remain: A Story of the End Times*. Grand Rapids: Zondervan, 1941.

Marsh, John. *You Work Tomorrow: An Anthology of American Labor Poetry, 1929–1941*. Ann Arbor: University of Michigan Press, 2007.

Massumi, Brian. *Parables of the Virtual: Movement, Affect, Sensation*. Durham: Duke University Press, 2002.

McCarthy, Mary. "The Man in the Brooks Brothers Shirt." In *The Company She Keeps*. 1942; New York: Mariner, 2003.

McCullers, Carson. *The Heart Is a Lonely Hunter*. 1940; reprint, New York: Mariner, 2000.

McPhail, Clark. "Blumer's Theory of Collective Behavior: The Development of a Non-Symbolic Interaction Expansion." *Sociological Quarterly* 30.3 (1989): 401–23.

Michaels, Walter Benn. *The Beauty of a Social Problem: Photography, Autonomy, Economy*. Chicago: University of Chicago Press, 2015.

Miller, John E. "Townsend Plan." *Encyclopedia of the Great Depression*, Vol. 2 New York: Thomson Gale, 2004: 982–5.

Milne, Richard. *That Man Townsend*. Indianapolis: Prosperity Publishing, 1935.

Minehan, Thomas. *Boy and Girl Tramps of America*. New York: Farrar and Rinehart, 1934.

Munro, Keith. "Full House: My Life with the Dionnes." In *The Aspirin Age, 1919–1941*, ed. Isabel Leighton, 297–312. New York: Simon and Schuster, 1949.

Neuberger, Richard L. and Kelley Loe. *An Army of the Aged: A History and Analysis of the Townsend Old Age Plan*. Caldwell: Caxton Printers, 1936.

Neuberger, Richard L. and Kelley Loe. "The Old People's Crusade," *Harper's*, December 1935.

Ngai, Sianne. *Ugly Feelings*. Cambridge, Mass.: Harvard University Press, 2007.

Norris, Frank. *McTeague*. 1897; reprint, New York: Signet Classics, 2011.

Nussbaum, Martha. *The Fragility of Goodness*. 1986; revised ed., New York: Cambridge University Press, 2001.

Nussbaum, Martha. *Upheavals of Thought: The Intelligence of Emotions*. New York: Cambridge University Press, 2001.

O'Connor, Alice. "Social Security Act." *Encyclopedia of the Great Depression*, Vol. 2, 896–904. New York: Thomson Gale, 2004.

O'Hara, John. *BUtterfield 8*. 1935; reprint, New York: Penguin, 2013.

Öhman, Arne. "Fear and Anxiety: Overlaps and Dissociations." In *Handbook of Emotions*, 3rd ed., eds. Michael Lewis Jeannette M. Haviland-Jones, and Lisa Feldman Barrett, 709–29. New York: Guilford Press, 2008.

Oiler, Forrest Loman. *Be Thou Prepared for Jesus Is Coming*. Boston: Meador, 1937.

"Old Age Security: Staff Report." Social Security Administration. Accessed July 23, 2018. https://www.ssa.gov/history/reports/ces/ces2armstaff.html.

Park, Robert E. "Collective Behavior." In *Encyclopedia of the Social Sciences*, Vol. 3, ed. Edwin R.A. Seligman, 631–3. New York: Macmillan, 1930.

Park, Robert E. *The Crowd and the Public*. 1904; reprint, Chicago: University of Chicago Press, 1982.

Park, Robert E. and Ernest W. Burgess. *Introduction to the Science of Sociology*. Chicago: University of Chicago Press, 1921.

Peale, Norman Vincent. *The Art of Living*. New York: Abingdon Press, 1937.

Perkins, Frances. *The Roosevelt I Knew*. New York: Viking, 1946.

Perkins, Frances. "The Roots of Social Security," speech, Baltimore, Maryland, October 23, 1962. Social Security Administration. Accessed July 23, 2018. https://www.ssa.gov/history/perkins5.html.

Phillips-Fein, Kim. *Invisible Hands: The Businessmen's Crusade against the New Deal*. New York: W.W. Norton, 2009.

Pitkin, Walter B. *Life Begins at Forty*. New York: Blue Ribbon Books, 1934.

Pooley, Jefferson D. and Michael J. Socolow. "Checking up on *The Invasion from Mars:* Hadley Cantril, Paul F. Lazarsfeld, and the Making of a Misremembered Classic." *International Journal of Communications* 7 (2013): 1920–48.

Powell, Lawrence, Alfred John B. Williamson, and Kenneth J. Branco. *The Senior Rights Movement: Framing the Policy Debate in America*. New York: Twayne Publishers, 1996.

Prescott, Edward C. and Ellen R. McGrattan. "The 1929 Stock Market: Irving Fisher Was Right." *International Economic Review* 45.4 (2004) 991–1009.

Reis, Harry T. and Arthur Aron. "Love: What Is It, Why Does It Matter, and How Does It Operate," *Perspectives on Psychological Science* 3.1 (2008): 80–6.

Report to the President of the Committee on Economic Security. Washington, D.C.: Government Printing Office, 1935.

Reynolds, Quentin. *The Fiction Factory, Or from Pulp Row to Quality Street*. New York: Random House, 1955.

Rhine, J.B. *New Frontiers of the Mind: The Story of the Duke Experiments*. New York: Farrar and Rhinehart, 1937.

Roosevelt, Eleanor. "First Lady Pleads for Old Age Pensions." *Social Security* 8 (February 1934): 3–4.

Roosevelt, Franklin D. "Address to Advisory Council of the Committee on Economic Security," speech, November 14, 1934. American Presidency Project. Accessed July 23, 2018. https://www.presidency.ucsb.edu/documents/address-advisory-council-the-committee-economic-security.

Roosevelt, Franklin D. "Annual Message to Congress," speech, January 4, 1935. American Presidency Project. Accessed July 23, 2018. https://www.presidency.ucsb.edu/documents/annual-message-congress-3.

Roosevelt, Franklin D. "Message to Congress on Social Security," speech, January 17, 1935. American Presidency Project. Accessed July 23, 2018. https://www.presidency.ucsb.edu/documents/message-congress-social-security.

Roosevelt, Franklin D. "Statement on Signing the Social Security Act," speech, August 14, 1935. American Presidency Project. Accessed July 23, 2018. https://www.presidency.ucsb.edu/documents/statement-signing-the-social-security-act-0.

Roth, Benjamin. *The Great Depression: A Diary*, eds. James Ledbetter and Daniel B. Roth. New York: Public Affairs, 2013.

Ruskin, John. *Seven Lamps of Architecture*. 1849; reprint New York: D. Appleton and Co. 1901.

Salant, Walter S. "The Spread of Keynesian Doctrines and Practices in the United States." In *The Political Power of Economic Ideas: Keynesianism Across Nations*, ed. Peter A. Hall, 27–51. Princeton: Princeton University Press, 1989.

Schaap, Jeremy. *Triumph: The Untold Story of Jesse Owens and Hitler's Olympics*. New York: Houghton Mifflin, 2007.

Schiller, R.J. "Investor Behavior in the October 1987 Stock Market Crash: Survey Evidence." NBER Working Papers Series. Accessed July 20, 2017. http://www.nber.org/papers/w2446.pdf.

Schlesinger, Arthur M. *The Coming of the New Deal, 1933–1935*. 1958; reprint, Boston: Mariner, 2003.

Schlesinger, Arthur M. *The Crisis of the Old Order, 1919–1933*. 1957; reprint, Boston: Mariner, 2003.

Schlesinger, Arthur M. *The Politics of Upheaval, 1935–1936*. 1960; reprint, Boston: Mariner, 2003.

Schmitter, Lyle L. and Betti C. Goldwasser. "The Revised Benefit Schedule under Old Age Insurance." Social Security Administration. Accessed July 23, 2018. https://www.ssa.gov/history/reports/1939no2.html.

Schopenhauer, Arthur. *The World as Will and Representation. Vol. 1. 1818*. New York: Dover, 1969.

Schumpeter, Joseph. "Depressions." In *Economics of the Recovery Program*, 3–21. New York: Whittlesey, 1934.

Schwartz, Delmore. "In Dreams Begin Responsibilities." In *Once and for All: The Best of Delmore Schwartz*, ed. Craig Morgan Teicher, 1–10. New York: New Directions, 2016.

Sedgwick, Eve Kosofsky. *Touching Feeling*. Durham: Duke University Press, 2003.

Server, Lee. *Encyclopedia of Pulp Fiction Writers*. New York: Facts on File/Checkmark Books, 2002.

Shouse, Eric. "Feeling, Emotion, Affect." *M/C Journal* 8.6 (2005). http://journal.media-culture.org.au/0512/03-shouse.php.

Siegel, Jerome and Joe Schuster. "Superman." In *The Superman Chronicles, Vol. 1, The Superman Chronicles*, 31–44. New York: DC Comics, 2006.

Sitkoff, Harvard. *A New Deal for Blacks: The Emergence of Civil Rights as a National Issue*. New York: Oxford University Press, 1978.

Smith, Bruce. *The History of Little Orphan Annie*. New York: Ballantine Books, 1982; Washington, D.C.: Smithsonian Institution Scholarly Press, 2003.

Social Security in America: The Factual Background of the Social Security Act as Summarized from Staff Reports to the Committee on Economic Security. Washington, D.C.: Government Printing Office, 1937.

Socolow, Michael J. "The Hyped Panic over 'War of the Worlds," *Chronicle Review*, October 24, 2008, 16–17.

Starrett, Paul. *Changing the Skyline*. New York: Whittlesey House, 1938.

Steinbeck, John. *The Grapes of Wrath*. 1939; New York: Penguin, 2006.

Stockbridge, Frank Parker. "Social Security, Or De Levee Done Bust." *Saturday Evening Post*, March 7, 1936.

Stockbridge, Frank Parker. "Social Security, Or De Levee Done Bust." *Saturday Evening Post*, March 14, 1936.

Stockman, David A. *The Great Deformation: The Corruption of Capitalism in America*. New York: Public Affairs, 2013.

Sutton, Matthew Avery. "Was FDR the Antichrist? The Birth of Fundamentalist Antiliberalism in a Global Age." *Journal of American History* 98.4 (2012): 1052–74.

Szalay, Michael. *New Deal Modernism: American Literature and the Invention of the Welfare State*. Durham: Duke University Press, 2000.

Temin, Peter. See *Lessons from the Great Depression*. Cambridge, Mass.: MIT Press, 1989.

Townsend, Francis E. *New Horizons: An Autobiography*. Chicago: J.L. Stewart, 1943.

Tressler, Irving. *How to Lose Friends and Alienate People*. New York: Stackpole Sons, 1937.

Trilling, Lionel. "Greatness with One Fault in It," *Kenyon Review* 4.1 (1941): 99–102.

United States. *Farm Tenancy: Report of the President's Committee*. Washington, D.C.: Government Printing Office, 1937.

United States. *Handbook of Labor Statistics*. Washington, D.C.: Government Printing Office, 1941.

Van Wienen, Mark W. *American Socialist Triptych: The Literary-Political Work of Charlotte Perkins Gilman, Upton Sinclair, and W.E.B. Du Bois*. Ann Arbor: University of Michigan Press, 2012.

Vieira, Mark A. *Sin in Soft Focus: Pre-Code Hollywood*. New York: Harry N. Abrams, 1999.

Wagner, David. *The Poorhouse: America's Forgotten Institution*. Lanham: Rowman and Littlefield, 2005.

Walker, Margaret. "Lineage." In *For My People*, 7. 1942; reprint New York: Arno Press, 1968.

Watts, Steven. *Self-Help Messiah: Dale Carnegie and Success in Modern America*. New York: Other Press, 2013.

Welles, Orson and Peter Bogdanovich. *This Is Orson Welles*. New York: De Capo Press, 1998.

West, Nathanael. *Day of the Locust*. 1939; reprint, New York: New Directions, 2009.

West, Nathanael. *Miss Lonelyhearts*. 1933; reprint, New York: New Directions, 2009.

Wicker, Elmus. *The Banking Panics of the Great Depression*. Cambridge: Cambridge University Press, 1996.

Willard, Josiah Flint. "Homosexuality among Tramps." Sexual Inversion, Havelock Ellis and John Addington Symonds. 1897; reprint, 252–7. New York: Arno Press/ New York Times, 1975.

Williams, Gareth. *Paralysed with Fear: The Story of Polio*. New York: Palgrave Macmillan, 2013.

Williams, Susan A. *The People's King: The True Story of the Abdication*. New York: Palgrave Macmillan, 2004.

Willis, Carol. "Building the Empire State." *Building the Empire State*, ed. Carol Willis. New York: Norton, 1998.

Wilson, Edmund. *The American Earthquake*. Garden City: Doubleday, 1958.

Wilson, Robert Anton. *Cosmic Trigger. Vol. 1, Final Secret of the Illuminati*. San Francisco: And/Or Press, 1977; reprint, Las Vegas: New Falcon Publications, 1991.

Wilson, Robert Anton. *Cosmic Trigger. Vol. 2, Down to Earth.* Tempe: New Falcon Publications, 1991.

Witte, Edward. "Why the Townsend Old Age Plan Is Impossible." Social Security Administration. Accessed July 23, 2018. https://www.ssa.gov/history/reports/ces/ces2witte6.html.

Wright, Richard. "How Bigger Was Born." In *Native Son.* 1940; reprint, 431–62. New York: Harper Perennial, 2005.

Wright, Richard. *Native Son.* 1940; reprint, New York: Harper Perennial, 2005.

Yutang, Lin. *The Importance of Living.* New York: John Day, 1937.

Ziegler, Philip. *King Edward VIII: The Official Biography.* London: Collins, 1990.

Zinn, Howard. *A People's History of the United States.* 1980; reprint, Harper Perennial, 1995.

Index

Note: Figures are indicated by an italic '*f*', respectively, following the page number.

For the benefit of digital users, indexed terms that span two pages (e.g., 52–53) may, on occasion, appear on only one of those pages.